BUILDING THE UK'S NEW SUPREME COURT
NATIONAL AND COMPARATIVE PERSPECTIVES

Building the UK's New Supreme Court

National and Comparative Perspectives

Edited by

ANDREW LE SUEUR

OXFORD

UNIVERSITY PRESS

OXFORD
UNIVERSITY PRESS

Great Clarendon Street, Oxford OX2 6DP

Oxford University Press is a department of the University of Oxford.
It furthers the University's objective of excellence in research, scholarship,
and education by publishing worldwide in

Oxford New York

Auckland Bangkok Buenos Aires Cape Town Chennai
Dar es Salaam Delhi Hong Kong Istanbul Karachi Kolkata
Kuala Lumpur Madrid Melbourne Mexico City Mumbai Nairobi
São Paulo Shanghai Singapore Taipei Tokyo Toronto

Oxford is a registered trade mark of Oxford University Press
in the UK and in certain other countries

Published in the United States
by Oxford University Press Inc., New York

British Library Cataloguing in Publication Data

Data available

Library of Congress Cataloging in Publication Data

Data available

ISBN 0-19-926462-7

1 3 5 7 9 10 8 6 4 2

Typeset by Kolam Information Services, Pvt. Ltd, Pondicherry, India
Printed in Great Britain
on acid-free paper by
Biddles Ltd, King's Lynn

Preface

This collection of essays stems from two seminars on 'Reforming the UK's Top Courts: Lessons from Comparative Policy', held in London and Edinburgh in 2001 under the auspices of the Economic and Social Research Council (ESRC) Future Governance Programme. None of the participants could have predicted that two years later the government would make its surprise announcement in June 2003 that a new supreme court for the UK was to be established. There is no ideal time to publish a book during a fast moving constitutional reform, but many of the contributions to this volume have been revised in the light of government's decision of 12 June 2003. I hope that the essays have a longevity that will make them relevant, or at least interesting, even after the foundations (both literal and metaphorical) of the new supreme court have been laid.

The two ESRC Future Governance seminars in 2001 were jointly organized by Richard Cornes (Essex University) and me. They could not have taken place without the substantial funding provided by the ESRC and the support of the programme director, Professor Edward Page. The Canadian High Commission in London gave additional financial support and hospitality for the speakers, as did the Délégation générale du Québec à Londres. Mrs Nadene Bryan of the School of Law at the University of Birmingham provided efficient administrative support throughout.

It was in 1999 that the Constitution Unit in UCL's School of Public Policy, with characteristic prescience by its director Professor Robert Hazell, started a study of possible models for reform of the UK's top courts. I joined the research team shortly afterwards and we were ably assisted by Roger Masterman (now at the University of Durham). The research carried out with Richard Cornes, funded by an ESRC grant (R000222908) and a British Academy grant (APN30026), led to several publications including the report A Le Sueur and R Cornes *The Future of the United Kingdom's Highest Courts* (UCL Constitution Unit London 2002 and online at <http://www.ucl.ac.uk/ constitution-unit>).

I am particularly grateful to Keith Vincent for his assistance in preparing the typescript for this volume. Above all my thanks go to the contributors.

Andrew Le Sueur
University of Birmingham
August 2003

Contents

INTERMEDIATE COURTS OF APPEAL AND TOP-LEVEL
NATIONAL COURTS

List of Contributors

David Anderson QC is a practising barrister at Brick Court Chambers, London, and a visiting professor of law at King's College London.

Charles Blake is a solicitor, former head of civil litigation at the Departments of Health and of Social Security and a part-time immigration adjudicator.

Dr Ignacio Borrajo Iniesta is *Letrado* (senior staff attorney) at the *Tribunal constitucional* (the Spanish constitutional court) in Madrid. He is professor of law at the Public University of Navarra and teaches at University Institute Ortega y Gasset, Madrid.

Professor Brice Dickson is Chief Commissioner of the Northern Ireland Human Rights Commission and professor of law at the University of Ulster.

Professor Gavin Drewry is Professor of Public Administration and Director of the Centre for Political Studies at Royal Holloway, University of London.

Dr Kay Goodall is a lecturer in law at the University of Glasgow.

Richard Gordon QC is a practising barrister at Brick Court Chambers, London, and a visiting professor of law at University College London.

Professor Andrée Lajoie is research professor at the Center of Research on Public Law at the Faculty of Law of the University of Montreal.

Professor Andrew Le Sueur is Barber Professor of Jurisprudence at the University of Birmingham. He is also an honorary senior research fellow at UCL's Constitution Unit and editor of the journal *Public Law*.

Dr Kate Malleson is a senior lecturer in law at the London School of Economics.

Warren J. Newman is General Counsel in the Constitutional and Administrative Law Section of the Canadian Department of Justice, Ottawa. He is also an adjunct professor of law at the University of Ottawa.

Dr Rainer Nickel is assistant professor (*wissenschaftlicher Assistent*) at the Wilhelm-Merton-Centre for Global Governance, Institute for Public Law, Johann Wolfgang Goethe-University, Frankfurt am Main. He was legal advisor at the *Bundesverfassungsgericht* (Federal Constitutional Court) from 1998 to 2001.

Aidan O'Neill QC practises as an advocate at the Scottish Bar and is an Associate Member of Matrix Chambers, London.

Dr Russell Wheeler is Deputy Director of the Federal Judicial Center, Washington DC (the research and education agency of the US federal judicial system established by Congress in 1967).

Table of Cases

Germany

Denmark

Table of Legislation

INTRODUCTION

1

The Conception of the UK's New Supreme Court

ANDREW LE SUEUR*

The Government believes that the establishment of a separate Supreme Court will be an important part of the package of measures which will redraw the relationship between the Judiciary, the Government and Parliament and increase our judges' independence.

> Department for Constitutional Affairs *Constitutional Reform: A Supreme Court for the United Kingdom* (July 2003), para 7

Frankly, I'm personally fed up with having to deal with a situation where Parliament debates issues and the judges then overturn them.

> Rt Hon David Blunkett MP, Home Secretary, quoted in *The Independent*, 20 February 2003

In June 2003, the Labour government surprised almost everybody by deciding to abolish the office of Lord Chancellor and to establish a new supreme court for the UK. The manner in which the decision was made—without any prior consultation and amidst the political intrigue surrounding the annual Cabinet reshuffle—provoked criticism. It did not help that the timing of the announcement coincided with some of the worst relations between central government and the judiciary since the days of Michael Howard's tenure as Home Secretary in the last Conservative government in the mid 1990s.[1] Nevertheless, the decision was broadly welcomed. With hindsight, the oddity is perhaps that it took an otherwise reform-minded government so long to be convinced of the arguments of principle and pragmatism in favour of reform of the Law Lords. Prominent think tanks and campaign groups had long argued in favour of reforms along

---

* Barber Professor of Jurisprudence, University of Birmingham.
[1] See A Bradley 'Judicial Independence under Attack' [2003] *Public Law* 397.

lines broadly similar to those proposed by the government,[2] as had some senior judges,[3] many academics[4] and a few parliamentarians.[5]

1. CONCEIVING A NEW COURT

In a few generations' time, when it is decided to celebrate a significant anniversary of the supreme court of the United Kingdom, the party planners will perhaps pick the date of royal assent of the Bill creating the court, or the court's first sitting day, or the day on which it handed down its first judgment, or the day it moved into its new premises. There is however another possibility: 12 June 2003. Like many conceptions, it was a day of fumbling behind closed doors.

The announcements made from 10 Downing Street on 12 June 2003 were part of the Prime Minister's annual Cabinet reshuffle. By means of a press release, we were told that (a) the office of Lord Chancellor was to be abolished, (b) a new Cabinet post of Secretary of State for Constitutional Affairs had been created, (c) there was to be a new judicial appointments commission for England and Wales, and (d) that the government planned to establish a new supreme court of the UK and remove judicial business from the House of Lords. While there was some forewarning of government thinking on the new judicial appointments commission,[6] the other changes were unexpected in their timing if not their substance. The blunt fact is that the government's new policies on the ending of the office of Lord Chancellor and establishing a new supreme court was a dramatic U-turn. Political memoirs, or the release of official records in 30 years' time, may reveal answers to many questions that deserve answers about the reasons for the change in policy. Clearly, they are not unconnected with the retirement from the government of Lord Irvine of Lairg (Lord Chancellor from 1997 to 12 June 2003).

---

[2] eg Institute of Public Policy Research *Written Constitution for the United Kingdom* (Mansell London 1991), 14–18, 101–105 and ch 9; JUSTICE 'A Supreme Court for the United Kingdom Policy Paper' (November 2002, available at <www.justice.org.uk>).

[3] eg Lord Bingham 'A New Supreme Court for the United Kingdom' The UCL Constitution Unit Lecture 1 May 2002 (UCL Constitution Unit London 2002); Lord Steyn 'The Case for a Supreme Court' (2002) 118 *Law Quarterly Review* 382, 383–384. During the parliamentary debates on the devolution Bills in 1998, Lord Cooke of Thorndon supported the radical idea of a constitutional court of the UK, but he later recanted: 'The Law Lords: An Endangered Heritage' (2003) 119 *Law Quarterly Review* 49.

[4] eg R Brazier *Constitutional Reform* (2nd edn Oxford University Press Oxford 1998) 178–182; C Gearty 'What are Judges For?' *London Review of Books*, 25 January 2001; K Ewing 'A Theory of Democratic Adjudication: Towards a Representative, Accountable and Independent Judiciary' (2000) 38 *Alberta Law Review* 208; D Oliver *Constitutional Reform in the United Kingdom* (Oxford University Press Oxford 2003) 348.

[5] Most notably, the Liberal Democrat peer Lord Lester of Herne Hill QC.

[6] Lord Irvine had given evidence to the House of Commons Select Committee on the Lord Chancellor's Department on 2 April 2003 and had said, 'I am prepared to conduct a wide consultation . . . It will extend to *the possibility* of a judicial appointments commission' (emphasis added). HC 611–i Q73. That announcement was however itself a 'surprise' to most informed commentators, see eg C Dyer 'Irvine May Drop Role on Judges' *The Guardian*, 3 April 2003.

2. A COURT BORN OF SECRET MINISTERIAL CABAL AND A PRESS RELEASE

It *could* have been a different, more dignified beginning for the new supreme court. Some of us regretted that so significant a constitutional reform had not been born of recommendations from a Royal Commission rather than a surprise press release and a hastily written departmental consultation paper published shortly before Parliament's summer recess.[7] If not a matter for a Royal Commission, then the proposal for a new court *could* have been the subject of normal political processes. All other major constitutional reforms initiated by the Labour government have merited mention in its election manifestos, but of the new supreme court and the abolition of the Lord Chancellor's office, there was nothing in the 2001 manifesto. Moreover, one might have expected senior members of the judiciary to be consulted or at least forewarned of the June 2003 announcement, but this did not happen.[8] Even the Cabinet was taken unawares. A Sunday newspaper said that the 'Cabinet was not consulted about any of the major constitutional changes ..., despite meeting only a few hours before the decisions were made public'.[9] Though there were repeated protestations by the Prime Minister's Official Spokesman that these 'were proposals which had been thought about for some time',[10] it is difficult to resist the conclusion that the reforms were the product of policy making on the hoof. They do not square with statements from government ministers in the preceding months about the value of having the Lord Chancellor as head of the judiciary and the lack of any plans for a new supreme court.[11] The proposal for a new supreme court is also at odds with the government's previously stated plans for parliamentary reform. In its November 2001 White Paper on reform of the House of Lords, the government enthusiastically supported the idea of keeping the Law Lords as part of the reformed second chamber, stating:[12]

---

[7] A Le Sueur 'The Government's (surprisingly quick) next steps in constitutional reform' [2002] *Public Law* 368.

[8] House of Commons Liaison Select Committee, Evidence presented by the Rt Hon Tony Blair MP, Prime Minister, on Tuesday 8 July 2003, HC 334–ii Q277 (21 July 2003); House of Commons Select Committee on the Lord Chancellor's Department, Uncorrected oral evidence of Rt Hon Lord Falconer of Thoroton QC, HC 903–i Q37–Q52 (30 June 2003); Hansard HL col 641 (14 July 2003) Lord Falconer; F Gibb 'Lord Chief Justice Warns Ministers He is not Crying Wolf' *The Times*, 2 August 2003, 6: 'Lord Woolf, the Lord Chief Justice, is reported to have told Lord Falconer at the annual judges dinner, three weeks after the announcement that "it must be a 'cause for concern' that the decision to abolish a historic office [that of the Lord Chancellor]," with its pivotal role in the administration of justice as head of judiciary, can be taken without any consultation with the judiciary"'.

[9] K Ahmed 'Cabinet Ignored over Historical Legal Reforms', *The Observer*, 15 June 2003, who went on: 'The issue of the departure of Derry Irvine, one of Tony Blair's oldest friends and mentor, was so sensitive that the Prime Minister would allow it to be discussed only by a small circle of his closest advisers. He never even set up a Cabinet sub-committee to scrutinise and improve policies before they were made public, as is customary'.

[10] eg Press Briefing 12 June 2003 at 5.45 pm. Summaries of Press Briefings are available at <http://www.number-10.gov.uk>.

[11] Le Sueur (n 7).

[12] *The House of Lords—Completing the Reform* (Cm 5291), para 81 (emphasis added).

The Government *is committed to maintaining judicial membership within the House of Lords.* In practice, it has been recognised that the formal judicial function constrains the capacity of active Law Lords to comment on legislation and issues of the day. However, Law Lords represent a significant body of expertise and experience, which can benefit the House beyond the period when they can sit judicially. As a result of recent changes Law Lords are now appointed formally to the age of 70. Between the age of 70 and 75 they continue to be eligible to sit judicially as circumstances require. The Government proposes that once the reform is implemented [ie that relating to the House of Lords generally], all those appointed as judicial members should continue to be members of the Lords until age 75, whether or not they sit judicially. This retirement provision will replace the term appointments of the other appointed members.

Ministers could not hide their irritation at the speculation about the backroom manoeuvrings that led up to the 12 June announcement. Speaking in a television interview 48 hours after the announcements were made, the new Lord Chancellor/Secretary of State for Constitutional Affairs (Lord Falconer of Thoroton) complained that 'people were wrongly judging the reshuffle on the basis of the misplaced newspaper speculation which preceded it. Instead, the focus should be on the "substance of the changes", he said'.[13] It was, perhaps, worrying that the minister responsible for constitution seemed not to recognize that the *process* of constitutional change—especially where the independence of the judiciary is at stake—is as important as the end result. It was not an encouraging start.

3. The concept of the new supreme court

On 14 July 2003, the Department for Constitutional Affairs (DCA) published a 48-page consultation paper[14] and there were question and answer sessions in both chambers of Parliament on the same day. It envisaged that the 'functions currently performed by the Appellate Committee [of the House of Lords] will be vested instead in a new supreme court, quite separate from Parliament'.[15] 'On balance' the government took the view 'that it would be right to transfer the jurisdiction on devolution cases from the Judicial Committee [of the Privy Council] to the new supreme court with arrangements which enable additional Scottish and Northern Ireland judges to sit in cases raising devolution issues where that is appropriate'.[16] No further changes were envisaged in the role of the supreme court,[17] and 'the initial members of the new Supreme Court will be the existing Lords of Appeal in Ordinary'.[18]

In promoting this model for the new court, the DCA rejected other options. Despite some early press comment to the effect that the new court would be 'like

---

[13] Lord Falconer on BBC1 'Breakfast with Frost' 16 June 2003, reported on BBC News Online <http://news.bbc.co.uk/1/hi/uk_politics/2991546.stm>.

[14] Department for Constitutional Affairs *Constitutional Reform: A Supreme Court for the United Kingdom* (DCA London 2003). See also another consultation paper released at the same time: *Constitutional Reform: A New Way of Appointing Judges* (DCA London 2003).

[15] ibid para 18.   [16] ibid para 21.   [17] ibid para 22.   [18] ibid para 29.

the United States Supreme Court'—with powers to strike down Acts of the UK Parliament incompatible with the Human Rights Act 1998 (rather than merely make 'declarations of incompatibility')—it was clear that such an institution was never contemplated. The idea that there ought to be a specialist constitutional court 'on the lines of some other European countries' was also dismissed as 'a departure from the UK's constitutional traditions'.[19] The government also rejected a model for the top-level court which postulated that rather than having an appellate function, the new court should give preliminary rulings on questions of UK law referred to it from the courts of appeal of England and Wales, Scotland, and Northern Ireland.[20]

4. THE REASONS FOR REFORM

The DCA presented its proposal for change as being part of the government's 'continuing drive to modernise the constitution and public services'.[21] Two specific pressures for change seemed to compel the 'conclusion that the present position is no longer sustainable'.[22]

First, the current institutional arrangements at the apex of the UK's court system 'raise questions about whether there is any longer sufficient transparency of independence from the executive and the legislature to give people the assurance to which they are entitled about the independence of the judiciary'.[23] Prior to 12 June 2003, the government had robustly rejected all suggestions that the role of the Lord Chancellor (as a government minister sitting as a judge), or the position of the Law Lords as members of the legislature,[24] breached Article 6(1) of the European Convention on Human Rights.[25] While Lord Irvine was Lord

---

[19] ibid para 23.
[20] ibid para 24. The inspiration for this model is of course the European Court of Justice. I first floated this idea in ch 10 of A Le Sueur and R Cornes *The Future of the United Kingdom's Highest Courts* (UCL Constitution Unit 2001). Without expressly acknowledging this source, Lord Bingham discussed and rejected this model in the Constitution Unit Spring Lecture 2002, published as 'A New Supreme Court for the United Kingdom' (UCL Constitution Unit 2002) 7. Lord Falconer agreed that this model 'is contrary to the whole notion of the common law': House of Commons Select Committee on the Lord Chancellor's Department, Uncorrected oral evidence of Rt Hon Lord Falconer of Thoroton QC, HC 903–i Q24 (30 June 2003).
[21] DCA consultation paper (n 14) para 1.
[22] ibid para 5.   [23] ibid para 2.
[24] On Art 6 ECHR and the Law Lords, see R Cornes '*McGonnell v United Kingdom*, the Lord Chancellor and the Law Lords' [2000] *Public Law* 166. cf Lord Lloyd of Berwick (a former Law Lord): 'It is sometimes said that for the Law Lords to sit in the Upper House is contrary to the theory of the separation of powers. I regard that as a nonsense argument. It could possibly be said to apply to the noble and learned Lord the Lord Chancellor as a member of the executive, but it does not apply to the Law Lords': Hansard HL col 615 (21 January 2003).
[25] eg Lord Irvine, Hansard HL col 655 (2 March 2000). His point in essence was that the question in any given case was whether there was a lack of independence and impartiality on the given facts. As Lord Chancellor he would never sit in a case relating to legislation that he had been involved with in his roles as a government minister or presiding officer of the House of Lords' chamber during debates on Bills.

Chancellor, he cherished and defended his role as head of the judiciary and from time to time exercised his right to sit on and preside over the Appellate Committee of the House of Lords.[26] With his departure from government, the DCA was free to accept the growing consensus that there were indeed broad problems relating to perceptions about the independence and impartiality. In so doing, it ensured that a clash with the Council of Europe was avoided.[27]

A second entirely pragmatic, but important, consideration prompting reform was the need for suitable accommodation for the Law Lords. As the DCA points out, facilities for judicial business in the Palace of Westminster are inadequate: 'the Law Lords' administration works in cramped conditions: one Law Lord does not even have a room'.[28]

5. THEMES AND ISSUES IN THE ESSAYS

The creation of a new supreme court for the UK will inevitably prompt a great deal of academic writing. The present volume aims to make an early and modest contribution to that scholarly work. The essays are intended to be of interest to anyone interested in the work of the Law Lords as currently constituted, in the development of the UK's new supreme court, or more broadly still in the institutional arrangements of top-level courts in general.

Three broad and overlapping themes link many of the individual contributions to this book: (a) the complexities of attempting to accommodate national differences within the UK into the institutional design of the new supreme court; (b) the scope for comparative lesson-learning, or reflection, from courts in other legal systems; and (c) the connections between the new supreme court and other courts, especially intermediate courts of appeal, the European Court of Justice and the European Court of Human Rights.

6. NATIONAL PERSPECTIVES

The project to establish a new supreme court for the UK must grapple with the complexities of our union state. First, there are three separate legal systems (England and Wales, Scotland and Northern Ireland)—and, arguably, two others are emerging with the recognition that there is such a thing as an all-UK legal

---

[26] The last such occasion was in *AIB Group (UK) Ltd v Martin* [2001] UKHL 63; [2002] 1 WLR 94 on 13 December 2001.

[27] On 1 April 2003, the Council of Europe Parliamentary Assembly Legal Affairs and Human Rights Committee unanimously adopted a report calling for the judicial role of the Lord Chancellor to be ended and the Law Lords to be constituted as a court separate from Parliament: *Office of the Lord Chancellor in the Constitutional System of the UK* Doc 9798. Professor Erik Jurgens, the committee's rapporteur, gave evidence to the House of Commons Select Committee on the Lord Chancellor's Department: HC 584–i (27 March 2003).

[28] DCA consultation paper (n 14) para 4.

system and an inchoate Welsh legal order distinct in some respects from that of England (not least because of the use of the Welsh language in the law). Secondly, the new supreme court is likely to acquire jurisdiction over 'devolution issues', allocated to the Judicial Committee of the Privy Council by the 1998 devolution Acts, and thus have responsibility for adjudicating on divisions of power disputes between the various governments within the UK.

There are two competing sets of expectations, often unarticulated or half formed, about the constitutional and legal status of the UK's top-level court. On the one hand, there is a desire for a court which serves each of the three legal systems *primarily as a court of that particular legal system*—not a court of the 'whole UK'. Thus, the House of Lords, when it sits to hear a Scottish civil appeal, is said to sit as a Scottish court, applying Scots law, and creating precedent that formally is binding only in Scotland.[29] The same is true of Northern Ireland[30] and by default of England and Wales. It is for those responsible for each legal system to decide whether, and if so how, to use the House of Lords (or its successor) as its final court of appeal. The Scottish legal system chooses not to permit criminal appeals to the House of Lords; and civil appeals are made on a different basis (without the restriction of a general leave requirement) from that pertaining in the courts in the other two legal systems.

The existence of three separate legal systems in the UK long predates the 1998 devolution Acts, but the Acts confirm the aspiration for legal system autonomy within the UK. Should the Scottish Parliament choose to do so, it could enact legislation ending the right of litigants in civil claims to take their case on appeal to the House of Lords.[31] If and when devolution of administration of justice functions occurs in Northern Ireland, the same may apply. The work of the Northern Ireland Human Rights Commission in developing a Bill of Rights for Northern Ireland needs also to be considered.[32] This set of expectations implies acceptance of plurality within the UK, comfort with asymmetrical arrangements and a permissive attitude towards territorial diversity.

There is also a second and different set of expectations about the status of the UK's top-level court: a desire for it to be a *national institution of and for the whole UK*, exercising unifying (and possibly also centralizing) functions. In adjudicating on 'devolution issues' in the Privy Council, the Law Lords (and

---

[29] DM Walker *The Scottish Legal System: An Introduction to the Study of Scots Law* (7th edn W Green/Sweet & Maxwell Edinburgh 1997) 424.

[30] B Dickson *The Legal System of Northern Ireland* (3rd edn SLS Belfast 1993) 66.

[31] A view endorsed by Lord Hope of Craighead 'Taking the Case to London: Is it all over?' [1998] *Juridical Review* 143. Lord Hope argues that there are good reasons why the Scottish Parliament would wish to retain Scottish appeals to the House of Lords (and presumably to its successor). But S Tierney notes: 'Lord Hope's view that this matter is devolved is unlikely to be universally shared, and if the Scottish Parliament were to attempt to remove the right of final appeal to the House of Lords such a move could well be challenged before the Judicial Committee (as a "devolution issue")': 'Scotland and the New Legal Order' (2001) 5 *Edinburgh Law Review* 49, 59.

[32] Following on from the 1998 Belfast Agreement, the NIHRC is required by statute to advise the Secretary of State for Northern Ireland on the scope for defining, in a Bill of Rights for Northern Ireland to be enacted by UK legislation, rights supplementary to those in the ECHR.

other judges) are clearly exercising a whole-UK jurisdiction.[33] The House of Lords also has 'whole UK' attributes. Many of its judgments have the function of ensuring consistent interpretation of UK Acts of Parliament in all three legal systems. Appointments to it are currently in the hands of the UK government, with no formal role in the selection process for the devolved institutions established in 1998. Moreover, it is a committee of the UK Parliament. What is missing is a clear demarcation of a body of law that is for the whole UK. David Walker in his *Oxford Companion to English Law* explains that there are:

in many and important respects quite distinct systems and bodies of law, civil, administrative and criminal, substantive and adjective, in England and Wales, in Scotland and in Northern Ireland. There is, accordingly, no such thing as United Kingdom or British law, though there are some rules common to all parts of the UK and these terms may be used loosely for the law generally or particular branches of law as contrasted with, say, French or American law. In respects in which the law varies as between England, Scotland and Northern Ireland, e.g. land law, the terms 'United Kingdom law' or 'British law' are meaningless. But in respect of taxation or social security where the same or substantially the same rules apply in each part of the UK, such terms are meaningful.

Convention rights (as incorporated by the Human Rights Act 1998) and the 1998 devolution Acts can now be added to the list of areas of law which can 'meaningfully' be called UK law. There is, however, no clear sense (yet) of anything analogous to 'federal' law—law of the whole state—of the kind that exists in most other countries with plural legal systems within their borders. The absence of 'federal' law and a unified common law throughout the whole of the UK makes it more difficult than it otherwise would be to define the jurisdiction of a new top-level court which may be created.

There is, then, ambivalence in the status of the UK's top-level courts. Whether or not the proposed reforms are to involve an amalgamation of jurisdictions of the House of Lords and the 'devolution issue' jurisdiction of the Privy Council (and they should), the following question must be addressed: how best can a new top-level court for the UK be, simultaneously, a court of each of the three legal systems and a court for the whole UK?

7. COMPARATIVE PERSPECTIVES

A second broad theme in this volume is the value (and limits) of comparative approaches to thinking about and designing the UK's new supreme court. Essays

---

[33] See, for example, the following exchange in the House of Commons: '*Mrs. Ewing*: To ask the Secretary of State for Scotland if the Judicial Committee of the Privy Council must use Scots law practice and precedent in deliberating on disputes relating to the powers of the Scottish Parliament. *Mr. McLeish*: The rules of procedure for the Judicial Committee of the Privy Council will be made by an Order in Council under section 103 of the Scotland Act 1998. They will extend throughout the United Kingdom, as does the Scotland Act 1998 itself. Similarly, the Judicial Committee will not be restricted to applying Scots law in determining cases under the Scotland Act.' Hansard HC col 33 (7 December 1998).

in this volume deal with the experiences of the Supreme Court of Canada,[34] the *Tribunal constitucional* in Spain,[35] the *Bundesverfassungsgericht* (Germany's federal constitutional court),[36] the US Supreme Court and federal courts of appeal.[37] Comparisons and lesson learning may also be sought from supranational courts: the European Court of Justice and the European Court of Human Rights.[38]

In *Reforming the House of Lords: Lessons from Overseas,* which was about legislative rather than judicial functions, Meg Russell explained that:[39]

the debate on reform of the upper house has, in general, been very insular. For example, during the two-day debate which the House of Lords held on the White Paper, no reference was made by any of the speakers to the international context or to any second chamber outside the UK. Yet bicameral (two chamber) parliaments are common around the world, and follow a diverse range of models which the UK might want to follow.

The debates about the future of the *judicial functions* of the House of Lords and the Judicial Committee of the Privy Council have not suffered from this defect of insularity. On the contrary, there is an abundance of comparative endeavour. Perhaps any project to establish or reform a top-level court is almost inescapably a comparative activity?

Reference may be made to top-level courts in other jurisdictions for a variety of pragmatic and reflective purposes.[40]

---

[34] See chs 5 and 6. Canada's recent experience of implementing the Charter of Rights (in a parliamentary system), and longer experience of adjudicating on divisions of powers disputes between different governments within Canada, makes the Canadian court system a potential source of lesson learning and reflection for the UK. The Canadian legal system has also had to accommodate two official languages (something relevant for Wales) and a province where many laws are civilian rather than common law in character (an analogy may be drawn between Quebec and Scotland).

[35] See ch 7. Spain is a non-federal state which since 1979 has been implementing a programme of asymmetrical devolution. Spain is also a country which, as with the UK, is subject to centrifugal tendencies (in the Basque country and Catalonia) which the *Tribunal constitucional* has had to mediate.

[36] See ch 8. The *Bundesverfassungsgericht* enjoys a reputation as Europe's pre-eminent constitutional court. Its institutional structure and procedures were a source of inspiration in several other legal systems (including Spain) designing new courts as part of democratization processes. Like other courts in Europe, it faces the challenges of responding to the growing influence exerted by pan-European constitutional norms as enunciated by the European Court of Justice and the European Court of Human Rights.

[37] See ch 11. If there is a mother of all supreme courts, it is the US Supreme Court. It is one of the most studied of all courts in the world and is therefore an obvious source of comparison. Interestingly from the UK's perspective, it has managed dramatically to reduce its caseload over the past 10 years.

[38] See ch 9.

[39] M Russell *Reforming the House of Lords: Lessons from Overseas* (Oxford University Press Oxford 2000) 1.

[40] For a theoretically informed account see A Riles 'Introduction: The Projects of Comparison' in A Riles (ed) *Rethinking the Masters of Comparative Law* (Hart Publishing Oxford 2001) esp 11–15.

A. Comparisons for institution-building and policy transfer

First, comparisons may be used for practical purposes of 'policy transfer',[41] seeking to identify institutional arrangements and procedures that might usefully be transferred from one system to another—or rejected as unfeasible or undesirable.[42] For instance, as already noted, the various basic institutional models alluded to, and rejected, in the DCA's consultation paper—a 'US style' supreme court, a constitutional court, and a court of justice for the UK giving preliminary rulings rather than hearing appeals—have roots in arrangements in other jurisdictions.[43] Other illustrations of the penetration of comparative approaches to policy arose during 1998 when the possibility of creating a special constitutional court to deal with 'devolution issues' was briefly on the policy agenda. Thus, during the passage of the Scotland Bill in the House of Commons in 1998, Alex Salmond MP (of the Scottish Nationalist Party) moved an amendment seeking to replace the Privy Council with a constitutional court, saying:[44]

We have chosen a model based on the German constitutional court, which has been exported recently to Spain and Mexico. We propose that, like the German model, the court's membership should be widely drawn from legal and academic experts.

A further illustration of a comparative approach is that, in searching for models for the implementation of a Northern Ireland Bill of Rights, a working group of the Northern Ireland Human Rights Commission considered the experience of South Africa and Germany.[45] Much of the policy-making in relation to new methods for appointing judges has also drawn heavily on comparative studies.[46]

In his classic statement on comparative law as a tool of law reform, 'On Uses and Misuses of Comparative Law', Sir Otto Khan-Freund argued for a distinction between the transplant of rules of substantive law and institutional arrangements. He was blunt: 'Comparative law has far greater utility in substantive law than in the law of procedure, and the attempt to use foreign models of judicial organisation may lead to frustration and may thus be a misuse of the

---

[41] A term of political science. For an excellent introduction see the work produced under the auspices of the ESRC Future Governance Project, online at <http://www.futuregovernance.ac.uk/> (8 August 2003).

[42] See eg ch 12 (on methods for selecting which appeals to hear), ch 13 (on methods for appointing judges).

[43] See text at nn 19–20.

[44] Hansard HC col 204 (12 May 1998).

[45] Bill of Rights Implementation Working Group 'Report Bill of Rights for Northern Ireland: Reports of the Independent Working Groups to the Northern Ireland Human Rights Commission' (NIHRC Belfast 2001) para 11.2.

[46] eg C Blair 'Judicial Appointments (Research Paper 5) for the Criminal Justice Review Group in Northern Ireland which investigated the Republic of Ireland, the USA and Canada: see *Review of the Criminal Justice System in Northern Ireland* (HMSO Belfast 2000) ch 6; the recent initiative by the Scottish Executive, *Judicial Appointments: An Inclusive Approach* (Scottish Executive Edinburgh 2000) where Annex D, entitled 'Comparative Information on Judicial Appointments', refers to France, Italy, Spain, Portugal, Germany, and the Netherlands.

comparative method'.[47] One reason for this, he believed, was that institutions and procedures 'express the power of the legal profession and the distribution of power within the legal profession'. The importation of courts which do not 'fit into the accustomed distribution of power between Bar and Bench' will fail, he said. Clearly, Khan-Freund was writing at a time when Europe and the wider world were very different from how they are now. The experiences of constitution building in post-Communist states suggest that less scepticism is needed in relation to transfer of ideas about reforming courts. Nevertheless, his stricture about the need to consider the role of the legal profession, as one factor in deciding appropriate comparators, remains an important one.

Richard Rose has drawn a particularly useful set of distinctions between different types of 'learning' that may take place as part of a process of policy transfer:[48]

(a) Most simply, 'the *adaptation* of the model to the circumstances of the importing nation'—Here there is 'a close correspondence between the original source' and the institution/programme based on it.

(b) There may be *hybrid* lesson learning, 'combining compatible elements from institutions/programmes in effect in two or more countries'.

(c) A lesson 'can be a *synthesis*, combing in a distinctive way elements familiar in similar programmes in different countries'.

(d) Finally, *inspiration* is 'the most artful and loosest form of lesson-drawing'.

Nobody suggests that mere 'copying' is an option in lesson learning in the process of designing the institutional and procedural arrangements for the UK's new supreme court. There is however potential for all the different types of learning enumerated above to be used.

B. Comparison for prospective evaluation

In the UK, we do not (at the time of writing) know what 'it will be like' to have a new supreme court. The supposition, or hope, behind the DCA's July 2003 consultation paper appears to be that little will be different, except perhaps that in the medium term the bench of the supreme court will better reflect the demographic make-up of the UK as a whole (or at least its legal profession). Obviously, it is impossible to run a pilot study to test how the new supreme court will operate, interact with other parts of the government machine, and develop the law. The process of looking at the experience of top-level courts elsewhere may, however, provide some basis for speculating about how the court will operate and what problems it may encounter.[49]

---

[47] (1974) 37 *Modern Law Review* 1, 20.

[48] R Rose 'Ten Steps in Lesson Learning from Abroad' (Future Governance Discussion Paper 1 ESRC Hull 2001) 12–13 online at <http://www.futuregovernance.ac.uk/> (8 August 2003).

[49] See further K Mossberger and H Wolman 'Policy Transfer as a Form of Prospective Policy Evaluation' (Future Governance Discussion Paper 2 ESRC Hull 2001).

C. Comparison of legal rules

Reference to legal concepts and rules developed in other jurisdictions is becoming part of the stock-in-trade of lawyers in the UK. This is a worldwide phenomenon. Even the US Supreme Court, long immune from interest in comparative law, has recently leant on Strasbourg jurisprudence in striking down state legislation criminalizing sex between gay men. Citing *Dudgeon v United Kingdom*, the US Supreme Court said, 'Authoritative in all countries that are members of the Council of Europe (21 nations then, 45 nations now), the decision is at odds with the premise in *Bowers* that the claim put forward was insubstantial in our Western civilization'.[50] The impact of Strasbourg case law on UK law generally, and the way it is controlled and directed by the Law Lords, has increased since the coming into force of the Human Rights Act 1998. In relation to the mainstay of top court cases—fundamental rights adjudication and adjudication on disputes over the division of legislative or executive power between different governments within a State—reference to the legal concepts adopted by other courts may assist in developing our own.[51]

D. Comparison as a mirror

Most basically, comparison helps us simply to reflect more deeply on our own legal system. By understanding how and why other courts operate in the ways they do, our awareness of the political, social, and cultural character of UK law and courts may be heightened, quite apart from any interest in borrowing ideas, institutional structures or processes.

8. INTERRELATIONSHIPS WITH OTHER COURTS

A third broad theme linking some of the essays is the 'connectedness' of top-level national courts to other parts of the legal systems they serve. As TR Powell reportedly said, 'if you can think about something which is attached to something else without thinking about what it is attached to, then you have what is called a legal mind'.[52] It is desirable to avoid having too much of a legal mind in relation to questions of top court reform. The DCA's consultation on the

---

[50] 539 US—(2003). cf Justice Scalia dissenting: 'The Court's discussion of these foreign views (ignoring, of course, the many countries that have retained criminal prohibitions on sodomy) is therefore meaningless dicta. Dangerous dicta, however, since "this Court...should not impose foreign moods, fads, or fashions on Americans." *Foster v Florida* 537 US 990 (2002) (Thomas J., concurring in denial of certiorari)'.

[51] See eg ch 6 in which Warren Newman examines the conceptual tools of division of powers adjudication in the Canadian Supreme Court, much of which originated in the case law of the Privy Council, which was Canada's final court of appeal until 1949.

[52] D Horowitz 'Decreeing Institutional Change: Judicial Supervision of Public Institutions' [1983] *Duke Law Journal* 1265, 1307.

jurisdiction of the UK's new supreme court considered the important issue of the relationship between the House of Lords and the Privy Council. In chapter 2, below, Aidan O'Neill examines the problematic nature of the dual apex to the UK's court systems and calls for a 'new and intellectually coherent structure for our top courts'. In chapter 3, Brice Dickson considers the interface between the Northern Irish courts and the Law Lords.

All UK courts are inescapably connected to the European Court of Justice and the European Court of Human Rights. Indeed, the processes of European integration challenge the whole notion of a 'top court' in a national legal order. The nature of these relationships is examined in chapter 9 by David Anderson, who suggests a range of practical reforms. In chapter 8, Rainer Nickel considers the response of the *Bundesverfassungsgericht* to the growing influence of European Union and European Convention law on constitutional norms.

In common law jurisdictions, top-level appellate courts typically determine only a small number of cases compared with intermediate appeal courts. Clarity is needed as to the respective functions of these courts. In chapter 10, Charles Blake and Gavin Drewry consider the work of the Court of Appeal in England and Wales and in chapter 11 Russell Wheeler examines the relationships between the US Supreme Court and the federal appeal courts in the USA.

9. OVERVIEW OF THE ESSAYS

Brief summaries cannot adequately capture the chapters which follow. Nevertheless, readers may find the following accounts helpful in navigating around the book.

In chapter 2, Aidan O'Neill examines the constitutional foundations of adjudication on 'devolution issues' and the role and character of the Judicial Committee of the Privy Council ('to date, a substantially Scottish enterprise'). His conclusion is that the 1998 devolution Acts caused a lack of clarity and confusion at the apex of the UK's legal systems of Byzantine complexity and that 'for the sake of constitutional and democratic stability in post-devolution UK' a better arrangement is needed.

Writing from Northern Ireland, in chapter 3 Brice Dickson charts the relationship between the legal system of the province and the Law Lords. Relatively few appeals from Northern Ireland are heard by the House of Lords and only three of the 105 Law Lords appointed since 1876 have previously served as judges in Northern Ireland. He draws attention to the fact that politically and legally important appeals are, in the absence of more Northern Ireland judges on the UK's top-level court, decided by a 'particularly "English" group of judges' with no first-hand knowledge or experience of adjudicating within Northern Ireland itself. Two models for reform are outlined.

What is at stake in discussions of 'representation' of Scotland and Northern Ireland among the Law Lords and the proposed supreme court? In chapter 4,

Kay Goodall considers whether it is a legal system, more broadly a 'legal tradition', or wider still a 'nation'. She argues, through a historical survey, that the situations of Northern Ireland and Scotland are radically different. To an extent challenging some of the premises in the O'Neill's and Dickson's essays, Goodall concludes that 'visions of law are . . . no longer a predominately national concern'. Whereas 'the primary work in the previous century was seen to be the clarification of the law, today the constitutionalization of rights is said to have brought about a revolution in the role of the senior judges'. She invites us to move away from 'the functionalist presumption that the roles of the Law Lords were ever clearly defined, or the teleological presumption that their roles evolved for some primary purpose which they exhibit today'.

If, however, we accept the on-going importance of difference within the UK, is it possible for this to be accommodated within the institutional design of the proposed new UK supreme court? In chapter 5, Andrée Lajoie argues that the answer to that question is emphatically 'no'. She examines the Canadian experience of attempts to incorporate minority interests (principally those of francophone Canadians and the civilian legal traditions of Quebec) within the court system through (i) bilingualism, (ii) 'bijuridism'—practices of legislative drafting and judicial interpretation aimed at harmonizing common law and civilian law concepts in Federal law and (iii) territorial representation on the bench of the supreme court. Her conclusion is that, despite these attempts, 'accommodation of regional difference has not happened for Quebec where it mattered, that is on issues relating to the Canadian version of "devolution", the constitutional division of legislative and executive powers. The score of the supreme court in this respect in almost a century and a half has been one of relentless centralization'. She suggests that far from being an exceptional failure, the experience of the Canadian court system is typical of that in any legal order.

In chapter 6, Warren Newman also writes about Canada. In 1998, in the UK, one of the reasons given for selecting the Judicial Committee of the Privy Council as the court for 'devolution issues' under the Scotland Act, Northern Ireland Act and Government of Wales Act, was that the Privy Council held that the government 'thought it appropriate to use its experience of handling cases that raise constitutional issues' from various commonwealth dependencies and colonies.[53] In fact, the Privy Council had no experience of 'division of powers' adjudication, as opposed to fundamental rights issues, since Canada stopped sending appeals to London in 1949 (when the Supreme Court of Canada became the highest court for all purposes). Newman shows that the Privy Council:

established, case by case, the complex and intricate framework of principles of constitutional interpretation—pith and substances, leading feature, true purpose, double aspect,

---

[53] Win Griffiths, Hansard HC col 927 (3 February 1998). The Attorney-General of South Australia has written that 'it is surprising to many of us to see that body given a new lease of life as a constitutional court, particularly seeing as it was so inadequate in that role when hearing appeals from Australia': BM Selway 'The Constitution of the UK: a Long Distance Perspective' (2001) 30 *Common Law World* 3, 22.

occupied field, paramountcy, reading down, colourability, severability, and so on—that still governs and shapes most of Canada's constitutional jurisprudence on the division of powers today.

The case law of the 1930s was not met with universal praise in Canada, but Newman argues that the Canadian experience in the adjudication of division of powers issues is a useful reference point for the UK's developing case law on devolution.

Chapter 7, by Ignacio Borrajo Iniesta, concerns the role of the Spanish constitutional court, especially its function in relation to the 'State of autonomies' (the form of devolution adopted since 1979). The *Tribunal constitucional*, established as part of the post-Franco constitutional settlement of 1978, is an example of comparative lesson learning in action: Borrajo explains that it was modelled on the post-World War II German and Italian constitutional courts rather than Spain's own Tribunal of Constitutional Guarantees that briefly existed in the Second Republic (1931–39). Borrajo shows how the constitutional court 'plays a vital role in the equilibriums established by the Constitution to decentralize public power'. An important context is the failure of the upper house of the Spanish parliament (the *Senado*) to fulfil its function as a chamber of 'territorial representation'. Instead, its electoral system duplicates that of the lower house: this 'failure to integrate the autonomous communities' interests and political forces into the general fabric of the State has many perturbing consequences', including to overload the constitutional court with conflicts that in other systems are solved at the federal chambers (the US Senate or the German *Bundesrat*)'.

The *Bundesverfassungsgericht* (German constitutional court) occupies a pre-eminent position in the world's constitutional courts in civilian jurisdictions. In chapter 8, Rainer Nickel assesses its current state and the future challenges it faces in a changing Europe. He shows how the court 'plays a central role in German jurisprudence and politics alike'. He argues that the court faces two pressures: those 'from a strong federal system, on the one hand, demand a clear concept of constitutional federalism, and the challenges connected with "ever closer Union" and with the growing human rights adjudication, on the other, threaten the function of the *Bundesverfassungsgericht* as an integrative social factor'. Upon analysis, however, the European Court of Human Rights is not a threat to the *Bundesverfassungsgericht*. The ECtHR is still 'only' an instrument of international law and only rarely extends a higher standard for protection than that provided by the German constitution. The position of the European Union's court is different, Nickel suggests. Although it has largely been 'business as usual' in the relationship between the *Bundesverfassungsgericht* and the ECJ since the latter's landmark 1993 judgment on the Maastricht Treaty—'the first time that a constitutional court of an EU Member State seriously challenged the construction of the EU and its democratic legitimacy'—Nickel argues that 'the ever growing law production will slowly but certainly erode the central position of the *Bundesverfassungsgericht* as *the* fundamental human rights court of

Germany'. The adoption of a constitution for the EU, a 'superior European constitutional order', may mean that national constitutional courts 'shrink to the second row'.

David Anderson, in chapter 9, continues to examine the relationship between the ECJ, the ECtHR and top-level national courts by providing a 'snapshot' of the practical interaction between the House of Lords and the two European Courts. He calls into question whether the preliminary ruling procedure under Article 234 EC is any longer an effective way of achieving the undoubtedly necessary goal of ensuring the proper application and uniform interpretation of Community law in Member States. Though perhaps too radical to be contemplated at the moment, Anderson suggests that more effective precautions against judicial error by top-level national courts in relation to their decisions in EU law might include liability in damages or infringement proceedings by the Commission in respect of national jurisprudence that is inconsistent with EU law. In relation to the ECtHR, Anderson argues that the 'Strasbourg case law is much better known in the UK than it is in most other Contracting States, including established Council of Europe members such as Germany'.

Continuing the theme that top-level national courts operate within networks of relationships with other courts, in chapter 10 Blake and Drewry consider the role of the Court of England and Wales as an 'intermediate court'. The fact is, they explain, 'the Court of Appeal is normally the final port of call for the minute proportion of cases that are first litigated and then appealed. It necessarily follows that the House of Lords must be performing a different appellate function to that of the Court of Appeal'. The functions of an appeal include (i) review, correcting mistakes of lower courts, and (ii) supervision, managing the development of precedent for the guidance of lower courts. The role of the Court of Appeal 'is mainly one of review although if a case stops there, as most do, the court is bound to act as a supervisory body in many instances, particularly on points of procedure where the House of Lords is normally reluctant to take appeals'. They go on to examine practices in relation to the grant of permission to appeal to the Court of Appeal and House of Lords. Recent rule changes have 'considerably raised the threshold for permission' to bring an appeal to the Court of Appeal. Blake and Drewry point to 'an oddity at work in the permission process': the Court of Appeal is encouraging of first instance courts to make decisions as to whether an appeal to the Court of Appeal should take place ('the court below is often in the best position to judge whether there should be an appeal', the Court of Appeal says in a practice direction). In relation to access to the House of Lords, however, the Court of Appeal has in recent years adopted a self-denying ordinance and rarely itself grants permission for a case to proceed upwards, instead leaving such decisions to the Law Lords. Blake and Drewry also comment on early findings of an empirical study of the Court of Appeal.

The position described by Blake and Drewry as pertaining to England and Wales—with a nominally 'intermediate' appeal court in reality being the final court of appeal for the vast majority of cases—is one familiar in many other common law jurisdictions. In chapter 11, Russell Wheeler examines the dynamics in the relationship between the US federal courts of appeal and the US Supreme Court. Over past decades, the Supreme Court has obtained almost total control over its docket (caseload) through the discretion to select which cases to hear. Having described the jurisdictional framework and main operational arrangements for the courts of appeal and the US Supreme Court, Wheeler examines the different, but overlapping, roles played by the two levels of courts. Form is shaped by function, he argues. Thus, characteristics of the US Supreme Court's institutional design follow on from its main function, namely 'resolution of important federal legal questions': the court should sit en banc not in panels; the Court should be small enough to allow collegial deliberation among its members; although the Court cannot and should not decide every case presented to it, Congress should not create other national appellate bodies to decide some of the cases that the Supreme Court does not decide; decisions of which cases the Court should review should be made by the Court itself; the Court can police the courts of appeals even though it reviews only a very small percentage of court of appeals decisions; and the Court also needs discretion as to its operations. Wheeler concludes by making it clear that 'although much of the debate over possible change in the US federal appellate system is cast in technical terms, the status quo and revisions to it also implicate important political questions about the distribution of power and government services'.

Chapter 12 looks in more detail at the question of how top-level courts select which cases to hear. In common law systems, supreme appellate courts give judgment in only a relatively small proportion of the cases brought to them. During 2001, the House of Lords disposed of 269 petitions for leave, allowing only 68 to go to a full hearing. Anecdotal evidence suggests that it is often far from clear to those involved first-hand why some cases are selected for a full hearing and others rejected. It is suggested the function of the leave requirement has changed over time. When instituted in the 1930s, it was conceived as a way of promoting access to the court. During the 1960s, the concerns were mainly managerial ones to prevent the House of Lords being 'flooded' with criminal appeals. Today, it is argued, a different or further purpose of the leave requirement ought to be emphasised: it has a constitutional function of helping the court define its role. The new practice of the House of Lords to give reasons for refusing leave is welcomed, but consideration is given to additional ways in which the important case selection task can be made more transparent and subject to greater accountability.

In chapter 13, Kate Malleson considers questions relating to the reform of the appointments process for the UK's top-level court. She argues that 'the quality of the judges in the UK's top courts in terms of intellectual ability and integrity is probably higher now than at any time in the 20th century, yet the judicial appointments process is facing an unprecedented challenge to its legitimacy'. A number of models are examined, including election, parliamentary confirm-

ation, and the possible roles of a judicial appointments commission in relation to
the UK's highest court.

Finally, in chapter 14, Richard Gordon provides reflections of his experiences
as an advocate before the Law Lords. Will the leisurely 'seminar' type advocacy
currently used before the Appellate Committee give way to the far shorter times
allowed for oral argument in other top-level courts such as those in the USA and
Canada? He also considers 'the anomaly' that in England and Wales cases are
often dealt with by less specialist judges as they progress on appeal (for instance
from a nominated judge in the Administrative Court, then a three-member Court
of Appeal, to a five-member Appellate Committee).

TOP-LEVEL NATIONAL COURTS IN DEVOLVED AND FEDERAL CONTEXTS

2

Judging Democracy: the Devolutionary Settlement and the Scottish Constitution

AIDAN O'NEILL*

1. INTRODUCTION

The Scotland Act 1998 is sometimes represented by politicians and writers of romantic, if unhistorical, disposition as effectively re-establishing the pre-1707 Union Parliament of Scotland. It does not, of course. The 1707 Parliamentary Union of England and Scotland is not dissolved: section 37 of the 1998 Act specifically provides that the English Union with Scotland Act 1706 and the Scottish Union with England Act 1707 continue to have effect, subject to the new Act. And section 1(1) of the 1998 Act which states that 'there shall be a Scottish Parliament' does not restore the old Estates of Scotland but rather establishes the new Scottish Parliament as a subordinate legislative body ultimately remaining, like parish councils in England, subject to the control of the Parliament of the UK at Westminster. The power of the Parliament of the UK to make laws for Scotland is unaffected by the Scotland Act (see section 28(7)). But the constitutional significance of the Scotland Act for the UK as a whole should not be underestimated, as Lord Rodger of Earlsferry has pointed out:

> The Scotland Act is a major constitutional measure which altered the government of the United Kingdom. This is reflected in the fact that, apart from section 25, the whole Act applies throughout the United Kingdom: section 131. So, not only the Union with England Act 1707 but also the Union with Scotland Act 1706 has effect subject to the Scotland Act: section 37. Sections 29(2)(d) and 57(2) of the Act put it beyond the power of the Scottish Parliament to legislate, and of a member of the Scottish Executive to act, in a way that is incompatible with any of the Convention rights. These are provisions of cardinal importance in the overall constitutional structure created by the Act.[1]

It is crucial to any proper understanding of the role of the judiciary (and of the top courts) under the new devolution dispensation that it be recognized that the new Parliament established at Holyrood is *not* an independent sovereign body. Notwithstanding that they require specific Royal Assent as a condition of their

---

* QC; Advocate at the Scottish Bar; Associate Member of Matrix Chambers, London.
[1] *HM Advocate v 'R'* [2002] UKPC D3; [2003] 2 WLR 317; 2003 SLT 4.

validity, the Acts of the Scottish Parliament are defined in the Human Rights Act 1998 as 'subordinate legislation'. The powers of the Scottish Parliament and Executive are delimited and circumscribed by the provisions of the statute which set them up. As the then Lord President Rodger robustly (if not uncontentiously) observed in the first case to reach the courts concerning the rights and duties of the devolved Holyrood Parliament:

[T]he [Scottish] Parliament [i]s a body which—however important its role—has been created by statute and derives its powers from statute. As such, it is a body which, like any other statutory body, must work within the scope of those powers. If it does not do so, then in an appropriate case the court may be asked to intervene and will require to do so, in a manner permitted by the legislation. In principle, therefore, the Parliament like any other body set up by law is subject to the law and to the courts which exist to uphold that law. . . .

[I]n many democracies throughout the Commonwealth, for example, even where the parliaments have been modelled in some respects on Westminster, they owe their existence and powers to statute and are in various ways subject to the law and to the courts which uphold the law. The Scottish Parliament has simply joined that wider family of parliaments. Indeed, I find it almost paradoxical that counsel for a member of a body which exists to create laws and to impose them on others should contend that a legally enforceable framework is somehow less than appropriate for that body itself. . . .

While *all* United Kingdom courts which may have occasion to deal with proceedings involving the Scottish Parliament can, of course, be expected to accord all due respect to the Parliament *as to any other litigant,* they must equally be aware that they are *not* dealing with a Parliament which is sovereign: on the contrary, it is subject to the laws and hence to the courts. For that reason, I see no basis upon which this court can properly adopt a 'self-denying ordinance'[2] which would consist in exercising some kind of discretion to refuse to enforce the law against the Parliament or its members. To do so would be to fail to uphold the rights of other parties under the law.[3]

What has been created in the Scottish Parliament is a democratic legislature whose acts (including questions regarding its internal workings) are, however, subject to control by the judiciary. In French constitutional writing, the idea of the judiciary having the power to review and strike down provisions of laws which have been duly passed by the legislature has been termed '*un gouvernment des juges*'.[4] This is how the French would characterize the American constitutional position under which, since the seminal judgment in 1803 of the US Supreme Court in *Marbury v Madison*,[5] the courts of that country have claimed the power to declare 'a legislative act contrary to the constitution' as 'not law'. By contrast, on the French constitutional model there can be no possibility for

---

[2] *R v Parliamentary Commissioner for Standards, ex p Al Fayed* [1998] 1 WLR 669 (CA), 670 (Lord Woolf MR).

[3] *Whaley v Lord Watson of Invergowrie and The Scottish Parliament* 2000 SC 125 (OH); 2000 SC 340 (IH), 348H, 349D-E, 350B-C (emphasis added).

[4] H Davis Michael 'A Government of Judges: an historical review' (1987) 35 *American Journal of Comparative Law* 559.

[5] *Marbury v Madison* 5 US 368, 389 (1803).

the judicial review of legislation once formally enacted. The separation of powers as understood in post-revolutionary France (given the experience during the *Ancien Regime* of judicial review of laws by a variety of regional courts, termed the *Parlements*) meant that the duty of judges was seen to be one of applying the law, rather than questioning it.[6] Since the adoption of the Constitution of the Fifth Republic in 1958, however, the French model has allowed for a narrow window of opportunity for limited constitutional review of proposed legislation, after its passage through Parliament but prior to its formal promulgation, which may be carried out by the *Conseil Constitutionnel* on a reference from the President of the Republic, the Prime Minister, the presidents of the two assemblies or 60 members of either the National Assembly or the Senate.[7]

The Scotland Act 1998 has perhaps surprisingly gone for a belt and braces approach. Section 33 of the Act gives the Advocate General, the Lord Advocate and the Attorney-General the power to refer Bills which have been passed or approved by the Scottish Parliament but not yet submitted for Royal Assent to the Privy Council for a ruling as to whether or not the provisions of the Bill fall within the legislative competence of the Scottish Parliament. This new role for the Privy Council—carrying out a form of 'pre-legislative' judicial review— would appear to be modelled on the current French provisions relating to the *Conseil Constitutionnel*.[8] But the French constitution, in contrast to that of the USA, continues to bar the courts from any possible judicial review of measures once these have been duly passed into law by the legislative assembly.[9] By contrast, sections 98 to 102 of and schedule 6 to the Scotland Act clearly envisage that *all* courts in the UK hierarchy will also have the power to carry out post-enactment judicial review of Scottish legislation, on the US constitutional model.

The granting of such wholesale powers of legislative judicial review creates a challenging new role for the judges. It raises large questions as to the interrelationship between the principle of judicial respect for the democratic will of the Scottish people (as expressed by the Scottish Parliament) and the enforcement by the judges of the limits laid down on that legislature in accordance with the democratic will of the peoples of the UK (as expressed by the UK Parliament and government in the provisions of the Scotland Act).

---

[6] N Carey 'Judicial Review of Acts of Parliament: the French Experience' [1998] *Trinity College Law Review* 71.

[7] P Linseth 'Law History and Memory: "Republican Moments" and the legitimacy of Constitutional Review in France' (1996/97) 3 *Columbia Journal of European Law* 49.

[8] See JE Beardsley 'Constitutional Review in France' (1975) *Supreme Court Review* 189 and Vroom 'The Constitutional Protection of Individual Liberties in France: the *Conseil Constitutionnel* since 1971' (1988) 63 *Tulane Law Review* 265.

[9] See H Davis Michael 'The Law/Politics Distinction, the French *Conseil Constitutionnel*, and the US Supreme Court' (1986) 34 *American Journal of Comparative Law* 45 and B Neuborne 'Judicial Review and Separation of Powers in France and the United States' (1982) 57 *New York University Law Review* 363.

Since the limits of the new legislative body are set out in statute, the task of ensuring that the Parliament stays within the powers granted to it is one for the courts. Section 29(1) of the Scotland Act provides that 'an *Act* of the Scottish Parliament is not law so far as *any provision* is *outside* the legislative competence of the Parliament'. Possible conflict between the UK Parliament and the Holyrood Parliament on claims that the new body is exceeding its limited powers is thus made into a juridical rather than a nakedly political matter.

The danger is, of course, that in giving the task of policing the Scottish Parliament to the courts, the judges come to be seen or to be presented as acting in a broadly political role, holding the ring between the demands of the UK Parliament and the expectations of the Holyrood Parliament. The juridicalization of what is essentially political conflict will inevitably lead to a perception of the politicization of the judiciary.

2. IDENTIFYING THE TOP COURT AFTER DEVOLUTION

Prior to the coming into force of the devolution statutes, one could relatively easily identify the top courts within the UK. It was clear that:

- the House of Lords was the final court of appeal for England, Wales, and Northern Ireland in both criminal and civil matters;
- the House of Lords was also the final court of appeal in civil cases appealed from the Court of Session in Scotland;
- the High Court of Justiciary was the final court of appeal from criminal matters in Scotland. Decisions of the House of Lords did *not* bind the High Court of Justiciary[10] and Scots criminal law developed entirely independently from that of the English and English derived systems;
- in matters of substantive European Community law under the EC Treaty and associated treaties, UK courts were and are obliged to decide cases 'in accordance with the principles laid down by, and any relevant decision of, the European Court of Justice'.[11]

With the coming into force of section 2(1) of the Human Rights Act 1998, UK courts were placed under a statutory obligation to 'have regard to' the decisions

---

[10] cf the statement of the High Court of Justiciary in *Lord Advocate's Reference (No 1 of 2000) Re Nuclear Weapons* 2001 JC 143 (a case concerning possible reliance on norms derived from customary international law by way of defence to a prosecution for criminal damage to government property associated with the Trident missile defence system) at para 60: 'In our view it is not at all clear that if this issue had been fully debated before us the incorporation of Trident II in the UK's defence strategy, in pursuance of a strategic policy of global deterrence, would have been regarded as giving rise to issues which were properly justiciable. *Chandler* [*v Director of Public Prosecutions* [1964] AC 763, HL] *remains binding authority in this court*. Such developments as have taken place seem to have left untouched the status of the prerogative in matters relating to the defence of the realm. However, we have not been asked to dispose of the case on this basis, and we see no alternative but to reserve the issue for another occasion' (emphasis added).

[11] European Communities Act 1972, s 3(1).

of the European Court of Human Rights (ECtHR) in matters concerning Convention rights.[12] The UK courts have interpreted this as meaning that the jurisprudence of the ECtHR, while of persuasive authority, is not to be regarded as formally binding upon them under domestic law.[13] At the level of public international law, however, the decisions of the ECtHR specifically pronounced against the UK *are* binding upon all its political institutions—legislative, executive and judicial.[14] Under the European Convention for the Protection of Human Rights and Fundamental Freedoms 1950 (ECHR) national courts are regarded by the ECtHR as organs or emanations of the Contracting States, and therefore themselves bound, under Article 1 ECHR, to secure to everyone within their jurisdiction the rights and freedoms set out in the Convention and required, under Article 13 ECHR, to ensure that there exists an effective remedy against what the ECtHR consider to be violations of the Convention rights and freedoms.[15]

The already complicated picture has, however, been further complicated by the coming into force of the devolution statutes—the Scotland Act 1998, the Government of Wales Act 1988 and the Northern Ireland Act 1998—all of which make reference to and define a new category of legal questions, 'devolution issues', arising out of the creation of devolved governments for the non-English parts of the UK.[16] Devolution issues are boundary markers. They are concerned with questions as to whether or not the devolved assemblies and administrations have transgressed the limits of the powers granted them under their founding acts—for example, by entering into areas reserved to the UK Parliament, or by being in breach of Community law, or in being *incompatible with any Convention rights* or by otherwise being out with the legislative competence of the devolved institutions.

As we have seen, questions as to the 'constitutionality' of the acts or omissions of the devolved institutions and administrations (in the sense of whether or not these conform to the limits set out in their founding statutes) may, if relevant to the matter at hand, competently be raised in any proceedings before any courts in the UK: such matters are *not* reserved for decision by the higher courts. In principle, devolution issues may arise within any of the legal jurisdictions of the UK: thus, questions as to the *vires* of a Welsh measure might be raised before a Scottish court; while Scottish legislation may be challenged in Northern Ireland or in England. Schedules 6, 8, and 10 to the Scotland Act, Government of Wales

[12] Human Rights Act 1998, s 1(1)–(2). See also n 26.

[13] *Brown v Stott* 2001 SC (PC) 43; [2001] 2 WLR 817 [43] in which the PC declined to follow the ECtHR's developing case law, notably *Saunders v UK* (1997) 23 EHRR 313 on the privilege against self-incrimination.

[14] *Montgomery v HM Advocate* 2001 SC (PC) 1; [2001] 2 WLR 779, 785 (Lord Hoffmann). See also R Higgins 'The Relationship between International and Regional Humanitarian Law and Domestic Law' (1992) 18 CLB 1268, 1268.

[15] *R v Kansal (No 2)* [2001] UKHL 62; [2002] 2 AC 69 (HL) [55], [79] (Lord Hope).

[16] For the various definitions of 'devolution issues' see para 1 of each of: sch 6 to the Scotland Act 1998; sch 8 to the Government of Wales Act 1998; and sch 10 to the Northern Ireland Act 1998.

Act and Northern Ireland Act respectively set out the procedures to be followed when devolution issues are raised before courts in the UK. All provide that frivolous or vexatious challenges to the competence of devolved legislation or administrative action or omissions need not, however, be taken up by the courts.[17]

A. The Privy Council as the top court in devolution issues

While the devolution statutes have put it within the power of all UK courts to review and strike down on grounds of competence both primary and subordinate legislation emanating from the devolved institutions, the three devolution statutes have also created a new role for the Privy Council in that they have given it, rather than the House of Lords, jurisdiction on the question of the final domestic resolution of any 'devolution issues'.

But it is only those Privy Councillors who hold or have held the office of a Lord of Appeal in Ordinary, or high judicial office as defined in section 25 of the Appellate Jurisdiction Act 1876 (that is to say English and Northern Ireland High Court and Court of Appeal Judges and, in Scotland, Senators of the College of Justice) may sit and act as a member of the Committee in proceedings under the Act. In effect, what this means is that Privy Councillors who were Commonwealth but not UK judges (for example the New Zealander Lord Cooke of Thorndon) are excluded from sitting in the Privy Council on devolution issue proceedings notwithstanding that they could continue to sit in the House of Lords even where devolution issues were raised. Secondly, although the pool of potential members of the UK Judicial Committee of the Privy Council is much wider than that of the potential members of the Appellate Committee of the House of Lords (which is restricted to holders of high judicial office in the UK who also have a peerage), unless Court of Appeal and Inner House judges—now *ex officio* appointed as Privy Councillors—are specifically called upon to sit on a particular hearing of the UK Judicial Committee (as the Court of Session judge, Lord Kirkwood was in *Brown v Stott*)[18] there will, in practice, be a high degree of overlap between those who are active House of Lords judges and those who sit as Privy Council judges in devolution cases.[19]

---

[17] Para 2 of each of sch 6 to the Scotland Act 1998, sch 8 to the Government of Wales Act 1998 and sch 10 to the Northern Ireland Act 1998.

[18] 2001 SC (PC) 43; [2003] 1 AC 681 in which the PC upheld the Crown appeal and *reversed* the unanimous decision of the High Court of Justiciary (reported at 2000 SLT 379) to the effect that the proposal by the Crown to lead and rely in court upon evidence of the admission which the accused was compelled to make to the police under s 172(2)(a) of the Road Traffic Act 1988 contravened her Convention right against self-incrimination implicit in Art 6.

[19] Lord Hope of Craighead 'Edinburgh v Westminster & Others: resolving constitutional disputes—inside the crystal ball again?' (1997) 42 *Journal of the Law Society of Scotland* 140 for a discussion of the differences between the House of Lords and the Judicial Committee of the Privy Council.

B. The Privy Council as the top court in UK human rights issues?

Section 103 of the Scotland Act, section 82 of the Northern Ireland Act and paragraph 32 of schedule 8 to the Government of Wales Act all assert the binding nature of decisions of the Privy Council in proceedings under these Acts in *all other courts and legal proceedings*, apart from later cases brought before the Privy Council.

These statutory provisions have reversed the previous common law rule to the effect that that the House of Lords in its judicial capacity is *not* bound by decisions of the Privy Council.[20] The position is now, instead, that when the Privy Council pronounces in a case brought under its devolution issue jurisdiction—but not its Commonwealth jurisdiction—it will bind even the House of Lords.[21] The precise reason for this provision is unclear. It may be that the purpose of this new provision was to ensure uniformity of approach across the UK on matters of Convention rights, among others. It may be that it was intended as a counter-weight to the idea of introducing, for the first time, an appeal outside Scotland in matters of criminal law from decisions of the High Court of Justiciary.[22]

For whatever reason we have, however, a *new* supreme court for the UK. It is a new court, too, in its method: in contrast to the traditional approach of the Privy Council advising with one voice the Sovereign in Empire and Commonwealth cases,[23] the devolution issue Privy Council has multiple and sometimes sharply dissenting judgments.[24]

In the first four years of the devolutionary settlement (May 1999 to April 2003) there were a total of 12 cases which had come to the Privy Council

[20] *London Joint Stock Bank v MacMillan and Arthur* [1918] AC 777 (HL), 807 (Finlay LC).

[21] For extra-judicial reservations about the appropriateness of using the Judicial Committee of the Privy Council in this way, rather than the HL, see Lord Steyn 'Incorporation and Devolution—a Few Reflections on the Changing Scene' [1998] *European Human Rights Law Review* 153. The nine-judge bench decision of the HL hearing the appeal from the decision of the Court of Appeal in *Attorney-General's Reference (No 2 of 2001)* [2001] 1 WLR 1869 was, however, awaited at the time of writing. This decision concerns the same substantive Convention issue arising in English as was determined in Scots law by the PC in *HM Advocate v 'R'* [2002] UKPC D3; [2003] 2 WLR 317; 2003 SLT 4—namely, whether the proper remedy for a breach of the reasonable time requirements of Art 6(1) ECHR in criminal prosecutions should be a stay in those proceedings. The constitutional question arises as to whether or not the nine judges of the HL will indeed consider themselves to be bound to follow the reasoning of the three majority (Scots) judges in the earlier PC decision.

[22] It has been suggested that the then Secretary of State for Scotland responsible for the drafting and promotion of the Scotland Bill, Donald Dewar MP, wished to soften the constitutional innovation of allowing for appeals in Scottish criminal cases outside Scotland by specifying a re-vamped Judicial Committee of the Privy Council as the appropriate court for this rather than the House of Lords.

[23] The tradition of unanimity has been abandoned even in Commonwealth cases before the PC: see eg the dissenting judgment of Lord Scott of Foscote in *R v A-G of England and Wales* [2003] UKPC 22, a decision on appeal from the Court of Appeal of New Zealand concerning the enforceability of MoD contracts requiring SAS members to maintain post-service confidentiality.

[24] R Munday 'Judicial Configuration, permutations of the court and properties of judgment' (2002) 61 *Cambridge Law Journal* 612, for discussion of this constitutional innovation of multiple and dissenting judgment in the PC.

under its new devolution issue jurisdiction.[25] All of these cases came from Scotland, all but one of them on appeal from the High Court of Justiciary acting as the court of criminal appeal in Scotland. Two of these cases were preliminary hearings before a three judge panel considering applications for special leave to appeal to the Privy Council cases after such leave had been refused by the court in Scotland. The remaining 10 cases were substantive appeals before five judges. In *all* of these devolution hearings before the Privy Council, there was a substantial Scottish presence on the bench hearing the application— Lord Hope, indeed, sat in all of these Privy Council's devolution cases. In both the preliminary applications for special leave and in two substantive cases— *Brown v Stott* and *HM Advocate v 'R'*—Scots judges formed a majority of the judges.

All of these devolution issue cases before the Privy Council concerned disputes over *Convention rights*, rather than any other disputes over the legal competences of the devolved institutions. Only one of the cases before the Privy Council was by way of direct reference to it on the application of the Lord Advocate using his powers under paragraph 33 of schedule 6 to the Scotland Act[26] after the special leave which had been granted by the Privy Council from the decision of the High Court lapsed, because the instance in the original case had fallen.[27] The Crown appealed to the Privy Council from the High Court of Justiciary in three of the cases and in two of these appeals the Crown was successful.[28] Of the six other substantive cases brought on appeal to the Privy Council by individuals, only two were successful.[29] Both the reported prelimin-

---

[25] The substantive decisions are, respectively: *Montgomery v HM Advocate* 2001 SC (PC) 1; [2003] 1 AC 641 (Art 6 ECHR and pre-trial publicity); *Brown v Stott (Procurator Fiscal, Dunfermline)* 2001 SC (PC) 43; [2003] 1 AC 681 (Art 6 and the privilege against self-incrimination); *McIntosh (Robert) v HM Advocate (No 1)* [2001] UKPC D1; 2001 SC (PC) 89; [2001] 3 WLR 107 (Art 6, drug confiscation orders and the presumption of innocence); *McLean v Buchanan (Procurator Fiscal, Fort William)* [2001] UKPC D3; 2002 SC (PC) 1; [2001] 1 WLR 2425 (Art 6, legal aid and the equality of arms between prosecutors and criminal defence lawyers); *Millar v Dickson* [2001] UKPC D4; 2002 SC (PC) 30; [2002] 1 WLR 1615 (Art 6 and possible waiver of the right to an independent and impartial tribunal); *Anderson v Scottish Ministers* [2001] UKPC D5, 2002 SC (PC) 63; [2002] 3 WLR 1460 (Art 5(1)(e) and the detention of persons of unsound mind); *Dyer v Watson and HM Advocate v K* [2002] UKPC D1; 2002 SC (PC) 89; [2002] 3 WLR 1488 (Art 6 and the factors indicating unreasonable delay); *Mills v HM Advocate (No 2)* [2002] UKPC D2; [2002] 3 WLR 1597, 2002 SLT 939 (Art 6 unreasonable delay between conviction and hearing of appeal and the remedy of a reduction in sentence); *HM Advocate v 'R'* [2002] UKPC D3; [2003] 2 WLR 317; 2003 SLT 4 (Art 6 unreasonable delay in bringing charges and remedies under the Scotland Act); *Clark v Kelly* [2003] UKPC D1; [2003] 2 WLR 1586 (Art 6 and the independence and impartiality of the district court). There have also been two decisions of the screening committee refusing special leave to appeal, namely: *Hoekstra v Her Majesty's Advocate (No 5)* 2001 SC (PC) 37; [2001] 1 AC 216 and *Follen v HM Advocate* [2001] UKPC D2; 2001 SC (PC) 105; [2001] 1 WLR 1668.

[26] *Clark v Kelly* (n 25).

[27] *Clark v Kelly* 2001 JC 16 (HCJ).

[28] *Brown v Stott* (n 25) and *McIntosh v HM Advocate* (n 25) were the successful Crown appeals against decisions of the High Court of Justiciary. *Dyer v Watson and HM Advocate v K* (n 25) was the unsuccessful Crown appeal.

[29] *Millar v Dickson* and *HM Advocate v 'R'* (n 25) were the two successful appeals by individuals to the PC against the High Court of Justiciary.

ary applications brought by individuals for special leave to appeal to the Privy Council were unsuccessful.[30]

The Privy Council had, at the time of writing, overturned the decision of the High Court of Justiciary in *four* of the *nine* substantive cases which have been brought before it from that court.[31] At almost one-half this is a very significant rate of reversal of the decisions of the High Court of Justiciary, a court from which there had been *no* appeal prior to the devolutionary settlement.

This new UK Privy Council—which has primacy over the House of Lords—has then, to date, been a substantially Scottish enterprise. This must present the non-Scottish members of the Privy Council with certain difficulties, given that there will doubtless be a sensitivity on the part of the non-Scots participants on the Judicial Committee to try not to offend the sensibilities of the Scots—or to tread on Scottish toes—in coming to their decisions (although the South African educated Law Lords, Lord Hoffmann and Lord Steyn seem to have been more robust in this regard). But it gives the Scottish members of the committee undoubted power (and, indeed perhaps an unfair advantage) in that the Scots law dimension can be used, as it were as a trump card, in the course of the Committee's deliberation in coming to its decisions.[32] To date, it seems that the Scottish card has been used in at least two ways.

First, in order to give a broad interpretation to the term 'devolution issues'—in the face of initial scepticism and indeed hostility in the analysis of the non-Scots judges in the Privy Council[33]—to include within the ambit of the Convention right to a fair trial the acts of the Lord Advocate and the Procurator Fiscal Service in bringing and pursuing criminal prosecutions in Scotland.[34] After the significant internal dissent seen in its decision *Montgomery v HM Advocate*,[35] a differently constituted Board of the Privy Council in *Brown v Stott*[36] (shorn of the doubting non-Scots judges seen in *Montgomery* but with the addition of a Court of Session judge in Lord Kirkwood, thereby producing a majority of Scottish judges on the Privy Council bench) held—this time, unanimously—that the manner in which both summary or solemn procedure prosecutions are conducted by the prosecuting authorities in Scotland may be said to raise devolution issues. This view is reached on the basis that all criminal prosecutions in Scotland concern the exercise of the functions of the Lord Advocate[37] and that

---

[30] *Hoekstra v Her Majesty's Advocate (No 5)* and *Follen v HM Advocate* (n 25).

[31] These four cases in which the PC has reversed the High Court of Justiciary are: *Brown v Stott*; *McIntosh v HM Advocate*; *Millar v Dickson*; and *HM Advocate v 'R'* (n 25).

[32] eg *Montgomery v HM Advocate* (n 25) 12D-E, 13A-C (Lord Hope).

[33] ibid 7B-C (Lord Hoffmann).

[34] *Brown v Stott* (n 25) 71G-H (Lord Hope).

[35] (n 25) a decision in which Lord Slynn, Lord Nicholls of Birkenhead and Lord Hoffmann expressed a degree of reservations (against the certainties of Lord Clyde and Lord Hope of Craighead) over the question as to whether the devolution jurisdiction of the PC had properly been invoked.

[36] (n 25), a decision in which Lord Clyde and Lord Hope of Craighead stayed in post with the remainder of the Board consisting of Lord Bingham of Cornhill, Lord Steyn and the Rt Hon Ian Kirkwood (Lord Kirkwood).

[37] (n 25) 17H-18E (Lord Hope); see also *Brown v Stott* (n 25) 71D-E (Lord Hope).

the Lord Advocate—and all those prosecuting on his behalf[38]—are said to owe a general duty of ensure that individuals receive a fair trial within a reasonable time before the courts.[39] This is a duty which runs concurrently with, and is not displaced by, the court's own duty to ensure the fairness of trials. The Lord Advocate's duty to ensure that any appeal against conviction be heard speedily is not so clear cut, however.[40]

But the Scottish card has also been played in the Privy Council not to ensure uniformity of approach but also to ensure difference, most clearly in relation to remedies available when a breach of a Convention right is established. On the question of remedies, particular emphasis has placed on the peculiar and specific constitutional settlement which Scotland has been afforded under the Scotland Act which is said to be distinct from the constitutional settlement applying in England as a result simply of the application of the Human Rights Act. In *HM Advocate v 'R'*,[41] the procedural provisions of the Scotland Act were said to take precedence as *lex specialis* over the Human Rights Act such that Convention rights complaints against the Lord Advocate and other members of the Scottish Executive have to be taken as devolution issues rather than simply as human rights issues under the Human Rights Act. This question of procedural exclusivity and the devolution status will be discussed more fully below. At this stage, it is enough to observe that such an interpretation of the statutory provisions also maintains, of course, a live and broad jurisdiction for the UK Privy Council in Convention law matters.

---

[38] In *Brown v Stott* 2000 JC 328, the following concession was noted by Lord Justice General, Lord Rodger of Earlsferry: '[T]he Lord Advocate had issued an instruction that the Crown should present *no* argument to the effect that, when acting under summary procedure, a procurator fiscal does not act as his representative and hence does not act as the representative of a member of the Scottish Executive for the purpose of s 57(2) of the Scotland Act. The Lord Advocate's instruction relieves us of any need to explore the exact nature of the relationship between the Lord Advocate and procurators fiscal in summary cases. I therefore proceed on the basis that, subject to s 57(3), the *procurator fiscal* in this case has no power to do any act which would be incompatible with the appellant's Convention rights' (emphasis added). In *Starrs v Ruxton (Procurator Fiscal, Linlithgow)* 2000 JC 208, the High Court was advised by the Solicitor-General that: '[T]he *Lord Advocate expected the Procurator Fiscal to be bound by the Convention as he is*, and that he would not take any point that something which was done by the procurator fiscal was not his act as Lord Advocate and as a member of the Scottish Executive' (emphasis added).

[39] In *Montgomery v HM Advocate* (n 25) 19G (Lord Hope):'But *the approach which that Act has taken is that the right of the accused to receive a fair trial is a responsibility of the Lord Advocate as well as of the court*' (emphasis added). See too 8H-I in which Lord Hope relies in part on Hume's *Commentaries on the Law of Scotland Respecting Crimes* (Bell and Bradfute Edinburgh 1844) vol 2, 134.

[40] *Mills v HM Advocate (No 2)* (n 25) [38] (Lord Hope): '[I]t should be borne in mind that the position of the prosecutor is *not* the same at the stage of an appeal as it was during the trial: *Howitt v HM Advocate* 2000 SCCR 195, 200B *per* the Lord Justice Clerk (Cullen). During the trial he is the master of the instance: Alison *Practice of the Criminal Law of Scotland* (1833) 88–90. What happens to a conviction thereafter is the responsibility of the court. It may be more difficult in these circumstances to identify an 'act' of the Lord Advocate which can be said to have caused delay in the hearing of an appeal' (emphasis added).

[41] (n 25).

The problem with this use of the Scottish trump card in decisions of the Privy Council is that it may be thought to pre-empt or upstage consideration of or decision on similar issues by the House of Lords in non-Scottish (particularly in purely English) law matters. It may also be thought to be contrary to the intent of the devolution settlement for the Privy Council to operate primarily as a further Scottish appeal court instead of a court for the whole of the UK, giving guidance and binding rulings on, inter alia, the interpretation and application of Convention rights after taking full and due account of the impact of their rulings on *all* the legal system of the UK, and not simply the Scottish legal system.

The significance of the statutory provision in the devolution statutes giving primacy throughout the UK to the decisions of the UK Privy Council over those of the Appellate Committee of the House of Lords is one which was, apparently, been little understood or appreciated prior to the coming into force of the devolutionary settlement.[42] But because of the way in which the devolution jurisdiction of the Privy Council has been developed we now have a situation in which particularly on questions of the effect and scope of *Convention rights* (which have been duly raised under the devolution statutes) the House of Lords has been superseded as the final court of appeal in the UK. The English final court of appeal in civil and criminal matters, the House of Lords, has itself been placed at level lower in the judicial hierarchy by another court, the Privy Council, which a developing constitutional convention seems to indicate, will be a court composed substantially (and at times by a majority) of Scots lawyers deciding cases brought primarily from Scotland. This must come as a great shock to many English human rights lawyers, who have engaged in litigation over Convention rights issues since the coming into force of the Human Rights Act in England at the beginning of October 2000.

The somewhat surprising (and surely unintended) result of this might be thought to be an effective Scottish take-over of English law when matters of Convention rights are raised in the UK Privy Council, and the exclusion of the majority of English lawyers and English judges effectively to reach final and binding decisions on Convention points. Thus, while the English Court of Appeal[43] decided in December 2000 on the compatibility with Convention rights of the procedure for property confiscation orders to be made in drug trafficking cases, the final decision on this question of Convention compatibility was effectively taken, not on any subsequent appeal by the parties to that case the House of Lords,[44] but by the supervening decision of February 2001 of the Privy Council in the Scottish case of *HM Advocate v McIntosh*[45] which reversed the majority finding of the High Court of Justiciary (sitting in Edinburgh as a court of criminal appeal) to the effect that the legal regime

---

[42] A O'Neill 'Judicial Politics and the Judicial Committee: the devolution jurisprudence of the Privy Council' (2001) 64 *Modern Law Review* 603.

[43] *R v Karl Benjafield* [2001] 3 WLR 75 (CA).

[44] *R v Karl Benjafield* [2002] UKHL 2; [2002] 2 WLR 235 (HL) [9]–[10] (Lord Steyn).

[45] (n 25).

governing such confiscation was incompatible with the fair trial requirements of Article 6.[46]

A further example may be given. In *HM Advocate v 'R'*, the UK Privy Council considered the question as what remedy could be pronounced by the court where it was found that there had been a breach of his Article 6 right to be brought to trial within a 'reasonable time'. The Judicial Committee in this case was composed of a majority of Scottish judges—Lord Hope, Lord Rodger and Lord Clyde—and in its decision split 3:2 with the three Scottish judges holding that the *only* remedy which could be pronounced was to order that the proceedings in Scotland brought by or in the name of the Lord Advocate be discontinued, since the act of continuing to prosecute charges after a reasonable time was incompatible with Article 6 and the Lord Advocate had, by virtue of section 57(2) of the Scotland Act, *no power* to act in a Convention incompatible manner.

The two non-Scots (the South African educated Lord Steyn and the Englishman, Lord Walker) were clearly unhappy with this result fearing, perhaps, that the decision in the Scottish case would mean that a similar result would have to be reached in English proceedings[47] which they were unwilling to countenance, given that the Strasbourg jurisprudence appeared to allow, rather than the quashing of all charges, a lesser remedy for breach of the reasonable time requirement, such as civil damages or a reduction in sentence. The concern of the non-Scots on the Committee appears also to have been that human rights should not be brought into public disrepute by too 'black letter' or absolutist an approach in their application. Lord Steyn observed:

A characteristically elegant observation of L'Heureux-Dubé J in *R v O'Connor* [1995] 4 SCR 411 is relevant. She said p 461, (para 69): 'It is important to recognize that the Charter has now put into judges' hands a scalpel instead of an axe—a tool that may fashion, more carefully than ever, solutions taking into account the sometimes complementary and sometimes opposing concerns of fairness to the individual, societal interests, and the integrity of the judicial system.

The moral authority of human rights in the eyes of the public must not be undermined by allowing them to run riot in our justice systems. In working out solutions under the Scotland Act 1998 and the Human Rights Act 1998 courts in Scotland and England should *at all times* seek to adopt proportionate remedies. In my view there is nothing in the open-textured language of section 57(2), read in context, which rules out the application of such an approach in this case.[48]

Lord Rodger of Earlsferry countered:

Judges, commentators and members of the public may have different views as to whether Parliament went too far when it prescribed these radical consequences for the infringement of this particular right of the appellant—even though the right is one of 'extreme

---

[46] *McIntosh v HM Advocate* 2000 SLT 1280 (HCJ).

[47] *AG's Reference (No 2 of 2001)* [2001] EWCA Crim 1568; [2001] 1 WLR 1869 (CA) (on appeal to the House of Lords at the time of writing, unprecedentedly to a bench of nine judges made up of all the Lords of Appeal in Ordinary, with the exceptions of Lords Saville and Hutton, both otherwise engaged in judicial inquiries, and the most junior Law Lord, Lord Walker).

[48] In *HM Advocate v 'R'* (n 25) para 18 (emphasis added). See also Lord Steyn's remarks in *Brown v Stott* (n 25) 839.

importance' for the proper administration of justice. [...] In enacting a constitutional settlement of immense social and political significance for the whole of the UK, Parliament has itself balanced the competing interests of the Government of the UK, of the Scottish Executive, of society and of the individuals affected. Having done so, Parliament has decided that members of the Scottish Executive should have no power to do acts that are incompatible with any of the Convention rights. In this case that means that the Lord Advocate has no power to continue the prosecution on charges 1 and 3. *If this is to use an axe rather than a scalpel, then Parliament has selected the tool. Your Lordships' Board cannot re-open the exercise that Parliament undertook and re-balance the competing interests for itself.* Rather, it must loyally give effect to the decision of Parliament on this sensitive matter, even if—or perhaps especially if—there are attractions in a different solution.[49]

But the Privy Council decision in the case of 'R' might now conceivably open arguments in English criminal proceedings to the effect that a failure to give persons charged in England at least as good a remedy for breach of the reasonable time requirement in criminal prosecutions as is available to those charged in Scotland is itself a breach of Article 14 ECHR which provides that 'the enjoyment of the rights and freedoms set forth in this Convention shall be secured without discrimination on any ground such as ... race ... national or social origin, birth or other status.' The English do, after all, constitute a distinct racial group from the Scots for the purposes of the Race Relations Act 1976.[50]

C. Top court in European matters?[51]

From the point of view of the national courts of the EU there are effectively two final human rights courts in Europe—one based in Luxembourg as regards matters of European Community law (the ECJ) and another, based in Strasbourg, as regards non-Community law matters (the ECtHR).[52] This potentially places the EU Member States in a difficult position—in particular, the existence of two distinct means of reference to fundamental rights, either under reference to the Human Rights Act 1998 or under reference to the general principles of Community law, in fact exacerbates the possibility of conflict for national courts between competing fundamental rights considerations and interpretations.[53]

---

[49] *HM Advocate v 'R'* (n 25) [152], [155] (emphasis added).

[50] *BBC Scotland v Souster* 2001 SC 458 (IH).

[51] For fuller discussion of this aspect see A O'Neill 'Fundamental Rights and the Constitutional Supremacy of Community Law in the UK after Devolution and the Human Rights Act' [2002] *Public Law* 724.

[52] Opinion 2/94 *Accession of the Community to the European Human Rights Convention* [1996] ECR I-1759.

[53] cf the Opinion of AG Jacobs in Case C–168/91 *Konstantinidis v Stadt Altensteig Standeasamt* [1993] ECR I-1191 [50]–[51] where he states: '[I]f the Court of Justice were to extend the circumstances in which the Convention may be invoked under Community law, the result would simply be to increase the likelihood of a remedy being found under domestic law, without the need for application to the organs established by the Convention'.

The authorities in the Contracting States may be found by the ECtHR to have breached the requirements of the Convention even where the matter at issue comes within the sphere of Community law and the Member State has in fact no discretion or power to do other than what is required of them under Community law.[54] It would appear that in such a situation the authorities of the Member State will be damned by the ECtHR if they act in accordance with Community law but in breach of Convention rights, but they will be damned by the ECJ if they act in breach of the requirements of Community law.[55]

Except in the case of the Lord Advocate in prosecuting any offence or acting in his capacity as head of the systems of criminal investigation of deaths in Scotland, the Scottish Parliament and Scottish Ministers are bound in absolute terms by sections 29(2)(d) and 57(2), respectively, of the Scotland Act 1998 to act in a manner compatible with Convention rights. In contrast to other public authorities, including the devolved institutions of Wales and Northern Ireland, it is not open to the Scottish Parliament or the Members of the Scottish Executive to rely upon section 6(2) of the Human Rights Act to justify any breaches of Convention rights on the grounds that they were required to do so by provisions of primary UK legislation.

In effect, this would seem to mean that neither the Scottish Parliament nor the Scottish Executive can justify any action incompatible with a Convention right on the grounds that they were required so to act by Community law. They are required to respect the Convention, which arguably means as interpreted and understood by the ECtHR. The devolved administration and parliament in Scotland will accordingly be bound *under the Scotland Act* by potentially incompatible judgments on fundamental rights of both the ECJ and the ECtHR.

Thus, the resolution of 'devolution issues' by the domestic courts in the UK may result in their being impelled by the logic of the new constitutional settlement to be the final arbiters in any divergence on fundamental rights issues as between the ECJ and the ECtHR in much the same way as the German constitutional courts, the *Bundesverfassungsgericht*, has reasserted against the claims of the ECJ that it and not the ECJ is the final arbiter on matters concerning the protection of fundamental rights in German territory, even within the field of Community law.[56] As Paul Kirchhoff, Justice of the German Constitutional Court, has noted extra-judicially:

---

[54] See eg *Matthews v UK* (1999) 28 EHRR 361; *Cantoni v France* 15 November 1996, RJD 1996-V, 1614; (App 51717/99) *Guérin Automobiles EURL v Member States of the European Community*, decision of 4 July 2000 ECtHR.

[55] I Canor '*Primus Inter Pares*: Who Is the Ultimate Guardian of Fundamental Rights in Europe?' [2000] *European Law Review* 3.

[56] eg *Maastricht Urteil* BVerfGE 89, 155. Translated in to English as *Brunner v European Union Treaty* [1994] 1 CMLR 57, [55]: 'The Federal Republic of Germany, therefore, even after the Union Treaty comes into force, will remain a member of an association of States (*Staatenbund*), the common authority of which is derived from the Member States and can only have binding effects within the German sovereign sphere by virtue of the German instruction that its law be applied'. See further ch 8.

If ... *Community law* were to seek to abridge the *fundamental rights* protection deemed immutable by [the German Constitution] the *Grundgesetz*, [German] constitutional law would then have the mandate and the power to reject this imposition as not being legally binding.[57]

In similar vein, Laws LJ observed, in the context of an appeal the conviction of traders who had been prosecuted for continuing to sell their goods in Imperial avoirdupois rather than in metric measures:

In the event, which no doubt would never happen in the real world, that a European [Community] measure was seen to be repugnant to a fundamental or constitutional right guaranteed by the law of England, a question would arise whether the general words of the European Communities Act 1972 were sufficient to incorporate the measure and give it overriding effect in domestic law.[58]

D. Preliminary reference procedure to the Privy Council in devolution issues

The UK Attorney-General, the Attorney-General for Northern Ireland, the Westminster based Advocate General for Scotland, and the Lord Advocate (ex officio a member of the Scottish Executive) are given a variety of powers and rights relative to the institution, defending and receiving of intimation of proceedings concerning the determination of any devolution issue. Mandatory references directly to the Privy Council may be made of devolution issues in proceedings in which any of the Law Officers are parties, on their application.[59]

The devolution statutes all provide for the possibility of preliminary references on a devolution issue being made from the lower courts to higher courts; a procedure modelled, in part, on Article 234 EC (formerly Article 177 of the EC Treaty). Under this procedure provision is made *for the House of Lords* to refer any devolution issues arising in judicial proceedings before it to the Privy Council 'unless the House considers it more appropriate, having regard to all the circumstances, that it should determine the issue'.[60]

This provision is perhaps intended to parallel the '*acte clair*' doctrine in the ECJ case law[61] under which national courts against whose decisions there is no further right of appeal[62] are relieved of their duty to make a preliminary reference to the ECJ where the answer to the question at issue is so obvious as to leave no room for any reasonable doubt. But it also underscores the scheme of the devolution statutes to make the Judicial Committee of the Privy Council the

---

[57] P Kirchhoff 'The Balance of Powers between National and European Institutions' (1999) 5 *European Law Journal* 225, 227

[58] *Thoburn v Sunderland City Council* [2002] EWHC Admin 195; [2003] QB 151 [69].

[59] paras 33–35 of sch 6 to the Scotland Act 1998; paras 30–31 of sch 8 to the Government of Wales Act 1998; and paras 33–35 of sch 10 to the Northern Ireland Act 1998.

[60] para 32 of sch 6 to the Scotland Act 1998; para 29 of sch 8 to the Government of Wales Act 1998 and para 32 of sch 10 to the Northern Ireland Act 1998.

[61] See ch 9.

[62] *HM Advocate v Orru and Stewart* 1998 SCCR 59 for an example of the application of this doctrine by the Scottish Criminal Appeal Court.

UK top court, taking precedence over the House of Lords, at least in matters concerning devolution issues.

E. Procedural exclusivity and the devolution statutes

The Human Rights Act and the three devolution statutes of 1998 were all, it seems, separately drafted under instructions from different government departments. The result of this has been that on certain issues the question as to how these various constitutional measures interrelate is sometimes quite obscure.[63] In particular, it was not clear from the terms of the various statutes under which statute or rules of procedure a court should be acting in considering a claim that an act or omission of a devolved executive or legislature contravenes a Convention right. There are particular rules to be followed in raising and pursuing Convention rights issues under, for example, the Scotland Act[64] but, on the face of it, section 7(1)(b) of the Human Rights Act allows a person who claims that a public authority (defined in section 6(3)(b) as 'any person certain of whose functions is of a public nature') has acted or proposes to act in a way which is incompatible with a Convention right to 'rely on the Convention right or rights concerned in *any* legal proceedings' before any court in the UK and section 7(9) envisages rules of court to cover this procedure.[65]

Since both the Acts of the Scottish Parliament and Northern Ireland Assembly and any secondary legislation issued by members of the Scottish Executive, Northern Ireland Minister or Northern Ireland Department or Welsh Assembly are defined as 'subordinate legislation' for the purposes of the Human Rights Act, it would seem to follow that any provision of such devolved legislation which appears to any court before which the matter is raised to contravene a Convention right may be treated as invalid and unenforceable under and in terms of section 3 of the Human Rights Act. And if a provision of devolved legislation is challenged under the Human Rights Act the courts will not make a declaration of incompatibility under section 4 since there is nothing in the devolution statutes, the primary UK legislation, which prevents the removal by the court of incompatible provisions of the devolved legislation. In contrast to the position under the devolution statutes, however:

[63] As Lord Rodger of Earlsferry observed in *HM Advocate v 'R'* [2002] UKPC D3, [2003]2 WLR 317, [116]: 'I must say something about the relationship between the Human Rights Act 1998 and the Scotland Act 1998, *a relationship which Parliament has not spelled out particularly clearly*' (emphasis added). And Lord Hope noted at [43]: 'The precise relationship between the remedies available under the Scotland Act 1998 and those which are available under the Human Rights Act 1998 *is still in the course of being worked out*' (emphasis added).

[64] See the Act of Sederunt (Devolution Issue Rules) 1999, SI 1999/1345 (now forming Chapter 25A of the Rules of Court) in relation to civil proceedings before the Court of Session; the Act of Adjournal (Devolution Issue Rules) 1999, SI 1999/1346 in relation to criminal proceedings before the High Court of Justiciary; the Act of Sederunt (Proceedings for Determination of Devolution Issue Rules) 1999, SI 1999/1347 in relation to proceedings before the Sheriff Court; and the Judicial Committee (Devolution Issues) Rules Order 1999, SI 1999/665 in relation to procedure before the Privy Council.

[65] Now the Human Rights Act 1998 (Jurisdiction) (Scotland) Rules 2000, SI 2000/301.

- there is a general one-year time-limit from the date of the act or omission complained of within which court proceedings alleging breach of Convention rights must be brought;[66]
- there is no provision under the Human Rights Act for filtering out frivolous or vexatious arguments;
- there is no provision in the Human Rights Act for any variation by the court of the retrospective effect of the court's decision on incompatibility;
- there is no possibility for a fast track reference on the issue raised to higher courts;
- final appeal against any decision on compatibility of devolved legislation with the Human Rights Act 1998 would lie either with the House of Lords or, if the question were raised in Scotland in the course of criminal proceedings, with the High Court of Justiciary acting as a criminal appeal court.

If, however, the incompatibility of the devolved legislation with the Convention right, as raised in the course of legal proceedings, is characterized by the courts as a 'devolution issue', then:

- the question of the time within which an action raising a devolution issue is left unspecified in the Scotland Act, presumably allowing the matter to be regulated simply by the existing principles of mora, taciturnity and acquiescence as applied in judicial review in Scotland.[67] There have to be specific averments by the respondents taking the plea showing how they would be prejudiced if the action were allowed to proceed.[68] It is not enough simply to allege that there has been unreasonable delay[69] or that the principles of good administration would be breached by the action proceedings,[70] since it has been held that delay without any material alteration of position on the part of the respondents or some inference of acquiescence on the part of the petitioner would not be sufficient to uphold the plea of mora,[71] notwithstanding the general requirement for judicial review applications to be brought with due expedition;[72]

---

[66] Human Rights Act 1998, s 7(5)(a).

[67] eg *King v East Ayrshire Council* 1998 SC 182 (IH, Lord President) 196C-D: 'It is recognised that the public interest in good administration requires that public authorities and third parties should not be kept in suspense as to the legal validity of a decision for any longer than is necessary in fairness to the person affected by it'. See, too, *Swan v Secretary of State for Scotland* 1998 SC 479 (IH).

[68] *Shennan v Glasgow District Council* 1994 SLT 440 (IH).

[69] *Noble v Glasgow City Council* 2001 SLT 2 (OH, Lord Eassie).

[70] *King v East Ayrshire Council* 1998 SC 182 (IH).

[71] *Gurjit Singh v Secretary of State for the Home Department* 2000 SLT 533 (OH). cf *Mackay-Ludgate v Lord Advocate* 2002 SCLR 109 (OH, Lord Phillip) where a three-year delay in applying for judicial review was characterized as excessive and unreasonable such as to justify dismissal of the petition.

[72] *Uprichard v Fife Council* 2000 SCLR 949 (OH, Lord Bonomy) and *Devine v Moray Council* 2002 SLT 312 for examples of the need for particular expedition in challenges to grants of planning permission.

- the matter has to be intimated to the relevant law officer(s) for the jurisdiction of the UK in which the proceedings in question take place;[73]
- the courts are enjoined to consider whether and to what extent any decision on incompatibility of devolved legislation (but not administrative action) should be made retrospective;[74]
- the court may also suspend its judgment to allow the identified defect in devolved legislation to be corrected;[75] and
- the final decision on the question of the compatibility of devolved legislation with the Convention rights, when this matter is raised as a 'devolution issue' would lie with the Privy Council.[76]

It seemed inherently unlikely that the UK Parliament would have intended that the complex systems of checks, references, and balances that has been put in place in relation to the resolution by the courts of 'devolution issues' could simply be overridden in the case where it is alleged in the course of any legal proceedings that a provision of devolved legislation is incompatible with the rights incorporated by the Human Rights Act. But as Lord Rodger of Earlsferry noted:

Taking the Human Rights Act 1998 route [in challenges to the Convention compatibility of acts of the Lord Advocate] seemed to have certain advantages, especially in avoiding the requirements for lodging a devolution issue minute in due time in terms of rule 40.2 of the Act of Adjournal (Criminal Procedure Rules) 1996 and for intimating the matter to the Advocate General in terms of paragraph 5 of Schedule 6 to the Scotland Act 1998. On 1 August 2001, however, in *Mills v HM Advocate (No 2)* 2001 SLT 1359, 1364–1365, para 19, the Appeal Court held in substance that any allegation that an act of the Lord Advocate was incompatible with the accused's Convention rights raised what was, by definition, a devolution issue in terms of paragraph 1(d) of Schedule 6. It followed that an accused person had to observe the requirements of the Scotland Act 1998 and of the Act of Adjournal relating to devolution issues.[77]

It had been argued by some commentators that since the Scotland Act and the Northern Ireland Act both post-date the Human Rights Act by some 10 days (the first two statutes having received Royal Assent on 19 November, the last on 9 November 1998), then the provisions of these Acts should be taken as impliedly repealing those of the Human Rights Act, insofar as there is any conflict between them: thus, anything which falls within the scope of the term 'devolution issue' must be dealt with under the relevant schedules to the Scotland Act. Such a line of argument, based on the traditional English constitutional claim that the UK Parliament cannot bind itself or its successors, seems to under-play the fundamental constitutional change wrought by the Human Rights Act and its domestication of the Convention rights. It also fails to take into account the fact that the

---

[73] eg ch 25A of the Rules of the Court of Session 1994 and ch 40 of the Criminal Procedure Rules 1996.

[74] Scotland Act 1998, s 102(2)(a).

[75] Scotland Act 1998, s 102(2)(b).

[76] Judicial Committee (Devolution Issues) Rules Order 1999, SI 1999/665.

[77] *HM Advocate v 'R'* (n 25) [112].

third devolution statute, the Government of Wales Act, was passed on 31 July 1998. It also may be thought to require a somewhat mechanistic view of the hierarchy to be accorded UK statutes, with the later always displacing the earlier in a manner which is difficult to reconcile with the general acceptance of the claims of European Community law, as mediated through the European Communities Act 1972, to overrule and require the disapplication of provisions of UK statutes (for example the Merchant Shipping Act 1988) passed subsequent to the entry of the UK into the EU.[78]

It seems clear now that the underlying logic and tenor of the approach of the Privy Council in the cases decided by it since *Montgomery and Coulter* under its devolution jurisdiction—which emphasize the role of the Privy Council in maintaining a uniformity of interpretation across the UK to, in particular, matters of Convention rights in criminal trials—would point inexorably to such a ruling in favour of procedural exclusivity: that is to say if a question concerning compatibility of (in)action with a Convention right can be analysed as raising a devolution issue then it must be raised by way of the devolution procedure set out in the relevant statute, rather than by means of direct reliance on the Human Rights Act's procedures. If such an approach to procedural exclusivity had not been taken by the Privy Council then the possibility arose of Scotland and England developing separate human rights jurisprudence since there, unless a devolution issue is properly raised under and in terms of the Scotland Act, there is no appeal from the decisions of the High Court of Justiciary acting as a court of criminal appeal and decisions of this court, while binding in Scots criminal law, are, at best, only of persuasive authority in the rest of the UK.

In sum, in order to preserve the scheme of schedule 6 to the Scotland Act, schedule 8 to the Government of Wales Act and schedule 10 to the Northern Ireland Act will be preserved in the case of challenges based on incompatibility with Convention rights, either the UK Parliament or the courts will have to stipulate that for the purposes of section 7(1)(b) of the Human Rights Act, the *only* reliance that can in law be placed on Convention rights in relation to provisions of devolved legislation is in the context of the matter raising a 'devolution issue' for the purposes of the devolution statutes.

This is in effect what the Privy Council decided in *HM Advocate v 'R'* where Lord Hope noted that it 'is not open to an accused person who seeks to rely on his Convention rights against the Lord Advocate to pick and choose between the Scotland Act 1998 and the Human Rights Act 1998. His challenge *must* be brought under the Scotland Act 1998'.[79] Lord Rodger stated:

[I]nsofar as an act is indeed incompatible with a party's Convention rights, any of these provisions of the Human Rights Act 1998 and of the Scotland Act 1998 that may be applicable may be engaged. Therefore, an accused person cannot conduct proceedings on

---

[78] Case C–213/89 *R v Secretary of State for Transport, ex p Factortame Ltd (No 2)* [1991] AC 603 (HL); [1990] ECR 2433.

[79] (n 25) [50] (Lord Hope).

the basis that he wants the court to consider the question of the incompatibility of an act of the Lord Advocate only in terms of section 6(1) of the Human Rights Act 1998. That would be to ask the court to fail to apply the law that Parliament has enacted in the Scotland Act 1998 for such cases of incompatibility. What must be ascertained in any given case is the actual legal position: that is determined by applying the relevant legislation enacted by Parliament, not by applying merely those parts of the relevant legislation which a particular party may have chosen to rely on. It is for this reason that, as the High Court held in *Mills v HM Advocate (No 2)* 2001 SLT 1359, a question of the incompatibility of any act of the Lord Advocate with Convention rights is necessarily a question under the Scotland Act 1998 and one which constitutes a devolution issue for the purposes of Schedule 6.[80]

One paradoxical result of this approach is that secondary legislation passed by members of the devolved executives will receive more procedural protection from being set aside by the courts than would subordinate UK legislation made by ministers of the Crown.

3. CONCLUSION

With the granting of a new domestic jurisdiction to the Privy Council under the devolution statutes, the precise hierarchical relationship among the various top courts of the UK, namely between the High Court of Justiciary, the Privy Council, and the House of Lords, has become unclear and confused.

Although it is a court of last instance, the Judicial Committee has stressed that the Privy Council is *not* a UK *constitutional* court of general jurisdiction.[81] The Judicial Committee has also stated that, in the ordinary course, it is confined to deciding appeals on 'devolution issues' only on matters which have been the subject of a specific determination by the court appealed against,[82] unless the issue in question may be said to be reasonably incidental to or following consequentially upon the determination of the devolution issue question—such as the appropriate remedy.[83]

On the other hand, although the Privy Council is limited to adjudication on devolution issues, what constitutes a 'devolution issue' has been interpreted broadly. It might be suggested that the broad interpretation of 'devolution issue' to include all Convention claims raised against the prosecution authorities in the course of criminal proceedings in Scotland was *necessary* in order to ensure that the Privy Council played its proper role of ensuring a uniformity of interpretation and application of Convention rights across the UK. If the Privy Council had not interpreted its jurisdiction on devolution issue broadly then there would arguably be a completely different approach as between Scotland

[80] ibid [50] (Lord Hope) and [118] (Lord Rodger of Earlsferry).
[81] See *Hoekstra and others v Her Majesty's Advocate (No 5)* (n 25) 221 (Lord Hope).
[82] See *Follen v HM Advocate* (n 25) [9] (Lord Hope).
[83] See *Mills v HM Advocate (No 2)* (n 25) [34] (Lord Hope).

and England as regards, say the right against self-incrimination in road traffic cases[84] or the presumption of innocence in applications for confiscation orders against persons convicted of drug trafficking,[85] both cases in which the Privy Council reversed, on Crown appeals, the previously unappealable decisions of the High Court of Justiciary.[86]

But the result of these approaches is that to date the Privy Council seems to have become less a general constitutional court for the whole of the UK post-devolution, and more a third-tier court of appeal in Scottish criminal matters. This expansive approach to devolution issues which has resulted in the 'capturing' by the Privy Council of a wide jurisdiction in Scottish criminal law issues is a matter on which Lord Bingham has, in his evidence to the Joint Parliamentary Committee on Human Rights, expressed some surprise. As he observed:

> When Scotland was united with England and Wales in 1707 it was clearly implicit in the Act of Union that there was no criminal appeal from Scotland to London...There was originally a doubt as to whether there was even a civil appeal from Edinburgh to London, but it was very quickly established that there was and indeed extensive use of it was made to such an extent that there was very little time to hear English appeals! But what is important is that *the Scots criminal system has always been self-contained and has had no English input at all. One of the anomalous, and to me surprising and unexpected, results of devolution is that for the first time one does have judges, Scots prominently among them but nonetheless judges, sitting in London ruling on questions relating to Scots criminal trials.*[87]

At the same time, this expansive approach to jurisdiction by the Privy Council has important implications for Convention rights law and procedure in the rest of the UK, given that the devolution statutes have made the decisions of the Privy Council (notably on the scope of Convention rights) formally binding on all UK courts and tribunals, including the House of Lords. As we have seen, the courts of England, Wales, and Northern Ireland will thus be bound, and UK human rights law developed, by a tribunal in which lawyers from the non-Scottish jurisdictions in the UK, particularly in England where it seems unlikely that 'devolution issues' will regularly arise before its courts, have little opportunity directly to participate. It is suggested that this is not a stable long-term constitutional arrangement.

Of course, provisions of the Scotland Act may themselves be subject to human rights challenge under the Human Rights Act. Aside from the suggestion of the constitutional 'tail wagging the dog syndrome'—which *may* be how some English lawyers would see a Scottish dominated Privy Council having precedence over an English dominated House of Lords—there are at least stateable arguments as to the very Convention compatibility of the Judicial Committee of the

---

[84] See *Brown v Stott* 2000 JC 328 (HCJ).
[85] *McIntosh v Lord Advocate* 2000 SCCR 1017 (HCJ).
[86] *Brown v Stott* (n 25) and *McIntosh v HM Advocate* (n 25).
[87] Minutes of Evidence taken on 26 March 2001, HL 66-ii/HC 332-iii Q110 (Lord Bingham of Cornhill) (emphasis added).

Privy Council as it is currently constituted by judges who also happen to be Privy Councillors: see, among others, the decisions of the ECtHR in *Procola v Luxembourg*[88] and *McGonnell v UK*.[89]

In *Starrs v Ruxton*[90] the High Court of Justiciary upheld a challenge to the structural independence and impartiality of temporary sheriffs from the Executive, in that they were appointed by the Lord Advocate in whose name criminal prosecutions were brought before those same part-time judges.[91] The Lord Advocate of the day, Lord Hardie, decided not to appeal against this decision to the Judicial Committee of the Privy Council. The consequence of this finding was, as the Privy Council ruled in *Millar v Dickson*,[92] *all* criminal proceedings before temporary sheriffs from 20 May 1999 fell to be quashed because afflicted by fundamental nullity.[93]

If the decision of the High Court of Justiciary in *Starrs v Ruxton* is correct[94] then questions must arise as to whether the Judicial Committee of the Privy Council, whose members qua Privy Councillors are appointed solely at the pleasure of the Crown without formal grant or letters patents and who may be removed or dismissed from the Privy Council at the pleasure of the monarch (albeit on advice from the Prime Minister) simply by striking their names from the Privy Council book, themselves satisfy the Article 6(1) requirements as understood by the ECtHR of the appearance of an independent and impartial tribunal established by law. This would mean that at the very least the appeals by the Lord Advocate to the Judicial Committee could not competently have been before the court, by virtue of the operation of section 57(2) of the Scotland Act.

The answer may of course be simply that since all the members of the Judicial Committee are tenured judges then no questions as to their independence and impartiality may arise. It might indeed be said, following the spirit of the recent decision of the Privy Council in *Clark v Kelly*[95] upholding the Convention compatibility of the District Courts, that this is just another example of lawyers' ingenuity going too far and the *reality* of the situation is that we *can* trust our judges who are Privy Councillors to be independent and impartial. But it remains at least a theoretical possibility that these appeal provisions of schedule 6 to the Scotland Act could be declared to be incompatible with the Convention under reference to section 4 of the Human Rights Act. After all, appeals to reality and past experience were rejected in the successful challenge to the Convention

---

[88] (1996) 22 EHRR 193.   [89] (2000) 30 EHRR 209.

[90] *Starrs v Ruxton (Procurator Fiscal, Linlithgow)* 2000 JC 208 (HCJ).

[91] A O'Neill 'The European Convention and the Independence of the Judiciary—the Scottish Experience' (2000) 63 *Modern Law Review* 429.

[92] [2001] UKPC D4, 2002 SC (PC)30, [2002]1 WLR 1615.

[93] See, however, *Lochridge v Miller* 2002 SLT 906 (HCJ) finding that even Convention based competency challenges to criminal proceedings have to be brought promptly.

[94] In *Clark v Kelly* (n 25) [34] Lord Hoffmann noted: '[I]n *Starrs and another v Ruxton (Procurator Fiscal, Linlithgow)* ... Lord Reed said that *if*, as was held by the High Court (*and as to which I make no comment*) a temporary sheriff is not an independent tribunal, it does not help that an appeal lies to the High Court of Justiciary which is undoubtedly independent' (emphasis added).

[95] (n 25).

compatibility of temporary sheriffs in both the decision of the High Court of Justiciary in *Starrs v Ruxton* and of the Judicial Committee of the Privy Council in *Millar v Dickson* where it was held that the lack of sufficient formal proced-ural safeguards guaranteeing structural independence and impartiality was such as to vitiate the decisions of the temporary sheriffs. We now have a situation post-devolution in which:

- the Judicial Committee of the Privy Council (shorn of its Commonwealth judges but with the possibility of other UK lower court judges who have been made Privy Councillors may—on what basis is not known—be called upon to sit), is the top appellate court in cases in which the lower court has made a determination of a devolution issue;
- where the lower court has made no determination of the particular devolution raised, the Privy Council has no power or jurisdiction to hear and determine the appeal since it has no original jurisdiction, except where cases are referred directly to it by the Law Officers;
- the definition of a devolution issue has been expanded to cover the conduct of criminal prosecutions in Scotland, with the result that the Privy Council has become a third-tier court of criminal appeal from Scotland but, only in appeals which can be presented as involving action (but *not* inaction) by the prosecution which is incompatible with an individual's Convention rights, otherwise there exists no right of appeal from the decision of the High Court of Justiciary;
- litigants are now bound, where they can, to raise Convention law issues as 'devolution issues' rather than simply unlawful breaches of the Human Rights Act with the result that appeal lies from a determination by the Court of Session or the High Court of Justiciary to the Privy Council rather than to the House of Lords;
- we have a top court in the form of the Privy Council entrusted to give final decisions on the proper interpretation of Convention rights which itself may not be regarded as properly structurally independent and impartial of the Executive as to be Convention compatible;
- finally the status of the ECJ as the top court in matters concerning Community law may itself be under threat at least in matters concerning the interpretation and application of Convention rights, given that the Scottish Parliament and Executive are bound under the Scotland Act to respect both Community law *et separatim* Convention rights.[96] The resolution of such conflicts will, it is suggested, require the courts of this country to make profound legal/political

---

[96] As C Boch has noted in *EC Law in the UK* (Longman Harlow 2000) 199–200: 'It is conceivable that once the UK incorporates the European Convention . . . the validity of some Community action or legislation will be challenged in the UK courts as being incompatible with the Convention. Even if the [European] Union respects fundamental rights and freedoms such as that contained in the Convention, given the real possibility of diverging interpretation between the Luxembourg and Strasbourg courts such challenge to the validity of Community law could also be mounted before UK courts. In this way new challenges to the supremacy of Community law in the UK may arise'.

choices which will shape the future development of the form and structure of the ever changing and dynamic relations between the European and national constitutions.

What has resulted is an appeal structure which is both under- and over-determined, in that a system of Byzantine complexity and obscurity which contains lacunae. What all these arguments, it seems to me, point to is the need for a re-consideration of the current arrangements for our top courts. That opportunity has now been afforded by the announcement by the government in June 2003 of its intention to abolish the office of Lord Chancellor and to establish a new supreme court for the UK.

The devolution issue case law of the Privy Council to date shows certain internal tensions in the way that the current arrangements are working. The review conducted by the Scottish High Court judge, Lord Bonomy, into the practice and procedure of the High Court of Justiciary recommended that, because of the delays and disruption caused to criminal trials in Scotland by the devolution issue procedure, the right of appeal from decisions of the Scottish criminal appeal court to the Privy Council should now be withdrawn. He stated:

The only practical reason for ever categorising such issues as devolution issues was to ensure that recognition was given to the Convention rights during the period between the implementation of the Scotland Act and the implementation of the Human Rights Act, but even there it was a rather artificial way of introducing Convention rights to Scottish criminal procedure. That interim period is now over. Schedule 6 of the Scotland Act should be amended to make it clear that acts or failures to act by the Lord Advocate as prosecutor, and anyone acting on his authority or on his behalf as prosecutor, are excluded from the definition of a devolution issue. The Scottish Executive should urge the United Kingdom Parliament to make that amendment.[97]

Ultimately, it is suggested that, for the sake of constitutional and democratic stability in post-devolution UK, we will need a new and intellectually coherent structure for our top courts. The most Convention compatible and constitutionally stable structure is, I would argue, a new UK supreme court which may combine the current functions of the Appellate Committee of the House of Lords and the devolution functions of the Judicial Committee of the Privy Council, and one in which the constitutional principle of the separation of powers is made evident by there being no overlap between this new supreme court—either in its members or in the building where it is housed—with the legislature or with the Executive. The fact that the Appellate Committee is currently—in terms of its membership and location—a part of the Second Chamber of the Legislature and the Judicial Committee—again in terms of its formal membership and

---

[97] *Improving Practice: the 2002 Review of the Practices and Procedure of the High Court of Justiciary by the Honourable Lord Bonomy,* para 17.14. The report is also available online at <http://www.scotland.gov.uk/library5/justice/rppj-00.asp> (6 August 2003).

location—sits in Downing Street and is, in constitutional theory at least, a part of the Executive—is unsustainable, in these post Human Rights times.

And yet the suggestion, contained in the July 2003 UK Government consultation paper on a new UK supreme court, that the proposed new court should combine the existing jurisdictions of the Appellate Committee of the House of Lords with the Judicial Committee of the Privy Council, has been rejected by the current Law Lords in their published collective response to the Government's consultation paper. Although they accept that it would be 'consistent' with the role of the proposed new UK supreme court that 'it should be the final arbiter of devolution issues', they note that under the devolution statutes the Privy Council may, in effect, call in on a case-by-case basis other judges 'drawn from the devolved jurisdictions', who would not otherwise be eligible to sit as House of Lords judges. The Law Lords then suggest that this is a feature of the devolution settlement which the devolved administrations would not wish to see abrogated and accordingly they conclude, 'with a measure of reluctance' that the two jurisdictions should not be combined in the one supreme court.[98] It is, perhaps, surprising (and disappointing) that the present Law Lords should consider the presumed political views of the devolved administrations (in reality of the Scottish Executive) are to be regarded by their Lordships as determinative of an issue of such general constitutional importance for the UK as a whole, when there are clearly important legal arguments which strongly point against their conclusion that the status quo should be maintained on this matter.

The logic of the on-going constitutional change requires the setting up of such a properly established supreme or constitutional court for the UK, with properly identified, tenured, and explicitly independent judges—perhaps, indeed, appointed after parliamentary hearings along the lines of the US Supreme Court.[99] The djinn of constitutional reform is out of the bottle and has acquired its own dynamic. It is clear that our legislators have not yet completed the task of writing the constitution in Scotland, or in the UK as a whole.

[98] See 'The Law Lords response to the Government's consultation paper on Constitutional reform: a Supreme Court for the United Kingdom' November 2003 at paragraph 9 (paper available online at http://www.parliament.uk/documents/upload/JudicialSCR271003.pdf).

[99] The case for a properly constituted UK supreme court physically and legally separated from the legislature and executive has been argued for by Lord Steyn in 'The Case for a Supreme Court' (2002) 118 *Law Quarterly Review* 382 and by Lord Bingham of Cornhill in 'The Evolving Constitution' [2002] *European Human Rights Law Review* 1 and 'Dicey Revisited' [2002] *Public Law* 39. For the contrary argument, see Lord Cooke of Thorndon 'The Law Lords: An Endangered Heritage' (2003) 119 *Law Quarterly Review* 49.

3

A Constitutional Court
for Northern Ireland?

BRICE DICKSON*

1. CURRENT ROUTES OF APPEAL

At the time when the Appellate Committee of the House of Lords was formed, in 1876, the whole of Ireland was, of course, still an integral part of the UK. Provision was therefore made at that time for appeals to go from the highest court in Ireland (the Court of Appeal) to the House of Lords.[1] During the following 40 years or so, several such appeals were indeed heard, as a glance at the contents pages of the appeal cases for those years will testify.

When Ireland was partitioned by the Government of Ireland Act 1920 the intention was to create not just a new Supreme Court of Judicature in both Southern Ireland and Northern Ireland (comprising a High Court and a Court of Appeal in each jurisdiction) but also a new High Court of Appeal for Ireland with appellate jurisdiction throughout the whole island.[2] This High Court of Appeal was to sit in either Northern Ireland or Southern Ireland depending on where the appeal in question came from, and if the Lord Chancellor of Ireland was not available to hear the appeal it was to be presided over by the Lord Chief Justice of the part of Ireland where the court was sitting.[3] But the Government of Ireland Act made clear that there was to continue to be a right of appeal from the final appeal court in Ireland to the House of Lords in London.[4] At least one case was taken on appeal to the Lords, *Cooper v General Accident Assurance Corporation*,[5] where Viscount Cave LC wryly remarked that this was the first instance coming before the House of the working of the judicial sections in the Government of Ireland Act 1920, 'by which in the wisdom of Parliament no less than four appeals are competent to a litigant in cases of this kind. The amount involved in this appeal is £250.'[6] In fact, the High Court of Appeal for Ireland existed for only a year or so, being superseded when the Irish Free State was

---

* Chief Commissioner of the Northern Ireland Human Rights Commission; Professor of Law, University of Ulster. This chapter is written in a personal capacity and is not intended to represent the views of the Northern Ireland Human Rights Commission.

[1] Appellate Jurisdiction Act 1876, s 3(3).
[2] Government of Ireland Act 1920, s 38.
[3] ibid s 42(3).   [4] ibid s 49.   [5] [1922] IR 214.
[6] ibid 214–15. The appeal was dismissed with costs.

formed in 1922.[7] Under that State's Constitution the link with any judicial structures in the UK was completely severed and a new court hierarchy was established by the Courts of Justice Act 1924.

In Northern Ireland, however, the link with London was maintained and to this day the court structure in the six counties of Northern Ireland is very similar to that in England and Wales, even if the legislation which has created it is different.[8] As far as final appeal rights are concerned, the routes to the House of Lords are also similar.[9] Thus, a litigant who loses in a civil case in the High Court of Northern Ireland can appeal first to the Court of Appeal of Northern Ireland and then, with the leave of either the Court of Appeal or the House of Lords, to the House of Lords,[10] as in *McGrath v Chief Constable of the RUC*.[11] The possibility of a leapfrog appeal in civil cases, from the High Court to the House of Lords, exists as well,[12] although there has never been such a case in Northern Ireland. But civil cases begun in the magistrates' courts or the county courts of Northern Ireland cannot be appealed beyond the Court of Appeal.[13]

As regards criminal cases, a defendant charged with an indictable offence who loses in the Crown Court of Northern Ireland can appeal first to the Court of Appeal of Northern Ireland and then, if the Court of Appeal certifies that a point of law of general public importance is involved and either that Court or the House of Lords grants leave for an appeal, to the House of Lords,[14] as in *R v Bingham*.[15] Likewise a defendant charged with a summary offence who loses in a magistrates' court can ultimately appeal, via the county court and Court of Appeal, to the House of Lords,[16] as in *Seay v Eastwood*.[17] When either side in a criminal case asks a magistrates' court or county court to 'state a case' to the Court of Appeal on a point of law, the matter can again be pursued beyond there to the House of Lords, under the same conditions.[18] Occasionally the Court of Appeal's decision on whether to certify that a point of law of general public importance is involved is reported, as in *R v Fox*.[19] And it was a case from

---

[7] In 1922 the first Lord Chief Justice of Northern Ireland, Sir Denis Henry, who took up his position on 1 October 1921, attended four sittings of the High Court of Appeal in Dublin: AD McDonnell *The Life of Sir Denis Henry, Catholic Unionist* (Ulster Historical Foundation Belfast 2000) 106.

[8] The main legislation is the Judicature (NI) Act 1978.

[9] For details, see B Dickson *The Legal System of Northern Ireland* (4th edn SLS Belfast 2001) 26–28, 198, 212, 237, and 261–262. The opportunities for taking cases to either the ECJ or the ECtHR are the same in Northern Ireland as in other parts of the UK.

[10] Judicature (NI) Act 1978, s 42.

[11] [2001] 2 AC 731. The same route to the HL is available if the case begins in an industrial tribunal in Northern Ireland, as in *Shamoon v Chief Constable of the RUC* [2003] UKHL 15; [2003] 2 All ER 26, or is heard by a Special Commissioner of Income Tax, as in *IRC v McGuckian* [1997] 1 WLR 991.

[12] Administration of Justice Act 1969, s 13 and Judicature (NI) Act 1978, s 43.

[13] County Courts (NI) Order 1980, Arts 28 and 60–62.

[14] Criminal Appeal (NI) Act 1980, s 31(2).

[15] [1999] 1 WLR 598.

[16] Judicature (NI) Act 1978, s 40.

[17] [1976] 1 WLR 1117.

[18] Judicature (NI) Act 1978, s 41(1)(b).

[19] [1996] Northern Ireland Judgments Bulletin (NIJB) 181. See too *R v McCann* [1996] NIJB 222 and *R v Thain* [1985] 11 NIJB 76.

Northern Ireland, *Attorney-General for Northern Ireland v Gallagher,*[20] which led the House of Lords to adopt the general principle that its jurisdiction in criminal appeals is not necessarily limited to the point of law of general public importance that has been certified by the Court of Appeal.

As in England and Wales, appeals from a decision in a criminal matter in judicial review proceedings can go straight from the Divisional Court of the Queen's Bench Division to the House of Lords,[21] as in *R v Chief Constable of the RUC, ex parte Begley.*[22] References to the Court of Appeal by the Attorney-General can also be appealed to the House of Lords, as in *Attorney-General for Northern Ireland's Reference.*[23]

But, whatever the theory, and whatever the route available, in practice very few cases reach the Lords from Northern Ireland. Going by the figures published annually in the *Judicial Statistics for England and Wales,* in the 30 years from 1973 to 2002 the total number of such appeals was just 44, making an average of one case every 8 months or so.[24] The rate of appeal has remained fairly constant over that period, except for the years 1987 to 1992, when 15 cases were appealed.[25] The decisions of the Lords in Northern Irish cases are not always reported in the official Law Reports or in the All England Law Reports (although, when they are, they are sometimes also reported in series such as the Industrial Cases, the Criminal Appeal Reports, or Tax Cases). More strangely, not all of the cases are reported in the Northern Ireland Reports. The majority of the cases taken are civil, not criminal, although a number of the civil law cases have been judicial reviews arising out of criminal proceedings. Many more than half of the cases have had some connection with the troubles in Northern Ireland. Livingstone has sought to argue that in handling the 13 troubles-related cases between 1969 and 1992 their Lordships were not as understanding of the relevant context as their brethren in the Court of Appeal of Northern Ireland[26] but, against that, it could be argued that in more recent years the House of Lords has shown a more understanding attitude than the Court of Appeal of Northern Ireland to some of the problems of statutory interpretation which have confronted the Northern Ireland judges.[27]

Throughout the period of the Northern Ireland Parliament (1921 to 1972) litigants in Northern Ireland could also invoke the jurisdiction of the Privy Council if they wished to argue that a law passed by that Parliament was beyond

---

[20] [1963] AC 349.   [21] Judicature (NI) Act 1978, s 41(1)(a).
[22] [1997] 1 WLR 1475.   [23] [1977] AC 105.
[24] In the first seven months of 2003 there were four further appeals from Northern Ireland decided by the HL: *Russell v Devine* [2003] UKHL 24; [2003] 1 WLR 1187; *Shamoon v Chief Constable of the RUC* (n 11); *Re Shields* [2003] UKHL 3; *Cullen v Chief Constable of the RUC* [2003] UKHL 39; [2003] 1 WLR 1763.
[25] The figures are: 2 (2002), 1 (2001), 1 (2000), 2 (1999), 1 (1998), 1 (1997), 1 (1996), 2 (1995), 1 (1994) and 1 (1993).
[26] S Livingstone, 'The House of Lords and the Northern Ireland Conflict' (1994) 57 *Modern Law Review* 333.
[27] eg *McCartan Turkington Breen (a firm) v Times Newspapers Ltd* [2001] 2 AC 277 and *Beaufort Developments (NI) Ltd v Gilbert-Ash (NI) Ltd* [1999] 1 AC 266.

its powers because it had not been given the express or implied authority to make such a law.[28] This avenue of redress appears to have been used only once[29] but it has been retained for the so-called 'devolution issues' which might now arise under the Northern Ireland Act 1998.[30] This means that if the Northern Ireland Assembly were to enact legislation allegedly outside its competence, this could be raised in any relevant court or tribunal proceedings in Northern Ireland and that court or tribunal could then refer the issue to the Court of Appeal in Northern Ireland; the Court of Appeal may itself refer such an issue to the Judicial Committee of the Privy Council and if the Court of Appeal determines such an issue there can be an appeal to the Judicial Committee. However, although the equivalent process under the Scotland Act 1998 has been invoked no fewer than 12 times,[31] it has not yet been used in Northern Ireland. Declarations of incompatibility cannot be made in respect of Acts passed by devolved parliaments because these Acts are by definition secondary legislation within the terms of the Human Rights Act itself. By implication they can be declared invalid under section 3 of the Human Rights Act, but not incompatible under section 4. The Human Rights Act 1998 makes it clear[32] that this applies as well to Orders in Council made under the 'direct rule' arrangements for Northern Ireland contained in the Northern Ireland Act 1974.[33] On the one occasion when a declaration of incompatibility has been issued in Northern Ireland under the Human Rights Act 1998, it was made with respect to a section of a UK Act.[34]

2. THE HOUSE OF LORDS AND THE NORTHERN IRELAND JUDICIARY

Since the formation of Northern Ireland in 1921 significant deference has been paid by the judges in Northern Ireland to decisions of the House of Lords. No

---

[28] s 51 of the Government of Ireland Act 1920. This allowed provisions in both Bills and Acts to be referred to the Privy Council and a variety of people were empowered to make such references, including the Lord Lieutenant. The provision would have applied in Southern Ireland as well had the Irish Free State not been established in 1921 after the Civil War.

[29] *Re Section 3 of the Finance Act (NI) 1934* [1936] AC 352. Cf s 18 of the Northern Ireland Constitution Act 1973, but this power of the Secretary of State to refer matters to the PC was never exercised.

[30] s 79 and sch 10; see too the Judicial Committee (Devolution Issues) Rules 1999.

[31] s 98 and sch 6; A O'Neill 'Scotland's Constitution and Human Rights' (a paper delivered at a Law Society of Scotland conference on human rights Edinburgh 28 March 2003). See also s 109 and sch 8 in the Government of Wales Act 1998, but no devolution issues have yet reached the PC from that principality.

[32] s 21 under 'subordinate legislation'.

[33] s 1(3) and sch 1.

[34] *Re McR* [2003] NI 1 concerning s 62 of the Offences Against the Person Act 1861. At the time of writing there had been 11 declarations of incompatibility issued in England and Wales: see K Starmer, 'Two Years of the Human Rights Act' [2003] *European Human Rights Law Review* 14, 18–19, *R v Secretary of State for the Home Department, ex parte D* [2003] EWHC 2805 (Admin); [2003] 1 WLR 1315, [2003] UKHRR 221; and *Bellinger v Bellinger* [2003] UKHL 20; [2003] 2 WLR 1174.

judge in Northern Ireland has ever questioned that the House's decisions are binding on the Court of Appeal of Northern Ireland as well as on all lower courts there, even when the decisions in question are ones made in cases which have reached the House of Lords from England or Wales. To that extent the House of Lords was, and remains, not just the highest appellate court within the legal system of Northern Ireland but also a font of new common law not prompted by Northern Irish litigation. This makes it all the more strange, perhaps, that, contrary to the practice concerning Scotland, there is no constitutional convention that any of the Law Lords at any particular time needs to have experience of adjudicating within Northern Ireland.

Of the 105 Law Lords appointed to date since 1876,[35] only three have served as judges in Northern Ireland (although some others have had different roots in Northern Ireland[36]). These are Lord MacDermott, Lord Lowry, and Lord Hutton. Sir John MacDermott was plucked from the High Court of Northern Ireland in 1947 and appointed as a Law Lord at the age of 51. On the retirement of Sir James Andrews as Lord Chief Justice of Northern Ireland four years later, Lord MacDermott was appointed as his successor and he remained in that post until 1971. But during that 20 year period he served on several occasions as a Law Lord. After his retirement as Lord Chief Justice he continued to serve for a few years as an occasional Law Lord as well as an occasional High Court judge in Northern Ireland.[37] There was a gap of 17 years before the next full-time Northern Ireland appointment to the House, Lord Lowry in 1988. He too had served as Lord Chief Justice of Northern Ireland, as the successor to Lord MacDermott. When he retired from the House in 1994 there again followed a gap, although this time only for three years, when no Northern Irish judge sat in the House. This was rectified when Sir Brian Hutton, the judge who had succeeded Lord Lowry as the Lord Chief Justice of Northern Ireland, was appointed a Lord of Appeal in 1997. If he wishes to do so, Lord Hutton can stay in office until 2006 (when he will be 75[38]), at which time the current Lord Chief Justice of Northern Ireland, Sir Robert Carswell, will be 72.[39] Whether he will then be appointed to fill Lord Hutton's shoes remains to be seen. If he is there would then be good grounds for arguing that a constitutional convention has indeed now been established whereby the retiring Lord Chief Justice of Northern Ireland is appointed as a Lord of Appeal provided that there is a vacancy, that he

---

[35] The 100th and 101st Law Lords to be appointed were Lord Hobhouse and Lord Millett (from 1 October 1998), the 102nd Lord Phillips (from 12 January 1999—appointed as Master of the Rolls 6 June 2000), the 103rd Lord Scott (from 17 July 2000), the 104th Lord Rodger (from 1 October 2001) and the 105th Lord Walker (from 1 October 2002).

[36] Lord Russell of Killowen, for instance, a Lord of Appeal from 1929 to 1946, had strong connections with County Down.

[37] eg the Chancery Division case of *McKeown v McKeown* [1975] NI 139 (9 and 23 June 1975). Lord MacDermott's son, another Sir John MacDermott, also became a judge in Northern Ireland, rising to serve as a Lord Justice of Appeal from 1987 to 1998.

[38] He was born on 29 June 1931. Under s 26(7)(b) of the Judicial Pensions and Retirement Act 1993 no one can sit to hear an appeal, or a petition for leave to appeal, after attaining the age of 75.

[39] He was born on 28 June 1934.

or she is not 75, and that no other Northern Ireland judge is still serving in that position.

On account of the fact that British governance of Northern Ireland has been contested by the Irish state since 1921—and that a sizeable proportion of the population of Northern Ireland would prefer to live in a re-united Ireland rather than in the UK—it is obvious that the role of the judges in Northern Ireland is an extremely sensitive one. More than anywhere else in these islands judicial practices, pronouncements and decisions are subjected to the closest of scrutiny for any hint of political prejudice.[40] Opinions differ as to how unbiased they have managed to be, particularly since the outbreak of the most recent bout of troubles in 1968, but in this writer's view they have performed remarkably well in the face of enormous pressures. Given the extremely restrictive security measures which the judges have had to live with (two magistrates, two county court judges and one Lord Justice of Appeal have been murdered by the IRA) and the *comparative* financial sacrifices which they have had to make to accept a position on the bench (their salary is probably at least 50% less than what they could earn as QCs), it is genuinely surprising that so many high calibre candidates have been prepared to serve on the bench. When one adds to this the very controversial cases which sometimes have to be decided (especially in more recent years with the growth in judicial review proceedings), and the convention that judges do not defend themselves in public whenever they are criticized, one can see that the judicial role in Northern Ireland is not an altogether enviable one. Over the years many commentators of a nationalist or republican disposition have been negative about the record of the Northern Irish judiciary (although often in rather unspecific terms), while many unionist politicians have argued that the judges have not been tough enough on terrorists and other criminals. A more balanced view, I would submit, is that, almost without exception, judges in Northern Ireland have done their duty as upholders of the rule of law in what has been a very troubled society. Unlike many other institutions of the legal system they have not manipulated the law for political ends. The worst that can be said of them (apart from noting the occasional unfortunate remark uttered during a trial or when passing sentence) is that, like nearly all judges everywhere, they have tended to be pro-establishment, pro-law and order, and innately conservative. Whether for security reasons or not, they have for the most part kept their heads below the parapet as much as possible, rarely venturing into the public domain to make speeches, participate in debates, or give interviews to journalists. They have preferred to remain sound legal technicians rather than become public figures. The contrast with senior judges in England and Wales over the last decade or so could hardly be more noticeable.

---

[40] For the author's own assessment, in 1992, see B Dickson 'Northern Ireland's troubles and the judges' ch 9 in B Hadfield (ed) *Northern Ireland: Politics and the Constitution* (Open University Press Milton Keynes 1992).

The Belfast (Good Friday) Agreement 1998,[41] perhaps surprisingly, said nothing at all about the future role or composition of the judiciary of Northern Ireland, let alone about whether the existing system of appeals to the House of Lords in London should be interfered with in any way. But the Agreement did say, in its section on policing and justice, that one of the matters which would be dealt with by a supplementary body was a wide-ranging review of criminal justice, and amongst the topics included in the terms of reference of the review, in Annex B of the same section of the Agreement, was 'the arrangements for making appointments to the judiciary and magistracy and safeguards for protecting their independence.' A review team was indeed established (within the Northern Ireland Office but with some external advisers) and a researcher was commissioned by the review team to produce a report analysing the different options regarding the appointment of judges.[42] In March 2000, only some six months later than the Belfast Agreement envisaged, the review team published a large report with detailed proposals for reform, including reform of the system for appointing judges. Many of the recommendations were subsequently enacted in the Justice (NI) Act 2002, including those dealing with appointments.[43] The relevant provisions are not yet in force but when they do commence they will provide for a Northern Ireland Judicial Appointments Commission to advise the First Minister and Deputy First Minister of Northern Ireland on appointments to all judicial posts. In the meantime a Judicial Appointments Commissioner has been appointed to review the way in which appointments are currently made in Northern Ireland and he liaises closely with the Judicial Appointments Commission headed by Sir Colin Campbell in England and Wales. The new Northern Ireland system, when it is fully operational, will not be as radical as the new Scottish system (where the Commission actually interviews the candidates for appointment), but it will be a great improvement on the rather opaque system which has existed heretofore. Whether it will be further reformed once a full-blown judicial appointments commission has been created for England and Wales, as promised in the government announcement of 12 June 2003, remains to be seen.

3. NEW CONSTITUTIONAL CHALLENGES

The post-Agreement landscape in Northern Ireland, especially when an Assembly and Executive are operational, means that the potential for significant legal challenges being raised against politically important decisions and practices is not inconsiderable. Given the sensitivities surrounding the outcome of some of these challenges, the position of the judges involved in adjudicating upon them is

---

[41] (1998) Cm 3883.
[42] See C Blair, *Judicial Appointments* (Research Paper 5, published in conjunction with the Report of the Criminal Justice Review March 2000).
[43] ss 2–5 and sch 2.

delicate indeed. They inevitably become the focus of media attention, as well as having their judgments carefully scrutinized by political activists and academics. An important question to consider here is whether the judges who have the final say on those issues should have any connection with Northern Ireland other than the fact that they happen to sit in the highest UK court.

In the five years or so since the Belfast (Good Friday) Agreement was reached, two important cases involving its interpretation have gone as far as the House of Lords. Several other cases could have gone that far had leave to appeal from the Court of Appeal been applied for and granted. Amongst this latter category[44] are cases such as *Re Williamson*,[45] where a woman whose parents had been killed by the IRA challenged the Secretary of State's refusal to certify that that organization was not maintaining its ceasefire, *Re Tweed*,[46] where the Orange Order challenged a decision of the Parades Commission to impose restrictions on a traditional parade to and from a church in Dunloy, and *Re de Brún and McGuinness*,[47] where two Sinn Féin Ministers challenged the refusal of David Trimble, the First Minister, to nominate them as representatives of the Northern Ireland Executive Committee at meetings of the North–South Ministerial Council. In June 2003, by a two to one majority (Carswell LCJ dissenting), the Court of Appeal of Northern Ireland held that the Army Board had not had the required 'exceptional reasons' to allow two soldiers convicted of murder in Northern Ireland to continue serving in the army after their release from prison.[48] This decision is unlikely to be appealed further, since the judges agreed that the Army Board could not be directed to dismiss the soldiers.

The first of the two cases which did reach the House of Lords was one where the Northern Ireland Human Rights Commission sought a ruling that, contrary to the conclusions reached by the High Court and Court of Appeal in Belfast,[49] the Commission had the implicit power to ask courts to allow it to intervene in court proceedings so that it might give those courts the benefit of its analysis of the human rights points at issue in those proceedings. Four of their Lordships (Lords Slynn, Woolf, Nolan and Hutton) gave speeches granting such a ruling, mainly relying on the Commission's explicit power to promote awareness and understanding of the importance of human rights.[50] In doing so they were well aware that they were reaching a different conclusion from that reached within the courts of Northern Ireland. Lord Woolf, for example, said:

---

[44] Several other 'constitutional' cases have been resolved at the High Court level, eg *Re Morrow and Campbell* [2001] NI 261 (Kerr J), where two DUP Ministers applied unsuccessfully for leave to bring judicial review proceedings to challenge the decision of the First and Deputy First Ministers to withhold Executive Committee papers from the applicants.

[45] [2000] NI 281.

[46] [2001] NI 165.

[47] [2001] NI 442.

[48] *Re McBride* judgments of 13 June 2003 <http://www.courtsni.gov.uk/judgments/judgments+2003.htm> (6 August 2003).

[49] *Re Northern Ireland Human Rights Commission* [2001] NI 271; Carswell LCJ in the High Court and McCollum LJ, Sir John MacDermott and (dissenting) Kerr J in the Court of Appeal.

[50] Northern Ireland Act 1998, s 69(6).

I am, however, acutely conscious that together with the majority of your Lordships I am disagreeing with the views of Lord Hobhouse of Woodborough, the Lord Chief Justice of Northern Ireland and the majority of the Court of Appeal in Northern Ireland. Furthermore we are doing so as to the interpretation of the Northern Ireland Act 1998, which was enacted in particularly sensitive political circumstances, in relation to the powers of the Northern Ireland Human Rights Commission.[51]

Lord Hutton, himself from Northern Ireland, gave the most detailed judgment, carefully examining the authorities on how courts had interpreted Lord Watson's statement in *Attorney-General v Great Eastern Railway Company*[52] that the objects which a statutory body may legitimately pursue must be ascertained from the Act itself but that the powers which the corporation may lawfully use in furtherance of these objects must either be expressly conferred or derived by reasonable implication from its provisions. He concluded:

In my opinion the liberal approach stated in the authorities is applicable to the determination of the powers of the Commission as well as to the determination of the powers of local authorities and commercial companies, notwithstanding that the Commission was established pursuant to the Belfast Agreement.[53]

But the majority's lack of scruples at glossing the express words of the Belfast Agreement was not shared by Lord Hobhouse, who dissented. He was of the view that the Belfast Agreement was a very carefully crafted document and that by omitting to confer it explicitly the drafters must have specifically intended to deny the Human Rights Commission a power to apply to intervene in court proceedings. In relation to the authorities cited by Lord Hutton, he said:

The authorities helpfully cited in the opinion of my noble and learned friend Lord Hutton show how far removed the context of that type of statute is from the context of the Northern Ireland Act 1998. The Belfast Agreement was an intensely political act where, after very difficult negotiations and a referendum campaign, agreement was finally obtained for a document which then fell to be given effect to in an Act of Parliament. Matters which might easily be thought to be reasonable for inclusion in the Belfast Agreement may well not have been included for some political reason not apparent subsequently to lawyers who have not been privy to what occurred. The question whether a human rights body should be empowered to intervene in litigation otherwise than on behalf of a legitimate party to that litigation could be an activity with considerable political significance so long as sectarian divisions persist. It must have been a political judgment how proactive and interventionist a Commission would be acceptable to the people of Ulster as a whole . . . In declining to be drawn into the extension of the powers of the Commission, I consider that the Lord Chief Justice and the majority of the Court of Appeal correctly understood the intent of the Belfast Agreement and the implementing legislation and their place in the constitutional framework of the Province.[54]

---

[51] *Re Northern Ireland Human Rights Commission* [2002] UKHL 25; [2002] NI 236 [29].
[52] (1880) 5 App Cas 473.
[53] *Re Northern Ireland Human Rights Commission* (n 51) [58].
[54] ibid [66].

This disagreement within the House of Lords as to the interpretation of an important aspect of the Belfast Agreement, and of the subsequent Northern Ireland Act 1998, illustrates well the overtly political dimension to this kind of adjudication. It inevitably leads one to think carefully about who should be charged with the responsibility of carrying out such adjudications.

The second House of Lords case provokes the same thoughts even more readily. In *Robinson v Secretary of State for Northern Ireland*[55] the Democratic Unionist Party MP, Peter Robinson, sought a declaration against the Secretary of State for Northern Ireland that the latter had acted unlawfully in not calling elections to the Northern Ireland Assembly within a certain time period, as supposedly required by section 16(8) of the Northern Ireland Act 1998. The High Court in Belfast,[56] and the Court of Appeal by a majority,[57] refused the declaration. In the Lords the decision was three to two against the applicant and again the prevailing judicial attitudes to the interpretation of the Agreement were crucial. Lords Bingham, Hoffmann, and Millett held for the Secretary of State, while Lords Hutton and Hobhouse sided with the applicant. All five judges gave judgments and, apart from Lord Millett, alluded directly to the political significance of their decision. Lord Bingham allowed himself to be persuaded not just by the underlying purpose of the Belfast Agreement but also by the idea that constitutional documents such as the Northern Ireland Act 1998 cannot cater for every eventuality and must be interpreted 'generously and purposively'. In answer to the point that the resolution of political problems by resort to the vote of the people in a free election lies at the heart of any democracy and that this democratic principle is one embodied in the Northern Ireland Act, he said, in words which are perhaps surprising in the mouth of the country's most senior judge:

[E]lections held with undue frequency are not necessarily productive. While elections may produce solutions they can also deepen divisions. Nor is the democratic ideal the only constitutional ideal which this constitution should be understood to embody. It is in general desirable that the government should be carried on, that there be no governmental vacuum. And this constitution is also seeking to promote the values referred to in the preceding paragraph.[58]

Lord Hoffmann, after expressing similar views to those of Lord Bingham concerning the constitutional nature of the point at issue,[59] held that:

... in choosing between the two constructions of section 16 which have been put forward, I think it is reasonable to ask which result is more consistent with a desire to implement the

---

[55] [2002] UKHL 32; [2002] NI 390.   [56] [2002] NI 64 (Kerr J).
[57] [2002] NI 206 (Nicholson and McCollum LJJ, Carswell LCJ dissenting).
[58] *Robinson v Secretary of State for Northern Ireland* (n 55) [11]. In the preceding paragraph Lord Bingham pointed out that the Belfast Agreement was an attempt to end decades of bloodshed and centuries of antagonism, that it was based on participation by the unionist and nationalist communities in shared political institutions and that, before seeking a popular decision at some time in the future on the ultimate political status of Northern Ireland, these shared institutions had to have time to operate and take root.
[59] ibid [24], [25].

Belfast Agreement... In my opinion the rigidity of the first alternative [that fresh Assembly elections must be held if no First and Deputy First Minister have been elected by the Assembly within six weeks] is contrary to the Agreement's most fundamental purpose, namely to create the most favourable constitutional environment for cross-community government. This must have been foreseen as requiring the flexibility which could allow scope for political judgment in dealing with the deadlocks and crises which were bound to occur.[60]

The opposing view was ably put by Lord Hutton. He too referred to the purpose and context of the Belfast Agreement[61] but he concluded:

I think it is necessary to bear in mind that the Belfast Agreement was drafted in a spirit of hope that the cross-community institutions of government which it proposed would succeed... [but] the Agreement contains no express provision stating what would happen if cross-community government was not established or did not continue... Parliament has laid down a procedure to be followed in the event of the Assembly resolving that it should be dissolved or failing to elect a First Minister or deputy First Minister within the specified period of six weeks, and whilst those sections continue in force unamended I consider that the objective of the Belfast Agreement cannot operate to alter the meaning of their words.[62]

Lord Hobhouse, also dissenting, as he had done in *Re NIHRC*, expressed himself more bluntly:

Another argument deployed in favour of the Secretary of State is to say that the Belfast Agreement supports the view that the Assembly should not be dissolved if it would be expedient, in the interests of stability, not to do so... [This argument does] not sufficiently recognise that the Northern Ireland Assembly is a statutory body governed by specific statutory provisions. The six week period is part of that structure. It is not acceptable to say that a longer period might have been better; in fact, in the present case, it was some 18 weeks, three times as long as the specified period... The Secretary of State's refusal to perform the duty to hold an extraordinary Assembly election must be political in character since it is bound to be seen to favour one political party or another; it thus fails to reflect the inclusive aspirations of the Belfast Agreement for the democratic institutions of Northern Ireland.[63]

Without taking a position on which of these judicial approaches to constitutional adjudication in Northern Irish cases is to be preferred, it is remarkable that of the eight Law Lords who were involved in deciding the two cases outlined above only one, Lord Hutton, had any first-hand knowledge and experience of adjudicating within Northern Ireland itself. It was, in other words, a particularly 'English' group of judges. Some might therefore ask whether it was an entirely appropriate forum for the interpretation of an Agreement which is specifically founded on a much more inclusive approach to the difficulties facing Northern Ireland. If the resolution of disputes over the legislative competence of devolved parliaments and assemblies has been allocated to the Privy Council, why should

---

[60] ibid [29], [30].   [61] ibid [52]–[54].   [62] ibid [61].   [63] ibid [74].

disputes over the actions of the UK government in relation to those devolved institutions not similarly be referred to a special court? In the case of Northern Ireland, where the interests of another state are obviously of some weight in the resolution of such disputes, should the composition of that special court not in some way reflect those interests?

4. OPTIONS FOR REFORM

When one reflects on what changes could be made to the current appeal system from Northern Ireland to the House of Lords, there are basically two options which arise for consideration, each with a variety of sub-options:

(a) Retain the current House of Lords (or the new UK supreme court) but add or substitute one or two judges from Ireland (North and/or South) whenever some (or all) cases from Northern Ireland are being heard.

(b) Set up a special court, separate from the House of Lords (or any new UK supreme court), to deal either with all issues which would otherwise have gone from Northern Ireland to the House of Lords or with specified issues, such as those requiring interpretation of the Belfast (Good Friday) Agreement or the related Northern Ireland Act 1998. This new court could be composed in a variety of ways. It could have judges only from Northern Ireland or a mixture of judges from Great Britain, Northern Ireland, the Republic of Ireland and/or elsewhere (such as Europe or the USA).

The merits and demerits of each of these options, and of their sub-options, will now be briefly examined.

A. The UK supreme court with additional or substitute judges from Northern Ireland or Ireland

The first of the two options is the less radical. To all intents and purposes it would maintain the status quo while acknowledging more explicitly the Northern Irish dimension to the House's jurisdiction. It would remove the anomaly whereby many appeals from Belfast are not heard by any Law Lords who have personal experience of the Northern Ireland legal system.[64] Of course such a lack of experience is not necessarily a flaw, since the vast majority of appeals are on questions of law which deserve a common solution in both Northern Ireland and England and Wales or which at any rate have no peculiar Northern Irish dimension to them justifying a different solution from that required in England and Wales. But on matters to do with the special constitutional position of Northern Ireland, including the Belfast (Good Friday) Agreement, it could be

---

[64] Of the 13 appeals from Northern Ireland decided by the HL since Lord Hutton was appointed as a Law Lord in 1997, he has sat in only six of them.

argued that it should be mandatory for at least one of the judges in the top court to have some direct experience of life in Northern Ireland. Indeed, given the importance of some of these decisions to the peace process in Northern Ireland, it may be appropriate to include two or more such ad hoc judges, perhaps in an overall bench of seven.[65] Against this, of course, it could be said that the provenance of the judges is of much less importance than the quality of the legal argument put to them and that so long as it is likely that counsel for the litigants have substantial experience of the Northern Ireland legal system (and they almost invariably do[66]) all the relevant arguments about the special character of that system can be put to the judges. Some would see it as a positive advantage, a virtual guarantee that local prejudices would not intrude into the decision-making process, if all the judges were required *not* to have a connection with Northern Ireland. But is it then appropriate, if that is correct, for all the judges to be entirely British in their background?[67]

If in a particular case there were more than one judge appointed with direct knowledge of Northern Ireland some might then argue that there should be at least one judge appointed who has knowledge of the Republic of Ireland (although this does not appear to be a current demand from either Sinn Féin or the Social Democratic and Labour Party). It could be said that this would help to counter any risk that judges from within the Northern Ireland legal tradition would be inclined to be pro-unionist in their interpretation of the Agreement or other constitutional legislation. Such an inclination is not to be taken for granted, however, not least because, if judges were chosen from within the current senior bench in Northern Ireland there are almost as many judges with a Catholic background to choose from as those with a Protestant background. But the presence of a judge with knowledge of the Republic's legal system could still be said to help counter *perceptions* of bias (which can be just as important as realities in Northern Ireland) as well as ensure that a perspective from south of the border is brought to bear as and when appropriate in the decision-making process.[68] There would, though, be very significant opposition to this idea from those of a unionist persuasion in Northern Ireland.

However there is no tradition—or provision—for ad hoc judges to sit in the House of Lords, in the way that there is, for example, in the Constitutional Court of South Africa or the European Court of Human Rights (albeit in situations where one or more of the 'ordinary' judges happen to be unavailable). An

---

[65] Benches of seven judges are, of course, not unheard of in the HL. The two most recent examples are *R v Bow Street Metropolitan Stipendiary Magistrate, ex p Pinochet Ugarte (no 2)* [2000] 1 AC 119 and *R v Secretary of State for the Home Department, ex p Anderson* [2002] UKHL 46, [2003] 1 AC 837.

[66] Very occasionally counsel from England are engaged, eg *IRC v McGuckian* (n 11).

[67] Of course two of the current Law Lords, Lords Steyn and Hoffmann, have a significant South African dimension to their legal background, but this is purely accidental.

[68] Two of the judges currently serving on Ireland's Supreme Court are from a Protestant background, even though the Protestant population of the country is considered to be approximately 2%.

amendment to the Appellate Jurisdiction Act 1876 would be required to create such a role. A possible model to follow would be that used for some appeals to the Privy Council, where occasionally an effort is made to involve an eligible judge with experience of the jurisdiction from which the appeal in question has been brought.[69] Given that the government has announced its intention of transforming the Appellate Committee of the House of Lords into a new supreme court for the UK, there will be an opportunity when the relevant legislation comes to be debated for this peculiar Northern Ireland dimension to the jurisdiction of the court to be given particular consideration.

B. The creation of a separate top-level court for Northern Ireland

The second of the two options—to create a wholly separate special court—is obviously a much more drastic one. It would mean depriving the existing House of Lords of some of its current jurisdiction as the UK's supreme court, offloading that work to a more specialized tribunal. Yet of course this is exactly what was done in order to accommodate the devolution arrangements in 1998: the Scotland Act, the Government of Wales Act and the Northern Ireland Act of that year all make provision for disputes over 'devolution issues' to be submitted, ultimately, to the Judicial Committee of the Privy Council, not to the Appellate Committee of the House of Lords.[70] The reasoning behind this is none too clear, especially as the judges entitled to sit in the two courts are almost identical. But the rules do allow for judges other than Law Lords to sit in the Privy Council and in the 12 devolution cases that have so far gone from the Scottish courts to the Privy Council an additional Scottish judge has occasionally been appointed, thereby giving the Scots a majority in the tribunal.[71] To date no great difficulties seem to have been encountered through the Privy Council issuing judgments that are odds with those issued by the House of Lords. If that were to happen it would presumably be dealt with in a similar way to conflicts between two judgments of the House itself.[72] The problem can be partly avoided by having the House of Lords refer devolution issues to the Privy Council in line with the provisions in the legislation.[73]

---

[69] PC judgments can be accessed at <www.privy-council.org.uk> (6 August 2003).

[70] See nn 30 and 31. The PC's decisions in devolution cases are listed separately on the website referred to in the previous note.

[71] eg *Brown v Stott* [2003] 1 AC 681, where the Rt Hon Ian Kirkwood joined Lords Hope and Clyde. See further ch 2.

[72] Here one thinks of how the HL in *R v Kansal (no 2)* [2001] UKHL 62; [2002] 2 AC 69 responded to the decision a few months earlier in *R v Lambert* [2001] UKHL 37; [2002] 2 AC 545: although three of the five Law Lords thought that the earlier decision was wrong, only one of them was prepared to depart from it.

[73] Northern Ireland Act 1998, sch 10 para 32; Scotland Act 1998, sch 6 para 32; Government of Wales Act 1998, sch 8 para 29. The common wording of this paragraph is: 'Any devolution issue which arises in judicial proceedings in the House of Lords shall be referred to the Judicial Committee unless the House considers it more appropriate, having regard to all the circumstances, that it [or they] should determine the issue.'

The Privy Council could of course be tasked with deciding a range of disputes over and above those already entrusted to it. It could, for example, be required to serve as the ultimate appeal court for all questions of interpretation concerning the Belfast (Good Friday) Agreement. The difficulty with this, however, is that the Privy Council, being technically a body which advises Her Majesty, is every bit as 'establishment-based' as the House of Lords, even if we are talking in each case about a legal committee of those institutions. It would, one imagines, be just as difficult for some nationalists and republicans in Northern Ireland to 'submit' to the jurisdiction of the Privy Council as it is for them to accept the jurisdiction of the House of Lords.

A more realistic course of action would be to establish an altogether new court—let's call it the Constitutional Court of Northern Ireland[74]—to deal with issues specifically assigned to it. Provision could be made for prohibiting any further appeal to the House of Lords, thereby making the Constitutional Court the final court of appeal for these designated matters. One of these could be disputes over the interpretation of the Belfast (Good Friday) Agreement or the Northern Ireland Act 1998, including the interpretation of the legislative competence of the Northern Ireland Assembly, which is currently within the purview of the Privy Council.

Another designated matter could be disputes over the interpretation of the Bill of Rights for Northern Ireland. The content of such a Bill of Rights is currently being considered by the Northern Ireland Human Rights Commission, which was charged, under the Belfast (Good Friday) Agreement and the Northern Ireland Act 1998,[75] with advising the Secretary of State for Northern Ireland on what rights, if any, should be contained in a Bill of Rights for Northern Ireland, supplementing the rights in the European Convention on Human Rights and reflecting the particular circumstances of Northern Ireland. In its consultation document on a proposed Bill of Rights, the Commission has raised the question whether the Bill should be enforced by a special court set up in Northern Ireland.[76] The Commission has not yet taken a final position on this question but one of the many options it may consider in this context (even if coming to a conclusion on the point is not essential for the purposes of advising on the content of the Bill of Rights) is whether such a special court should in effect become a constitutional court for Northern Ireland, replacing altogether the current appeal mechanism to the House of Lords. Some of the organizations which responded to the Commission's consultation document called for a Human Rights Court to be established to enforce the Bill of Rights, but they were not specific as to how this new court would relate to the House of Lords

---

[74] There is of course already a Supreme Court of Judicature in Northern Ireland, comprising the High Court, the Crown Court and the Court of Appeal: Judicature (NI) Act 1978, s 1.

[75] s 69(7).

[76] Northern Ireland Human Rights Commission *Making a Bill of Rights for Northern Ireland* (Belfast 2001) 100–2, available at <www.nihrc.org> (6 August 2003).

(or indeed how it would affect the current enforcement arrangements under the Human Rights Act 1998). Other respondents argued that rather than create a special Human Rights Court every court should be encouraged to be one which applies human rights standards, thereby mainstreaming them. This is also the writer's present view. He does not see how 'rights issues' can be disentangled from legal disputes and siphoned off to a special tribunal for adjudication. It would cause great confusion and complexity. If the whole case were to be referred to the specialist tribunal, would it have the requisite expertise to decide the non-rights issues that might require to be decided? If, on the other hand, the Human Rights Court were to be a court to which questions of law are referred for an advisory opinion (as with the referral procedure to the European Court of Justice under Article 234 of the (amended) Treaty of Rome), which court would be the final court of appeal if the application of the advisory opinion to the facts of the case were called into question? A way out of this conundrum is to refer these rights issues not to a Human Rights Court but to a constitutional court with a more broad-ranging judicial competence.

In favour of the proposal for a special constitutional court it can be argued that the Belfast Agreement has altered the whole constitutional topography in Northern Ireland, making it very much 'a place apart' in constitutional terms, the only part of the country having a special relationship with another state, the Republic of Ireland. The fact that perhaps as many as 43% of the population of Northern Ireland (this being the proportion of the people who are Catholic[77]— although it is clear that not all of these would automatically be in favour of a united Ireland) want to see the Irishness of Northern Ireland recognized to at least the same extent as its Britishness, might in some eyes make the current appeal route to the House of Lords seem anomalous. Those with this opinion could say that the anomaly is multiplied by the fact that the House of Lords is itself something of an anachronism in the modern world. Even though the Law Lords are appointed because of their judicial experience, they can (and do) speak and vote in the House when it is operating as a legislature, and the Lord Chancellor, of course, is a walking contradiction of the separation of powers doctrine. The House of Lords is a quintessentially British institution and, as such, it rankles with many nationalists.[78] The recently announced intention of replacing the Appellate Committee of the House of Lords with a supreme court will go some way towards alleviating these concerns, but even this new institution, the features of which are still far from settled, may not quell nationalists' antipathy to having the North of Ireland so firmly plugged into the British judicial system.

---

[77] According to the results of the 2001 census. For details see <www.nisra.gov.uk/census/start.html> (6 August 2003).

[78] The only nationalist politician of any note to have accepted a peerage is Gerry Fitt, the socialist MP for West Belfast from 1966 to 1983. He became Lord Fitt in 1983 after he lost his Parliamentary seat to Gerry Adams of Sinn Féin.

5. CONCLUSION

The Belfast Agreement states, in its section on constitutional issues, that the political parties endorse the two governments' commitment that:

[W]hatever choice is freely exercised by a majority of the people of Northern Ireland, the power of the sovereign government with jurisdiction there shall be exercised with rigorous impartiality on behalf of all the people in the diversity of their identities and traditions and shall be founded on the principles of full respect for, and equality of, civil, political, social and cultural rights, of freedom from discrimination for all citizens, and of parity of esteem and of just and equal treatment for the identity, ethos and aspirations of both communities.

Given the brouhaha that arose over the clauses in the Justice (NI) Bill dealing with royal coats of arms in courthouses,[79] and the earlier court case over whether barristers appointed to be Queen's Counsel in Northern Ireland should be obliged to swear an oath to serve the Queen,[80] it is very likely that if the question of the most suitable final court of appeal for Northern Ireland were to be raised in inter-party or inter-governmental talks a majority of nationalists and probably all republicans would favour abandoning the route to the House of Lords and setting up a new local supreme court. This, they would say, would provide an opportunity to recognize the Irishness of a large proportion of the population by (under one option) allowing judges from the Republic of Ireland to sit on this court in conjunction with judges from Northern Ireland. At present, neither of the two large nationalist parties in Northern Ireland seem to be calling for the channel of appeal to the House of Lords to be removed, let alone arguing that a new supreme court should be established in Northern Ireland with representation on it from the Republic of Ireland, but such a position would be a logical progression of their current attitudes to flags and emblems in court-houses in Northern Ireland and of their call for a Human Rights Court in their responses to the Human Rights Commission's provisional recommendations on a Bill of Rights. The administration of justice is not yet a matter which has been transferred to the devolved administration in Northern Ireland (which at the time of writing has been in suspension for more than a year, since 14 October 2002) but when it does become an area of devolved power in Northern Ireland the position of the Appellate Committee of the House of Lords (or of any new supreme court for the UK) will be thrown into greater relief and its relevance as a final court of appeal for Northern Ireland is almost bound to be raised sooner or later.

Whatever one's political persuasion, one could also argue that because Northern Ireland has developed its own legal system since being created in

---

[79] eg Second reading debate in the House of Lords, 3 May 2002. See now s 66 of the Justice (NI) Act 2002.

[80] *Re Treacy and Macdonald* [2000] NI 330 (Kerr J). After the decision in this case, the wording of the oath to be sworn was soon changed so as not to cause any offence to nationalist barristers.

1920 it now deserves to have its own final court of appeal. Scotland has long had its own domestic supreme court for criminal matters. In the case of Northern Ireland the court would not have to be purely domestic—it could draw upon judicial experience in other jurisdictions in these islands or elsewhere and it would thereby attract greater credibility.

The main argument *against* altering the current arrangements for appeals to the Lords is the counter-political one—that it would weaken even further the links between this part of the UK and the rest of the country. There would be huge unionist opposition to cutting or varying this constitutional link, just as there has been to other proposals which tend in that direction.[81] They would point, as would others, to the fine record of the judges in the House of Lords, which is undoubtedly recognized as one of the most learned (and today one of the most liberal) final courts of appeal anywhere in the world. Although the Supreme Court of Ireland has in recent years established a high reputation for itself, it does not yet have the worldwide authoritativeness which the House of Lords has accumulated over much more than a century. Such opposition would lessen, although probably not significantly, if the Irishness of people in Northern Ireland were to be deemed worthy of recognition merely by providing for representation of this aspect of their identity on the highest court, as under the first option above.

[81] B Dickson 'A Unionist Legal Perspective on Obstacles in the South to Better Relations with the North' in Forum for Peace and Reconciliation *Building Trust in Ireland* (Blackstaff Press, Belfast, 1996) 55–83.

4

Ideas of 'Representation' in UK Court Structures

KAY GOODALL*

1. Introduction

It is often suggested that the judiciary in a modern democratic state should be representative of the population which it serves. What amounts to 'representation', though, is an interesting question. In the UK, there is a constitutional convention that there are two Scottish Law Lords in the supreme civil court, the Appellate Committee of the House of Lords. What do these positions represent? Is it the legal system of Scotland, legal tradition or the Scottish nation?[1] Similar questions need also to be asked about the practice of appointing a Law Lord from Northern Ireland. This essay will reflect on theoretical and practical issues relating to 'representation' of these kinds.[2]

There is a widely held, and largely undiscussed, presumption that the distinctive Scottish legal system requires representation on a UK panel of judges. It seems obvious that what is represented is a specialist knowledge and expertise in Scots law. Scotland has a separate legal system with distinct origins and a mixed common and civil law base. A Scottish Law Lord seems essential to represent a legal system with which a panel of English and Northern Irish Lords may be unfamiliar. The law of Northern Ireland is much more closely tied to that of England and Wales, but again one might think it appropriate for there to be a Northern Irish Law Lord who can understand and represent that legal system and political history.

It would seem straightforward to assume, then, that appropriate posts would have been created to allow legal experts to represent those two legal systems in nationwide legal debates, and to ensure consistency and coherence in the law in Northern Irish and Scots appeals. The actual history of the Northern Irish and Scottish Law Lords, however, looks stranger to modern readers, and more interesting.

Following the partition of Ireland in 1920 and the creation of the separate region of Northern Ireland, there has not constantly been a Northern-Irish

* Lecturer in law, University of Glasgow.
  Many thanks to Brigid Hadfield, Siobhan Ramage and Careena Bruen for their valuable contributions to improving this essay. Any errors are, as always, the sole responsibility of the author.

[1] See ch 2.   [2] See ch 3.

trained judge in the Lords. Over the periods when there has been such an individual available in the House, he has often been present as a life peer who falls within the broader pool of senior judges who are eligible to sit on appeals, rather than occupying a core full-time post of Lord of Appeal in Ordinary.[3] Certainly they are not required to sit on Northern Irish appeals merely by dint of those appeals originating from Northern Ireland. Many of these cases do not involve a distinctive point of Northern Ireland law and may be heard by a panel of whom none has a background in that legal system.[4] It may be that the practice of having a Northern Irish-trained judge in the Lords is now consolidating into constitutional convention, but if so it may have been encouraged in that direction largely because of the high calibre of the individuals themselves who have come to the Lords from that part of the world since partition.

In contrast, there is a constitutional convention that there be at least one Scottish Lord of Appeal in Ordinary[5] but this was initially a convention of Scottish membership of the court, rather than of presence on Scottish appeals. Even after the convention came into being, for many decades there was no guarantee that a Scots-trained judge would sit on Scottish appeals. Invariably today at least one will sit on a Scottish appeal, but this convention crystallized as late as the 20th century.

What was it of Scotland and Ireland that was 'represented', then, when a new House of Lords came together following the Union of Scotland and England in 1707 and the Union of Great Britain with Ireland in 1801? And what is 'represented' of Scotland and Northern Ireland today? To understand this odd state of affairs a little better, it is helpful to look back over its origins.

2. CHANGING CONTEXTS

Judicial roles in the 21st century are not now what they once were. The judicial work of the House of Lords at the creation of Great Britain in 1707 and the UK

---

[3] Lord MacDermott was a Lord of Appeal in Ordinary only between 1947 and 1951, after which he chose to return home to take up the post of Lord Chief Justice of Northern Ireland. This was not the end of his role in the HL, because as a life peer, he sat on the occasional appeal in the HL for many years afterwards: eg *Dingle v Turner* [1972] AC 601. It was, however, the end of his full-time involvement. Lord Lowry was made a life peer in 1979 and could hear Lords appeals from that date, but occupied the post of Lord of Appeal in Ordinary only between 1988 and 1994. As a life peer, he also remained eligible to sit after that: see for instance the 1995 decision of *C v DPP* [1996] 1 AC 1. Lord Hutton became a full-time Lord of Appeal in Ordinary in 1997 and remains in post to date. It is also worth mentioning Lord Carson, who had practised at the Irish bar in the early part of his career, until 1893, and after that at the English bar. He went to the Lords in 1921 as a Lord of Appeal in Ordinary, having been a member of government in the Commons. He remained in post until 1929. See 'The Irish Lords of Appeal in Ordinary' in DS Greer and NM Dawson *Mysteries and Solutions in Irish Legal History* (Dublin Four Courts Dublin 2001).

[4] eg *McCartan Turkington Breen v Times Newspapers Ltd* [2001] 2 AC 277. This case concerned a Northern Ireland statutory provision, but not a distinctive point of Northern Ireland law.

[5] It was not until 1867 that there was always at least one Scots Law Lord in the HL and not until 1947 that there were two or more.

in 1801 was not allocated to a distinct and separate professional court. The whole House of Lords at that time exercised an appellate authority over the country's superior courts, representing what was then the judicial authority of the sovereign and his or her council in parliament.[6] Not until 1876 was a definite line drawn between the House of Lords as a legislature and the House of Lords as a court. The forerunners of today's Scottish and Northern Irish Law Lords were not legally-trained judges, but aristocrats with seats in the wider House of Lords.

At the time when the union of the Scottish and English parliaments was being negotiated, the appellate role of the House of Lords was viewed in England as part of its wider political role in government. The English monarch had long exercised a judicial function which had gradually over the centuries been delegated to courts of first instance and then also to intermediate appeal courts. The monarch and his council of advisors continued to hear appeals, and eventually parliament, in the sense of a meeting of advisors, developed an appellate jurisdiction as the court of the monarch in Parliament, the House of Lords. The appellate work of the House of Lords was one part of the range of judicial and legislative responsibilities it possessed, and no sharp constitutional line was drawn between the judicial and the legislative function. Some constitutional theorists of the time portrayed the arrangements as a system of checks and balances between monarch, aristocracy (House of Lords), and democracy (House of Commons), and although this never accurately reflected the actual balances of power, what is interesting is the focus on power shared among these three institutions, rather than on any separation between legislature, executive, and judiciary.

This English House of Lords was composed of the Lords Spiritual (bishops and archbishops) and the Lords Temporal (possessing hereditary peerages). The Acts of Union with Scotland in 1707 and Ireland in 1800 created a third category of member, the representative peer.[7] Those peers were placed there originally to represent the Scottish and Irish political systems, rather than specifically their legal systems. They were politically representative in two senses: they represented the dismantled Scottish and Irish parliaments; and they represented the body of Scottish and Irish peers who had inhabited those parliaments. Not all the peers of Scotland and Ireland were permitted to participate and vote in the new united House of Lords. Instead, by statute, 16[8] Scottish and 28 Irish peers were

---

[6] There are many detailed discussions of the history of the HL, eg L Blom-Cooper and G Drewry *Final Appeal: A Study of the House of Lords in its Judicial Capacity* (Clarendon Press Oxford 1972) and R Stevens *Law and Politics: The House of Lords as a Judicial Body, 1800–1976* (Weidenfeld and Nicolson London 1979).

[7] Act of Union with Scotland 1707, Arts 22, 23 and Act of Union with Ireland 1800, Art 4. See also B Hadfield 'Whether or Whither the House of Lords?' (1984) 35 *Northern Ireland Legal Quarterly* 313, 316–317 and CRA Howden 'The House of Lords. Its History and Constitution' (1909–10) 21 *Juridical Review* 358, 360.

[8] In 1963, the Peerage Act permitted all the Scottish peers to sit in the Lords.

elected by their fellows to represent them. The Scottish peers were elected to serve for the duration of a parliament, while the Irish peers were elected for life.

When they joined the House of Lords, these peers could participate in hearing appeals to the House of Lords in its judicial function. It was common for members without legal qualifications to sit on these appeals in the 18th and early 19th centuries. In many cases it seems that their actual influence on the outcome was minimal and that in effect the decisions were made by the legally qualified peers. There were, however, occasions when lay members went their own way and by force of numbers were able to outweigh the balance of legal opinion. Turberville cites two examples of decisions where the majority of the legal experts was outnumbered by lay opponents. One in 1783 was dominated by bishops supporting one of their own number, while another in 1805–6 left the Lord Chancellor in the minority when friends of the Prince of Wales packed the House of Lords in a case involving an orphan child in the care of his wife. There were also cases heard with no legally-qualified peers present, the last in 1834.[9]

3. SCOTTISH CIVIL JURISDICTION

The modern Appellate Committee of the House of Lords has a civil appellate jurisdiction for Scotland, but not a criminal one. The story of how this came about is complex. The legal justification for its existence originates in the right of appeal to the 'three estates' of the old (unicameral) Scottish Parliament.[10] That right of appeal might never have made its way into the post-Union court procedure, however, had it not briefly flamed into significance shortly before the Union took place.

Scotland, with its separate monarchy, had also developed a traditional right to appeal to the monarch's own court. This had been a corrective to the endemic corruption and incompetence of the local courts. By the 17th century, though, the judicial jurisdiction of the Scottish Parliament had not been called upon for centuries. In 1674, however, a dispute rocked the Court of Session. Outrage broke out at a decision in which one of the parties was believed to have influenced the judges.[11] The losing party immediately appealed to the King and Parliament, and a raging argument ensued. The judges insisted that this appeal was not competent, while the appellant's counsel held fast to their insistence that it most certainly was. Those counsel were then suspended from practice, only to be followed in a voluntary 'strike' by forty other members of the Faculty of

---

[9] *Bishop of London v Ffytche* (1783) 36 Lords Journals 587 and *Seymour v Lord Euston* (1805–6) 45 Lords Journals 296 and a third decision which Turberville does not name: see AS Turberville 'The House of Lords as a Court of Law 1784–1837' (1936) 52 *Law Quarterly Review* 189, 203–204. The 1834 decision is also referred to in A Lyall 'The Irish House of Lords as a Judicial Body, 1783–1800' (1993–95) 28–30 *Irish Jurist* 314, 341.

[10] For a detailed discussion of the history, see ARG McMillan 'The Evolution of the Scottish Judiciary' (1940) 52 *Juridical Review* 1, 126, 293 (in three parts).

[11] ibid.

Advocates.[12] Further threats of permanent suspension eventually brought them all back into line, although not before the sole copy of the relevant book of procedure, which they claimed settled the matter in their favour, mysteriously vanished never to reappear.[13]

Having reawakened the right, influential Scots decided to ensure that it was protected. The Estates of Scotland forcefully enumerated the right in the 1689 Claim of Right, which specifically stated that: 'It is the right and privilege of the subjects to protest for remeid of law to the King and Parliament against sentences pronounced by the Court of Session', adding that 'all imprisonments and prosecutions for such petitioning are contrary to law.' The right of appeal from this civil court was only exercised six more times before 1707,[14] and its existence was deplored by lawyers as doughty as Lord Stair,[15] but it had been sufficiently established to allow the civil jurisdiction to be later taken on by the House of Lords.

Famously, the Treaty of Union made no mention of this potential civil jurisdiction. Article 19 of the Treaty was cleverly worded. It ensured that no decision of the Court of Session could be appealed to any of the English courts 'in Westminster Hall', or in any other court 'of the like nature'. The House of Lords, however, did not sit in Westminster Hall and, as the court of Parliament, it had a separate status of its own and was not a court 'of the like nature' to the other superior courts of England. By a deft process of omission, then, a corridor was left open which could lead from the Court of Session to the House of Lords.

It is often assumed that the commissioners who drew up the Treaty fully intended the appeal to exist, but wished to avoid saying so in case it enraged the Scottish people, many of whom who were already unenthusiastic about union and might be furious were they to discover that their highest civil court was to be made subservient to any court located in England. Opponents of union were to be found among both the wealthy and the rest of the populace. The merchant elite of the royal burghs were politically and economically conservative and saw the entrepreneurial possibilities following from union with England as a threat rather than an opportunity.[16] Powerful interest groups—legal, clerical, and aristocratic—had to be offered concessions[17] and there was rioting in Edinburgh.[18] The negotiation of the Treaty was a matter to be handled delicately and it seems straightforward to assume that the commissioners had no desire to add any further fuel to the flames of Scottish discontent.

---

[12] Advocates are Scotland's near-equivalent to barristers and the Faculty of Advocates comprises their professional association.

[13] McMillan (n 10) 297.

[14] McMillan (n 10) 298.

[15] AD Gibb *Law From Over the Border* (W Green Edinburgh 1950)

[16] David McCrone *Understanding Scotland: The Sociology of a Stateless Nation* (Routledge London 1992) 40–42.

[17] RM White and DM Willock *The Scottish Legal System* (Butterworths Edinburgh 1993) 27.

[18] DM Walker *The Scottish Legal System: An Introduction to the Study of Scots Law* (6th edn W Green Edinburgh 1992) 154.

Nevertheless, there were those who saw advantage in wresting power from the Scottish courts, whose senior judges were political appointees. The opposition to an appeal to the House of Lords was not unanimous among the Scots.[19] In a fascinating discussion of the negotiations,[20] AJ MacLean indicates that the commissioners had indeed considered the issue and saw the House of Lords as the one English superior court which would at least contain Scottish representatives, the 16 Scottish peers. But MacLean also argues cogently that there was another, more powerful reason for the sleight of hand: one which had to be concealed from the English, not the Scots. The Court of Session was a court of equity; the House of Lords was not. Scots law has never chosen to separate equity out from law and so its courts hear the two together.[21] The House of Lords had only recently emerged from a bitter battle over whether it had the jurisdiction to hear appeals from courts of equity. To have re-opened the debate by examining the House's jurisdiction over the Court of Session could have been deeply damaging, so it was quietly played down.

Within the first session of Parliament after the Union, the first appeal from the Scottish Court of Session was brought to the House of Lords, although it attracted relatively little attention. More important were the Order of 19 April 1709 which created a stay of execution for the period of the appeal, and the 1710 case of *Greenshields v Magistrates of Edinburgh* in which the House of Lords overturned the decision of the Court of Session and thus brought to public attention the now established right of appeal.[22]

Whatever the pragmatic reason for not mentioning the right of appeal in the Treaty of Union, the creation of an appeal to a London court was certainly a matter of political sensitivity. And although the Court of Session was far from incorruptible,[23] the House of Lords was not held in great respect either.[24] The judicial work of the Lords was not viewed as alluring and the lay members had to be forced to take part.[25] The appellate work of the Lords was not the major

[19] AJ MacLean 'The House of Lords' in *Stair Memorial Encyclopaedia* (Butterworths Edinburgh 1988) vol 6, paras 811–812.

[20] AJ MacLean 'The 1707 Union: Scots Law and the House of Lords' (1983) 4 *Journal of Legal History* 50. The discussion which follows is taken from this article.

[21] For more discussion of this, see DM Walker 'Equity in Scots Law' (1964) 66 *Juridical Review* 103.

[22] The first case brought to the HL was that of the *Earl of Roseberie v Inglis*. For a discussion of this and the other initial developments, see *Law and Politics* (n 6) 8 and *Law From Over the Border* (n 15) 9–11.

[23] JA Lovat-Fraser 'The Constitutional Position of the Scottish Monarch Prior to the Union' (1901) 17 *Law Quarterly Review* 252, 254–255. See also AD Gibb *Judicial Corruption in the United Kingdom* (W Green Edinburgh 1957) and MacLean (n 20).

[24] AA Paterson 'Scottish Lords of Appeal, 1876–1988' (1988) 33 *Juridical Review* 236. See also *Law From Over the Border* (n 15) 10–12. In another article, Gibb observes wryly that one of the earliest Scottish appeals to the Lords, the *Greenshields* case 1710, went in favour of the appellant after the Lords had been treated to 'the most shameless canvassing': AD Gibb 'The Inter-relation of the Legal Systems of Scotland and England' (1937) 29 *Law Quarterly Review* 61, 64.

[25] RB Stevens 'The Role of a Final Appeal Court in a Democracy: the House of Lords Today' (1965) 28 *Modern Law Review* 509, 511.

element of its judicial work and it was not at that time a particularly significant feature of the English appeals structure.[26] The seminal works of Scots law were not to be found in English law libraries[27] and the Lords' role as an appellate court for Scotland must have seemed unpromising to many. It is hardly surprising that in the early days, neither the Scots judiciary nor the members of the Lords were unanimously keen on the idea of Scottish civil cases being added to the workload of the Lords. Only five years after the Union, one law reporter, who it seems was finding insufficient space to record the many details, was already complaining that 'this number of appeals, we see increase every year, to the great impoverishing and detriment of the nation'.[28] We may assume that the writer meant the *Scottish* nation, but in any case it soon turned out that his views were not shared by all.

The guardians of Scots jurisprudence may not have much liked the idea of an interjection of a London influence, but those with more pragmatic aims thought otherwise. While jurists might have been interested in the implications of the supervisory function of the Lords, others were interested in its powers of review and were quick to spot its possibilities in Scotland. Wealthy Scots litigants soon became notably enthusiastic about appealing to the Lords, and by the end of the 18th century the majority of appeals to the Lords were coming from Scotland, not England; so much so that legislative attempts (largely unsuccessful) were made to reduce the attraction.[29] A Lords appeal offered not only the chance of getting a decision overturned, but also the stay of execution of the judgment of the lower court meanwhile—not a Scottish practice. Soon there were many frivolous appeals. Various remedial reforms were introduced, allowing lower courts to give interim effect to decrees and limiting the categories of appeal which could be made from the Inner House. Nevertheless, these changes failed to make the attraction pall. The wealthy and unscrupulous found it highly convenient to extend the proceedings for as long as they could, finally agreeing to settle out of court at the eleventh hour.

While the individual litigants liked the advantages an appeal to the Lords brought, the decisions were often less welcome to Scots lawyers. Neither legal training nor a Scots law background was necessary for the parties' representatives (let alone the judges themselves) in Lords appeals in the earlier days.[30] The backlog of Scots appeals grew ever worse and by the start of the 19th century, grumbling lay peers who were only there to make up the numbers were being

---

[26] *Law and Politics* (n 6) 6–8.

[27] *Law From Over the Border* (n 15) 15.

[28] Fountainhall's *Decisions of the Lords of Council and Session* (Hamilton & Balfour Edinburgh) vol ii , 734, where he lists 13 additional cases he describes in the barest form. This quote is also cited in *Law From Over the Border* (n 15) 5 and Lord Hope of Craighead 'Taking the Case to London: Is it all over?' (1998) 43 *Juridical Review* 136, 137–138.

[29] AA Paterson, T StJ N Bates and MR Poustie *The Legal System of Scotland: Cases and Materials* (4th edn Sweet & Maxwell Edinburgh 1999) 86.

[30] AA Paterson notes that cases were typically argued by English-trained counsel 'during much of the eighteenth and nineteenth centuries': Paterson (n 24) 236.

ordered on to a rota under a penalty of £50 for non-attendance.[31] There is considerable juristic testimony in a range of fields of Scots civil law that during the 18th and much of the 19th centuries, decisions were reached to the serious detriment of Scots law.[32] Hart notes that Scottish cases were sometimes remitted back to the Court of Session for its opinion: '[t]he supreme court was so distrustful of its knowledge of the law it was supposed to administer that *at the litigants' expense* it had to resort to the lower Court for illumination.'[33] Walker adds crisply that '[s]ometimes in cases of doubt this tribunal obtained the assistance of the *English* judges. As late as 1904 the English judges were called in to advise on the disposal of a Scottish appeal.'[34] Walker (writing in the 1950s) also remarked pointedly on

... the practice, which is still all too common, of saying and frequently assuming that the point at issue involved nothing peculiar to Scots law or that the laws of England and Scotland were the same on the point. This was rarely the case and the speakers were seldom qualified to say so ... The House still utilises substantially the same trick and whenever in a modern case one is assured that the laws of the two countries do not differ sceptical Scots prepare for a piece of judicial legislation.[35]

The Court of Session was none too happy either about the loss of its definitive status. A range of delaying tactics were used to discourage appeals from getting into the hands of the Lords.

The increasing pressure of work and the backlog of cases forced change on the Lords, and most clearly threw the spotlight of attention on the increasingly anomalous role of the lay peers. The growing importance of the House of Lords as an appellate court brought into focus the need for a core body of legally-qualified judges, and by the 1830s enough Law Lords were available in the House of Lords to make this practicable (although as we saw above, even as late as 1834 there was a case heard by lay peers alone[36]). By then they dominated the outcome of decisions and when in the Irish appeal against conspiracy of the Irish politician, Daniel O'Connell,[37] lay peers attempted to outvote the majority of the Law Lords who were in favour of allowing his appeal, the Law Lords objected. The Prime Minister intervened and after debate the lay peers abstained from the vote. After that they continued frequently to make up the numbers in appeal hearings, but did not have their votes counted. By the 1850s there were

[31] Lord Fraser 'The House of Lords as Court of Last Resort for the United Kingdom' (1986) *Scots Law Times* 33, 35. See also RB Stevens 'The Final Appeal: Reform of the House of Lords and Privy Council 1867–1876' (1964) 80 *Law Quarterly Review* 343, 344. See also *Law and Politics* (n 6) pt I.

[32] *Law From Over the Border* (n 15). See also many comments by TB Smith, for instance in *Studies Critical and Comparative* (W Green Edinburgh 1962).

[33] WO Hart 'The Inter-relation of the Legal Systems of Scotland and England' (1937) 29 *Law Quarterly Review* 61, 67.

[34] DM Walker 'Some Characteristics of Scots Law' (1955) 18 *Modern Law Review* 321, 332–333 (emphasis in original). See also *Studies Critical and Comparative* (n 32).

[35] Walker (n 34) 333.

[36] See n 9.

[37] *O'Connell v R* 11 Cl & F 155. See also the discussion in *Law and Politics* (n 6) 32–34.

usually three or more Law Lords available to hear appeals and it became rare for lay peers to make up the quorum.[38] The last attempt by a lay peer to vote was made in 1883 in *Bradlaugh v Clarke* by Lord Denman, who did have some legal background but no judicial experience. His vote was ignored.[39]

These changes were to the benefit of Scots law, but the problems were not wholly resolved. A comment in the *Scots Law Times* in 1950 describes appeals from Scotland up until 1876 as 'resembling a passage from Alice in Wonderland'.[40] To cite only one example, the comment of Lord Cranworth in *Bartonshill Coal Co v Reid* in 1858 has regularly been singled out by enraged Scots: 'But if such be the law of England on what ground can it be argued not to be the law of Scotland? The law as established in England is founded on principles of universal application not on any peculiarities of English jurisprudence'.[41] Gibb observes that with this blithe introduction of the English concept of common employment into Scots law, '[t]he result was to plague Scotland for 100 years with an unfair and irksome rule'.[42]

And yet, despite the obvious risks to the integrity of Scots legal practices, up until the mid-19th century many Scots lawyers were not particularly keen to see Scots-trained judges deciding Scots appeals in the Lords. In 1856 a Lords committee looked into the matter of its appellate jurisdiction and sought the opinion of various senior Scottish lawyers. Some maintained that there should be no Scottish judge in the Lords, while others took the opposite view and averred that the current situation was highly unsatisfactory.[43] Gibb wondered if some feared that the creation of a Scottish Law Lord might have made such an individual in effect 'a one-man tribunal of appeal' because the other Law Lords allowed him to dominate Scottish decisions,[44] while Lord Hope quotes a comment from a witness that a good Scottish judge was 'infinitely more use in Scotland' than in the House.[45] As a result of the split views, no formal change was made for another 20 years until the Appellate Jurisdiction Act of 1876, although in 1867 a retired Scots judge (Lord Colonsay) was finally elevated to the House as a peer and began advising the lords in Scottish appeals.[46] The 1876 Act however was the foundation for a professionalized court. For some time before that, legally qualified peers had carried out the House's judicial work, but it was not until then that separate Lords of Appeal in Ordinary were created,

---

[38] DEC Yale records that there were around 200 cases decided between 1833 and 1856 by the Lord Chancellor or a single Law Lord, with lay peers present to make up a quorum. 'The Third Lord in *Rylands v Fletcher*' (1970) 86 *Law Quarterly Review* 311–312.

[39] (1883) 8 AC 354. See Lord du Parcq 'The Final Court of Appeal' (1949) *Current Legal Problems* 1, 7–8.

[40] TB Smith 'The House of Lords as Supreme Court of Appeal' (1950) *Scots Law Times News* 98.

[41] (1858) 3 MacQueen's cases 266, 285.

[42] *Law From Over the Border* (n 15) 58–59.

[43] AJ MacLean (n 19) paras 801–812. See also *Law and Politics* (n 6) 43.

[44] *Law From Over the Border* (n 15) 79.

[45] Lord Hope of Craighead (n 28) 146.

[46] For a discussion of the Scots involvement in the HL before this time, see *Final Appeal* (n 6) 30–35.

with attendant salaries. A Scottish judge, Lord Gordon, was appointed to one of the two new posts. Lord Gordon's health was poor, but his successor, Lord Watson, elevated in 1880, was a talented lawyer who was able to make his mark. Although the Scottish Law Lord was not required to sit on all Scottish appeals, that Scottish legal presence began to exercise an influence on the court, not only in Scottish appeals but also in those from the other jurisdictions.[47]

It is interesting to see the fear regarding the dominance of Scottish judges in Scottish appeals being reprised again in the 1930s, in a discussion of the House in the early 20th century:

...there has been no 'inferiority complex' among Scottish Law Lords in English cases. The complex has been rather the other way round as regards cases where Scottish law was involved. It is perhaps unfortunate that English Law Lords do not always, to use a favourite expression of the late Lord Stormonth Darling, 'lay their lugs into it' in the case of a Scottish appeal.[48]

Sands observed that the view of at least one Scottish Law Lord prevailed in every case between 1875 and the date at which he was writing, 1931.

On the other hand, a Scots-trained Law Lord was not always present at Scottish appeals. Today, if a Scottish Law Lord is free it is usual that he will sit on the panel in a Scottish appeal: the normal representation in such appeals is two Scottish lords on the panel of five.[49] This expectation is however very much a modern one. Certainly, from 1947 onwards there were always two Scottish Law Lords in the House of Lords, if not sitting on all Scottish appeals, and there were occasions in the early 20th century where not only two but a majority of Scots-trained judges decided the outcome of an appeal to the Lords: on occasion three Scottish Law Lords sat on a Scottish appeal, and indeed also on some English appeals.[50] Still, however, the intermittent absence of representation on Scots cases continued. Scottish appeals could be heard with no Scottish Law Lord present[51] and this still happened on occasion as late as the 1970s.[52] We can see that the perception that the presence of a Scots-trained judge is essential to ensure the best outcome in a Scottish appeal is a very recent one. Nor was that presence necessarily successful in preventing 'anglicization' of Scots law: Drewry and Blom-Cooper cite a few interesting cases which they see as clear examples of

[47] *Law and Politics* (n 6) 108–9.

[48] Lord Sands in an introductory note to DC Mackenzie 'Lord Colonsay and his Island' (1931) 43 *Juridical Review* 1.

[49] This is not invariably the case: in the 2000 appeal of *Caledonia North Sea Ltd (Respondents) v British Telecommunications Plc* [2002] UKHL 4; 2002 SLT 278, Lord Mackay was the only Scots Law Lord present. To have only one present is however unusual today.

[50] RE Megarry cites several instances from the 1930s in 'The House of Lords and Scottish Appeals' (1956) 19 *Modern Law Review* 95.

[51] Blom-Cooper and Drewry cite the case of *CIR v Albion Rovers FC* [1952] TR 327 in *Final Appeal* (n 6) 381.

[52] *The Legal System of Scotland: Cases and Materials* (n 29) 91. Note also the complaint of the editor of the *Scots Law Times* ([1904] *Scots Law Times News* 73) in the notorious Free Church decision in the HL, that only one Scottish judge took part despite widely publicized calls beforehand for other eligible Scots to be brought on to the panel.

anglicization or insufficient attention to Scots legal problems in Lords appeals, as late as the 1960s.[53]

The Scottish judges themselves were not at all keen to represent their nation in the Lords. In the early days following union, transfer to London amounted to a serious uprooting for ageing men at a time when it took many days to travel from London to Edinburgh. Gibb has pointed out that at the time of the Union between Scotland and England, it took a fortnight to travel to London, on a route beset by highwaymen.[54] Not only ordinary Scots but even the urban legal elite, including the judges, spoke a distinctive Scots dialect[55] and had a strong Scottish identity; England was a foreign and unfamiliar place, and Scots appeals in the House were conducted in English, not Scots.

It took centuries for this reluctance to disappear. In 1876, when the two nations had grown culturally much closer, the Appellate Jurisdiction Act created Lords of Appeal in Ordinary and the first Scottish Lord of Appeal was to be appointed. Scottish judges however did not want the job despite the generous salary. The first Scottish Lord of Appeal was the third choice after the first two to whom the post had been offered had refused it. Scottish judges continued to turn the post down or take it up reluctantly, even into the later 20th century.[56] As late as 1950 Thomas Smith described the post as one which was viewed by some Scottish judges as forcing them to 'uproot themselves late in life to live in exile in London'.[57] Alan Paterson provides evidence to suggest that few of the 16 Scottish Lords of Appeal appointed between 1876 and 1988 accepted the post without reluctance and were the first choice for the post. Lords President (the highest judicial post in the Court of Session) rarely showed interest in the post.

At one time there was a debate among Scots jurists about whether the House of Lords sat as a Scottish court when it heard Scots appeals, or whether it sat as a UK court applying the law of whichever legal system governed the case before it.[58] English jurists have sometimes described the House as having been effect-ively a Scottish court in the years when Scottish cases dominated the case roll, but whether it has ever been a Scottish constitutional court, a court of Scottish appeals, or neither, it was for a long time a place of exile in the eyes of Scottish judges.

---

[53] *Final Appeal* (n 6) ch 18. See also Claire MacDiarmid 'Scots Law: the Turning of the Tide' [1999] *Juridical Review* 156.

[54] *Law From Over the Border* (n 15) 12–13.

[55] ibid 13–14. See also TB Smith [1950] *Scots Law Times News* 98 for an amusing account of one satirical abuse of the language differences on an occasion when Scottish judges and politicians were called before the Lords.

[56] For the example of Lord Normand in the mid-20th century, see the editorial comments in [1953] *Scots Law Times News* 184. See also Paterson (n 24)

[57] TB Smith 'The House of Lords as Supreme Court of Appeal' [1950] *Scots Law Times News* 98.

[58] TB Smith *The Doctrines of Judicial Precedent in Scots Law* (W Green Edinburgh 1952) 49. A-G Donaldson also observes in a discussion of the identity of the court when hearing Northern Irish appeals that '[i]n view of the lengthy period during which the House of Lords has been the ultimate appellate tribunal for three different systems of law it is surprising that its precise function has never been specifically formulated.'

Since Paterson's observations in 1988, there appears at last to have been a change of heart, given the profile of those who have been appointed since then, including two Lords President who have accepted appointment to the Lords.[59] Although fast transport came to be available in the 20th century, it is only in recent decades that the judges have been willing to shuttle back and forth. Smith observed that this 'exile in London' cut them off from the everyday activities, and so some of the ongoing legal influence, of the Court of Session. The question remaining today, 53 years later, is not so much whether the judges lose their 'Scottish legal touch'—access to judgments and jurist debates in electronic form is easily available—but whether they miss out on the subtler updating of their knowledge when they are no longer immersed in the daily judicial work of Scotland. It would be a much more difficult question to answer.

4. A SCOTTISH CRIMINAL JURISDICTION?

So far we have examined only the Scottish civil jurisdiction of the House of Lords. Uniquely in its UK jurisdiction, the House has no jurisdiction over appeals from the Scottish criminal courts. It is commonly assumed today that the jurisdiction never existed, and that it was never intended that it should. Criminal cases, after all, were mostly not capable of being appealed to the old Scottish Parliament and so it would not have been competent to appeal them to the new British one.

AJ MacLean, however, concludes otherwise. He states that '[t]here can be little doubt that in the years following the 1707 Union the House of Lords did exercise a jurisdiction over the High Court of Justiciary . . . [the competence of which was] recognised by lawyers like Professor William Forbes, Lord Kames, Lord Bankton and John Erskine. It went unchallenged until 1765'.[60] In the early days it seems that there was a general view that criminal appeals to the House were competent, and it was only later that the existence of the jurisdiction was denied.

What follows is largely drawn from MacLean's fascinating investigation of the debates and the case law. MacLean notes that between 1709 and 1718 several criminal appeals from the High Court of Judiciary were composed and recorded but never got as far as being presented to the House of Lords. In the case of *Elgin* in 1713[61] the House of Lords reversed a judgment of the High Court of Justiciary in a combined civil and criminal appeal, while in *Munro* in 1724[62] the House received an appeal, although there is no record of its outcome.

---

[59] Lord Hope of Craighead was elevated in 1996 and Lord Rodger of Earlsferry took his seat in September 2003.

[60] AJ Maclean 'The House of Lords and Appeals from the High Court of Justiciary, 1707–1887' [1985] *Juridical Review* 192, 225.

[61] *Magistrates of Elgin v Ministers of Elgin* (1713) Rob 69, as cited in MacLean (n 60) 195.

[62] *Munro v Bayne, Lord Advocate and Anr*, 22 *Journal of the House of Lords* 357 as cited in MacLean (n 60) 198.

One interesting case in 1754 involved Archibald Macdonald, convicted of high treason following the Jacobite rebellion. The sentence passed on him stated that he was to be 'hanged on a gibbet, to be cut down alive, his entrails torn out and burnt',[63] after which he would be beheaded and quartered. Not surprisingly, Macdonald's legal advisers attempted to find a way to avoid this rather unpleasant execution. An imaginative appeal was made to the Lords on technical grounds involving English law and the question of competence, but before it could be established he was given a reprieve and then a pardon. Had the case proceeded it might have established a limited jurisdiction there and then, but even had it done so, it seems likely that legislative or other measures would have been taken to cut the development off at the pass. The reality was that the judges of both the High Court and the House of Lords were horrified at the prospect of a whole new flood of cases being appealed to London, with final judgments being left hanging.

The question was not only whether the jurisdiction existed, but also the extent to which it existed. There were a variety of debates. One concerned whether the old Scottish Parliament, having heard appeals against conviction for treason, had also been a competent forum in which to hear other criminal appeals: perhaps there was a continuing jurisdiction to hear only treason cases. Another dispute contrasted appeals against interlocutory decisions with appeals against decisions of a jury. Yet another considered whether capital cases should be distinguished from non-capital cases. And so on. In 1765 it happened that a Patrick Ogilvie, sentenced to death by hanging, decided to bring an appeal to the House of Lords at a time when the Parliament was in recess, so could not hear the case in time to prevent his execution. He petitioned the King for respite and the case was examined in detail on the King's behalf by the Scottish solicitor-general who concluded that while there was some precedent to suggest the possibility of the existence of criminal appeal to the House of Lords, it was not so established that the Lords were bound to hear such appeals. He recommended that given the threat of the uncertainty which would be introduced in the administration of Scottish criminal justice by the proliferation of such appeals, the appeal should be refused. The Scottish Lord Advocate, his senior, then insisted (MacLean argues that he did so erroneously, given both the cases cited above and juristic writings of that period) that the jurisdiction had never existed and that the appeal was incompetent. Even this did not quite dispose of the issue altogether, however, and it was not until the decision of *Mackintosh* in 1876 that the House of Lords conclusively decided that no right of appeal existed to the House from the High Court of Justiciary. Lord Chancellor Cairns dismissed the attempt to establish that a criminal jurisdiction existed as 'a pure experiment.'[64] The matter was eventually dealt

---

[63] H Arnot *A Collection and Abridgement of Celebrated Criminal Trials in Scotland, 1536 to 1784* (W Smellie Edinburgh 1785) cited in MacLean (n 60) 199.
[64] *Mackintosh v Lord Advocate* 1876 SC 34, 37.

with in statute[65] by the enactment of section 72 of the Criminal Procedure (Scotland) Act 1887 which conclusively reserved jurisdiction to the High Court of Justiciary.

For many years after Union, then, the position was rather less clear than it is now generally assumed to have been. Nor would it necessarily have been viewed by all Scots as the imposition of a foreign interference. At times when the decisions of the High Court were unpopular, an appeal to the Lords might well have been welcomed by some in Scotland: MacLean offers the example of the much-resented sedition trials in 1793.[66] It should be remembered that there remained the option of petitioning the sovereign directly for a reprieve or a pardon, so there was always the possibility that a death sentence could be commuted. This of course amounted at best only to mercy and not to a reversal of the original sentence. It was not a substitute for further appeal. Nevertheless, the House feared (with good reason) the development of a protracted appeal process which would be to the detriment of criminal justice in Scotland, and so the door was closed.

5. An Irish and Northern Irish jurisdiction

In contrast to Scotland, Ireland's legal connection with England long preceded union. From the 13th century onwards, English law had gradually made its way throughout Ireland and by the 17th century it was well-established. Ireland also had its own bicameral parliament and the existence of an appeal to the Irish House of Lords was first established by a declaration of the Irish Houses of Lords and Commons in 1641. This declaration came about as the result of a conflict over which parliament held appellate jurisdiction from the impeachment trial of the counsellor of King Charles I, the Earl of Stafford.[67] The matter did not end there and two cases in 1698 and 1699 were appealed to first the Irish and then the English Houses of Lords, the Irish asserting its jurisdiction and the English denying it. This did not stop the Irish House hearing appeals, however. This unsatisfactory state of affairs could not last and in 1719 it was resolved in a most dramatic fashion. Following a battle of jurisdiction in the case of *Annesley v Sherlock*,[68] the Irish House of Lords directed that three judges of the Irish Court of Exchequer be jailed for attempting to follow the decision of the Irish House rather than the British House. The incident led to the British Parliament passing a statute which removed the Irish House's jurisdiction.

---

[65] It was however dealt with sharply in the case of *Mackintosh v Lord Advocate* 1876 SC 34, 37, in which Lord Chancellor Cairns dismissed the attempt to establish that a criminal jurisdiction existed as 'a pure experiment.'

[66] MacLean (n 60) 221.

[67] FH Newark 'Notes on Irish Legal History' (1947) 8 *Northern Ireland Legal Quarterly* 121, 133 and A Lyall (n 9) 318. Much of what follows is taken from Lyall's intriguing account.

[68] 1718 Journal of the House of Lords 55.

It was not restored until 1783, only 17 years before the House was abolished entirely by the Union.[69]

As the Irish House of Lords had had a role similar to the British House of Lords in hearing appeals and so it was a relatively straightforward matter after Union to transfer that judicial role to the newly-constituted UK House. The Irish Lords had possessed the power to hear both civil and criminal appeals, so both jurisdictions were carried on. This may not however have been welcomed by the Irish common law judges. The nation had already some decades before experienced the unwelcome imposition of English doctrine on the Irish law of equity by the British House of Lords, a messy situation which had later to be corrected by the Irish Parliament.[70] And as we have seen above, the Irish peers after Union with Ireland in 1801 joined the House of Lords at a time when lay peers could vote in appeals, and were still on occasion outvoting the legally-qualified peers. As Lyall has observed, this lay involvement was in marked contrast to the position in the Irish House of Lords, which had already reached the stage where its judicial work was carried out by a core of professional judges. Although lay peers occasionally took part in appeals in the Irish House, they had come to be viewed as unqualified to comment on technical legal points.

In the light of this background, it can be imagined that after Union the Irish judges preferred to see as much as possible of the nation's judicial work kept within its own borders. Indeed it seems that Ireland was careful to enhance its own court structure before Union so that it could limit the number of cases which might be appealed to the London House of Lords. The Irish Parliament created a separate appeal court of the common law judges, in the form of the Irish Court of Exchequer Chamber. Whatever the representative role of the Irish peers in London was intended by the abolished Irish Parliament to be, it appeared not to be the development of a significant judicial function.[71] What exactly their representative role was we shall perhaps never know for certain. The mystery is not easy to piece together and many of what additional clues there might have been were comprehensively destroyed when the Four Courts were bombed and 'the legal records of seven centuries were literally scattered over the City of Dublin'.[72] When the matter was raised by their descendants more than a

---

[69] Lyall (n 9).

[70] Lyall (n 9) 350–351 cites the British HL's decisions in *Kane v Hamilton* 1784 and *Bateman v Murray* 1779, in which it adopted a restrictive interpretation of the doctrine of Irish equity in the area of equity to renew leases: he states that the 'development caused great concern in Irish law where the equity had long been recognised' and cites robust criticisms made by senior Irish judges regarding the decisions.

[71] The Irish impression of the HL's abilities did not improve in the decades which followed: see *Final Appeal* (n 6) 28, *Law and Politics* (n 6) 130, *Law From Over the Border* (n 15) 83. The peers of the House also sat on the Judicial Committee of the PC, which was competent to hear appeals from the Irish Free State until 1932. For further criticism of that work, see T de V White *Kevin O'Higgins* (Anvil Dublin 1948) 220, citing a speech by O'Higgins in the Dáil in which he referred to Lord Dunedin's admission of ignorance with an Irish statute on which he was adjudicating.

[72] FH Newark (n 67). See also Newark's comments in 'The Constitution of Northern Ireland: the First Twenty-Five Years' (1948) 8 *Northern Ireland Legal Quarterly* 52.

century and a half later, long after the island of Ireland was divided and the Irish Free State came into being in 1922,[73] and shortly after the last Irish representative peers had vanished from the House of Lords,[74] a distinguished committee of Law Lords and lay peers decided that they had no instant answer to the question of whether the Irish peers had represented the Irish peerage, the realm of Ireland, or the territory of Ireland.[75] The Irish peers had joined the Parliament[76] and they had left the Parliament, and what exactly their political role had been in the interim years remains hard to say.

Nevertheless, after Union, Irish litigants were not averse to trying out their appeals to the House of Lords. Common law and equity appeals had returned to the House of Lords following the abolition of its Irish counterpart, adding to the burden of work on the Lords which we have already considered above.[77] Fortunately the Irish appeals did not follow the nightmarish precedent of the Scottish appeals, because (as with English appeals) execution of the judgments was not stayed so there was less incentive for eager litigants to flood the House with appeals as a delaying tactic. Also, problems of integrating Irish and English law were far fewer because so much of Irish law was shared with England. Lord Fitzgerald was the first Lord of Appeal in Ordinary to be appointed from Ireland, in 1882.[78] He was followed by the Irish Lord Morris and Killanin, but this did not establish a practice of appointing an Irish Lord of Appeal, and they were not appointed with any specifically Irish judicial brief.

When Ireland was partitioned, Northern Ireland remained a part of the UK. Statute ensured that a continued civil right of appeal to the Lords was provided for.[79] A criminal right of appeal to the Lords was later added by section 6 of the Criminal Appeal (Northern Ireland) Act 1930, although only in cases where the Attorney-General certified that the case involves 'a point of law of exceptional public importance, and that it is desirable in the public interest that a further appeal should be brought'.[80]

---

[73] Formal independence was brought about by Irish and British legislation. The Irish government enacted the Constitution of the Irish Free State (Saorstát Éireann) Act 1922. The British government combined a Royal Proclamation with the Constitution of the Irish Free State Act 1922 to make the new state a member of the Commonwealth.

[74] The Irish peers held their posts in the HL for life. B Hadfield explains that Lord Chancellor of Ireland was responsible for administering their election to the Lords, and in 1922 when that office was abolished by Irish legislation, no further elections were held. The remaining peers continued to sit until the death of the last remaining peer in 1961: 'Whether or Whither the House of Lords?' (1984) 35 Northern Ireland Legal Quarterly 313, 316–317.

[75] See the discussion in CE Lysaght 'The Irish Peers and the House of Lords' (1967) 18 Northern Ireland Legal Quarterly 277.

[76] Along with Irish members of the House of Commons and several Irish positions in the government, of course.

[77] Blom-Cooper and Drewry indicate that 10% or more of cases in that period originated from the Irish courts in the first century after Union: Final Appeal (n 6) 36.

[78] Law and Politics (n 6) 109.

[79] Government of Ireland Act 1920, ss 49 and 50 (as amended). For additional information see AS Quekett The Constitution of Northern Ireland Parts II (HMSO Belfast 1933) 80–82. See also FH Newark's discussion (n 72).

[80] The Constitution of Northern Ireland Parts II (n 79) 82.

One might have expected a convention to develop that there be a Northern Irish Lord of Appeal in Ordinary, similar to that of the Scottish one. Certainly there was a legislative lacuna which could have been filled, and as Harry Calvert observes, what representation there is of Northern Ireland interests generally in the House is 'entirely fortuitous'.[81]

The legal system of Northern Ireland however has little to compare with the historical or ideological separation which the Scottish legal system possesses. The English legal system is its parent and in many fields, legal provision is largely undifferentiated among England, Wales, and Northern Ireland. We should be cautious about any drawing any analogies between the histories of Northern Ireland and Scotland: the constitutional role created for the organs of government in the Northern Ireland legal system at the time of partition (as indeed has again happened today) was rightly described by Megaw J in the Court of Appeal as having 'no exact parallel'.[82]

Northern Ireland's courts and judges also occupy a notably different position in its judicial hierarchy when compared with the Scottish courts and judiciary. In the majority of civil and criminal cases, the right of appeal lies beyond the Northern Ireland Court of Appeal, making it predominantly a second-tier, penultimate court rather than a final court of appeal. The Northern Ireland Court of Appeal does not possess extensive powers of ultimate jurisdiction other than in the majority of civil cases begun in the lower courts of the magistrates' and county courts. Although only a tiny number of cases go from the Northern Ireland Court of Appeal to the House of Lords each year,[83] its whole body of case law is small[84] in comparison with that of the House of Lords and the English Court of Appeal together,[85] whose appeal workload effectively creates a body of decisions binding or influential upon most aspects of Northern Ireland law. Decisions of the Court of Appeal in England are persuasive although not binding on the Northern Ireland Court of Appeal.[86] Decisions of the House

---

[81] H Calvert *Constitutional Law in Northern Ireland: A Study in Regional Government* (Stevens London 1968) 84. This remains the case today, particularly given the increasingly problematic consequences which may result from a Law Lord participating in legislative debate, as discussed below. A Northern Irish Law Lord is no substitute to wider regional representation in the House, particularly now when the devolved Northern Ireland Assembly and Executive was dissolved on 28 April 2003, returning the devolved legislative responsibility to the UK Parliament, to be addressed by the making of orders in council. For an excellent discussion of the democratic deficiencies and legislative weaknesses of this arrangement, see B Hadfield *The Constitution of Northern Ireland* (SLS Belfast 1989).

[82] *Attorney-General v Jaffé* [1935] NI 97, 126–127.   [83] See ch 3.

[84] Northern Ireland judicial statistics indicate that between 1993 and 2000, the court heard between 33 and 110 criminal appeals each year. Similar historical figures are not given for the civil appeals, but 34 were heard in 2000. Northern Ireland Court Service *Judicial Statistics 2000* (HMSO Belfast 2001) 16–19.

[85] UK judicial statistics for 2001 indicate that the HL heard 88 appeals in 2001, of which one came from the Northern Ireland Court of Appeal. The Criminal Division of the Court of Appeal heard 2,110 appeals and the Civil Division heard 1,386.

[86] In addition to the cases which will be discussed below, see *In re Northern Ireland Road Transport Board and the Century Insurance Co Ltd* [1941] NI 77, 106–107 and *Russell v Thompson* [1953] NI 51, 68.

of Lords are not strictly binding upon the Court of Appeal in Northern Ireland other than in cases which originate in Northern Ireland, but would normally be followed.

When the question of its status has been discussed in judgments, it seems that the Northern Ireland higher judiciary regards the court as occupying a status for the most part equivalent to that of the English Court of Appeal.[87] Lord Lowry, the then Lord Chief Justice of Northern Ireland, in *R v Flynn and Leonard*, for example, spoke of his 'brother judges in criminal trials' and listed English and Northern Ireland examples without in any way distinguishing them.[88] Judgments have not been very explicit on the subject, but there appears to be little suggestion that the judges of the Court of Appeal possess or have possessed a greater power or significance in the Northern Ireland legal system, other than in constitutional cases which involved the Government of Ireland Act 1920 [89] and in those cases where no appeal lies to the House of Lords.

Briefly, following the Government of Ireland Act 1920, there existed a High Court of Appeal for Ireland (with jurisdiction over both Northern and Southern Ireland). It regarded itself as 'the supreme guardian of the constitution' and stated that it had a more important constitutional role than the old Irish Court of Appeal.[90] The corollary of this was that it was not bound by the old court's decisions. Calvert in 1968 argued that the Northern Ireland courts which remained after this short-lived court ceased to function had also taken on that more significant constitutional role. Accordingly they should never have felt it necessary to assume the doctrine of binding precedent which limited the power of the English Court of Appeal, at least in the area of constitutional review, which was a power available to the Northern Irish court but not to its English counterpart.[91] However, as Calvert himself admitted,[92] this flexibility of constitutional precedent was never accepted by the Northern Ireland Court of Appeal.

Furthermore, there is no higher panel of Northern Ireland judges beyond the Court of Appeal, although individual judges may of course be elevated to the Lords. Thus while there have undoubtedly been distinctive and highly talented Law Lords who have risen to the post from Northern Ireland, there has not been a national panel possessing a broad and final review to take a critical or challenging approach to Northern Ireland law and to draw out any national legal identity. As with the Scots jurisdiction, it is not clear whether the House of Lords sit as a Northern Irish court or a UK court when hearing Northern Irish appeals, although the similarity between much of English and Northern Irish law

---

[87] The standard authority for this is the old Irish Court of Appeal case of *McCartan v Belfast Harbour Commissioners* [1910] 2 IR 470, 494.

[88] *R v Flynn and Leonard* (1972) 11 NIJB (May) 1, 3.

[89] See the discussion of *O'D Cars Ltd v Belfast Corporation*, below.

[90] *Leyburn v Armagh County Council* [1922] IR 15. The court sat for only a year between 1921 and 1922 and heard nine appeals during that time: see *The Constitution of Northern Ireland* (n 81) 41.

[91] *Constitutional Law in Northern Ireland* (n 81) 119.

[92] ibid 112–119.

does make the question less significant.[93] On the other hand, FH Newark noted, in 1973:

It is true that there does not appear to be any instance of a Northern Ireland court ignoring a decision of the House of Lords in a case coming from England and Scotland, or even suggesting that any such decision could be ignored ... [but] a case 'on all fours' with another case is a rare commodity, and judges have a great capacity for 'distinguishing'.[94]

Developments in the doctrine of precedent in the UK have however slightly altered the relationship of the Northern Ireland Court of Appeal with the English courts over the period since 1920. In the early days post-partition, the Northern Irish court was strongly loath to declare any divergence from the decisions of the English Court of Appeal. Holmes LJ had declared previously in *McCartan v Belfast Harbour Commissioners*:

It is true that although we are not technically bound by decisions in the co-ordinate English Court [of Appeal] we have been in the habit, in adjudicating on questions as to which the law of the two countries is identical, to follow them. We hold that uniformity of decision is so desirable that it is better, even when we think the matter doubtful, to accept the authority of the English Court, and leave error, if there be error, to be corrected by the tribunal whose judgment is final on both sides of the Channel.[95]

In *Cash v Rainey*, Babington LJ remarked: 'This Court is not bound to follow the English Court of Appeal but does so as a matter of practice and in order to maintain uniformity of decision unless it entertains a very strong opinion to the contrary'.[96]

In later years the position taken by the Northern Ireland Court of Appeal developed in a less restrictive direction. In the 1950s the Court of Appeal led by Lord MacDermott was willing to state its opposition to English decisions,[97] a position later expressed in the lower courts too, as when in 1996 Girvan LJ stated:

If the Court in this jurisdiction after a careful analysis of the law is convinced the decision of the English Court is wrong then it should be and in my view is free to take a different view from that adopted by the English Court. As a matter of strict legal theory the decisions of the English Court of Appeal are not binding upon the Courts in this jurisdiction although obviously great weight is put upon them.[98]

What is interesting in his statement is the absence of any reference to the need for comity or uniformity; this was also absent when Carswell LJ reached a similar

---

[93] AG Donaldson *Some Comparative Aspects of Irish Law* (Duke University Press Durham 1957) 28.

[94] FH Newark *Elegantia Juris: Selected Writings* (Faculty of Law Queen's University; *Northern Ireland Legal Quarterly* Belfast 1973) 253.

[95] [1910] 2 IR 470, 494.

[96] [1940] NI 52, 64.

[97] See eg Porter LJ in *McGuigan v Pollock* [1955] NI 74, 100 and Lord MacDermott LCJ in *R v Bailey* [1957] NI 15, 19.

[98] *National and Provincial Building Society v Lynn and Lynn* Chancery Division 28 June 1996.

conclusion in a 1986 decision.[99] Girvan LJ backed his arguments by a careful reading of the legislation in its statutory context, thus preferring his reading of legislative policy over the alternative formal weight of precedent. Formal reasoning not surprisingly is emphasized in these divergent decisions: in another (rare) example of explicit divergence from a decision in the English Court of Appeal, the Northern Ireland Court of Appeal in *R v Harper* justified the divergence with references to literal interpretation, to English precedent on rules of construction and on English dicta and analogous authority.[100]

While there was a parliament in Northern Ireland, there were also interesting developments during the later period in some devolution judgments in the Court of Appeal during the period in which Northern Ireland had a parliament of its own. In *O'D Cars Ltd v Belfast Corporation*, for instance, the Court of Appeal turned to the constitutional law of other Commonwealth countries for aid in interpreting the 1920 Act. Lord MacDermott LCJ made reference to US cases and indicated that the 1920 Act had given the Northern Ireland courts a power of constitutional review regarding the validity of enactments governed by that Act. He also stated that 'its interpretation should be sufficiently liberal to let [the Parliament of Northern Ireland] be "mistress in her own house".'[101] The House of Lords gave support to Lord MacDermott's approach. Viscount Simonds noted that 'a flexibility of construction is admissible in regard to such [constitutional] instruments which might be rejected in construing ordinary statutes or inter partes documents.'[102]

The divergences have been rare, and today at a time when devolution arrangements have failed in Northern Ireland there is all the less compass in which to develop distinctive areas of Northern Ireland law. Nevertheless, significant legal developments in the region, such as in the areas of fair employment and judicial appointments, make the Northern Ireland legal system rather more than a branch of the English parent and provide a fruitful area of legal study for jurists in the other UK legal systems. Both the Northern Ireland legal system and the powers of Northern Ireland's Court of Appeal are distinctive and no simple direct comparison can be made between it and any other part of the UK, even on a formal level. The institutional role of a Northern Irish Law Lord is not quite like that of the Scottish Law Lords: indeed, one can ask whether such a thing as a 'Northern Irish Law Lord' exists in the UK's constitution, or whether there are simply Law Lords who happen to originate from Northern Ireland and may contribute usefully to judicial and legislative work concerning that region.

While many of the questions asked about the Scottish judiciary are relevant to queries about the judges of Northern Ireland, it is important to consider the two separately. Not only Northern Irish legal identity but also Northern Irish political identity (or identification) have been described by political scientists as

[99] *Re Broderick (a bankrupt)* [1986] 6 NIJB 36.
[100] [1990] 4 NIJB 75.
[101] [1959] NI 62, 87.
[102] *Belfast Corporation v OD Cars Ltd* [1960] NI 61, 86 (HL).

relatively weak in comparison to that of, say, Scottish identity or identification. It lacks historical and cultural depth and it lacks a clear definition. 'Northern Irishness' is part of a constellation of potential identifications alongside Irishness and Britishness which the region's citizens can adopt, reject, hold singly, or hold together.[103] What a Northern Irish Law Lord represents is even more difficult to identify than that represented by a Scottish Law Lord. So instead, perhaps we can only ask what qualities or expertise is a Scots-trained or Northern Ireland-trained judge thought to bring to the Lords today, and how has that perception altered over the centuries?

6. THE COURT WITHIN PARLIAMENT

As noted above, the House of Lords was the court of the sovereign and his or her council in parliament at the time the UK was being formed, and that link has never quite been broken. Blom-Cooper and Drewry amusingly described the House as 'something of a constitutional anachronism, a feudal relic preserved in the interests of judicial ancestor-worship.'[104] As recently as 1948 the court heard its appeals in the chamber of the House itself: judicial business was heard for the first part of the day, then the whole House convened to consider non-judicial business. It was only moved out of the chamber to make room for the House of Commons during rebuilding after wartime bombing. At this point the court became a temporary 'Appellate Committee', made permanent a few years later. Even today the Appellate Committee still hears appeals in the chamber for a week at the end of the summer recess, before the other Lords reconvene. It then returns to its separate committee rooms. Nor is the link only geographical: the Appellate Committee remains a committee of the House of Lords in more than name only. The decisions it reaches are not actually binding until they are agreed to by the House, although in practice this is done at a sitting of the Law Lords in the House. In the course of a recent celebrated appeal against prosecution popularly known as the 'metric martyrs' case, the appellant Mr Thoburn contemplated that, were the case to go to the House of Lords, he could ask the whole House to hear the case, in place of the Law Lords.[105] There was nothing in statute to prevent this: the Appellate Jurisdiction Act 1876 requires that three Law Lords be present on the panel but does not state that lay peers cannot also participate.[106] The force of constitutional convention, however, was of course entirely against Mr Thoburn's proposal and in any event the application to appeal to the House of Lords was refused.

---

[103] For a discussion of this, see eg J Whyte *Interpreting Northern Ireland* (Clarendon Press Oxford 1990) ch 4.

[104] *Final Appeal* (n 6) 15. 11 August 2003.

[105] J Rozenberg 'Trying to Keep the Scales of Justice Imperial' *Daily Telegraph*, 30 January 2001.

[106] See also the historical discussion in R Stevens 'The Final Appeal: Reform of the House of Lords and Privy Council 1867–1876' (1964) 80 *Law Quarterly Review* 343, 368.

Nevertheless, although by convention the wider House cannot today join the Law Lords to hear appeals and the Appellate Committee is no longer in practice a 'court of Parliament',[107] the Law Lords and others eligible to sit on the Appellate Committee are life peers, not only ex officio members of the House. They can join the wider House to participate in the process of making and scrutinizing legislation. Even today the Scottish and Northern Irish Law Lords have a parliamentary role as well as an appellate one. This is not in any way a duty of regional representation. The power to participate is one which they can exercise or not by choice and on topics of their choosing (within conventional limits).[108] While several have carried out the work with flair, there is no convention or even practice burdening them with any such responsibility, and there are many more lay peers who can represent the nations and regions.

7. The Scottish and Northern Irish contribution

Blom-Cooper and Drewry astutely asked back in 1972 what exactly a 'Scottish case' and a 'Scottish judge' might be (indeed one of the most famous, Lord Reid, was trained in Scots law but practised at the English Bar before elevation to the Lords). How long does a judge remain fully 'Scottish' after joining a UK court, and is every case originating in Scotland a 'Scottish' case even if it never raises any issues on which the law of Scotland and the other constituent nations of the UK differ? When a Scottish Law Lord decides a particular way, is this because of his Scottish legal background or for some other unrelated reason?[109] The question is all the more difficult when we look at the Northern Irish Law Lords: although their contribution as individuals has been very significant,[110] the 'Northern Irishness' of it would be difficult to discern. Their judicial work has often been excellent, but it has been a general contribution to shared English and Northern Ireland law rather than a specifically 'Northern Irish' one.

---

[107] cf the Committee for Privileges which hears claims relating to hereditary peerages and questions relating to the orders, customs, and privileges of the HL. This committee must include at least three Law Lords.

[108] There is a convention regarding participation in certain legislative debates where this might be seen to conflict with judicial responsibilities. The senior Law Lord, Lord Bingham, made a formal statement in the House on 22 June 2000 regarding this (see Hansard HL Deb vol 614 col 419), stating that it would not be regarded as appropriate by the Law Lords for them to participate in debates where there might be a 'strong element of party political controversy' and they would also consider the possibility that offering an opinion might render them ineligible to sit judicially in a related appeal: JUSTICE 'A Supreme Court for the United Kingdom Policy Paper' (JUSTICE London 2002). This convention is coming under increasing scrutiny: consider the recent impartiality ruling in *Davidson v Scottish Ministers (No 1)* 2002 SC 205.

[109] *Final Appeal* (n 6) 7–8.

[110] For some interesting examples, see Lord Lowry's spirited piece, 'The Irish Lords of Appeal in Ordinary' in DS Greer and NM Dawson (eds) *Mysteries and Solutions in Irish Legal History* (Four Courts Dublin 2001). Lord Lowry of course omits his own contribution to the Lords in his time as a Lord of Appeal in Ordinary, a contribution which was very highly regarded.

It is all too easy to creep into an atomistic reductivism, focusing on individual legal players and elevating their personal contributions into structural explanations while overlooking the roles of other factors in developing the law. The best of the modern commentators have been careful to avoid this, and it is interesting to examine what conclusions they have reached about the character of the 'regional' Law Lords. Unfortunately, these have mostly been restricted to comments about the Scottish-trained judges.

Today, Lord Hope suggests that the 'primary role' of the Scottish Law Lords is 'to ensure that appeals in the Scottish cases will be decided according to the principles and practice of Scots law.'[111] In the early days, though, it is not clear at all what contribution Scottish judges brought to the Lords. It might be assumed that they were appointed to contribute a detailed working knowledge of Scots law, but it is not clear that that has been seen as their most important contribution, particularly given that for much of the history of the Lords after 1876, Scottish judges did not always sit on Scottish appeals. There has also been a perception in the past that Scottish judges living and working in England tended to forget the details of Scots law, so that their contribution was more in terms of the *principled* approach of the Scottish jurist, rather than the detailed supervision of the implementation of individual legal norms. However, that perception was challenged by Alan Paterson[112] and as we saw above it seems even less convincing now.

It was also argued in the past that the Scottish Law Lords contributed a distinctive principled approach to appeals from the common law jurisdictions.[113] Lord Hope argues that that Scottish contribution was once important but has declined due to the influence of the 'European tradition' on all the UK judges.[114] So, what do they bring?

Stevens and Paterson argued that the Scottish judges are distinctive 'generalists' on Lords appeals because (as remains the case today) as advocates they do not specialize at the Bar in the same way English barristers do. Stevens argued that they have added a distinctive breadth to Lords decisions.[115] Due to their greater length of service in comparison with their English counterparts, Paterson noted that they also tended to achieve disproportionate seniority and so influenced not just outcomes of decisions but also who is allotted to which case.[116] Writing in 1988, he observed that the Scottish Law Lords had served for an average of 12 years compared with the English eight. Whether this will continue to be the case is of course dependent on the individuals, and as Paterson noted, since 1984 the selection of the senior Law Lord is no longer dependent solely on

---

[111] Lord Hope of Craighead (n 28) 146.   [112] Paterson (n 24) 246–247.

[113] ibid 246 observes, regarding Lord Reid's contribution, that 'one suspects that the English had rather more to complain about in relation to "Scottification" than the Scots had of anglicisation at the hands of Lord Reid'.

[114] Lord Hope of Craighead (n 28) 145.

[115] Paterson (n 24) 248; *Law and Politics* (n 6) 130 and 269.

[116] Paterson (n 24) 250–251.

length of service as a Lord of Appeal. Looking at the pattern since Paterson wrote this, we see that Lord Keith served 19 years and was the last Scots-trained senior Law Lord to date, but that Lord Jauncey served only six and while Lord Mackay served 16, 10 of those were as Lord Chancellor, in practice a predominantly administrative rather than appellate role (albeit a powerful one in other ways, for instance in his role in judicial appointments for England and Wales, including the House of Lords). Lord Clyde served for seven years (he retired in September 2003), while Lord Hope has served seven to date.

Paterson also maintained that the Scots judges had tended to be the ones who pushed the Lords from its older tendency to multiple opinions to a later tendency to single opinions, and they have also been less prone to deliver dissents. On the other hand, Blom-Cooper and Drewry's study 16 years prior to Paterson's suggested that Scottish judges were inclined to dissent just as much as the English judges were.[117] Today, the single opinion tendency is prevalent among the Law Lords generally, not only the Scottish Law Lords. I think that when we look at the relatively small number of individuals involved, there is insufficient evidence available to come to a conclusion in a complex issue such as this: it would be hard to be certain whether there is something distinctively Scottish about a collectivist approach, even if a survey of more recent cases confirmed Paterson's thesis. It is probably fair to say that the Scottish judges have a generalist approach, something which is not unique to the Scottish legal system and wholly explained by lack of specialism at the Bar, but which can be found in other smaller legal systems such as Ireland. There is more scope for substantive reasoning and less of a need for definitive decision-making in the small legal system where there is less risk of a multiplicity of future cases which would make strict delineation of rules necessary from the outset: indeed, a breadth of vision is important in decisions which may have to do service over a wide area of law for many years.[118] Paterson also refers to the related influence which certain Scottish judges such as Lord Reid possessed, resulting in 'opinion deference' by judges of lesser stature, and the continuing importance of the Scottish Law Lords as 'specialists' in the Scottish appeals.[119] This latter is undoubtedly significant, whatever one concludes regarding the Scottishness of a collectivist approach.

All these are useful attributes, but other than the 'specialist' contribution, they do not seem fundamental reasons for keeping Scots-trained judges in the Law Lords. So let us consider instead what disadvantages and advantages their presence, and that of the Northern Irish Law Lords, brings today. The disadvantages seem to be mainly experienced by the Scots and Northern Irish themselves: the delay brought about by a further tier in the appeals structure; the expense; and, for some, the cost and inconvenience of travelling to London. Perhaps the most serious disadvantage today, though, is the elevation of two small

---

[117] *Final Appeal* (n 6) 184.
[118] See also K Goodall 'What defines the Roles of a Judge? First Steps towards the Construction of a Comparative Method' (2000) 51 *Northern Ireland Legal Quarterly* 535.
[119] Paterson (n 24) 252.

jurisdictions' best judges to an appeal court where so few of their cases are decided each year. Smith has remarked on this in Scotland[120] and Sir John MacDermott observed that it was fortunate for Northern Ireland that Lord Lowry was elevated to the House much later in his career than he might have been.[121]

The other complaints have come mostly from Scots. The first is resentment expressed regarding decisions on Scottish matters being taken by a mixed panel outwith national borders. A decision of five or more Scots judges in the Court of Session can be overturned by a panel in the Lords with only one or two Scots judges on it.[122] As Smith has observed, this 'might be thought to give [the Scottish Law Lords] theoretically too much power in relation to the judges of the Court of Session and too little power in relation to the English and Irish Law Lords.'[123]

There are many advantages for Scotland and Northern Ireland in the present arrangements. Other than the one usually cited, which is avoiding error in deciding questions of distinctive Northern Ireland and Scots law, we can also consider the great benefit of being represented in nationwide decision-making. Given that the larger English and Welsh legal system produces so many more precedents than do the smaller systems, many of which will be adopted by courts elsewhere because of their persuasiveness, it is valuable to the smaller systems to be involved in the decision-making process. Also, given that in some areas of law, such as fiscal, it is important to have consistency across the UK, it is important that judicial interpretations in such fields are perceived as legitimate. If there were no Northern Irish or Scots judges in the House, law might be perceived to be 'imposed on' those regions not only by unelected judges, but unelected judges from other nations and other legal systems. In addition, so long as there is a UK Parliament, enacting legislation for the whole UK, then it is valuable for there to be a single court able to give consistent interpretation throughout the UK.

There are benefits too for all the legal systems in providing the opportunity for distinctive concepts and case law from different legal systems to be examined when reaching decisions.[124] This of course assumes that the House takes any notice of these distinctive concepts and case law. These days it is generally believed that it does, but as we have seen above, it was not always so.

Assuming that the Scottish Parliament will not decide to remove a large part of the House's jurisdiction in Scots civil law, and that a constitutional reform of the House of Lords would still leave it to hear Northern Irish and Scottish appeals,

---

[120] TB Smith *A Short Commentary on the Law of Scotland* (W Green Edinburgh 1962) 88.

[121] Sir John MacDermott, tribute to Lord Lowry in (1999) 50 *Northern Ireland Legal Quarterly* 8, 9.

[122] Paterson (n 24) 252–253. The majority of cases in the Inner House of the Court of Session (its appeal court) are heard by three judges, but five or more can be convened, and occasionally are, for cases of particular difficulty or importance.

[123] See also *A Short Commentary on the Law of Scotland* (n 120) 88.

[124] See *A Short Commentary on the Law of Scotland* (n 120) and *Law and Politics* (n 6) 270–271 and 490 (citing Lord Denning's enthusiasm for the Scottish principled approach).

what representation might continue to be required? Lord Bingham remarked in 2002 on 'the desirability of including Scottish and Northern Irish law lords on committees hearing appeals from those jurisdictions respectively'.[125] For Northern Ireland, with perhaps one or two appeals a year, not necessarily in distinctive Northern Ireland points of law, a full-time Lord of Appeal does not seem necessary—if we are considering only the appellate work which Law Lords carry out. The representation from Scotland has dropped over the last century. At first, the Scots judge was one of the two judicial peers. In 1913 it was two out of six and now that there are 12 Law Lords there is still no requirement for there to be more than two Scots-trained judges among them. The concern now is to have enough Scots judges to hear both devolution issues before the Privy Council and Scots appeals to the House of Lords.[126] The question will be whether this requires more Law Lords to be appointed, or for there instead to be a wider pool of eligible persons holding high Scottish judicial office.[127] Even if the Scottish Parliament did decide to reduce the number of areas of law in which a right of appeal existed to a court beyond the Court of Session, there would still need to be Scots judges to serve in the Privy Council to hear devolution cases, and cases involving the Human Rights Act 1998 would still continue to be appealed to the House of Lords.

There is very little continuity between the original peers who represented Scotland and Ireland in the House and the professional judges from those legal systems who are elevated today: as Blom-Cooper and Drewry put it, the House after 1876 'was a phoenix from the ashes, completely new, resembling the old tribunal only in name and venue'.[128] At the time of Union with Scotland, Court of Session judges gave decisions without giving reasons, while Lords' decisions were given by panels which included lay peers. Four hundred years ago, a Scottish judge needed primarily to be a God-fearing man of independent means who was too wealthy to be bribed.[129] By the late 19th century, first the Irish legal system then the others had moved towards an ethos of a professional judiciary. As Stevens has explained, the changing constitutional ideology which moved from a 'balance among King, Lords and Commons to a balance among executive, judicial, and legislative institutions' had created a perception of a need for a final court of appeal for the UK which was separate from the executive and legislature;[130] the judicial function of the House of Lords many times came close

---

[125] Lord Bingham 'A New Supreme Court for the United Kingdom' (UCL Constitution Unit London 2002) 13.

[126] Lord Hope of Craighead (n 28) 144–145.

[127] Particularly given the provision in Scotland Act 1998 s 103(2) that in appeals on devolution issues, the membership of the Judicial Committee of the PC is effectively excludes the Commonwealth judges who are members of the Committee, confining it to UK judges. See A Page, C Reid and A Ross *A Guide to the Scotland Act 1998* (Butterworths Edinburgh 1999) 159–160.

[128] *Final Appeal* (n 6) 37.

[129] Scottish Executive *Judicial Appointments: An Inclusive Approach* (Consultation Paper 20 HMSO Edinburgh) 5.

[130] *Law and Politics* (n 6) 5.

to being excised from the House. By the early 20th century, nevertheless, a typical Lords judge was being rewarded with the post for his political work and it was not until later in the century that the legal pedigree of a candidate became formally the single most important criterion for the post.[131]

The primary work in the previous century was seen to be clarification of the law; today the constitutionalization of rights is said to have brought about a revolution in the role of the senior judges. Whether the public perception of the judiciary has changed so radically, though, is another question. The judiciary themselves have been slow to adapt to the modern discourse of transparency and accountability which brings with it expectations of accessibility. A professional public relations apparatus has been the last element to find its way into the normal administration of judicial work at senior levels across the UK. Representation is a major component of modern conceptions of judicial legitimacy, and discussions about representation will need to link into debates about legitimacy. As I have noted elsewhere,[132] the judiciary in most parts of the UK[133] has had both a discursive and an institutional invisibility, in which even today, with the advent of new judicial roles in interpreting constitutional legislation, the approach to legal reasoning remains relatively formal and is accompanied by a discursive minimizing of the importance of judicial discretion. Even now that the creative and law-making power of the judge has been recognized in higher court discourse for decades, there remains very little formal institutional recognition of that power within law-creating procedures. The debate about representation in the highest courts of appeal has awoken in Scotland in particular with the devolution work of the Privy Council, but the debate has been a political one which has not penetrated deeply into legal discourse. In many ways the situation in Northern Ireland has not been so different, with critiques of judicial work being discussed within nationalism debates rather than being examined through discussion about visions of law.

Visions of law are also no longer a predominantly national concern. With the growing importance of European and other international legal influences on the law of the UK, there is an interesting debate to be had about the changing roles of the judiciary, and work to be done on developing comparative method in examining these. Comparative law in the UK has made good use of method but has lacked explicit methodologies and an acknowledgement of the implications

---

[131] Paterson (n 24) 242.

[132] K Goodall 'The Legitimacy of the Judge' in John Bell (ed) *Studies in UK Law 2002* (BIICL London 2002) 33.

[133] This has been a little less so in Northern Ireland where their work has been dogged by a lack of confidence in what is seen as the British institution of the justice system. Significant changes have taken place recently: following the Good Friday Agreement in 1998, a Review Group was appointed to consider among other things judicial appointments and the institutional protection of judicial independence. Their *Review of the Civil Justice System in Northern Ireland—Final Report* (NICS Belfast 2000) recommended the establishing of an independent Judicial Appointments Commission, with an interim independent commissioner carrying out the work until the Commission is established. The first commissioner was appointed in December 2001.

which using different methods carries. In particular, we must start clearly defining our terms: one of the great pitfalls lies in not defining what appear to us to be our ordinary language terms. The issue of representation is complex. Here we have been considering regional representation; most commonly discussions about representation in the senior judiciary in the UK focus on specific conceptions of a cross-section of society. It is by no means clear what this would be. We have seen above the difficulty of identifying what regional representation in the House of Lords might be, and how the concept has changed over the centuries. We have not even begun to consider questions such as how Scottish or Northern Irish Law Lords can represent their respective communities of Gaelic speakers.

The issue of the ideological influence of regional Law Lords, one part of the juristic debate about what they represent, is equally complex. In discussions about the Law Lords, jurists have questioned to what extent the senior judiciary today have a judicial ideology. Critical theorists are quite convinced they have an ideology. But the concept of ideology has a huge history in political theory, from Adorno and Althusser, to Terry Eagleton and Foucault, to the Essex school of discourse analysis which argues that the word 'ideology' is too closely tied to Marxism and should be rejected in favour of the term 'discourse': and then when we start to look at discourse we find it can mean anything from state propaganda to the entire social structure, depending on whose theories one reads that day.

While we are aware that terms such as 'constitution', 'judicial independence', and 'accountability' can mean something quite different in France, Ireland, or Canada from what they signify here, we also need to be aware of the potential for confusion in the political concepts we use in our wider policy discussions. This is not work which public lawyers and policymakers can carry out by themselves: it is work for jurists and political theorists and we should be looking to bring them forward to carry out that kind of precise, time-consuming analysis. In asking what it is that Scottish and Northern Irish judges represent in the House of Lords, we should move away from the functionalist presumption that their roles were ever clearly delineated, or the teleological presumption that their roles evolved for some primary purpose which they exhibit today. It is time to examine the wider contexts of judicial roles: social ideas of authority, of legitimacy, the question of what a good Law Lord or a good Appellate Committee would be. It is no easy task, but it will be an interesting one.

5

Possible Means for an Impossible Task: Accommodating Regional Differences through Judicial Design—the Canadian Experience

ANDRÉE LAJOIE*

1. Introduction

At this point in time when the UK is restructuring its judicial system and creating a new 'top court' in the hope, perhaps, of accommodating regional differences, especially in the twin contexts of devolution and Europeanization, it might seem relevant to look for inspiration to other multinational countries. Canada would seem a prime target, being both a Commonwealth country with a British institutional heritage and the quintessential example of multiculturalism. Looking at its judicial system is consequently useful, if only to get insights about what not to do. For I am afraid there is no way the top-level court of a normal nation state can really accommodate significant regional differences through judicial institutional design.

As I will show later in this essay, this assertion is not supported just by my natural pessimism, but also by the findings of my recent research. In Canada, the Supreme Court will write minority values into law only when they overlap, in part, with the dominant ones, or at least are not incompatible with them. But first, I must explain that this is not for lack of institutional and other formal arrangements officially designed to accommodate regional differences.

2. Some possible means

The UK already has three legal traditions or systems, with a fourth one emerging,[1] and some in the legal community feel there is a consequent need to accommodate differences in language (Welsh), in legal traditions (civilian

* Research Professor at the Center of Research on Public Law, Faculty of Law, University of Montreal.

[1] Editor's note: on the emerging Welsh legal order, see A Sherlock 'Government in Wales and the development of a new legal system within a system' (2002) 8 *European Public Law* 16; R Rawlings

traditions in Scotland and common law elsewhere in the UK), and in 'devolution issues', no doubt relating to the respective interests of British, Northern Irish, Scottish, and Welsh components of the UK population, whether they be majority or minorities. It is suggested that this might be done by bilingualism,[2] territorial representation among the Law Lords (or whatever the justices of the UK supreme court will be called),[3] and involvement of devolved institutions in the process of selecting judges.[4] Canadian judicial institutional design, some of it even constitutionalized, encompasses these three features, and then some, so we must look at it in order to find out how far it has taken us on the road to accommodating not only regional differences but, more importantly, the minority values underlying them.

A. Bilingualism and even 'bijuridism'

In Canada, it is the Constitution that prescribes bilingualism in the judicial system:

[a]nd either of those Languages [English or French] may be used by any Person or in any Pleading or Process in or issuing from any Court in Canada established under this Act, and in or from all or any of the Courts of Quebec.[5]

and:

English and French are the official languages of Canada and have equality of status and equal rights and privileges as to their use in all institutions of the Parliament and government of Canada.[6]

These enactments have been recently reinterpreted by the Supreme Court, reversing an earlier decision,[7] as meaning that in Canada, 'any Person' has the choice of the language he/she wants to use in court, whether or not he/she is, in fact, bilingual,[8] because the Canadian Charter of Rights and Freedoms[9] has now given equality of status to the languages themselves. In these circumstances, the accessibility of judicial proceedings and legislative statutes seems guaranteed in both languages not only in these three provinces respectively harbouring a

---

'Taking Wales Seriously: Devolution, Human Rights and Legal System' in T Campbell, C Gearty and A Tomkins (eds) *Sceptical Approaches to Human Rights* (Hart Publishing Oxford 2001).

[2] Editor's note: see ch 1 and eg submission of Law Society for England and Wales to the Auld Commission Review of Criminal Courts available at: <http://www.lcd.gov.uk/criminal/auldcom/lorg/lorg5.htm>.

[3] See ch 4.

[4] See A Le Sueur and R Cornes *The Future of the United Kingdom's Highest Courts* (UCL Constitution Unit London 2001) para 13.3.3.

[5] Constitution Act 1867, s 133.

[6] Constitution Act 1982, s 16(1); Canada Act 1982, sch B.

[7] *Société des Acadiens v Association of Parents* [1986] 1 SCR 549.

[8] *R v Beaulac* [1999] 1 SCR 768. [Editor's note: cf Welsh Language Act 1993 and *Williams v Cowell (no 1)* [2000] 1 WLR 187].

[9] Constitution Act 1982, pt 1.

majority and important minorities of francophones, but also to all Canadians in other provinces as well.[10]

Moreover, the 1867 Constitution Act did not only ordain bilingualism in court proceedings. In a provision that was later extended to Manitoba[11] and New Brunswick[12]—and may now even apply to other provinces as well as a consequence of *Beaulac*,[13] where the reasoning is about linguistic rights in general, although the case arose in the context of legal rights in courts—it prescribed the publication of Canadian and Quebecois statutes in both languages: 'The Acts of the Parliament of Canada and of the Legislature of Quebec shall be printed and published in both those languages'.[14]

Yet the fact that litigants can be heard and addressed in the official language of their choice in court, applying a statute also available in that language, only accounts for basic fairness in the judicial process and does not guarantee that their claims will be accepted, let alone their values recognized. Far from it, it seems it might be better described as a condescending concession.

As an illustration, I would quote the very bilingual former Chief Justice of the Supreme Court of Canada, Justice Antonio Lamer, answering a question on how he chose the language in which he would write a decision in a case where one party was anglophone and the other francophone. He confided that, as a matter of politeness, he would write the original in the language of the party that had just lost the case...

So, however generous this protection of language rights, it has not seemed sufficient to the federal Department of Justice, which has recently promoted a policy of 'bijuridism'. Conceived as a tool for harmonizing federal statutes pertaining to private law—and particularly to real property based on common law—with corresponding legislation in Quebec civil law, and thus defined broadly as interaction between civil and common law, 'bijuridism' rests on a special methodology applicable to both legislative drafting and judicial interpretation.

According to the Associate Deputy Minister in charge of the programme,[15] a first methodological implication derives from an analysis of the interaction between federal statutes and the civil law. When legislation enacted by Parliament in relation to property and civil rights is silent and it becomes necessary to look for subsidiary rules to implement it in Quebec, civil law rules effective in that province will be supplementary and will serve to interpret the federal

---

[10] Such is the present extension of language rights as confirmed in *Beaulac* (n 7), a case originating from British Columbia, by Justice Bastarache, writing his conclusions for a unanimous Court.

[11] Constitution Act 1871, enacted as Manitoba Act 1870, s 23, interpreted by the Supreme Court in *Re Manitoba Language Rights* [1985] 1 SCR 721.

[12] Constitution Act 1867, s 133.

[13] *Beaulac* (n 8).

[14] Constitution Act 1867, s 133.

[15] M Dion *Canadian Bijuridism and Harmonization of the Law* (University of Ottawa Ottawa 20 October 2000), here adapted freely, with the authorization of the author, to serve the purposes of this essay.

legislation, unless otherwise indicated by Parliament. However, there are exceptions to such complementariness, described as dissociations, to be met by either a
'unijural' solution—when a statutory provision is based on a concept unique to
common law in both the English and French versions—or 'semi-bijural', where
the French version of a legislative provision is based on concepts specific to civil
law and the English version on notions or terminology specific to common law.

For instance, the use of the expressions 'special damages' in English and
dommages-intérêts spéciaux in French in section 31(3) of the Crown Liability
and Proceedings Act,[16] is an example of a 'unijural situation': the expression
'special damages' and the French equivalent *dommages-intérêts spéciaux* are
unique to the common law. In civil law, the correct expression would be
'pre-trial pecuniary loss' in English and *pertes pécuniaires antérieures au procès*
in French.

On the other hand, the use, for example, of the terms 'real property' in English
and *immeuble* in French in section 20 of the Federal Real Property Act[17] is a case
of 'semi-bijuralism'. You will note that, in this case, the terminology specific to
the civil law (*immeuble*) is used in the French version only, while the terminology
specific to common law (*real property*) is used in the English version only. This
provision then will only become 'really bijural' by incorporating the terms *biens
réels* as well as *immeubles* in the French version to take into account the French
common law and the word *immovable* alongside 'real property' in the English
version to take into account the English civil law.

The method is far more refined than I can account for here, and I will gladly
refer those interested in further details to Canadian jurists who are versed in this
technique. Yet, however experienced they may be in this new dialect, they all
admit it has its limits. To quote the Associate Deputy Minister again: '[It] is never
easy where the issues to be resolved are complex, because federal legislation must
target four audiences simultaneously, and in the process be not only bilingual but
bijural'. Yet those four audiences only account for transcription of common law
in English and in French, and transcription of civil law in French and in English: I
dare not count how many audiences that would mean for the UK, where at least
two languages and perhaps four legal traditions should be integrated into I do
not know how many versions of the same statute ...

To cope with the consequences that may derive for practising lawyers from
such a complex legal and judicial system, McGill University has already started
an integrated programme of common/civil law for its Bachelor of Law degree,
where professors of private law must consistently teach both civil and common
law concepts on each topic that law may address, either in Quebec or, division of
powers allowing, at the federal level. University of Montreal is following suit,
with a special MA programme in comparative common law (Canada/USA). I
dare not think of the consequences for the poor students submitted to such a
cruel and unusual treatment, let alone the integrity of either system of law, but it

---

[16] RSC 1985, c C-50.   [17] SC 1991, c 50.

may well be that this post-modern cross-cultural experiment will succeed. Even if this were the case however, these results would only deal with some accommodation of the civil and common law traditions, essentially in the realm of private law. For 'bijuridism', even if it succeeded beyond all expectations, would do nothing to accommodate irreconcilable differences in the interpretation of devolution, well anchored in the sphere of public law, where we are not only dealing with a matter of cultures in conflict, but of power at stake. Before analysing the limited effects of bilingualism and 'bijuridism', however, we must look at other means of accommodation in use in the Canadian legal context.

B. Territorial representation and even territorialization of the judicial system

Even if 'bijuridism' is of limited effect, and bilingualism can be a minimal—and even, at times, condescending—concession, one might think that territorial representation among judges might work better. In fact, in Canada, we have gone even further by setting alongside not only federal and provincial, but also 'joint', tribunals, in a very complex judicial system featuring all the appearances of territorial judicial autonomy for the provinces. If I say 'all the appearances', it is because the appeals geometry and the administrative structure responsible for the careers of judges take back all the apparent authority that the formal institutional design seems to give to the provinces over the judicial system. Without going into the arcane details of this complex structure, I will try to describe its general outline to show why it does not answer the problems of accommodation of territorial differences.

At first glance, reading the Constitution, it would seem that the administration of justice is a provincial responsibility, as the constitutional division of powers provides for the provinces to legislate on 'The administration of Justice in the Province, including the Constitution, Maintenance and Organisation of Provincial Courts, both of Civil and of Criminal Jurisdiction, including Procedure in Civil Matters in those Courts'. However, reading these words (especially 'in *those* Courts'), any lawyer will suspect that there might be other courts than provincial ones—and be right about it—since, a few sections further, the same Constitution enacts:

The Parliament of Canada may, notwithstanding anything in this Act, from Time to Time, provide for the Constitution, Maintenance and Organisation of a General Court of Appeal for Canada and for the Establishment of any additional Courts for the better Administration of the Laws of Canada.[18]

Consequently, a federal court system has emerged alongside the provincial one. But moreover, the Superior Court with its District and County components pre-existed Confederation,[19] and the Constitution Act 1867 preserved it and pro-

---

[18] SC 1991, s 101.
[19] An Act to amend the laws relative to the Courts of Original Civil Jurisdiction in Lower Canada 1849, c 38 (Province of Canada).

vided for the (federal) Governor General to appoint its judges, thus institutional-
izing a third, 'joint', judicial order in which the day-to-day management of
the court, including its costs, is of provincial jurisdiction, while not only the
appointment of its judges, but their careers,[20] fall within federal jurisdiction:
'The Governor General shall appoint the Judges of the Superior, District and
County Courts in each Province, except those of Probate in Nova Scotia
and New Brunswick'.[21]

It is moreover important to note that judicial interpretation of that section
by the Supreme Court has had the effect of freezing the jurisdiction of the
Superior Court as it was in 1867,[22] so that it has been impossible for
the provincial legislatures—although endowed with competence over the administration of justice—to give jurisdiction over any matter then comprised in the
Superior Court jurisdiction to a court whose judges are appointed by provincial
authorities.

So the result is that we indeed have what at first glance might seem like judicial
territorial autonomy for the provinces, including of course Quebec as a civil law
jurisdiction, but these provincial courts' jurisdiction—comprising, in Quebec,
the Quebec Court[23] (including, as a division, the Small Claims Courts[24]), the
Quebec Administrative Tribunal,[25] and the Municipal Courts[26]—only hears
claims regarding personal property under 30,000 Canadian Dollars. In contrast,
all cases related to real property, and to personal property over 30,000 Canadian
Dollars, are heard by the Superior Court,[27] constitutionalized as a joint tribunal
in 1867, and all appeals are deferred to the—also joint—Quebec Appeal
Court.[28] Also excepted from provincial judicial jurisdiction, of course, are all
matters within that of the Federal Court, created in 1971 to succeed the Exchequer Court[29] inherited from Britain, not to mention the final appeal's jurisdiction of the Supreme Court of Canada[30] over important decisions not only of
the Appeal division of the Federal Court, but of the Appeal Courts of the
provinces as well.

This is to say that provincial judicial institutions hear only rather minor cases,
and then only at trial level, important cases and appeals lying in the joint and/or
federal tribunals jurisdiction. Both their limited basic jurisdiction and the
appeals structure consequently deprive the provincial courts of the final word
even on what matters they do hear: in those circumstances, the autonomy of

[20] Constitution Act 1867.   [21] ibid s 96.
[22] *Vallin v Langlois* (1879) 3 SCR 1; (1879) 5 AC 115.
[23] Judges Act RSC 1985, c J-1.
[24] An Act to promote access to justice SQ 1971, c 86, amending the *Code of Civil Procedure* RSQ, c
C-25.
[25] Courts of Justice Act RSQ, c T-16.
[26] An Act respecting administrative justice RSQ 1996, c J-3.
[27] *Code of Civil Procedure* (n 24), ss 31 and 34.
[28] Courts of Justice Act (n 25); *Code of Civil Procedure* (n 23).
[29] Federal Court Act RSC 1985, c F-7.
[30] Supreme Court Act RSC 1985, c S-26.

interpretation of civil law is non-existent even when such cases do not reach the Supreme Court, where the majority of judges have been trained in the common law tradition.

C. Territorial involvement in the selection of judges

Finally, our judicial structures feature territorial involvement—both legal and de facto—in the selection of judges. First the Constitution provides for the nomination of judges of provincial courts by the relevant provincial government,[31] and for selection from the ranks of the Quebec Bar of judges appointed to the (joint) Superior Court, where the nomination rests with the federal government.[32] Moreover, even if it is not prescribed by the Constitution or the law, there is a well respected custom to the effect that three of the nine Supreme Court judges must come from Quebec, and that the Chief Justices alternate between a francophone and an anglophone.

So, having met all the conditions now under consideration in the UK to accommodate regional differences, and then some, one would think that indeed the Canadian system does meet the task. Yet, we shall see that unless one is satisfied with formal accommodation of territorial differences not involving the integration into the fabric of the law of the minority values underlying them, this is not so.

3. AN IMPOSSIBLE TASK

In order to find out whether the design of our judicial system has successfully accommodated the kinds of regional differences outlined in the framework of this essay, one must look at the reception our courts have reserved for the claims emerging from what is described in the UK as 'nations and regions', but that we must—internal 'multi-juridism' *oblige*—translate in Canadian lingo as 'territorial minorities'. Indeed there are regions in Canada, but the term refers to entities that are quite different from England, Northern Ireland, Scotland, and Wales, and we must ourselves go into a little 'bijuridism' here if we want the rest of the exercise to be meaningful. The mere size of the Canadian territory, the second largest mass of land in the world after Russia, implies the very existence of regions and, over the formal political division in 10 provinces and three Aboriginal territories, three larger geographical entities are generally recognized as regions: 'central Canada', a term coined by westerners to include Ontario and Quebec, 'the West', including all provinces and territories west of the Ontario/Manitoba border, and the 'Atlantic Provinces', comprising the four provinces east of the Quebec/New-Brunswick border. But these geographical regions, which do not, as such, benefit from any political recognition or devolution, are

---

[31] Constitution Act 1867, s 92(14).   [32] ibid s 98.

not characterized either by distinct cultures, languages, or legal traditions. Nor are most provinces which, however, enjoy such powers as the Constitution Act 1867 bestows on them.

What then, in Canada, would correspond to what is meant by 'nations and regions' in the UK are two 'territorialized' minorities speaking different languages, featuring distinct legal traditions and systems, and enjoying different degrees of what is referred to as devolution: Aboriginals, who form 2.8% of the Canadian population (1.1% in Quebec) and have recently obtained recognition of some degree of territorial control over James' Bay, Nunavut, and Nisga'a territories (together harbouring 5.6% of the Aboriginal population, 0.01% in Canada), and francophones, who form 23.2% of the Canadian population, 85% of which is located in Quebec, a province endowed with the powers devolved to provinces since Confederation. So if one wants to take the measure of what corresponds in Canada to 'regional accommodation', we must look at the reception that the Canadian judicial system has reserved for the claims emerging from such political—and at least partially—territorialized minorities,[33] that we will concern ourselves now, looking first at the net results yielded by this jurisprudence, before trying to find an explanation for them.

Because the link between the reception by the Court of the claims of political minorities and the territorial provenance of the claims of the Quebecois minority is stronger, and the related results, therefore, more relevant here, I will deal with them first, before I analyse the Aboriginal minority claims, which however, as we shall see, have fared no better for coming from a more dispersed population, long without a territorial basis recognized in Canadian law.

A. Net results: Quebec

To summarize the interaction of Canadian courts with the Quebec population as a territorialized minority, I would say that the design of our judicial system can claim some success at the procedural level—where language needs and, recently, those related to legal tradition, are increasingly being met—only to fail on the substantive level, where devolution issues (the 'division of powers' issues) have been decided to the detriment of Quebec litigants in a majority of cases—with a short but very politically significant exception between 1960 and 1975—with the consequent erosion of its territorially based legislative and executive powers. Such is the conclusion of a study I did for the Royal Commission on the Economic Union and Development Prospects for Canada (Macdonald Commission) in 1986,[34] updated since without invalidating its findings, far from it.[35]

---

[33] As distinct from 'social', non-territorialized minorities such as gays, lesbians, seniors, and women (a minorized majority), whose treatment by the courts is somewhat different.

[34] A Lajoie, P Mulazzi and M Gamache 'Political Ideas in Quebec and the Evolution of Canadian Constitutional Law, 1945–1985' in I Bernier and A Lajoie (eds) *The Supreme Court of Canada as an Instrument of Political Change* (University of Toronto Press Toronto 1986) 1–103.

[35] A Lajoie 'Égalité et asymétrie dans le fédéralisme canadien' in AM Le Pourhiet (ed) *Liberté et égalité locales* (Economica Presses universitaires d'Aix-Marseille Aix-en-Provence 1999) 325–340.

As it is not possible to reconstruct here the evolution of political thought in Quebec, as framed in constitutional claims to the Supreme Court of Canada since it became the final judicial arbiter of such conflicts after the Second World War, we will have to make do with a brief overview of these political claims expressed through litigation on the division of powers, before relating them to the relevant decisions of the Supreme Court since the Second World War. In succinct terms, these claims range from much more devolution of powers for provinces in general, and Quebec in particular, within a federation, to a union of equal nation states, to outright independence, with variable fluctuations.

But before we move to the reception of Quebec's constitutional claims by the Supreme Court, it is important to take note of the fact that from Confederation in 1867 to 1949,[36] the final court of appeal for important cases, and especially constitutional ones, was not our Supreme Court, even if it had been in existence since 1875,[37] but, as befitted a colony within the British Empire and even a member of the Commonwealth, the Judicial Committee of the Privy Council (UK).[38] These years are considered by Quebec constitutionalists[39] to have been the golden age of a decentralizing interpretation of Canadian federalism. This interpretation which had, for that period, the effect of restraining centralization within the Canadian federation and protecting the provincial legislative powers against erosion, can be best explained by the distant if not foreign status of the Privy Council. Indeed, London was not depriving itself of the powers that the Privy Council recognized as belonging to the provinces, contrary to the situation in which Ottawa would find itself later, when it would be appointing the judges of a Supreme Court adjudicating the same matters.

Nevertheless, the Privy Council's interpretation of federalism, generous as it was to provincial powers, was not entirely devoid of potential for centralization. For while refusing most of the time to apply them to the situations involved in the appeals they were hearing, the Law Lords were crafting the very instruments the Supreme Court would later use to centralize the Constitution: the 'ancillary and residuary powers' theories of interpretation, and what it saw as exceptions to the division of powers as stated in the constitutional text: the emergency powers and, even if the Privy Council wavered about it over time, the national dimensions theory.

Indeed, 1949 opens a new era in the interpretation of Canadian federalism. Appeals to the Privy Council were abolished,[40] the Supreme Court of Canada, now the last resort for the resolution of such constitutional conflicts resolved

---

[36] When appeals to the Privy Council are abolished: Act to amend the Supreme Court Act SC 1949, c 37.

[37] Supreme and Exchequer Courts Act SC 1875, c 11.

[38] See ch 6.

[39] See A Tremblay 'Judicial Interpretation and the Canadian Constitution' [1991–92] 1 *National Journal of Constitutional Law* 163.

[40] Supreme and Exchequer Courts Act 1875.

them, on the whole, by imposing solutions favourable to the interests of the federal state authorities. Moreover, this important change, both institutional and interpretive, is but a reflection of deeper political mutations: first a bolder Canadian nationalism, affirming itself in the context of a new world equilibrium where America trumps Europe, but more important yet, the lasting effect of the centralization brought about by the economic requirements of the war effort. It is in this context that the reception by the Supreme Court of Canada of the claims of the Quebecois minority—as a negative example of judicial accommodation of regional differences—must be analysed. Four periods can be carved out of the era that spans from then until now, in which federalism can successively be viewed as: unilateral (1949–60); bi-polar (1960–75); mono-polar (1976–82) and hidden (1982 to date).

1. Unilateral federalism (1949–60)

All cases decided by the Supreme Court during that period—save three, emanating from other provinces[41]—affirmed federal powers, which is not surprising in a situation where Quebec, influenced by both its distrust of the Supreme Court and its inclination towards a minimalist State, stayed away from the Supreme Court[42] and from interventions that would bring it there, while other provinces were already industrialized and in favour of centralization. Provincial powers were restricted in favour of federal ones first by instruments previously designed by the Privy Council, such as a broad interpretation of criminal law—an explicit federal competence said to include such provincial penal matters as prevention,[43] confiscation of the proceeds of crime and prohibition of slot-machines,[44] and even inobservance of religious holidays[45]—and the application, in the field of urban development, of emergency powers,[46] added to the national dimensions theory.[47] But in the fields of commerce and labour law, the Supreme Court had to invent new theories of its own, such as the 'pith and substance theory',[48] or its amalgamation with a broad definition of inter-provincial commerce and extra-provincial character of business enterprises.[49]

---

[41] *Duplain v Cameron* [1961] SCR 693; *John MM Troup Ltd v Royal Bank of Canada* [1962] SCR 487; *AG Ontario v Barfried Enterprises* [1963] SCR 570.

[42] Only two of the 33 cases the Court heard on the division of powers during that period came from Quebec.

[43] *Goodyear Tire and Rubber Co of Canada Ltd v The Queen* [1956] SCR 303.

[44] *Industrial Acceptance Corporation v The Queen* [1953] 2 SCR 273; *Johnson v AG Alberta* [1954] SCR 127; *DeWare v The Queen* [1954] SCR 182.

[45] *Birks v City of Montreal* [1955] SCR 799, somewhat attenuated by *Lieberman v The Queen* [1963] SCR 643.

[46] *Reference as to the validity of the Wartime Leasehold Regulations* [1950] SCR 124

[47] *Johannesson v Rural Municipality of West St-Paul* [1952] 1 SCR 292; *Munro v National Capital Commission* [1966] 57 SCR 663.

[48] *Commission du salaire minimum v Bell Telephone* [1966] SCR 767.

[49] *Winner v SMT* [1951] SCR 887; *Esso Standard (Interamerica) Inc v JW Entreprises* [1963] SCR 144; *Murphy v CPR* [1958] SCR 626.

2. Bi-polar federalism (1960–75)

Consequently, when the next period begins, a large chunk has already been carved out of provincial jurisdiction over property and civil rights. But political ideas and values were changing in Quebec, and brought the Supreme Court to an exceptional and temporary halt whereby it momentarily diminished the pace of centralization, a change all the more spectacular because it manifested itself only in cases originating from Quebec. Indeed, in comparison not only with the previous period where the only two decisions rendered in Quebec cases had been decided against it, but with the centralizing tendency of the findings in the vast majority of cases on appeal from other provinces in this same period, two-thirds of the decisions in cases submitted by Quebec parties were provincial gains. This change in the attitude of the Supreme Court coincided with new political trends then observed in Quebec, that have in common the rejection of the former period's state minimalism, together with the transformation of its nationalism into a more open pluralist liberal movement, where the state played an important role. An increased judicialization of the constitutional conflict between Quebec and Ottawa thus emerged as a second best alternative to outright independence, and was met with more openness from the Supreme Court than the political expression of the same claims would fetch from the political authorities, who negotiated them in parallel during the whole period. And probably for the same reason that explained the record of the Privy Council: the Supreme Court does not lose what powers it concedes to the provinces, while politicians are quite conscious of the contrary as far as they are concerned...

So while other provinces were successful only in one-third of their division of powers cases during that period, Quebec litigants won two-thirds of theirs. Moreover, the significance of this jurisprudence for Quebec is not only quantitative, but qualitative, for it has diminished the impact of three of the Supreme Court's most useful theories in terms of centralization: the extra-provincial character of business enterprises, somewhat mitigated;[50] the 'pith and substance' theory, that the Supreme Court refrains from applying to subsidiaries of federal companies,[51] and the national dimensions theory, that it refused to apply to the federal statute on anti-inflation,[52] thus agreeing to the kind of federalism that the non-independentist autonomists in Quebec were defending. It would seem that such results are not unrelated to the political context in which these cases arose. The constitutional claims of successive governments could not help but appear reasonable in comparison with actions of the anti-federalist opposition, involving the formation of a new party that became Her Majesty's loyal opposition, as well as extra parliamentary violent anti-democratic acts of protest.

But a quantitative analysis of the division of powers cases for the whole of Canada from that period indicates that the Supreme Court nevertheless wished

---

[50] *Reference Re Agricultural Products Marketing* [1978] 2 SCR 1198.
[51] *Construction Montcalm Inc v Minimum Wage Commission* [1979] 1 SCR 754.
[52] *Reference Re Anti-inflation Act* [1976] 2 SCR 373.

to preserve the federal government's jurisdiction, as more than half of its decisions in cases from all provinces taken together on these matters during that period favoured the federal legislative competence in such traditional fields as labour relations,[53] transport,[54] and matrimonial law,[55] as well as in new grounds like economics[56] and commerce,[57] communications,[58] planning,[59] and environment.[60] Amazingly, only criminal law, the single explicit federal power involved in this group of decisions, yielded a majority of provincial victories.[61]

3. Mono-polar federalism (1976–82)

The third period opens in November 1976, with the election of a sovereigntist government in Quebec which, one would have thought, might logically have

[53] *Letter Carrier's Union v CUPW* [1975] 1 SCR 178; *Canadian Labour Relations Board v City of Yellowknife* [1977] 2 SCR 729, but curtailed on the same grounds in *CNR v Nor-min Supplies* [1977] 1 SCR 322 and especially *Construction Montcalm Inc v Minimum Wage Commission* [1979] 1 SCR 754.

[54] *The Queen v Board of Transport Commissioners* [1968] SCR 118; *Registrar of Motor Vehicles v Canadian American Transfer* [1972] SCR 811; *Kootenay and Elk Railway Co v CPR* [1974] SCR 955; *CNR v Commissionners of Public Utilities* [1976] 2 SCR 112; *Saskatchewan Power Corporation v Trans-Canada Pipelines* [1979] 1 SCR 297; *Agence Maritime Inc v Conseil canadien des relations ouvrières* [1969] SCR 851 and *Three Rivers Boatman Ltd v Conseil canadien des relations ouvrières* [1969] SCR 607.

[55] *Jackson v Jackson* [1973] SCR 205 and *Zacks v Zacks* [1973] SCR 891.

[56] Federal gains [*AG Ontario v Policy Holders of Wentworth Insurance* [1969] SCR 779; *Tomell Investments Ltd v East Marstock Lands Ltd* [1978] 1 SCR 974; *Martin Service Station v Minister of National Revenue* [1977] 2 SCR 996; *Canadian Industrial Gas and Oil Ltd v Saskatchewan* [1978] 2 RCS 545; *R v Air Canada* [1980] 2 SCR 303 and *Reference Re Anti-inflation Act* [1976] 2 SCR 373]; almost equal provincial ones [*Robinson v Countrywide Factors* [1978] 1 SCS 753; *Alworth v Minister of Finances* [1978] 1 SCR 447; *Reference re Agricultural Products Marketing* [1978] 2 SCR 1198; *Simpson-Sears v Provincial Secretary of New-Brunswick* [1978] 2 SCR 869; *Covert v Minister of Finances (NS)* [1980] 2 SCR 774].

[57] Six findings in favour of provinces [*Kootenay and Elk Railway Co v CPR* [1974] SCR 955; *Canadian Indemnity Co v AG BC* [1977] 2 SCR 504; *Multiple Access Ltd v McCutcheon* [1982] 2 SCR 163 (in part); *Carnation Company Ltd v Quebec Agricultural Marketing Board* [1968] SCR 238; *McDonald and Railquip Entreprises Ltd v Vapor Canada Ltd* [1977] 2 SCR 134; *Reference re Agricultural Products Marketing* (n 56)] and eight in favour of federal authorities [*Multiple Access Ltd v McCutcheon* [1982] 2 SCR 163 (in part); *PG Manitoba v Manitoba Egg and Poultry Association* [1971] SCR 689; *Caloil Inc v AG Canada* [1971] SCR 543; *Jorgenson v AG Canada* [1971] SCR 725; *Chamney v The Queen* [1975] 2 SCR 151; *Burns Foods Ltd v AG Manitoba* [1975] 1 SCR 494; *Reference re Agricultural Products Marketing* (n 56); *Central Canada Potash Co Ltd v Saskatchewan* [1979] 1 SCR 42].

[58] Based on federal supremacy theory: *Capital Cities Communications Inc v Canadian Radio-Television Commission* [1978] 2 SCR 141 and *Public Services Board v Dionne* [1978] 2 SCR 191 (cf *AG Quebec v Kellogg's Co* [1978] 2 SCR 211].

[59] Where results are the same, with two very important decisions going in opposite directions: *Reference re Offshore Mineral Rights of British-Columbia* [1967] SCR 792 and *Morgan v AG Prince-Edward Island* [1976] 2 SCR 349.

[60] Same pattern again: *Interprovincial Co-Operative Ltd v The Queen* [1976] 1 SCR 477 in favour of federal authorities, but also *Fowler v The Queen* [1980] 2 SCR 213 in favour of provincial powers.

[61] The Court confirmed provincial jurisdiction over penal law [in *Mann v The Queen* [1966] SCR 238; *McIver v The Queen* [1966] SCR 254; *Ross v Registrar of Motor Vehicles* [1975] 1 SCR 5; *Bell v P-E I* [1975] 1 SCR 525]; over administration of criminal justice [in *Faber v The Queen* [1976] 2 SCR 9 and *Di Iorio v Warden of the Montreal Jail* [1978] 1 SCR 152; *Ministre du Revenu national v Lafleur* [1964] SCR 412; *Batary v AG Saskatchewan* [1965] SCR 465; *AG British Columbia v Smith* [1966] SCR 719] and health [in *Fawcett v PG Ontario* [1960] SCR 776].

brought, if not outright secession, at least a rapid change in institutional design leading to a modification of the Constitution in favour of greater devolution. But this was not to be the case, probably because sovereigntist ideas, even if supported by the majority party that formed the government, were not dominant in the civil society, as the results of the 1980 referendum would show. Moreover, these ideas, now institutionalized in the democratic field appeared less dangerous and less forceful than when they emerged from an extraparliamentary and sometimes violent opposition within an effervescent civil society.

So there was indeed a constitutional change, but not in the expected direction: instead of more devolution, Quebec got 'patriation' of the Constitution, that is transference of the power to amend it from the British Parliament where it had rested since that Parliament had adopted the British North America Act as the Canadian constitution in 1867, to the Canadian authorities, far less generous towards Quebec, as we have already seen.

The jurisprudence of the Supreme Court in matters related to the division of powers reflected the same abrupt change towards Quebec. In a double somersault, it reversed its previous tendency in order both to increase centralization in the ROC[62] and to halt it in Quebec. In that completely symmetrical reversal, it found in favour of provinces in two-thirds of its decisions in cases originating from all other provinces than Quebec, in all fields where litigation had been brought before it (labour law,[63] transport,[64] taxation,[65] finance,[66] and commerce)[67]—save environment[68] and planning,[69] while two-thirds of the cases involving Quebec were decided in favour of centralization of power in the hands of the federal authorities.

Of course, one might be tempted to think that this was perfectly normal since most of these cases dealt with criminal law, an explicit federal competence to begin with. But this would entail overlooking the highly political content of half of them,[70] while minimizing the meta-constitutional character of the other two

---

[62] ie 'rest of Canada'

[63] *Four B Manufacturing Ltd v United Garment Workers* [1980] 1 SCR 1031; *Canada Labour Relations Board v Paul l'Anglais Inc* [1983] 1 SCR 147; *Canadian Pioneer Management Ltd v Labour Relations Board of Saskatchewan* [1980] 1 SCR 433.

[64] *Fulton v Energy Resources Conservation Board* [1981] 1 SCR 153.

[65] *AG British-Columbia v Canada Trust Co* [1980] 2 SCR 466; *Massey-Ferguson Industries Ltd v Government of Saskatchewan* [1981] 2 SCR 413; *New Brunswick Finance Minister v Simpsons-Sears* [1982] 1 SCR 144; *Newfoundland and Labrador Corporation v AG Newfoundland* [1982] 2 SCR 260; *Reference re Exported Natural Gas Tax* [1982] 1 SCR 1004.

[66] *Canadian Pioneer Management Ltd v Labour Relations Board of Saskatchewan* [1980] 1 SCR 433.

[67] *Dominion Stores Ltd v The Queen* [1980] 1 SCR 844; *Labatt v AG Canada* [1980] 1 SCR 914.

[68] *Northern Falling Contractors Ltd v The Queen* [1980] 2 SCR 291; *Moore v Johnson* [1982] 1 SCR 115.

[69] *Reference Re Upper Churchill Water Rights Reversion Act* [1984] 1 SCR 297; *Reference Re Newfoundland, Continental Shelf* [1984] 1 SCR 86; *Reference Re Ownership of the bed of the Strait of Georgia and related areas* [1984] 1 SCR 388.

[70] *AG Quebec and Keable v AG Canada* [1979] 1 SCR 218; *Bisaillon v Keable* [1983] 2 SCR 71; *Vignola v Keable* [1983] 2 SCR 117.

decisions involved, namely the *Reference Re the Constitution of Canada*[71] and the *Reference Re the Modification of the Constitution of Canada*,[72] whose weight on the future of the federation cannot be exaggerated.

Indeed, despite paying lip service to the provinces by admitting their consent was necessary for the 'legitimacy' of patriation, the Supreme Court nevertheless favoured the federal authorities irretrievably by adding that the consent of the provinces was unnecessary to the 'legality' of the operation, adding insult to injury towards Quebec by refusing to recognize its hitherto accepted veto over constitutional modifications.

4. Post-charter hidden federalism (1982 to date)

Moreover the patriated Constitution came from the UK Parliament with a last modification included: the Canadian Charter of Rights and Freedoms,[73] the interpretation of which would from then on monopolize most of the activity of the Supreme Court, to the detriment of the division of powers, whose substantial modification could then go relatively unnoticed.

Indeed, what actually happened was obscuring the centralizing activity of the Supreme Court regarding the division of powers, especially in the economic field. Founding its decisions on the general federal legislative power grounded in the 'peace, order and good government' clause, especially as interpreted in the light of the national dimensions' theory,[74] on the commerce power, which it extended beyond its previous limits,[75] on the declaratory power combined with the pith and substance theory,[76] on the spending power[77] and on the free circulation of goods—mentioned in section 121 of the Constitution Act 1867, but rarely invoked until then, that it elevated to the rank of 'fundamental constitutional principle',[78] the Supreme Court single-handedly federalized legislative and executive powers over the economy as it had already done for land planning. What we see emerging here is a federalization of the powers deemed necessary for the implementation of the Canadian Economic Union envisaged by the MacDonald Commission and, subsequently NAFTA and perhaps the FTAA.

This the Supreme Court achieved through severely curtailing the extra-territorial effects of provincial laws,[79] while increasing those of federal legislation[80] and by extending the scope of the federal supremacy theory even to 'potential' conflicts of jurisdiction, which was tantamount to rehabilitating the 'unoccupied field' theory, long dismissed not only by the Privy Council, but by the Supreme Court itself.[81]

---

[71] *Reference Re Objection to a Resolution to amend the Constitution* [1982] 2 SCR 793.
[72] *Reference Re Resolution to amend the Constitution* [1981] 1 SCR 753.
[73] Constitution Act 1982, pt 1.
[74] *The Queen v Crown Zellerbach* [1988] 1 SCR 401; *Hunt v T&N plc* [1993] 4 SCR 289.
[75] *General Motors of Canada v City National Leasing* [1989] 1 SCR 641.
[76] *Ontario Hydro v Ontario (Labour Relations Board)* [1993] 3 SCR 327.
[77] *YMCA Jewish Community Center of Winnipeg v Brown* [1989] 1 SCR 1532 and *Reference Re Canada Assistance Plan* [1991] 2 SCR 525.
[78] *Hunt* (n 74).   [79] ibid.   [80] *Bank of Montreal v Hall* [1990] 1 SCR 121.
[81] *Multiple Access v McCutcheon* (n 57).

To sum up: despite bilingualism, 'bijuridism', apparent territorialization of the judicial system and territorial involvement in the appointment of judges, accommodation of regional differences has not happened for Quebec where it mattered, that is on issues relating to the Canadian version of 'devolution', the constitutional division of legislative and executive powers. The score of the Supreme Court in this respect in almost a century and a half has been one of relentless centralization, except for the 15 years between 1960 and 1976, when Quebec enjoyed a power relationship it has not been able to reproduce since. Unfortunately, we cannot but note that this temporary *rapport de forces* was built on acts of protests one would not like to see replicated.

B. Net results: Aboriginals

The legal relationship of Aboriginals to the Canadian territory is complex and reads differently depending on whether one takes a positivist or a pluralist perspective. Even if this is not the occasion to discuss these theoretical points at length, it is important to look at least at the big picture before analysing the reception the Supreme Court has reserved for Aboriginal claims as a measure of accommodating regional differences, whether or not these claims come from the territorialized groups among the Aboriginals. In my (pluralist) view, where there has been no conquest by the colonizers or surrender of the Aboriginals—which means almost all territory included in British Columbia and Quebec which is not covered by valid 'numbered' treaties—Aboriginals still own the territory and have retained political control over it. Needless to say, most Canadian political authorities, whether they be federal of provincial, do not quite see it that way, and recognize as Aboriginal territory only the 'reductions' or 'reserves' created by the Indian Act[82]—where devolution, if this is the proper word, is minimal and akin to municipal powers—and these parts of the country that have been designated as Aboriginal territories through more recent formal agreements: James Bay,[83] Nisga'a,[84] and Nunavut,[85] to which one might add Yukon and the North West Territories which, as older components of the federation, enjoy a more limited measure of autonomy, and where Aboriginals have traditionally formed an important proportion of the population.[86]

In the context of this paper, it would be appropriate to compare the reception that the Supreme Court has granted to claims regarding the division of powers

[82] RSC (1985), c I-5.

[83] James Bay and Northern Quebec Agreement of 1975, available on the Grand Council of the Crees' website at <www.gcc.ca>.

[84] *Nisga'a Final Agreement*, ratified by An Act to give effect to the Nisga'a Final Agreement SC 2000, c 7.

[85] Agreement between the Inuit of the Nunavut Settlement Area and Her Majesty the Queen in Right of Canada, ratified by An Act to amend the Nunavut Act and the Constitution Act SC 1998, c 15.

[86] Aboriginals represent 61.8% of the population of the North West Territories, 20.1% of that of Yukon, but the combined Aboriginal population of these two territories only counts for 5.5% of the total Aboriginal population of Canada.

between these entities and the federal—or even provincial—authorities, to its reception of the same coming from Quebec. However, to my knowledge, no case has ever been brought to the Supreme Court about such claims from those territories. This is not to say Aboriginals are content with their lot within the Canadian federation, far from it, but their claims in the judicial forum have not been formulated in terms of division of powers or devolution, but of other values, including in particular the content and meaning of the 'Aboriginal Title', an ideological device common law has invented to reduce the relationship of Aboriginals with the land to its patrimonial content and empty it of any control over the territory. So, what comparative material we have in this respect is framed in terms of the values that Aboriginals sought to insert into the fabric of Canadian law through the Courts—recognition of their collective identity, mother earth and related economic self-sufficiency, territorial and political content of Aboriginal title, respect for the environment—and it is in those terms that it has been analysed.[87]

The results of this recent research first point to the fact that the proportion of Aboriginal victories in the Supreme Court—43% over all since the creation of the Supreme Court in 1875—has increased importantly over time, rising from 33% (1880–1939) to 54% since 1990. They also show that some important values expressed by Aboriginals, in their briefs to the Supreme Court and in interviews their leaders gave to our research team, have been integrated into Canadian law, especially recognition of identity, protection of the environment and resources, but (of course...) not economic self-sufficiency, control of the territory, or—unless one takes into account a certain acceptance of legal pluralism in Yukon and the NWT—political self-determination...Indeed, that last value is mentioned only once by the Supreme Court, only to reject it outright.[88]

In fact this dichotomy between the political rights of the Aboriginals and their economic rights is paramount in the corpus of the Supreme Court regarding Aboriginal cases, and quite significant. In cases related to political rights where the Supreme Court only grants rights related to status[89] and never to political control,[90] Aboriginal defeats are nevertheless predominant (8:4)[91] and the same

---

[87] A Lajoie, E Gélineau, I Duplessis and G Rocher 'L'intégration des valeurs et des intérêts autochtones dans le discours judiciaire et normatif canadien' (2000) 29 *Osgoode Hall Law Journal* 143.

[88] *The Queen v Pamajewon* [1996] 2 SCR 821.

[89] *Re Eskimos* [1939] SCR 105; *The Queen v Drybones* [1970] SCR 282 and *Corbière v Canada* [1999] 2 SCR 203.

[90] *Four B Manufacturing Ltd v United Garment Workers* (n 63); *Native Women Association of Canada v Canada* [1994] 3 SCR 627 and *The Queen v Pamajewon* (n 88).

[91] **Defeats:** *AG Canada v Lavell* [1974] SCR 1349; *Native Women Association of Canada v Canada* (n 90); *Davey v Isaac* [1977] 2 SCR 897; *Four B Manufacturing Ltd v United Garment Workers* (n 63); *The Queen v Pamajewon* (n 88); *Jack and Charlie v The Queen* (1985) 4 DLR (4th) 96; *The Queen v Gladue* [1999] 1 SCR 688; *Natural Parents v Superintendent of Child Welfare* [1976] 2 SCR 751. **Gains:** *Re Eskimos* (n 89); *The Queen v Drybones* (n 89); *Corbière v Canada* (n 89); *The Queen v Sioui* [1990] 1 SCR 1025.

is true regarding real property (9:3),[92] whereas in cases related to economic rights, victories, including fiscal benefits refused to other minorities,[93] outnumber defeats (22:21).[94]

But numbers do not tell all, and one must pay attention to the very clever rhetorical approach the Supreme Court has used in Aboriginal cases, by which it has consistently and solemnly affirmed a principle integrating Aboriginal values into the law and favouring their interests, while denying it any application in the case at hand. Modalities have differed according to circumstances. The Supreme Court has affirmed the fiduciary obligation of the Crown only to deny that it had been violated[95] it has granted 'title' and curtailed it to the point of uselessness,[96] it has frozen rights in time so as to limit them,[97] thus taking back with the left hand what it had not yet finished giving with the right one.

In sum, the Supreme Court will grant freely to Aboriginals the recognition of their identity, some private money as damages and even some public funds, especially in the form of resources, the latter as quid pro quo for real political autonomy exercised in the form of control over territory and the net result is not very different from that obtained from the Supreme Court by Quebec. So the ultimate results of the interaction between the Supreme Court and the two 'territorialized minorities' that, in the Canadian context, represent what is

---

[92] **Defeats:** *The Queen v Bonhomme* [1918] DLR 690; *The Queen v Easterbrook* [1931] SCR 210; *Paulete and al v The Queen* [1977] 2 SCR 628; *Canadian Pacific Limited v Paul and The Queen* [1988] 2 SCR 654; *Ontario v Bear Island Foundation* [1991] 2 SCR 570; *Opetchesaht Indian Band v Canada* [1997] 2 SCR 119; *Calder v British-Columbia AG* [1973] SCR 313; *St Catherines Milling & Lumber Co v The Queen* (1887) 13 SCR 577; *Ontario Mining Co v Seybold* (1901) 32 SCR 1. **Gains:** *Delgamuukw v British-Columbia* [1997] 3 SCR 1010; *AG Canada v Giroux* (1916) 53 SCR 172; *Smith v The Queen* [1983] 1 RCS 554.

[93] *Nowegijick v The Queen* [1983] 1 SCR 29; *The Queen v Williams* [1992] 1 SCR 877.

[94] **Gains:** *Prince & Myron v The Queen* [1964] SCR 81; *Frank v The Queen* [1978] 1 SCR 95; *The Queen v Sutherland Wilson & Wilson* [1980] 2 SCR 451; *Moosehunter v The Queen* [1981] 1 SCR 282; *The Queen v Williams* (n 93); *Nowegijick v The Queen* (n 93); *Blueberry River Indian Band v Canada* [1995] 4 SCR 344; *Guerin v The Queen* [1984] 2 SCR 335; *Mitchell v Peguis Indian Band* [1990] 2 SCR 85; *Simon v The Queen* [1985] 2 SCR 387; *The Queen v Nikal* [1996] 1 SCR 1013; *The Queen v Adams* [1996] 3 SCR 101; *The Queen v Sundown* [1999] 1 SCR 393; *The Queen v Marshall* [1999] 3 SCR 456 and *The Queen v Marshall* [1999] 3 SCR 533; *Derrickson v Derrickson* [1986] 1 SCR 285; *Paul v Paul* [1986] 1 SCR 306; *Quebec AG v Canada (National Energy Board)* [1994] 1 SCR 159, and four partial victories: *Sparrow v The Queen* [1990] 1 SCR 1075; *The Queen v Gladstone* [1996] 2 SCR 723; *The Queen v Côté* [1996] 3 SCR 139 and *Badger Kiyawasew & Ominayak v The Queen* [1996] 1 SCR 771. **Defeats:** *Sikyea v The Queen* [1965] 2 CCC 129; *Sigeareak E1–53 v The Queen* [1966] SCR 645; *Daniel v White & The Queen* [1968] SCR 517; *Cardinal v Alberta AG* [1974] SCR 695; *Myran, Meeches and al v The Queen* [1976] 2 SCR 137; *The Queen v Derriksan* (1976) 71 DLR (3d) 159; *Kruger & Manuel v The Queen* [1978] 1 SCR 104; *Jack and al v The Queen* [1980] 1 SCR 294; *The Queen v McKinney* [1980] 1 SCR 1031; *The Queen v Mousseau* [1980] 2 SCR 89; *Elk v The Queen* [1980] 2 SCR 166; *Dick v The Queen* [1985] 2 SCR 309; *The Queen v Horse* [1988] 1 SCR 187; *Horseman v The Queen* [1990] 1 SCR 901; *The Queen v Lewis* [1996] 1 SCR 921; *The Queen v Van der Peet* [1996] 2 SCR 507; *The Queen v NTC Smokehouse Ltd* [1996] 2 SCR 672; *St Mary's Indian Band v City of Cranbrook* [1997] 2 SCR 657; *Westbank First Nation v BC Hydro and Power Authority* [1999] 3 SCR 134; *The Queen v George* (1966) 55 DLR 386.

[95] *Sikyea v The Queen* (n 94); *The Queen v George* (n 94); *Horseman v The Queen* (n 94).

[96] *Delgamuukw v British-Columbia* (n 91).

[97] *Sparrow v The Queen* (n 94).

referred to as 'nations and regions' in the UK, show that the Supreme Court will refuse most of devolution claims, whether they be related to the division of powers between Ottawa and Quebec, or to Aboriginal political autonomy in the form of control over territory. We now have to try to find an explanation of these results.

4. POLITICAL FACTORS IMMUNE TO JUDICIAL DESIGN

Looking at these results, one might think that the Canadian Supreme Court is particularly biased because of the Canadian political context or for whatever reason and has consequently not been able to accommodate adequately our minorities. But I do not think this is the case: far from being an exception, it only exemplifies the weight that dominant values exert in any society over judicial interpretation or, more generally, over any interpretive activity, be it in art, literature, or social sciences, only more so when law is concerned. This is indeed the conclusion I came to when I understood that to make sense of this pattern of the Supreme Court, one had to distance oneself from the narrow scene of judicial interpretation and refer to theories relative to the whole field of interpretive activities. After looking at several possible approaches in *Jugements de valeurs*,[98] in an analysis too long to even summarize here, I have chosen the perspective of contemporary hermeneutics. In this theoretical perspective, the judicial production of law results form the interaction of a judge/inter-preter—already holding a precast image,[99] a mental grid, derived from his/her personal values,[100] but informed by his/her interpretive community[101]—and a norm which he/she will interpret in context,[102] through a narrative,[103] under the influence of 'overdetermination',[104] exerted by the textual and historic 'hori-zons',[105] as expressed through the expectations of both universal and specialized 'audiences'.[106]

Yet, it is not sufficient to understand that judges, like any interpreters in other fields of knowledge, can make no sense but social sense. One must also note that

---

[98] A Lajoie *Jugements de valeurs: le discours judiciaire et le droit* (Presses Universitaires de France Paris 1997).

[99] KE Boulding *The Image* (University of Michigan Press Ann Arbor 1957); KVW Stone 'The Post-War Paradigm in American Labor Law' (1981) 90 *Yale Law Journal* 1509.

[100] L Hunter 'Bora Laskin and Labour Law: The Formative Years' (1984) 6 *Supreme Court Law Review* 431.

[101] S Fish 'La pensée juridique moderne' in *Respecter le sens commun* (LGDJ Paris 1995).

[102] P Ricoeur 'Le problème de la liberté de l'interprète en herméneutique générale et en herméneu-tique juridique' in P Amseleck (ed) *Interprétation et droit* (Editions Emile Brulyant Bruxelles; Presses Universitaires d'Aix-Marseilles Aix-Marseilles 1995).

[103] R Dworkin *Law's Empire* (Fontana London 1986).

[104] G Timsit *Les noms de la loi* (Presses Universitaires de France Paris 1991).

[105] HG Gadamer *Vérité et méthode* (Editions du Seuil Paris 1976).

[106] C Perelman and P Foriers *La motivation des décisions de justice* (Etablissements Emile Bruylant Bruxelles 1978).

their special position in society—within the normative field—puts even heavier constraints on them, because, contrary to literary or artistic interpretation, the meaning they give to norms affects the real day-to-day life of their addressees, who will consequently be inclined to deny them legitimacy if that meaning does not coincide with their own values or interests. In such circumstances, it is easy to understand that judges can readily write dominant values into law without any damage to their legitimacy, the credibility of the court they belong to, or the efficacy of their rulings. However, it does happen sometimes that they will instead support minority or marginalized values, as they have for non-territorialized social minorities[107] as well as territorialized political ones,[108] but only, as we have seen, when their values are not completely unacceptable to the dominant majority.

If these findings are true, three conditions must be present for a political minority to get its values integrated into the law through the judiciary. First, the gains involved must not infringe on dominant values such as social peace and the integrity of the State: neither real political power, nor control of territory shall be ceded. Second, these gains should not be obtained at the cost of affecting at least substantially other interests, especially economic ones, of the dominant majority. Finally, the threshold beyond which the majority will see these interests as infringed will vary with the power relationship each minority can establish at any given time.

As the weight of such factors makes them immune to the judicial system, it consequently can play no role in real accommodation, whatever its institutional design. Bilingualism and 'bijuridism' in court will only affect the expression of what minority values the dominant interpretive community will allow the judges to write into law. As for participation in the appointment of judges, it would no more take those appointees away from the social context in which they cannot but work under the 'implicit and inferential'[109] rule of the dominant group in that society. Only territorialization of the judicial system might entail some improvement, but only if it brought all matters subject to judicial decisions at all levels including appeals up to supreme courts under the aegis of a completely autonomous system that would put adjudication entirely within the interpretive community of the minority concerned, and outside the purview of the majority values. Yet this solution would only work if it is not mitigated by any possibility of restoring the balance in favour of the majority, such as transferring control of devolution to the central legislature instead of the courts, as seems to be the case

---

[107] A Lajoie, MC Gervais, E Gélineau and R Janda 'When Silence is no Longer Acquiescence: Gays and Lesbians under Canadian law' (1999) 14 *Canadian Journal of Law and Society* 101; A Lajoie, MC Gervais, E Gélineau and R Janda 'Les valeurs des femmes dans le discours de la Cour suprême du Canada' (2000) 34 *Revue Juridique Thémis* 563; A Lajoie 'I valori delle minoranze sociali nelle giurisprudenza costituzionale delle Corte suprema del Canada', in G Rolla (ed) *Lo sviluppo dei diritti fondamentali in Canada fra universalità e diversità culturale* (Giuffre Milano 2000).

[108] A Lajoie, E Gélineau, I Duplessis and G Rocher (n 87).

[109] RA MacDonald 'Pour la reconnaissance d'une normativité juridique implicite et inférentielle' vol XVIII no 1 *Sociologie et sociétés* 47.

for Scotland. It would then seem like a concession no nation state in its right mind would accept, for it might mean real devolution...

Even if this might count as a conclusion, I would like to add a last remark related to the very notion of 'regions'. Even when conceptual accommodation has been made to allow for the fact that regions in themselves do not need accommodation—only the population which inhabits them, and then only if it has common values different from those of the larger group established on the territory from which these regions have been carved—the territorial factor might have been overvalued in the current legal thinking in the UK, at least if the Canadian context can offer any insights. For indeed, it could be expected that a minority linked to a territory over which it enjoys some control through a federal division of powers or even more restrained devolution would have more clout and might obtain more from constitutional adjudication by a supreme court than a minority not anchored in its own territory or region. This assertion might prove true for social minorities such as gays, lesbians, women and perhaps even the elderly, although we have no data on this latter group, which gets less from the Supreme Court than political minorities. But the difference does not hold between political minorities, where territorialization seems to make no differ-ence, as our results show.[110] In comparable claims to political autonomy and control of territory, Quebec, territorializing 85% of Canadian francophones, did not fare any better than Aboriginals, who are territorialized only to a total proportion of 5.8%, and on three different territories at that. The significant variable does not seem to be territorialization but political clout and the estab-lishment of a favourable power relationship.

---

[110] See above.

6

Adjudicating Divisions of Powers Issues: a Canadian Perspective

WARREN J. NEWMAN*

1. INTRODUCTION

When the UK Parliament enacted the British North America Act in 1867, it bestowed upon Canada a constitution that was patterned both upon the British tradition of parliamentary government in accordance with unwritten principles and conventions, and the American experiment with a written constitution and a federal system. In countries with a federal system, legislative authority is constitutionally distributed between a central government on the one hand and provinces or local states on the other. Where a dispute arises as to whether the central or the provincial (or state) government has the constitutional *power* to carry out the policy it has purported to enact into law, the courts are almost invariably called upon to act as arbiters and to decide the legal aspects of the controversy, having regard to the terms and underlying principles of the constitutional text. US Supreme Court Justice Sandra Day O'Connor has observed that '[r]ecent constitutional changes in the UK raise the questions what effect the courts will have on devolution and, just as important, what effect devolution will have on the role of the courts'.[1] Given the mandate conferred upon the Judicial Committee of the Privy Council (hereinafter, the Privy Council) in the adjudication of divisions of powers matters under the devolution statutes, this essay devotes particular attention to the role played by that body in the development of federalism and 'the federal principle' in Canada's constitutional jurisprudence.

One must be mindful of the structural distinctions to be drawn between a federal constitution on the one hand and a unitary state on the other, whereby powers are delegated to local, subordinate bodies by the principal lawgiver—in the UK, the supreme Parliament at Westminster. Justice O'Connor puts the proposition baldly as follows: 'Federalism represents a true division of power, whereas devolution is simply a delegation'.[2] She adds: 'Further, devolution in

* General Counsel, Constitutional and Administrative Law Section, Department of Justice of Canada.

The views expressed in this essay are those of the author. An earlier draft of this essay appeared in The Supreme Court Law Review (2d), Vol 22 (Butterworths Toronto 2003).

[1] Sandra Day O'Connor 'Altered States: Federalism and Devolution at the "Real" Turn of the Millennium' (2001) 60 *Cambridge Law Journal* 493, 498.
[2] ibid 502.

the UK is asymmetrical, while federalism in America is almost perfectly symmetrical'.[3]

The Canadian experience, as we shall see, is perhaps more in keeping with the evolution of the UK's constitutional arrangements, notably because the Canadian Constitution, as interpreted by the Privy Council and the Supreme Court of Canada, has evolved from a structure designed to favour a central Parliament over subordinate local governments, to one that recognizes the autonomy of the provincial legislatures within their spheres of competence. It is a structure that has evolved to combine the principle of parliamentary sovereignty with the principle of federalism, and to harmonize the principle of the equality of the provinces with a recognition of the distinctiveness of Canada's regions, linguistic communities, history, interests, and peoples.[4] It is not a structure that has been free of the centripetal and centrifugal tensions that characterize most federations, but it is one that has dealt remarkably well with the challenges those tensions have presented, notably through resort to adjudication before the courts in accordance with the rule of law.

The late Dr Geoffrey Marshall, in his remarks on the human rights and devolution statutes, observed that 'the current legislation is only the latest stage in a process of transformation that has other sources and inspirations', and that '[o]ne such influence, in many ways unnoticed, has been the Commonwealth'.

In the first half of the 20th century, the trade in political institutions was mainly thought of in terms of the export of the Westminster model. In the second half of the century there has been a significant inspirational flow in the opposite direction. Think, for example, of the three key aspects of the British system that were set out in Professor AV Dicey's classic work on the constitution—the sovereignty of Parliament, the conventions of the constitution, and the rule of law. It is evident that their present shape has been strongly influenced by constitutional developments in Canada, New Zealand, Australia, and South Africa....

Politicians are now less, and judges more, in charge of our affairs. That is a considerable sea change for a nation whose tradition and culture have respected the rule of law while distrusting lawyers.[5]

In Canada, division of powers (or 'federalism') cases have been overshadowed for the past two decades by the sheer volume of human rights cases under the Canadian Charter of Rights and Freedoms,[6] as well as by the intrinsic interest

---

[3] Sandra Day O'Connor 'Altered States: Federalism and Devolution at the "Real" Turn of the Millennium' (2001) 60 *Cambridge Law Journal* 503.

[4] See ch 5.

[5] G Marshall 'Remaking the British Constitution' John Tait Memorial Lecture, Faculty of Law, McGill University, Montreal, 5 October 2000 (published jointly by the Department of Justice and McGill University).

[6] The Canadian Charter of Rights and Freedoms is one of the instruments of the Constitution of Canada. The Charter was enacted and proclaimed in force in 1982 as Part I of the Constitution Act 1982, itself a schedule to the Canada Act 1982 (UK). The Supreme Court of Canada has rendered more than 400 decisions in Charter cases since 1982.

and media attention that such cases naturally generate. One observer has remarked that this is also reflected in the relative dearth of recent commentary on division of powers questions, the groves of academe now overrun, it seems, with commentators eager to analyse Charter issues.[7] A division of powers case, like Dickens' description in *Bleak House* of a suit in Chancery, is too often perceived as 'a slow, expensive, British, constitutional kind of thing'. Arid though such matters may appear to be, an appreciation of the basic principles, rules, themes, and dynamics behind the adjudication of division of powers issues is essential for constitutional lawyers, political scientists, and other students of government.

2. THE TOUCHSTONES OF THE CONSTITUTION OF CANADA

As the British Constitution is the most subtle organism which has proceeded from the womb and long gestation of progressive history, so the American Constitution is, so far as I can see, the most wonderful work ever struck off at a given time by the brain and purpose of man.

British Prime Minister William Gladstone is often cited—often in the USA, at least—for that famous observation. What would Gladstone have thought of the Constitution of Canada (had he turned his mind to it)? Would he have remarked that the Canadian Constitution is a unique and judicious blend of the American and British models of constitutionalism? Or would he have thought it a curious amalgam of written and unwritten rules, of federal and unitary forms of government?

Certainly, the Constitution of Canada is similar in structure to that of the USA in that its broad outlines have been laid out in a pre-eminent written constitutional instrument—or in the Canadian case, a series of instruments, the Constitution Acts 1867 to 1982, and the amendments thereto. Like its American counterpart, the Canadian Constitution governs the relationships between the executive, legislative, and judicial branches of government; regulates and controls the division of legislative powers between the central government of the federation and the local legislatures; contains an entrenched bill of rights; sets out special and complex procedures for constitutional amendment; and declares that the Constitution is the 'supreme law' of the land.

The Constitution of Canada is also, however, as the preamble to the British North-America Act—now styled the Constitution Act 1867—confirms, 'a Constitution similar in Principle to that of the United Kingdom'. Canada is a constitutional monarchy 'under the Crown of the United Kingdom', and a parliamentary democracy on the Westminster model. The executive government and authority 'of and over Canada' is declared, by section 9 of the Act of 1867, 'to continue and

---

[7] A Wayne MacKay 'The Supreme Court of Canada and Federalism: Does/Should Anyone Care Anymore?' (2001) 80 *Canadian Bar Review* 241, 243.

be vested in the Queen', and section 12 constitutes the Queen's Privy Council for Canada. Section 17 of the Act establishes 'One Parliament for Canada,' consisting of the Queen; an appointed upper house of sober second thought, the Senate; and a popularly elected lower chamber, the House of Commons. The Queen's representative in Canada, the Governor General, and the other actors and institutions of the central state exercise their powers and carry out their duties in accordance with the conventions of responsible government, whereby the executive ministry is, in principle, accountable to the elected house. The Lieutenant Governors, provincial legislatures and cabinets operate in kind.

Canada's constitutional arrangements thus differ from its American counterparts in Canada's allegiance to the Crown, in the pattern of its democratic institutions, and in its adherence to British customs and traditions of governance. It is a constitution born of evolution, not revolution. This long and profound heritage of legal continuity is illustrated even by the fact that the Canada Act 1982—which gave legal effect to Canada's independence as a sovereign state (long recognized as a matter of convention by the Balfour declaration in 1926 and the preamble to the Statute of Westminster in 1931)—is itself an Act of the UK Parliament.

A 'Constitution similar in Principle to that of the United Kingdom', the courts have recognized, means that the Constitution of Canada is more than a collection of statutes and instruments. The *law* of the Constitution is, of course, to be found in the Constitution Acts and the rules of the common law. However, in accordance with the British (and Diceyian) model, the Constitution includes, in its broader analytical sense, the unwritten *conventions* that govern the way political actors exercise their powers under the written text of the Constitution. These conventions are political obligations, not rules enforceable at law, but the Supreme Court has recognized that in certain instances, they may be more important than the bare framework of the law itself in ensuring that the implementation of the text of the Constitution conforms to the prevailing values of Canadian society.

Straddling the divide between law and conventions are the organizing *principles* of the Constitution. These fundamental principles, our Supreme Court has declared, are the lifeblood of the Constitution. The principles infuse the *provisions* of the constitutional text with constitutional meaning, and they also provide the *raison d'être* for the unwritten rules of constitutional conventions. These principles are said to be 'not merely descriptive' but rather, 'invested with a powerful normative force' and 'binding upon both courts and governments'. Constitutional principles 'emerge from an understanding of the constitutional text itself, the historical context, and previous judicial interpretations of constitutional meaning'.[8]

---

[8] See *Reference Re Secession of Quebec* [1998] 2 SCR 217, [32] and [54]. For an examination of the normative scope of unwritten constitutional principles, see WJ Newman '"Grand Entrance Hall," Back Door or Foundation Stone? The Role of Constitutional Principles in Construing and Applying the Constitution of Canada' (2001) 14 *Supreme Court Law Review* (2d) 197.

3. Some fundamental principles and characteristics of the Canadian federation

In Canada, as former Chief Justice Lamer once wrote, our constitutional evolution 'has culminated in the supremacy of a definitive written constitution'.[9] He was later to add the following words of caution: 'There are many important reasons for the preference for a written constitution over an unwritten one, not the least of which is the promotion of legal certainty and through it the legitimacy of judicial constitutional review'.[10] Nonetheless, Lamer CJ was an exponent of the development of constitutional interpretation through resort to unwritten constitutional principles, many of them flowing ostensibly from the recitals in the preamble to the Constitution Act 1867. 'Indeed,' he stated, 'given that ours is a Constitution that has emerged from a constitutional order whose fundamental rules are not authoritatively set down in a single document, or a set of documents, it is of no surprise that our Constitution should retain some aspect of this legacy'.[11]

Fundamental, then, to an understanding of the Constitution of Canada, and to the adjudication of disputes arising thereunder, are its basic principles. These, the Supreme Court has said, work in symbiosis. No single principle can be said to trump the others. Certain principles are, however, broader and overarching in nature. They go to the very structure of the Constitution, or to what the Court has referred to as the Constitution's basic values and 'internal architecture'.

These principles include constitutionalism and the rule of law, federalism, democracy, the protection of minorities, parliamentary sovereignty, responsible government, parliamentary privilege, judicial independence, and the separation of powers. Several (and perhaps all) of these principles are relevant to the theme of this essay. Key amongst them are constitutionalism and the rule of law, and the federal principle.

4. Constitutionalism and the rule of law

The first principle of the Canadian Constitution is respect for the *rule of law* and *constitutionalism* itself. This principle is reflected both in the preambles to the Constitution Act 1867 and the Constitution Act 1982, and in section 52 of the latter Act, the supremacy clause. We have already noted that the preamble to the Act of 1867 speaks of 'a Constitution similar in Principle to that of the United Kingdom'. The preamble to the Constitution Act 1982 declares, 'Whereas Canada is founded upon principles which recognize the supremacy of God and the rule of law'. Section 52 of the Constitution Act 1982 begins with the following clause:

---

[9] *New Brunswick Broadcasting Co v Nova Scotia (Speaker of the House of Assembly)* [1993] 1 SCR 319, 355.

[10] *Reference Re Provincial Court Judges* [1997] 3 SCR 3, [93].

[11] ibid [92].

52. (1) The Constitution of Canada is the supreme law of Canada, and any law that is inconsistent with the provisions of the Constitution is, to the extent of the inconsistency, of no force or effect.

Section 52, in affirming that the provisions of the Constitution are supreme and render inconsistent laws invalid, expresses a rule of constitutional law that has always been recognized and applied by Canadian courts since 1867. By virtue of the Colonial Laws Validity Act enacted by the UK Parliament in 1865, any colonial law that was 'repugnant to the Provisions' of any imperial statute 'extending to the colony' was 'absolutely void and inoperative' to the extent of the repugnancy. The British North America Act of 1867(BNA Act) was therefore the supreme law of Canada. The courts would declare any law enacted by the Canadian Parliament or the provincial legislatures that was inconsistent with the BNA Act to be *ultra vires* and thus void and inoperative. The repeal of the Colonial Laws Validity Act in 1931, at the instance of the dominions, did not affect the status of the British North-America Acts 1867 to 1930. At the request of Canada, their pre-eminent position was preserved by section 7(1) of the Statute of Westminster.

The 'rule of law', the Supreme Court has stated, comprises three principal elements. The first is that 'the law is supreme over the acts of both government and private persons. There is, in short, 'one law for all'. The second is that the rule of law requires 'the creation and maintenance of an actual order of positive laws which preserves and embodies the more general principle of normative order'. The third element is that 'the exercise of all public power must find its ultimate source in a legal rule'; ie that 'the relationship between the state and the individual must be regulated by law'.[12]

The principle of 'constitutionalism', the Court has said, is similar but not identical to the rule of law. 'Simply put, the constitutionalism principle requires that all government action must comply with the Constitution. The rule of law principle requires that all government action must comply with the law, including the Constitution'. In Canada, the 'essence of constitutionalism is embodied in section 52(1) of the Constitution Act 1982';[13] that is, in the words and meaning of the supremacy clause set out above.

The Constitution binds all governments, including the executive branch . . . They may not transgress its provisions: indeed, their sole claim to exercise lawful authority rests in the powers allocated to them under the Constitution, and can come from no other source.[14]

Constitutionalism and the rule of law have been strengthened by structural amendments to the Constitution, most notably the enactment and proclamation of Part I of the Constitution Act 1982—the Canadian Charter of Rights and Freedoms—and Part V setting out the legal rules that henceforth govern constitutional amendment.

---

[12] *Quebec Secession Reference* (n 8) [71]; see also *Reference re Manitoba Language Rights* [1985] 1 SCR 721, 747–752, and *Provincial Judges Reference* (n 10) [10].
[13] *Quebec Secession Reference* (n 8) [72].   [14] ibid.

Prior to 1982, significant constitutional amendments required action by the UK Parliament. In order to effect such constitutional amendments, a political process had emerged over time whereby the two houses of the Canadian Parliament would adopt a joint address to Her Majesty, requesting that she place the proposed measure before the UK Parliament for enactment. The precedents were such that it could fairly be said that the Canadian government would not, as a rule, proceed with an amendment through the joint resolution process if it did not have the support of provincial premiers. The legitimacy of Canadian Prime Minister Pierre Trudeau's 1980–81 initiative to 'patriate' the Constitution and entrench a Charter of Rights occasioned much controversy, because initially it had the formal support of just two of the 10 provincial premiers. The eight dissenting governments mounted constitutional challenges to the process. A majority of the Supreme Court opined that the process was not unconstitutional in the legal sense, but that it would breach a constitutional convention if a substantial consensus amongst the premiers was not reached. The Court left it to the political actors to determine the degree of consensus that would be necessary.[15] In November 1981, after a final round of constitutional negotiations, nine provincial governments agreed to support the patriation package, and the joint address to the Queen (and through Her Majesty, to the UK Parliament) proceeded. The Canada Act 1982 was enacted by the UK Parliament in March of that year, and its schedule, the Constitution Act 1982, was proclaimed in force by Her Majesty in Ottawa on April 17.

The sole dissenting government was that of Quebec. In the meantime, it had renewed the constitutional challenge to the patriation process by submitting a new question to the Court of Appeal of the province as to whether, as a matter of constitutional convention, the consent of the Quebec government was required to move forward. The Court of Appeal ruled that what was required by the convention was a substantial degree of consensus, not unanimity, and that the government of Quebec had not demonstrated that it possessed a conventional power of veto over the process. The nine judges of the Supreme Court, in a *per curiam* opinion, confirmed the finding of Quebec Court of Appeal. In ruling that there had been no breach in the constitutional *convention* governing the process of patriating the Constitution, the Court also emphasized, *a fortiori*, the validity of the constitutional *law* resulting from the patriation process.

The Constitution Act 1982 is now in force. Its legality is neither challenged nor assailable. It contains a new procedure for amending the Constitution of Canada which entirely replaces the old one in its legal as well as in its conventional aspects.[16]

Two further attempts at major constitutional reform between 1987 and 1990, and 1990 and 1992, the Meech Lake and Charlottetown Constitutional

---

[15] *Re Resolution to amend the Constitution* [1981] 1 SCR 753.
[16] *Re Objection to a Resolution to amend the Constitution* [1982] 2 SCR 793, 806.

Accords, respectively, led to initial agreement amongst the Canadian Prime Minister and the provincial premiers, but the agreements ultimately failed to be ratified.[17] However, several less ambitious but still significant constitutional amendments have been enacted and proclaimed.[18]

The principles of constitutionalism and the rule of law have also been forged and strengthened by the crucible of two challenges of momentous proportions. In 1985, the Supreme Court struck down as invalid and of no force and effect almost 90 years of laws enacted by the legislature of Manitoba solely in English, in contravention of the requirement of bilingual enactment and promulgation in both English and French mandated by section 23 of the Manitoba Act 1870, which is part of the Constitution of Canada. Section 23 imposed a constitutional duty on the legislature with regard to the manner and form of its legislation; a duty which protected 'the substantive rights of all Manitobans to equal access to the law' in English and French. That constitutional duty conferred upon the judiciary 'the responsibility of protecting the correlative language rights of all Manitobans including the Franco-Manitoban minority'. The Supreme Court spoke deeply to the values at the heart of constitutionalism:

The Constitution of a country is a statement of the will of the people to be governed in accordance with certain principles held as fundamental and certain prescriptions restrictive of the powers of the legislature and government. It is, as section 52 of the Constitution Act 1982 declares, the 'supreme law' of the nation, unalterable by the normal legislative process, and unsuffering of laws inconsistent with it. The duty of the judiciary is to interpret and apply the laws of Canada and each of the provinces, and it is thus our duty to ensure that the constitutional law prevails.[19]

---

[17] Both agreements were intended, to a greater or lesser extent, to restore constitutional harmony between the government of Quebec and that of Ottawa and the other nine provinces, notably by amendments to the Constitution that would have expressly recognized Quebec as a distinct society within Canada. The agreements would also have provided for other constitutional reforms, including changes in relation to the Senate and the Supreme Court, and in the case of the Charlottetown Accord, the recognition of an inherent right of the Aboriginal peoples of Canada to self-governance. The packages of constitutional amendments proposed by both agreements required the application of the strictest of the amending formulae, ie unanimity amongst the Senate, the House of Commons, and the 10 provincial legislative assemblies, under s 41 of the Constitution Act 1982. Both federal Houses and nine provincial legislative assemblies approved the Meech Lake Accord; however, the Accord failed after the Newfoundland House of Assembly revoked its ratifying resolution and the resolution was never put to a vote in the Manitoba legislative assembly. The opinion of Canadian voters on whether to proceed with the amendments proposed in the Charlottetown Accord was solicited by the Governor in Council in October 1992 under An Act to provide for referendums on the Constitution of Canada SC 1992, c 30, but the Accord failed to win sufficient popular support and so the formal amendment process was never engaged.

[18] These include an amendment to the Canadian Charter of Rights and Freedoms recognizing the equality of the English and French linguistic communities of the province of New Brunswick and amendments to the Constitution Act 1867 and the Newfoundland Act in relation to denominational schools in the provinces of Quebec and Newfoundland, respectively. (The constitutional amendment procedure employed to effect those changes is more flexible, requiring the consent of the Senate, the House of Commons, and the legislative assembly of the province to which the amendment applies: see s 43 of the Constitution Act 1982.)

[19] *Manitoba Language Rights Reference* (n 12) 744–755.

The second challenge came to a head a decade later. Both prior to and in the aftermath of the October 1995 referendum on Quebec sovereignty, the Quebec government took the position that neither the Constitution nor the courts of Canada would have any role to play in determining the framework within which Quebec's 'process of accession to sovereignty' might unfold. The premises of the draft Bill, An Act respecting the sovereignty of Quebec, and its successor, Bill 1, insofar as it purported to authorize the National Assembly of Quebec to effect the *unilateral* secession of Quebec from Canada, represented a radical—indeed, revolutionary—threat of unprecedented proportions to the stability of the Canadian legal order and the rule of law. Although the Bill did not proceed after the failure of the Quebec government to obtain majority support for its proposal from the population of the province in the referendum, that government continued to claim that should it obtain a simple majority, on a question of its choosing, in a referendum organized at a time of its convenience, the right of self-determination at international law would lead to a right of secession, by a unilateral declaration of independence, if necessary.

In the circumstances, the Government of Canada sought a comprehensive opinion from the Supreme Court on the legal issues relating to unilateral secession. In its landmark judgment in August 1998,[20] the Court confirmed that unilateral secession would be an unlawful act under the Constitution and a violation of the Canadian legal order; a revolution. Nor was there any legal right at international law, whether as a matter of self-determination or otherwise, to unilateral secession in the circumstances of Quebec. Secession, to be lawful under the Constitution of Canada, would require a constitutional amendment. At the same time, the Court recognized that if a clear majority of Quebecers, on a clear question, expressed their desire to leave Canada, this would 'confer legitimacy on the efforts of the government of Quebec *to initiate the Constitution's amendment process* in order to secede by constitutional means'. Negotiations would be governed by the same constitutional principles identified by the Court at the outset as relevant to the question of secession: federalism, democracy, constitutionalism and the rule of law, and respect for minorities.

This balanced finding, marrying the need for constitutional legality with the search for political legitimacy, has been salutary for Canada's civic traditions and political culture. Those who favour sovereignty and independence over federalism have a stake in the proper operation and application of the Constitution of Canada, because it safeguards their legitimate interests, just as it does those of Canadians as a whole. However, those who would embrace the Court's finding of an obligation to negotiate must also accept the Court's rules as the circumstances in which such a duty would arise—a clear expression of a clear majority of a desire to secede from Canada—and the rules governing such negotiations: respect by all participants, including the sovereigntist government,

---

[20] *Quebec Secession Reference* (n 8).

of the underlying principles of the Constitution of Canada, and notably the rule of law and constitutionalism itself.[21]

5. FEDERALISM AND THE DIVISION OF POWERS

The second broad principle of the Canadian Constitution—in fact, the predominant one for many years, at least until the advent of the Charter of Rights—is the principle of *federalism*. The framers of the Constitution sought to achieve something unique for the governance of Canada. Unlike the UK, Canada would not be a unitary state; but by providing, it was thought, for a robust central government, the new country would also avoid the centrifugal tensions that had led to the recent civil war amongst the American states. Its structure would combine the features of a constitution similar in principle to the UK—a constitutional monarchy, parliamentary sovereignty, the conventions of responsible government, the rule of law—with provinces 'federally united into one Dominion under the Crown'.[22]

In contrast to the situation that prevailed in the US, where the state legislatures held the residue of power under the Constitution, in Canada, the powers of the provincial legislatures would be defined and therefore limited, whilst the Dominion Parliament would be empowered to make laws generally for 'the Peace, Order and good Government of Canada' in relation to all matters not assigned exclusively to the provinces. The federal power to regulate trade and commerce would be drafted in broader terms than its American interstate equivalent, and the criminal law power, which in the US was a state responsibility, would be conferred upon the central Parliament.[23] Stated Sir John A Macdonald, the first Prime Minister of Canada, during the Confederation Debates:

They [ie the Americans] declared by their Constitution that each state was a sovereignty in itself, and that all the powers incident to a sovereignty belonged to each state, except those powers which, by the Constitution, were conferred upon the General Government and Congress.

Here we have adopted a different system. We have strengthened the General Government. We have given the General Legislature all the great subjects of legislation. We have

---

[21] For further discussion of the events leading to the Reference and the wisdom of the Supreme Court's opinion, see WJ Newman *The Quebec Secession Reference—The Rule of Law and the Position of the Attorney General of Canada* (York University Centre for Public Law and Public Policy Toronto 1999). See, as well, An Act to give effect to the requirement for clarity as set out in the opinion of the Supreme Court of Canada in the Quebec Secession Reference SC 2000, c 26, enacted by the Parliament of Canada, and An Act respecting the exercise of the fundamental rights and prerogatives of the Quebec people and the Quebec State SC 2000, c 46, enacted by the Legislature of Quebec. The official opposition in the legislative assembly, the Quebec Liberal Party, voted against the enactment of the latter statute. The Liberals won the provincial election on 14 April 2003. The sovereigntist government of the Parti Québécois was thus replaced by a federalist one when the Lieutenant Governor of the province administered the oath of office to Premier Jean Charest and his ministry on 29 April 2003.

[22] Constitution Act 1867, preamble.

[23] Constitution Act 1867, ss 91 and 92.

conferred on them, not only specifically and in detail, all the powers which are incident to sovereignty, but we have expressly declared that all subjects of general interest not distinctly and exclusively conferred upon the local governments and local legislatures, shall be conferred upon the General Government and Legislature.

We have thus avoided that great source of weakness which has been the cause of the disruption of the US . . . [24]

Beyond this, the provinces would be, in certain respects, subordinate to the central government. The Lieutenant Governor of each province would be appointed by the federal Cabinet (the Governor in Council), as would the judges of the provincial superior and appellate courts.[25] The Bills passed by the legislatures would be subject to the reservation of assent by the Governor General, and the Acts of the legislatures to disallowance by the Governor General within one year of their enactment.[26] The Parliament of Canada could assume legislative jurisdiction over various provincial works simply by declaring them to be for the advantage of Canada or two or more provinces.[27]

In the early years of the federation, the powers of reservation and disallowance, as well as the declaratory power, were employed quite frequently.[28] Over time these powers fell largely into disuse,[29] particularly reservation and disallowance, as constitutional adjudication came to be seen—barring exceptional circumstances—as a more appropriate means of dealing with the enactment of *ultra vires* legislation.[30]

[24] Sir John A Macdonald, quoted in M Bliss *Right Honourable Men* (Harper Collins Toronto 1994) 13–14. States Bliss at 12: 'Like most politicians in the British tradition, he [Macdonald] did not like the idea of federations. The UK was a legislative union rather than a federation. One legislature, Parliament, under the Crown, governed all England, Ireland, Scotland, and Wales, and the system seemed to work wonderfully. By contrast, the world's most famous experiment in federalism, the United States of America, had fallen apart and into bloody civil war.'

[25] ss 58 and 96, respectively, of the Constitution Act 1867.

[26] s 90 read with ss 56 and 57 of the Constitution Act 1867.

[27] para 92(10)(c).

[28] This is partly a matter of historical perspective. In JEC Munro *The Constitution of Canada* (Cambridge University Press Cambridge 1889) the author observed: 'The power of disallowance has been exercised in a comparatively small number of cases. Of the 6000 Acts passed by the provincial legislatures up to 1882 only 33 have been disallowed, viz. in Ontario 5, Quebec 2, Nova Scotia 5, Manitoba 7, British Columbia 12 . . . [T]he Dominion government are conscious that the power of disallowance ought to be exercised with great care and caution'.

[29] The power of disallowance was employed 112 times and last exercised in 1943; the power of reservation in 1961. (This does not mean, of course, that the power has ceased to exist as a matter of law. 'It was not the courts but political forces that dictated their near demise': *Ontario Hydro v Ontario* [1993] 3 SCR 327, 371–372 (LaForest J).)

[30] On 17 July 1975, Prime Minister Pierre Trudeau, in refusing a public request for disallowance of Bill 22, the Official Language Act passed by the Legislature of Quebec and declaring French to be the official language of the province, wrote that '[I]t is only in rare cases that the federal government should avail itself of this power since its use represents a clear exception to the general principle that the federal and provincial legislatures are autonomous in their respective areas of legislative competence and are responsible for the policies they embrace . . . Not every provincial law which is contrary to federal policy or to the public interest, or which is "unwise and unjust" should be subject to disallowance. The responsibility for such laws should ordinarily be left with the province unless other elements are present: for example, that their effect cuts directly across the operation of federal law or creates serious disorder particularly beyond the boundaries of the province enacting them' (correspondence tabled in the House of Commons, 22 July 1975, Sessional Papers 301–5/185).

For provincial legislatures and governments, however, those early years were often marked by a struggle to assert 'provincial rights'—at any rate, provincial *powers*—in the face of the apparent dominance of the central Parliament and government. The provinces had little enthusiasm for the subordinate status that the formal constitutional arrangements appeared to have thrust upon them. They did not appreciate, for example, the disallowance of provincial legislation by the central government, which arguably placed the provinces in a position analogous to the colonial relationship that existed at the time between the British government and Canada (the latter also subject, in principle if not in practice, to the disallowance of its legislation by the former).

An increasing emphasis on provincial autonomy became an important object-ive for Premiers Oliver Mowat in Ontario and Honoré Mercier in Quebec, the latter province being the only one in which the French-Canadian population formed a majority. At the time of Confederation, the official use of the French language in the statutes, records, and journals of Parliament and the legislature of Quebec, as well as in the proceedings of the courts of Canada and of Quebec, was expressly guaranteed by section 133 of the Constitution Act 1867. The French civil law system and the freedom to practice the Roman Catholic religion, which had been restored to the province by the Quebec Act in 1774, were also preserved by the Constitution Act 1867. Provincial powers over property and civil rights, local affairs and education were essential to the legislature and government of Quebec's pursuit of protecting and developing its distinctive identity within Canada.[31]

The issue of identity would continue to shape the political and constitutional forces at play in Canada over the next 130 years. Much of the debate originally centred upon the nature of the Canadian federation itself. Did 1867 bring about, in John A Macdonald and Georges-Etienne Cartier's terms, the birth of a new nation? Or was it to be simply a pact between pre-existing provinces, a loose confederation of regional and sectarian interests? Was it an agreement between two 'founding peoples,' English-speaking and French-speaking? Could the Can-adian vision of citizenship accommodate multiple, cumulative identities, cultures and communities, and thereby cultivate a sense of belonging to a sum greater than the whole of its parts; 'unity in diversity'? How might provincial interests best be harmonized with 'the national interest'? These and related questions would later form the backdrop to many of the division of powers cases before the courts. The Judicial Committee of the Privy Council was alive to many of these questions and concerns.[32]

---

[31] For a sensitive study of attitudes in Quebec (ie Lower Canada) towards Confederation, see AI Silver *The French-Canadian Idea of Confederation 1864–1900* (University of Toronto Press Toronto 1982).

[32] It is not within the scope of this essay to rehearse the decisions of the Judicial Committee in regard to minority rights per se, notably in respect of the nature and scope of the denominational rights guaranteed by s 93 of the Constitution Act 1867 and s 22 of the Manitoba Act 1870. In an influential piece that appeared in *Queen's Quarterly* in 1930, FR Scott argued forcefully that the contention that the Privy Council was 'the defender of minority rights' did not fit the facts. 'What the

The Judicial Committee of the Privy Council established, case by case, the complex and intricate framework of principles of constitutional interpretation—pith and substance, leading feature, true purpose, double aspect, occupied field, paramountcy, reading down, colourability, severability, and so on—that still governs and shapes most of Canada's constitutional jurisprudence on the division of powers today. Nowhere, however, was its influence more markedly felt than in the balance it struck between the powers of the central Parliament on the one hand and the powers of the provincial legislatures on the other: in short, in articulating the federal principle underlying the Constitution. The Judicial Committee, and most notably Lords Watson and Haldane, buttressed the role of the provinces as co-equals, rather than subordinates, in the conduct of the affairs of the federation.

In *Liquidators of the Maritime Bank v Receiver General of New Brunswick*,[33] for example, Lord Watson stated that the appellants had argued that the effect of the Constitution Act 1867 had been 'to sever all connection between the Crown and the provinces; to make the government of the Dominion the only government of Her Majesty in North America; and to reduce the provinces to the rank of independent municipal institutions'. For this position, he replied, there was neither principle nor authority:

The object of the Act was neither to weld the provinces into one, nor to subordinate provincial governments to a central authority, but to create a federal government in which they should all be represented, entrusted with the exclusive administration of affairs in which they had a common interest, each province retaining its independence and autonomy. That object was accomplished by distributing between the Dominion and the provinces, all powers executive and legislative... But, in so far as regards those matters which, by sect. 92, are specially reserved for provincial legislation, the legislature of each province continues to be free from the control of the Dominion, and supreme as it was before the passing of the Act...

[T]he provincial legislature of New Brunswick does not occupy the subordinate position which was ascribed to it in the argument of the appellants... its status is in no way analogous to that of a municipal institution, which is an authority constituted for purposes of local administration. It *possesses powers, not of administration, merely, but of legislation, in the strictest sense of the word*; and within the limits assigned by sect. 92 of the Act of 1867, these powers are exclusive and supreme.[34]

Privy Council has done in our Constitution is to safeguard, not minority rights, but provincial rights... It is little comfort for the French-Canadian minorities in the Maritimes, in Ontario, Manitoba, and Saskatchewan to realize that the provincial governments on which they depend for their educational privileges and their civil rights have had their powers enlarged, and that the Dominion Parliament, in which the French-speaking members must always exercise a powerful influence, has been deprived of much of its former capacity. Provincial rights and minority rights would be identical if the minority were confined to the province of Quebec.' Reprinted in R MacGregor Dawson *Constitutional Issues in Canada 1900–1931* (Oxford University Press Oxford 1931) 347–353.

[33] [1892] AC 437.
[34] ibid 442–443 (emphasis added).

That powerful statement on provincial autonomy would later be embellished by Lord Haldane in *Re the Initiative and Referendum Act*:[35]

The scheme of the Act passed in 1867 was thus, not to weld the Provinces into one, nor to subordinate Provincial Governments to a central authority, but to establish a central government in which these Provinces should be represented, entrusted with exclusive authority only in affairs in which they had a common interest. Subject to this each province was to retain its independence and autonomy and to be directly under the Crown as its head. Within these limits of area and subjects, its local Legislature, so long as the Imperial Parliament did not repeal its own Act conferring this status, was to be supreme, and had such powers as the Imperial Parliament possesses in the plenitude of its own freedom before it handed them over to the Dominion and the Provinces, in accordance with the scheme of distribution it enacted in 1867.[36]

In 1998, in the *Quebec Secession Reference*, the Supreme Court of Canada recognized federalism as one of a series of fundamental structural principles relevant to the resolution of the issues in question. Because the Reference dealt with 'questions fundamental to the nature of Canada', the Court stated, 'it should not be surprising that it is necessary to review the context in which the Canadian union has evolved'.[37] History revealed that 'the evolution of our constitutional arrangements has been characterized by adherence to the rule of law, respect for democratic institutions, the accommodation of minorities, insistence that governments adhere to constitutional conduct and a desire for continuity and stability'.[38] Within that historical evolution, the significance of Confederation was that it was driven by a desire for a *federal* union, with a division of powers between the central and provincial governments that would reflect Canada's diversity:

Federalism was a legal response to the underlying political and cultural realities that existed at Confederation and continue to exist today. At Confederation, political leaders told their respective communities that the Canadian union would be able to reconcile diversity with unity...

The federal-provincial division of powers was a legal recognition of the diversity that existed among the initial members of Confederation, and manifested a concern to accommodate that diversity within a single nation by granting significant powers to provincial governments. The *Constitution Act, 1867* was an act of nation-building. It was the first step in the transition from colonies separately dependent on the Imperial Parliament for their governance to a unified and independent political state in which different peoples could resolve their disagreements and work together toward common goals and a common interest. Federalism was the political mechanism by which diversity could be reconciled with unity.[39]

Returning to this theme in its analysis of the relevant constitutional principles, the Court stated that although 'on paper, the federal government retained sweeping powers which threatened to undermine the autonomy of the

---

[35] [1919] AC 935.   [36] ibid 942.   [37] *Quebec Secession Reference* (n 8) [34].
[38] ibid [48].   [39] ibid [43].

provinces', in fact, '[o]ur political and constitutional practice has adhered to an underlying principle of federalism, and has interpreted the written provisions of the Constitution in this light'.[40] Citing, inter alia, the Privy Council's decision in *Liquidators of the Maritime Bank*, the Court stated that in a federal system, 'political power is shared by two orders of government', each with 'respective spheres of jurisdiction':

In interpreting our Constitution, the courts have always been concerned with the federalism principle, inherent in the structure of our constitutional arrangements, which has from the beginning been the lodestar by which the courts have been guided.

This underlying principle of federalism, then, has exercised a role of considerable importance in the interpretation of the written provisions of our Constitution. In the *Patriation Reference*, pp 905–9, we confirmed that the principle of federalism runs through the political and legal systems of Canada. Indeed, Martland and Ritchie JJ, dissenting in the *Patriation Reference*, at p 821, considered federalism to be 'the dominant principle of Canadian constitutional law'. With the enactment of the *Charter*, that proposition may have less force than it once did, but there can be little doubt that the principle of federalism remains a central organizational theme of our Constitution. Less obviously, perhaps, but certainly of equal importance, federalism is a legal and political response to underlying social and political realities.

The principle of federalism recognizes the diversity of the component parts of Confederation, and the autonomy of provincial governments to develop their societies within their respective spheres of jurisdiction. The federal structure of our country also facilitates democratic participation by distributing power to the government thought to be most suited to achieving the particular societal objective having regard to this diversity.[41]

The scheme of the Constitution Act 1867, the Court then affirmed, quoting the Judicial Committee in *Re the Initiative and Referendum Act*, was 'not to weld the Provinces into one, nor to subordinate Provincial Governments to a central authority...'

Finally, the Supreme Court made special reference to the place of Quebec in the context of federalism and the Canadian federal structure, and concluded this part of its opinion with another reference to autonomy and the provinces generally:

The principle of federalism facilitates the pursuit of collective goals by cultural and linguistic minorities which form the majority within a particular province. This is the case in Quebec, where the majority of the population is French-speaking, and which possesses a distinct culture. This is not merely the result of chance. The social and demographic reality of Quebec explains the existence of the province of Quebec as a political unit and indeed, was one of the essential reasons for establishing a federal structure for the Canadian union in 1867. The experience of both Canada East and Canada West under the *Union Act, 1840* (U.K.) 3–4 Vict., c. 35, had not been satisfactory. The federal structure adopted at Confederation enabled French-speaking Canadians to

---

[40] ibid [55]. The Court cited, as an example of this practice, the abandonment of the use of the disallowance power, now long dormant.

[41] ibid [56]–[58].

form a numerical majority in the province of Quebec, and so exercise the considerable provincial powers conferred by the *Constitution Act, 1867* in such a way as to promote their language and culture. It also made provision for certain guaranteed representation within the federal Parliament itself.

Federalism was also welcomed by Nova Scotia and New Brunswick, both of which also affirmed their will to protect their individual cultures and their autonomy over local matters. All new provinces joining the federation sought to achieve similar objectives, which are no less vigorously pursued by the provinces and territories as we approach the new millennium.[42]

These several passages from the Supreme Court of Canada's landmark opinion in the *Quebec Secession Reference* illustrate the extent to which the principle of federalism, as developed by the learned jurists of the Judicial Committee of the Privy Council and refined by our own high court, has come to be embraced as an integral part of the Canadian constitutional system.[43] Adherence to the federal principle is central to the legacy left to Canada by the Judicial Committee and its impressive body of constitutional jurisprudence.

6. The Supreme Court of Canada and the Canadian court system

The Supreme Court of Canada stands at the apex of the Canadian court system as the final arbiter of legal disputes. Section 101 of the Constitution Act 1867 granted to Parliament the power to constitute and maintain 'a General Court of Appeal for Canada', and the Supreme Court was established by statute in 1875. It was not until 1949, however, upon the abolition of civil appeals to the Judicial Committee of the Privy Council,[44] that the Supreme Court became truly 'supreme' as the court of last resort in Canadian constitutional adjudication.

Under the Supreme Court Act, the Court is composed of the Chief Justice of Canada and eight puisne judges, who are appointed by the Governor in Council from amongst the judges of the superior courts or members of the provincial bars with at least 10 years' standing. By law, three of the nine judges are appointed from the Court of Appeal or the Superior Court of Quebec, or from the advocates of that province; by practice, three of the other justices are appointed from Ontario, one from the Atlantic provinces and two from the Western provinces, respectively. [45]

---

[42] *Quebec Secession Reference* (n 8) [59]–[60].

[43] '[F]ederative jurisprudence has influenced Canadian federalism to such an extent that, based on the legal decisions which have established case law, a federal system very different from the almost unitarian system found in the 1867 Act has emerged. It was the constitutional arbitration of the Privy Council . . . which, more than any other arbitration, contributed to realizing the potential for federalism contained in the Canadian Constitution'. A Tremblay 'The Canadian Constitutional Reform Dilemma' (1992) 1 *National Journal of Constitutional Law* 163, 165.

[44] Criminal appeals to the Judicial Committee were abolished in 1933.

[45] Currently, five of the nine justices are francophones.

The Supreme Court exercises ultimate appellate jurisdiction in all civil and criminal matters arising before the courts of the provinces and territories, and before other courts established by Parliament for the better administration of the laws of Canada, notably the Federal Court. With the exception of certain classes of appeals as of right (for example, in criminal cases where one appellate court judge has dissented on a question of law), in most cases, appeals are heard by the Supreme Court only where leave to appeal is granted by the Court itself. Under section 40 of the Supreme Court Act, an appeal lies to the Supreme Court from any final or other judgment of the Federal Court of Appeal, or of the highest court of final resort in a province, where the Supreme Court is of the opinion that the question is, by reason of its public importance, or the importance of the issue of law or mixed law and fact at stake, one that ought to be decided by the Supreme Court. The Court also exercises special jurisdiction in references by the Governor of Council, under section 53 of the Act, of important questions of law or fact relating to the interpretation of the Constitution Acts, the constitutionality or interpretation of any federal or provincial legislation, the powers of Parliament or the legislatures of the provinces, or the governments thereof, whether or not the power in question has actually been exercised; and any other important question the Governor in Council deems fit to refer.[46] La Forest J, writing on behalf of the Court, has remarked appositely that:

In assessing constitutional issues, it is well to remember that the court system in Canada is, in general, a unitary one under which provincially constituted inferior and superior courts of original and appellate jurisdiction apply federal as well as provincial laws under hierarchical arrangement culminating in the Supreme Court of Canada established by Parliament under section 101 of the *Constitution Act, 1867*.[47]

In another matter, in which the validity of a provincial statute that had produced extra-provincial effects in another province was challenged before the latter province's courts, giving rise to issues of jurisdiction, La Forest J elaborated further on the impact of the Canadian Constitution on the court structure and constitutional adjudication:

It is well established that a range of Canadian courts and tribunals in Canada are empowered to consider the constitutionality of the laws they apply. In doing so, they are applying the principle of the supremacy of the Constitution confirmed by section 52(1) of the Constitution Act 1982 . . . The same principle applies with, if anything, more force to the provincial superior courts. These are the ordinary courts of the land having inherent jurisdiction over all matters, both federal and provincial, unless a different forum is specified . . . This jurisdiction must include a determination of whether the laws sought to be applied are constitutionally valid. In Laskin J's words in *Thorson v. Attorney General of Canada*, [1975] 1 S.C.R. 138, at p 151: 'The question of the constitutionality of legislation has in this country always been a justiciable question' . . .

[46] The validity of the reference power was upheld by the Judicial Committee of the Privy Council in *Attorney-General for Ontario v Attorney-General for Canada* [1912] AC 571, and more recently, by the Supreme Court in the *Quebec Secession Reference* (n 8).
[47] *Ontario(Attorney General) v Pembina Exploration* [1989] 1 SCR 206, 215.

[A]ll judges within the Canadian judicial structure must be taken to be competent to interpret their own Constitution. In a judicial system consisting of neutral arbiters trained in principles of a federal state and required to exercise comity, the general notion that the process is unfair simply is not legally sustainable, all the more so when the process is subject to the supervisory jurisdiction of this Court.[48]

The Supreme Court's position at the summit and its power to decide constitutional questions allows it to exercise a 'unifying jurisdiction' over the provincial courts, which is consistent with its mandate under section 101 of the Constitution Act 1867 as 'a General Court of Appeal for Canada'.[49]

At the same time, the Court has been careful to recognize that whilst 'the Canadian Constitution does not insist on a strict separation of powers',[50] the role of the judiciary is distinct from that of the legislature and the executive in our constitutional system, and there are boundaries that should ordinarily be respected.

In the *Provincial Court Judges Reference*, Chief Justice Lamer contended that an unwritten constitutional principle of judicial independence was 'recognized and affirmed by the preamble to the *Constitution Act, 1867*' and its reference to 'a Constitution similar in Principle to that of the United Kingdom'.[51] The same principle can be said to flow from the 'judicature' provisions in sections 96 to 101 of the Act of 1867 and the right to a fair hearing by an independent and impartial tribunal in section 11 of the Charter of Rights. Whatever the provenance of the principle, Lamer CJ emphasized that 'the institutional independence of the courts is inextricably bound up with the separation of powers, because in order to guarantee that the courts can protect the Constitution, they must be protected by a set of objective guarantees against intrusions by the executive and legislative branches of government':[52]

What is at issue here is the character of the relationships between the legislature and the executive on the one hand, and the judiciary on the other. These relationships should be *depoliticised*. When I say that those relationships are depoliticised, I do not mean that they are political in the sense that court decisions (both constitutional and non constitutional) often have political implications, and that the statutes which courts adjudicate upon emerge from the political process. What I mean instead is the legislature and executive cannot, and cannot appear to, exert political pressure on the judiciary, and conversely, that members of the judiciary should exercise reserve in speaking out publicly on issues of general public policy that are or have the potential to come before the courts, that are the

---

[48] *Hunt v T&N plc* [1993] 4 SCR 289, 311–315.

[49] ibid 318–319.

[50] *Quebec Secession Reference* (n 8) 15.

[51] *Reference re Provincial Court Judges* (n 10) 64. For criticism of the historical basis for this approach, see the dissent of La Forest J ([304] onwards), which is instructive. '[T]o the extent that courts in Canada have the power to enforce the principle of judicial independence, this power derives from the structure of *Canadian*, and not British, constitutionalism' ([319]; the emphasis is that of La Forest J).

[52] ibid [138] (Lamer CJ).

subject of political debate, and which do not relate to the proper administration of justice.[53]

'The institutional independence of the courts', the Chief Justice stated, 'emerges from the logic of federalism, which requires an impartial arbiter to settle jurisdictional disputes between the federal and provincial orders of government'.[54] In the *Quebec Secession Reference*, the Supreme Court recognized that in exercising its discretion to determine questions alleged to be non-justiciable, the Court must ask itself:

(a) if to do so would take the Court beyond its own assessment of its proper role in the constitutional framework of our democratic form of government; or
(b) if the Court could not give an answer that lies within its area of expertise: the interpretation of law.[55]

In the *Secession Reference*, the questions put to the Court by the Governor in Council did not 'ask the Court to usurp any democratic decision' that Quebecers might be called upon to make; rather, the questions, properly interpreted, were 'limited to aspects of the legal framework in which that democratic decision is to be taken'—a legal framework involving 'the rights and obligations of Canadians who live outside the province of Quebec, as well as those who live within Quebec'. The questions could clearly be construed as 'directed to legal issues', and thus the Court was in a position to answer them:[56]

The Reference questions raise issues of fundamental public importance. It cannot be said that the questions are too imprecise or ambiguous to permit a proper legal answer. Nor can it be said that that the Court has been provided with insufficient information regarding the present context in which the questions arise. Thus, the Court is duty bound in the circumstances to provide its answers.[57]

7. The Privy Council's influence on the division of powers

When the Supreme Court became the court of final resort for Canada in 1949, it inherited an impressive legacy of constitutional jurisprudence from the Judicial Committee of the Privy Council. During the course of its reign as Canada's highest appellate court, the Judicial Committee rendered over 170 decisions in Canadian constitutional law cases. In a series of significant rulings,[58] the Judicial

---

[53] ibid [140]. The emphasis is that of the Chief Justice.
[54] ibid [124].
[55] *Quebec Secession Reference* (n 8) [26]. See also *Reference Re Canada Assistance Plan (BC)* [1991] 2 SCR 525, 545.
[56] *Quebec Secession Reference* (n 8) [27], [28].
[57] ibid [31].
[58] *Citizens Insurance Co v Parsons* [1881–82] 7 AC 96; *Russell v The Queen* [1881–82] 7 AC 829; *Hodge v The Queen* [1883–84] 9 AC 117; *Bank of Toronto v Lambe* [1887] 12 AC 575; *Liquidators of the Maritime Bank v Receiver General of New Brunswick* [1892] AC 437, above; *Tennant v Union Bank of Canada* [1894] AC 31; *AG Ontario v AG Canada* [1894] AC 189; *AG Ontario v AG Canada*

Committee, and particularly Lords Watson and Haldane, had at once expounded and transformed the Constitution of Canada. The federal powers over trade and commerce and the criminal law were narrowed (although the latter power was to wax and wane); provincial powers over property and civil rights were expanded. Perhaps most significantly, the general—or residuary—power of Parliament, under the opening words of section 91 of the Constitution Act 1867, 'to make Laws for the Peace, Order, and good Government of Canada,' was progressively narrowed to matters of 'national concern' and then, in Viscount Haldane's hands in *Board of Commerce* and *Snider*, restricted to temporary circumstances of exceptional urgency: 'cases arising out of some extraordinary peril to the national life of Canada,'[59] such as war, famine, or pestilence.

The changes wrought by Lords Watson and Haldane led Professor (and later, Senator) Eugene Forsey, a leading constitutional expert in Canada, to affix their Lordships with the sobriquet of the 'wicked Stepfathers of Confederation'. In the early 1930s, with the passing of Viscount Haldane, the Judicial Committee, under Lords Sankey and Atkin, in the *Proprietary Articles Trade Association* case[60] and in the *Aeronautics*[61] and *Radio References*,[62] upheld Parliament's powers to legislate more broadly in the field of criminal law, and to regulate the new fields of aeronautics and radio communications, respectively. However, in the middle of the decade, when the Government of Canada was struggling to cope with the grave social and economic crises provoked by the severity of the Great Depression and its effects on employment, incomes and prices, in a series of decisions the Judicial Committee struck down most of Parliament's 'New Deal' legislation.[63] These decisions, which Professor Monahan describes as 'formalistic and dysfunctional',[64] provoked serious criticism at the time from constitutional scholar FR Scott:

[T]he Dominion residuary clause, while kept alive verbally by courtesy, is virtually non-existent, and the residue of power throughout Canada, in matters of national as well as of local importance, even in the midst of an emergency as great as that which befell us between 1925 and 1935, belongs exclusively to the provinces. For it may be contended

---

('*Local Prohibitions*' case) [1896] AC 348; *Union Colliery v Bryden* [1899] AC 443; *Re Initiative and Referendum Act* [1919] AC 935, above; *In re the Board of Commerce Act 1919 and the Combines and Fair Prices Act 1919* [1922] 1 AC 191; *Fort Frances Pulp and Power Co v Manitoba Free Press* [1923] AC 695; *Toronto Electric Commissioners v Snider* [1925] AC 396.

[59] *Snider* (n 58) 412.
[60] *Proprietary Articles Trade Assoc v AG Canada* [1931] AC 310.
[61] *In re the Regulation and Control of Aeronautics in Canada* [1932] AC 54.
[62] *In re Regulation and Control of Radio Communications in Canada* [1932] AC 304.
[63] *AG Canada v AG Ontario* [1937] AC 326 (the '*Labour Conventions*' case); *AG Canada v AG Ontario* [1937] AC 355 ('*Unemployment Insurance Reference*'); *AG British Columbia v AG Canada* [1937] AC 377 ('*Natural Products Marketing Act Reference*'); *AG British Columbia v AG Canada* [1937] AC 368 (*Criminal Code*); *AG British Columbia v AG Canada* [1937] AC 391 (*Farmers Creditors Arrangements Act*, upheld); *AG Ontario v AG Canada* [1937] AC 405 (*Dominion Trade and Industry Commission Act*, upheld).
[64] PJ Monahan *Constitutional Law* (2nd edn Irwin Law Concord 1997) 245.

that an emergency power which the world economic crisis does not justify using is no power at all... None but foreign judges ignorant of the Canadian environment and none too versed in constitutional law could have caused this constitutional revolution... the net result of the Canadian constitutional developments, culminating in the decisions under review, has been very greatly to weaken the central government, and to postpone indefinitely any further attempts at government regulation of the economy in the interests of stability and social security.[65]

Professor Scott reserved his sternest criticism for the finding of the Judicial Committee in the *Labour Conventions* case, and its implications for Canada's ability to implement its international treaty obligations effectively. Essentially, the Privy Council held that although the treaty-making power was vested in the Government of Canada, the implementation of treaties by legislation would be divided in accordance with the respective jurisdictions of Parliament and the provincial legislatures. Thus, Parliament could not enact legislation limiting hours of work and imposing minimum wages in order to give effect to draft conventions adopted by the International Labour Organization (ILO), because the impugned federal statutes affected property and civil rights, a provincial matter. Lord Atkin summed up his judgment with what Professor Scott sardonically termed 'the helpful reminder'[66] that, 'It must not be thought that the result of this decision is that Canada is incompetent to legislate in performance of treaty obligations. In totality of legislative powers, Dominion and Provincial together, she is fully equipped.'[67]

In his concluding words, his Lordship could not resist another 'unhappy metaphor' (as Professor JR Mallory put it[68]), that seemed to put aside entirely the double-aspect theory first advanced in *Hodge v The Queen*:

But the legislative powers remain distributed, and if in the exercise of her new functions derived from her new international status Canada incurs obligations they must, so far as legislation be concerned, when they deal with Provincial classes of subjects, be dealt with by the totality of powers, in other words by co-operation between the Dominion and the Provinces. *While the ship of state now sails on larger ventures and into foreign waters she still retains the water-tight compartments which are an essential part of her original structure.*[69]

Professor Scott was moved to the following statement of concern raised by this decision:

As party to a British Empire treaty Canada is therefore a unitary state; as an independent country she is composed of nine[70] (or is it ten?) sovereign states whose assent is required

---

[65] FR Scott 'The Privy Council and Mr Bennett's "New Deal" Legislation' and 'The Consequences of the Privy Council Decisions' (1937), articles combined and reprinted in FR Scott *Essays on the Constitution* (University of Toronto Press 1977) 90 onwards, 98–101.

[66] ibid 99.

[67] *Labour Conventions* (n 63) 353–354.

[68] JR Mallory *The Structure of Canadian Government* (Macmillan Toronto 1971) 346.

[69] *Labour Conventions* (n 63) 354; (emphasis added).

[70] There were, of course, only nine provinces when FR Scott was writing in 1937; Newfoundland became the 10th province in 1949.

before the obligations of certain treaties can be fully performed. The logical political consequence of this is that plenipotentiaries from the provinces will have to attend at the negotiating of treaties of this third category in order to insure their adoption and enforcement; which is equivalent to saying that Canada is practically incompetent to make any such treaties at all. Moreover, no one but the courts will be able to tell with certainty to what category a particular treaty belongs, and this, of course, cannot be decided until after the treaty is made. The only certainty lies in reverting to colonial status and never venturing beyond the imperial orbit; the fruits of independence are disunity and decentralization. The law of the Canadian constitution has now degenerated into this welter of confusion.[71]

While Scott may have, in retrospect, overstated his criticism,[72] Professor Peter Hogg agrees that the *Labour Conventions* decision was 'poorly reasoned' and that it produced an 'unduly narrow and literal interpretation' as well as an 'unquestionably anomalous' and 'highly inconvenient result'. However, he adds that 'it is much more difficult to be confident that the result is undesirable as a matter of policy within a federation such as Canada':

In defence of the constitutional rule laid down by the *Labour Conventions* case, it may be said that Canada's difficulty in making and fulfilling treaty obligations is one of the prices of federalism. Provincial autonomy would be seriously threatened if every treaty made by the federal government led to an automatic increase in the legislative authority of Parliament. One does not need to suppose that the federal government would act in bad faith, or would enter into colourable treaties simply to increase federal legislative power, to be disturbed at this prospect. The proliferation of multinational treaties concerning health, education, welfare, labour relations, human rights and other matters within provincial jurisdiction which have been sponsored by international organizations of which Canada is a member is sufficient reason for caution.[73]

Of the many other cases adjudicated by the Judicial Committee, one more stands out for special mention. For although it was decided near the end of the Privy Council's tenure as Canada's highest court, it dealt with constitutional issues canvassed in one of the Judicial Committee's first cases, and revisited periodically ever since. Moreover, as Professor Mallory observed, the case 'astonished constitutional lawyers by apparently abandoning completely the narrow and restrictive interpretation of federal power which had stemmed from the labours of Lord Watson and Lord Haldane'.[74]

The case was that of *Attorney-General for Ontario v Canada Temperance Federation*.[75] It arose by way of a provincial reference as to the validity of the Canada Temperance Act enacted by Parliament in 1878. The Act was upheld by a majority of the Ontario Supreme Court. The Attorney-General for Ontario,

---

[71] *Essays on the Constitution* (n 65) 94.

[72] In a subsequent piece he was no less dubious of the result: 'So long as Canada clung to the Imperial apron strings, her Parliament was all powerful in legislating on Empire treaties, and no doctrine of "watertight compartments" existed; once she became a nation in her own right, impotence descended': FR Scott, 'Labour Conventions Case' (1956) 34 *Canadian Bar Review* 114, 115.

[73] PW Hogg *Constitutional Law of Canada* (4th edn Carswell Scarborough 1997) 300–303.

[74] *The Structure of Canadian Government* (n 68) 348.   [75] [1946] AC 193.

supported by Alberta and New Brunswick, appealed to the Privy Council. The Attorney-General for Canada, the 'Canada Temperance Federation' and others supported the constitutionality of the legislation. The real object sought in the appeal was to reverse the decision of *Russell v The Queen*,[76] decided some 65 years earlier. The Judicial Committee had upheld the validity of the Canada Temperance Act in that case on the basis of the 'general' or 'residuary' power over peace, order and good government in the opening words of section 91 of the Constitution Act 1867. Since then, the ratio in *Russell* had been restricted, firstly by Lord Watson's 'national concern' test, and later, explained away entirely by Viscount Haldane's impending national 'disaster' rationale, as the Judicial Committee moved largely towards an interpretation of the POGG (peace, order, and good government) power founded exclusively on the emergency theory.

Viscount Simon delivered the judgment in the *Canada Temperance Federation* case. He carefully reviewed not only *Russell* but also Lord Watson's analysis in the subsequent *Local Prohibition* case and particularly, Viscount Haldane's characterization in *Snider*, in which Lord Haldane had affirmed that *Russell* could 'only be supported today... on the assumption... that the evil of intemperance at that time amounted in Canada to one so great and so general that at least for the period it was a menace to the national life of Canada so serious and so pressing that the National Parliament was called on to intervene to protect the nation from disaster'. Viscount Simon proceeded to debunk the basis for this elaborate hypothesis:

The first observation which their Lordships would make on this explanation of *Russell's* case is that the British North America Act nowhere gives power to the Dominion Parliament to legislate in matters which are properly to be regarded as exclusively within the competence of the provincial legislatures merely because of the existence of an emergency. Secondly, they can find nothing in the judgment of the Board in 1882 which suggests that it proceeded on the ground of emergency; there was certainly no evidence before the Board that one existed. The Act of 1878 was a permanent, not a temporary, Act, and no objection to it was raised to it on that account.[77]

Viscount Simon then went on to set out 'the true test' for the application of the peace, order, and good government clause (whilst invoking as illustrations the *Aeronautics* and *Radio References*, which had been distinguished and set aside by Lord Atkin in the *Labour Conventions* case):

In their Lordships' opinion *the true test* must be found *in the real subject matter of the legislation: if* it is such that *it goes beyond local or provincial concern or interests and must from its inherent nature be the concern of the Dominion as a whole* (as, for example, in the *Aeronautics* case and the *Radio* case), then it will fall within the competence of the Dominion Parliament as a matter affecting the peace, order and good government of Canada, though it may in another aspect touch on matters specifically reserved to the provincial legislatures. War and pestilence, no doubt, are instances; so, too, may be the drink or drug traffic, or the carrying of arms. In *Russell v The Queen*, Sir Montague Smith

---

[76] [1881–82] 7 AC 829.   [77] *AG Ontario v Canada Temperance Federation* (n 75) 205.

gave as an instance of valid Dominion legislation a law which prohibited or restricted the sale or exposure of cattle having a contagious disease. *Nor is the validity of the legislation, when due to its inherent nature, affected because there may still be room for enactments by a provincial legislature dealing with an aspect of the same subject* in so far as it specially affects that province.[78]

Viscount Simon noted that nowhere in *Snider* was *Russell* said to be wrongly decided. All *Snider* did was advance an explanation of the *Russell* decision; an explanation 'too narrowly expressed'.[79]

Viscount Simon advanced another reason why *Russell* should not be overruled: 'on constitutional questions it must be seldom indeed that the Board would depart from a previous decision which it may be assumed will have been acted upon both by governments and subjects'. The present decision had stood for over 60 years and 'must be regarded as firmly embedded in the constitutional law of Canada,' and 'impossible now to depart from it'.[80]

The *Canada Temperance Association* case did not put an end to the emergency branch of the POGG power. It was relied upon by Lord Wright in a subsequent case in 1946, *Co-operative Committee on Japanese Canadians v Attorney-General for Canada*.[81] Moreover, in the later *Margarine Reference (Canadian Federation of Agriculture v Attorney-General for Quebec* [1951] AC 179), Lord Morton set out everything that was said by Viscount Simon in the *Canada Temperance* case on the 'true test' of national concern;—only to conclude that '[t]his passage must, however, be considered with the words used by Lord Atkin when delivering the judgment of the Board in the *Labour Conventions* case'.[82]

Nonetheless, the *Canada Temperance Association* case did breathe new life into the 'national concern' branch of the peace, order and good government clause; a branch that was subsequently relied upon by the Supreme Court of Canada in several cases, including *Johannesson*,[83] *Munro*,[84] *Crown Zellerbach*,[85] and *Ontario Hydro*.[86] At the same time, the emergency branch continued to exist as the appropriate test in cases of exceptional circumstance, where sweeping measures might temporarily override the normal division of powers. Professor Hogg demonstrates that most of the cases can be explained by this contemporary analysis, which owes much to the work of Professor WR Lederman and is consistent with the need to preserve the integrity of the division of powers. Professor Hogg has put it very well:

[78] ibid 205–206 (emphasis added).   [79] ibid 206.   [80] ibid 207–208.
[81] [1947] AC 87.
[82] [1951] AC 179, 197.
[83] *Johannesson v West St Paul* [1952] 1 SCR 292 (upholding federal power over aeronautics on basis of national concern test).
[84] *Munro v National Capital Commission* [1966] SCR 663 (federal legislation could validly designate area around Ottawa as the National Capital Region and provide for Commission to regulate land use).
[85] *R v Crown Zellerbach* [1988] 1 SCR 401 (marine pollution a matter of national concern).
[86] *Ontario Hydro v Ontario* [1993] 3 SCR 327 (Parliament had regulatory jurisdiction over nuclear power).

The test [in the *Canada Temperance* case] is whether the matter of the legislation 'goes beyond local or provincial concern or interests and must from its inherent nature be the concern of the Dominion as a whole'. If this test is satisfied, then the matter comes within the p.o.g.g. power in its national concern branch. Of course, ... the emergency cases are still good law in the sense that an emergency will also provide a basis for legislation under the p.o.g.g. power. But the *Canada Temperance* case established that there was a national concern branch of p.o.g.g. as well as an emergency branch ...

One point has been settled by the course of decision since the abolition of appeals to the Privy Council. It is clear that the Privy Council was wrong in asserting that only an emergency would justify the invocation of the p.o.g.g. power. *Johannesson, Munro, Crown Zellerbach* and *Ontario Hydro* establish that the emergency test cannot be the exclusive touchstone ... The problem then is to draw the line between these two different classes ...

W.R. Lederman ... pointed out that such subject matters as aviation, the national capital region and atomic energy each has 'a natural unity that is quite limited and specific in its extent'. He contrasted these 'limited and specific' subject matters with such sweeping categories as environmental pollution, culture or language. If the sweeping pervasive categories were enfranchised as federal subject matters simply on the basis of national concern, then there would be no limit to the reach of federal legislative powers and the existing distribution of legislative powers would become unstable. Accordingly, in normal times such categories had to be broken down into more specific and meaningful categories for the purpose of allocating legislative jurisdiction; on this basis some parts of the sweeping categories would be within federal jurisdiction and other parts would be within provincial jurisdiction. Only in an emergency could the federal Parliament assume the plenary power over the whole of a sweeping category.[87]

Professor Lederman was able to test his theory as one of counsel in the *Anti-Inflation Reference*,[88] wherein he won over Beetz J, whose dissenting opinion had, on this point, the support of a majority of the bench. This was also the approach that was adopted by Le Dain J for the majority of the Supreme Court in *Crown Zellerbach*. It has ensured that the peace, order and good government power cannot be invoked lightly to disturb the prevailing balance in the division of federal and provincial powers.

8. SOME LATER ASSESSMENTS OF THE JURISPRUDENCE OF THE PRIVY COUNCIL

In 1951, MacDonald J of the Supreme Court of Nova Scotia summed up the opinion of many contemporary Canadian jurists[89] when he described the legacy of the Judicial Committee of the Privy Council in the following stark terms:

[87] *Constitutional Law of Canada* (n 73) 452, 470–471. (Professor Lederman's views are expressed in his article, 'Unity and Diversity in Canadian Federalism' (1975) 53 *Canadian Bar Review* 597.)
[88] *Reference re Anti-Inflation Act* [1976] 2 SCR 373.
[89] See, for example, the views of more than 30 commentators cited by FR Scott in 'Centralization and Decentralization in Canadian Federalism' (1951) 29 *Canadian Bar Review* 1095, 1108–1109, n 44, each authority having 'emphasized the degree to which the courts have departed from the original intention of the constitution'.

early in its career it formed a very definite view of the nature of the Federal Union effected by the [British North America] Act and has persistently sought to make the Act square with that view. That view was that Canada is a true federation resulting from a 'compact' between sovereign bodies the legislatures of which were intended to possess equal status and autonomy within their prescribed limits; and that it was the function of the courts to maintain this compact and make these legislative rivals hew to the line of division; and in particular to preserve provincial legislative 'autonomy' from encroachment.[90]

He continued:

The fact is that the B.N.A. Act does not embody a true federal system but a highly specialized kind of federalism; that both in executive and legislative terms it is deliberately weighted in favour of the central Government and Parliament; and in particular it reveals a scheme of legislative jurisdiction in which Parliament was to play the dominant part.

The truth is, also, that their Lordships never understood the kind of federalism intended to be given, and in terms given; and in revolt against contentions contrary to their own ideas, and against the pro-Dominion bias which underlay the distribution of powers, proceeded to establish a balance of jurisdiction more conformable to those ideas . . . In the result, as our most competent writers have agreed, it is incontestable that our Constitution, as it now exists in a text encrusted with decisions, is not what we sought or what the Imperial Parliament provided for us. It is history that, contrary to Lord Carnarvon's hopes, the Privy Council has not been a protector of minorities so much as it has been a protector of the provinces, and in that endeavour has distorted the whole scheme of legislative powers in the process of judicial fabrication of a constitution alien to that desired and enacted . . .

Misunderstanding of the nature of Canadian federalism and obsession with the idea of preserving provincial autonomy from encroachment led to the initial misinterpretation of the function of the various terms in sections 91 and 92, and to the debasement of Dominion heads and to the enlargement of provincial heads; and thereby to the fundamental result, which divorced jurisdiction from the practical ability to deal with grave problems in the form in which they presented themselves.[91]

In 'The Meaning of Provincial Autonomy',[92] Professor Louis-Philippe Pigeon, who would later be appointed to the Supreme Court of Canada, replied obliquely to this assessment from a very different perspective. Agreeing that the Judicial Committee of the Privy Council had 'fairly consistently adopted the autonomist conception of federation' in its rulings, he contended that '[a]ll of the arguments advanced against these decisions are based either on the "Peace, Order and good Government" clause or on the so-called "historical construction" of the Act'. Dealing with the POGG question, Professor Pigeon wrote:

In support of the first argument it is contended that the courts have failed to give full effect to the opening words of section 91 and that the authority thus conferred on the federal

---

[90] VC MacDonald 'The Privy Council and the Canadian Constitution' (1951) 29 *Canadian Bar Review* 1021, 1030.
[91] ibid 1031–1035.
[92] (1951) 29 *Canadian Bar Review* 1026.

Parliament should be broadly construed.[93] But it is significant that seldom do those who advance this contention quote the complete sentence. They speak of the importance of the grant of legislative authority for the 'Peace, Order and good Government of Canada'. They point out that such expressions were traditionally used to grant legislative authority; but they pay slight attention to the fact that these pregnant words are immediately followed by the all-important restriction: 'in relation to all Matters not coming within the classes of Subjects by this Act assigned exclusively to the Legislatures of the Provinces'. If due attention is paid to these words, it becomes impossible to construe the grant of residuary power otherwise than as saving provincial authority instead of overriding it.[94]

As for the 'pretended inquiry into the intentions of the framers of the Canadian constitution,' Pigeon countered that the Constitution Act 1867 was not the intention of one man, which might be gathered from extrinsic evidence with some certainty, but rather 'the expression of a compromise between many men holding different and opposed viewpoints. When agreement was reached on a text, are we justified in assuming that agreement was also reached on intentions?'[95] Waxing philosophically at some length on the nature of law, morality, and freedom, Pigeon explained what he considered to be the true meaning of provincial autonomy:

The true concept of autonomy is thus like the true concept of freedom. It implies limitations, but it also implies free movement within the area bounded by the limitations: one no longer enjoys freedom when free to move in one direction only. It should therefore be realized that autonomy means the right of being different, of acting differently. This is what freedom means for the individual; it is also what it must mean for provincial legislatures and governments... Just as freedom means for the individual the right of choosing his own objective so long as it is not illegal, autonomy means for a province the privilege of defining its own policies.

It must be conceded that autonomy thus understood allows the provinces on occasion to work at cross purposes. But it would be a grave mistake to assume that this is wrong in itself, or that it is necessarily against the national interest.[96]

For Pigeon, tests of constitutional validity invariably involve questions of judgment and degree, and broad principles rather than technical construction:

In my view it is wrong to read the generally accepted definition of legislative autonomy ('that the Dominion to a great extent, but within certain fixed limits, may be mistress in her own house, as the Provinces to a great extent, but within certain fixed limits, are mistresses in theirs') as implying limits defined with mathematical accuracy. To do so is to conceive political science as an exact science ascertainable in the same manner as the natural sciences.[97]

---

[93] Professor Pigeon (p 1128) cited an article by Professor Bora Laskin, '"Peace, Order and Good Government" Re-examined' (1947) 25 *Canadian Bar Review* 1054, as an example of this call for a broader construction of the federal power. Professor Laskin would also become a Justice of the Supreme Court of Canada (and ultimately, its Chief Justice).

[94] ibid 1128.   [95] ibid.   [96] ibid 1132–1133.

[97] ibid 1131. (The passage quoted parenthetically is from the '*Persons*' case: *Edwards v Canada* [1930] AC 124, 136.)

Professor Pigeon concluded his article by stating that the 'great volume of criticism' heaped upon the Privy Council (and the Supreme Court at that time) 'on the ground that their decisions rest on a narrow and technical construction of the B.N.A. Act' was 'ill-founded':

The decisions as a whole proceed from a much higher view... [T]hey recognize the implicit fluidity of any constitution by allowing for emergencies and by resting distinctions on questions of degree. At the same time they firmly uphold the fundamental principle of provincial autonomy: they staunchly refuse to let our federal constitution be changed gradually, by one device or another, to a legislative union. In doing so they are preserving the essential condition of the Canadian confederation.[98]

In the 100th anniversary year of Confederation, Professor GP Browne published a major reassessment of the work of the Judicial Committee. Browne concluded that 'whatever its practical defects, the Judicial Committee's interpretative scheme for the British North America Act is both fairly certain and generally congruous. This does not seem either a minor consideration or a mean achievement'.[99] To those who argued that the Judicial Committee had formulated a principle of balancing powers between sovereign legislatures, a principle not expressed in the Constitution Act 1867, Browne replied that 'it is just as likely that the "federal principle" was not imposed on the British North America Act, but derived from it'.[100] For Browne, the interpretation of sections 91 and 92 was generally consistent with the logic of federalism underlying the Act.

Senator Eugene Forsey, writing in 1970, provided a more balanced (if still acerbic) assessment than he had in earlier years:

The Judicial Committee of the Privy Council, the Stepfathers of Confederation, turned a good deal of the Fathers' work upside down, and, in effect, handed most of labour legislation and social security, and much of the regulation of trade and commerce, to the provinces. But even after the havoc they wrought, a good deal of the original division of powers remains. And a good many new things—interprovincial and international highway motor traffic, interprovincial and international telephone lines, radio, television, air transport—have in fact gone to the Dominion. Even the not-so-new grain trade, which a court decision fatuously assigned to the provinces, was rescued by the Fathers' far-sighted provision in section 92, head 10, paragraph (c) of the BNA Act, by which the Dominion Parliament can assert exclusive jurisdiction over any local 'work' simply by declaring it to be 'for the general advantage of Canada or of two or more of the provinces'.[101]

---

[98] ibid 1135. For a lucid analysis of the role of the Privy Council's jurisprudence in preserving Quebec's ability to protect its collective identity, see J Beetz 'Les Attitudes changeantes du Québec à l'endroit de la Constitution de 1867' in PA Crepeau and CB Macpherson (eds) *The Future of Canadian Federalism / L'avenir du fédéralisme canadien* (University of Toronto Press Toronto and Les presses de l'Université de Montréal Montreal 1965). Professor Beetz, like Professor Pigeon, went on to become a distinguished judge on the Supreme Court of Canada.

[99] GP Browne *The Judicial Committee and the British North America Act* (University of Toronto Press Toronto 1967) 170.

[100] ibid 32.

[101] EA Forsey 'Our Present Discontents' (1970), published as essay no 24 in EA Forsey *Freedom and Order* (McLellan and Stewart Toronto 1974) 310.

Professor JR Mallory pointed out that 'most of the criticism by historians and legal writers of the judicial interpretation of the constitution was written from the perspective of the 1920s and '30s, when the important cases of the period before 1914 had become awkward precedents in determining the constitutional arrangements of an age when the problems of government were much different'.[102]

Professor Hogg has captured the prevailing mood of most of the Canadian legal community towards the Judicial Committee's jurisprudence:

The denials of federal power in the 'p.o.g.g. cases' of the Haldane period and the new deal period had profound effects on the nature of the Canadian federation... The emergency period of the Privy Council thus wrote an exceedingly important chapter of Canadian constitutional law. While... the pendulum has subsequently tended to swing back to a position which allows larger use of the principal federal powers, it is likely that the broad lines of constitutional authority which were established by the Privy Council will continue to be controlling, and the expectations and patterns of legislative activity which they generated will certainly not be quickly revised. Recognizing this, constitutional lawyers have tended to lose interest in the once-heated debate over whether or not the Privy Council 'misread' the Constitution in so limiting federal power. One can debate a fait accompli for only so long.[103]

The Judicial Committee's influence on the interpretation of the division of powers under the Canadian Constitution is felt to this day. The Supreme Court of Canada has enlarged the scope of the trade and commerce power and the criminal law power, and has, as we have seen, resorted to the 'national concern' branch to uphold certain statutes under the residuary power of 'peace, order and good government'. On the whole, however, the judges of the Supreme Court have striven to maintain an appropriate balance between the powers necessary for a modern state and national (and international) economy, and the need to protect the distinctiveness and autonomy of the provinces and regions of Canada, in keeping with its status as a federation.

True, one can continue to cavil over whether, in specific instances of the application of the principle to the division of legislative powers under the Constitution, the Privy Council was too restrictive in its interpretation of the residuary power and the enumerated heads of federal jurisdiction, just as one can now attempt to claim (as some have) that the Supreme Court has been more than generous in construing, in specific instances, the scope of certain of

---

[102] *The Structure of Canadian Government* (n 68) 343: Mallory saw great benefits in the role played by the Judicial Committee as the head of a unified appellate system for the whole British Empire (336), but remained critical of the structural weaknesses he saw in the Committee (337–338). 'It is apparent from a study of the case law on Canadian federalism that few if any of the distinguished judges understood the constitutional difficulties of federalism, or even what federalism as a form of government is. Their minds were wholly patterned in the legal system of a unitary state in which Parliament (one Parliament, not eleven) is sovereign and free to modify the law at will if the courts make a mess of it... Those few who professed to understand it, like Lord Watson and Lord Haldane, acted as if they had never read the British North America Act through'.

[103] *Constitutional Law of Canada* (n 73) 464.

those powers. Professor Monahan has stated, 'The reality is that under the existing Canadian constitution there are very few social, political, or economic levers that are denied to the provinces. While the Supreme Court has in recent years broadened the authority of Parliament, it has continued to favour an expansive interpretation of provincial powers'.[104]

9. Conclusion

The Canadian experience in the adjudication of divisions of powers issues is likely to prove instructive in relation to the UK's devolution experiment. The Constitution of Canada, modelled as it is on those of Great Britain and the USA, provides an interesting vantage point for comparative law in this area. Still more pertinent is the fact that much of the development of the principle of federalism in Canada's constitutional jurisprudence has resulted from the work of the Judicial Committee of the Privy Council. Professor Vernon Bogdanor has noted that while, constitutionally, 'devolution is a mere delegation of power from a superior political body to an inferior', politically, it is a different matter, '[f]or power devolved, far from being power retained, is power transferred'. He contends that the relationship between Westminster and Edinburgh, for example, 'will be quasi-federal in normal times and unitary only in crisis times'. He posits that over time, as the adjudication of issues in relation to the transferred powers progresses, 'both Westminster and the Scottish Parliament will have come to depend upon the Judicial Committee for the protection of their sphere of action, a condition characteristic of federal systems of government'.[105]

Whether the adjudication of the devolution of powers effected under the UK legislation shall pursue a path similar to that followed in regard to the division of powers under the Constitution of Canada remains to be seen. That the Canadian experience will be a useful reference point is, however, undeniable.

---

[104] *Constitutional Law* (1st edn 1997) 366, and similarly, 2nd edn (n 64) 484.
[105] V Bogdanor *Devolution in the United Kingdom* (Oxford University Press Oxford 2001) 287, 291 and 293. For early analysis of the Judicial Committee's first decision on the validity of an Act of the Scottish Parliament, see BK Winetrobe 'Scottish Devolved Legislation and the Courts' [2002] *Public Law* 31.

7

Adjudicating in Divisions of Powers: the Experience of the Spanish Constitutional Court

IGNACIO BORRAJO INIESTA*

1. INTRODUCTION

This essay shares some thoughts and experiences on devolution of powers or, as we tend to say in Spain, decentralization and political pluralism. The UK and the Kingdom of Spain have some common memory and history, both of fighting each other and of working together (now as members of the EU and the Council of Europe). We are neighbours—with 'sea in the middle'—and live on the periphery of Europe. We also share some odd institutional arrangements, including monarchies and now, it seems, devolution of powers.

The UK has arguably been more successful in government institution building than has Spain. More than 10 constitutions have been adopted by Spain since 1812 (in Cadiz, surrounded by Napoleonic forces) or since 1808 (if you start counting from the Bonaparte charter of that year), and has endured more than four civil wars since then. The last one, fought in 1936–1939 as a forerunner of the Second World War, did not really end until 1977. The elections held in June that year opened a new era for Spain. The Spanish constitution adopted in December 1978 established a government structure we hope will last for many generations to come. In life, failures teach us how to behave. If that is true, Spain has some lessons to offer.

This essay begins by examining the Spanish constitution and the manner in which the 'state of autonomies' has been created since 1979. Very significant political and law-making powers have been devolved to the 17 'autonomous communities' (*comunidades autónomas*) that now exist throughout the whole of Spain. The essay then moves on to consider the role of the constitutional court (*Tribunal constitucional*) in adjudicating disputes over the division of powers between general institutions and the autonomous communities.

* Senior Staff Attorney, Spanish Constitutional Court; Professor of Law, Public University of Navarra; lecturer at University Institute Ortega y Gasset, Madrid. I am very grateful to several colleagues who commented on the draft, and especially to Andrew Le Sueur who made this readable in academic English.

2. THE SPANISH CONSTITUTION

The 1978 text of the Spanish constitution was adopted in a spirit of 'consensus'. *Consenso* among political forces, as well as socio-economic agents, religious institutions and different cultural elites was the key objective of more than 16 months of negotiation. The drafters wanted the constitution to last so it was imperative that everybody should accept it. In the end, almost all political forces did, although nobody felt very happy with the text and it was decried as ambiguous and complex. A small minority of Basque nationalists refused to accept the 1978 constitution, claiming as of right a Basque state that never existed, formed by territories from neighbouring provinces in both Spain and France. They have been killing since then: first military and police personnel; later, when the 1981 coup d'état failed, civil servants and civilians; lately, political leaders, judges, and journalists. Leaving aside that small minority (several hundred people supported by less than 10% of two million Basques)[1] the remaining 41 million Spaniards strongly support the constitution.

The Spanish constitutional compact has several essential elements. First, political pluralism is enshrined in the constitution as a fundamental principle along with freedom, justice and equality (article 1.1 CE).[2] The acceptance of pluralism is a key element in the whole constitutional pact and has deep significance for territorial arrangements, as we shall see.

Secondly, there is a strong attachment to the rule of law as legally binding commitments, starting with the constitution itself. The constitution is a legal document with the full force of law, superior to any legislative text past or future, and to be protected by all citizens and public authorities alike, especially by an independent judiciary and a specialized court of law—the constitutional court. Human dignity and respect for the law are the foundations of political order and social peace (article 10.1 CE, underlined by Spanish history). Any constitutional provision can be repealed or amended, but only through legal procedures and qualified majorities (articles 167 and 168 CE).

Thirdly, freedom of religion and thought is combined with a mandate for the government to co-operate with religious communities, the Catholic Church being specifically mentioned along with any other denomination accepted in Spanish society (article 16 CE). The more contested debate in this field, educa-

---

[1] Supporters of independence, even if violence is required, are less than the people forced to leave the Basque country in the last 20 years: estimates of more than 200,000 Basques forced to exile (10% of the population) have been given by no less that the political science professor head of the Euskobarometer, Francisco José Llera Ramo: 'La sangría etnicista' *El País*, 7 November 2002, 13. Available at <perso.wanadoo.es/laicos/2002/752S-etnicista.htm> (6 August 2003).

[2] An English translation of the Spanish constitution (CE) may be found at: <www.oefre.unibe.ch/law/icl/sp00000_.html> (6 August 2003) or at <www.spainemb.org/information/constitucioninn.htm> (6 August 2003); historical texts may be found at: <www.cervantesvirtual.com/portal/constituciones>(6 August 2003).

tion, ended up with a tie: a mixed system of public and private schools, both safeguarded by the constitution (article 27 CE).

Fourthly, there is freedom to work, to create and join labour unions and to strike, as well as to hold private property and to inherit, freedom of enterprise within a market economy, and authorization for government to nationalize resources and sections of the economy and to introduce planning in the general interest (articles 35 and 28 CE; also 33, 38, 128, and 131 CE).

Fifthly, there is political decentralization embodied in the so-called 'state of autonomies' (*estado de las autonomías*). This has proved to be extremely difficult to settle. Nationalist parties, especially strong in Catalonia and the Basque Country, but also in many other territories in Spain, were close to proposing the splitting up of the country: nothing less than accepting each of them as nations, subject to Castile imperialism in history, and free to exercise self-determination rights, would be acceptable. The leading opposition party, the Spanish Workers Socialist Party (PSOE, later in the majority 1982–1996) espoused a federalist agenda: Spain should become a federation, resembling the Austrian dynasty confederation of kingdoms in a modern political structure. The ruling Centrist coalition (UCD) would never accept the breakdown of the Spanish nation, but were willing to contemplate political formulae to accommodate diversity with different accents in its several groups. And the conservatives (AP, later the Popular Party, running the national government since 1996) would not even hear of any loosening of the national government, so laboriously built since the War of Succession (ended in 1714) and in the 19th century.

Eventually, a constitutional pact was reached in this difficult area, so full of feeling and perceptions of identity. It is embodied in article 2 of the constitution and worked out in title VIII (articles 137–158, plus many additional, transitional and repealing provisions). Article 2 CE sets the stage with baroque prose:

The Constitution is based on the indissoluble unity of the Spanish nation, the common and indivisible homeland of all Spaniards, and recognizes and guarantees the right to autonomy of the nationalities and regions which make it up and the solidarity among them all.

The long and complex title VIII, on the 'territorial organization of the state', sets down the rules according to which 'bordering provinces with common historical, cultural, and economic characteristics, insular territories, and provinces with a historical regional status may accede to self-government'. The new autonomous communities to be created could cover the whole Spanish territory, or just a part of it; they could also be very different: from self-governing administrative regional bodies to fully fledged political entities, endowed with a president, a legislative assembly and an executive (but no judicial power). By 1983, these initial doubts had been dispelled: all of Spain was divided into 17 autonomous communities. All of them exercise legislative authority and they are responsible for a growing number of public services.

3. Jurisdictional arrangements under the Spanish constitution

The constitution is a binding text, having the force of law. All courts and public servants, from the King downwards, only take office after a solemn oath or promise to uphold it. The courts are bound to apply it in any litigation or criminal case (articles 9.1, 53, 117 CE). The constitution stands above any legislation of the national parliament (*Cortes Generales*) or any decision adopted by any public authority, which are always bound to comply with the constitution, even in time of public emergency or war (articles 95, 164, and 116 CE).

This is a sharp departure from Spanish tradition, where all constitutional texts were deemed to be political documents with no direct legal effect. Only legislation passed by the national parliament or, as was often the case, by government would create rights and duties, to be enforced by the courts. As a matter of fact, some early decisions by the Spanish Supreme Court declared the 1978 constitution to be a political document, having no more than a non-binding 'programmatic effect' in litigation before the courts of law. Some of those judicial rulings were reversed by the constitutional court in judgments stressing the full legal effect of the constitution.[3]

The ordinary courts were entrusted with the duty to enforce the constitution, especially the fundamental rights and freedoms written into it (articles 53 and 117 CE).[4] Spain has had an independent and professional judiciary since late 19th century; the 1985 law in force today safeguards the judges from removal and provides for selection through objective competitive exams.[5] Authoritarian rule had been achieved, in different periods of the 20th century, through military courts, special judicial committees, administrative tribunals, and granting large powers on family law to Catholic Church courts, leaving ordinary courts to deal with private property and 'ordinary' crimes in a fairly independent atmosphere. The 1978 constitution was therefore careful to remove any possibility for the creation of 'special' courts, and to confine military courts within strict limits (articles 117 and 24 CE). Nevertheless, the drafters were intent on making sure that the new constitution would be given full judicial guarantee by a body of men with a clear understanding of the constitutional pacts embodied in the 1978 text and a clear commitment to the new democratic and decentralized system.

---

[3] STC *Yébenes Carrillo* (80/1982, 20 December) [1]; STC *Capitán Pitarch* (21/1981, 15 June) [17]; also STC *Caballero Villanueva* (204/1988, 7 November) [4]. 'STC' signifies a *sentencia* (judgment) of the *Tribunal constitucional*.

[4] On the relationship between the constitutional court and the ordinary courts, see below.

[5] The judiciary became independent and professional since late 19th century, when the 1870 'provisional' Act on Judicial Power (embodying the liberal tenets of the 1869 constitution) had been given full effect; the 1870 Act was in force until 1985. See F Tomás y Valiente *Manual de historia del Derecho español* (4th edn 1983) in *Obras completas* vol II (CEC Madrid 1997) 1369– and 1457–; J Sainz Guerra *La Administración de justicia en España (1810–1870)* (Eudema Madrid 1992); JM Romero Moreno *Proceso y derechos fundamentales en la España del siglo XIX* (CEC Madrid 1983); J-M Scholz (ed) *El tercer poder: hacia una comprensión histórica de la justicia contemporánea en España* (V Klostermann Frankfurt am Main 1992); JF Lasso Gaite (ed) *Crónica de la codificación española* (5 vols Ministerio de Justicia Madrid) (1970–1979).

Accordingly, a constitutional court (*Tribunal constitucional*) was created (articles 159–165 CE). The Supreme Court continues to be at the head of the ordinary courts: it is the highest judicial body 'except in matters concerning constitutional guarantees' (article 123 CE), where the constitutional court takes precedence.

The Spanish constitution follows the Kelsen model of a 'negative legislator'[6] with the addition of additional jurisdiction, notably: the protection of fundamental rights and freedoms, specifically guaranteed through an individual appeal procedure (*recurso de amparo*); and the preservation of the territorial distribution of powers between the central government and autonomous communities.

The role of the court to preserve the equilibrium between central and territorial authorities cannot be overestimated. The organic law[7] on the constitutional court (*Ley Orgánica del Tribunal Constitucional*) was hastily passed in October 1979, and the court itself quickly nominated and staffed by February 1980, so that it could be in operation when the new autonomous communities were established. (Acts for the Basque Country and Catalonia were passed in December 1979 and elections held in March 1980.) Some of the earliest more important judgments adopted by the constitutional court had to deal with the new system of decentralized powers. This is still the case, as can be glimpsed in the Court Reports and the media coverage of court rulings.

Now let us have a look into the basic features of the new Spanish decentralized system, the 'state of autonomous communities' or, more simply, the 'state of autonomies'. Later, we shall review some basic data on the court and its procedures when exercising its vital role as umpire of the 'autonomic state'.

4. The creation of the 'state of autonomies'

A. Constitutional pact

As we have seen, article 2 of the Spanish constitution embodies conflicting views on Spain: one nation, 'common and indivisible homeland of all Spaniards', which is redundantly declared to be based on 'indissoluble unity'; and also one state, formed of 'nationalities and regions' endowed with a right to autonomy or self-government. Spanish nationalists would accept a 'national government' and several 'regions' with 'regional governments'. Peripheral nationalists (mostly Catalonian, Basques, Galicians, Andalusians, Valencians, and Canarians) would only agree to a 'central state government' and 'national governments' in the

---

[6] See H Kelsen 'Judicial Review of Legislation: A Comparative Study of the Austrian and the American Constitution' (1942) 4 *The Journal of Politics* 183.

[7] Under art 81 CE, 'organic law' (in distinction to ordinary parliamentary legislation) is a type of legislation requiring, for its approval, modification or repeal, an absolute majority of the lower house (*Congreso de los diputados*) of the national parliament (*Cortes Generales*). Organic laws deal with matters such as fundamental rights and the organization of the major institutions of Spain.

diverse territories. This is the reason for this new term, 'autonomous community', as well as for the fact that the word 'state' is used with two different meanings, sometimes referring to the whole of the government structure (formed by three levels: general, autonomic, and local), and sometimes the national authorities only. The constitutional court has acknowledged this 'amphibology'.[8]

The details of this convoluted pact are set out in the complex title VIII of the Spanish constitution. It encompasses 22 articles (articles 137–158), some of them several pages long.[9] Title VIII is further developed by a complex list of additional, transitional and repealing provisions, some of them of deep symbolic significance, and most of them of the greatest political impact. It is important to notice that no direct substantive decisions were adopted in the constitutional text itself. Title VIII provided *procedures* to create autonomous communities, and provides a general framework for a new state, which was federal in all but name.[10] But in 1978, everything was left to the future.

Title VIII allows Spain one autonomy or three, or a few, or all, or none, according to the will expressed by the people or the representatives of a given territory; and allows that autonomy to be wide or restricted, and that different communities should have the same or different degrees of self-government, and that they organize themselves homogeneously or heterogeneously; it also allows for the mistakes made while in the process to be amended.[11]

The key feature for this constitutional pact was the deferral of all substantial decisions to the 'statutes of autonomy' (*estatutos de autonomía*), to be drafted and proposed by each Spanish 'territory' (be it nationality or region), and passed by the national parliament (*Cortes Generales*) with an absolute majority in the lower house. It was for each of the *estatutos de autonomía* to: define the boundaries of the new autonomous community (based on the 50 provinces [*provincias*] created in 1833); to establish the institutions to rule the autonomous community; and to define the extent of the legislative (if any) and executive powers vested in the self-governing institutions (articles 147 and 149.3 CE).

Before we go into more detail, it is important not to overlook that the 1978 constitution adopted some significant provisions besides the creation of autonomous communities. It declared local government (*municipios*) not only democratic in their organization, but also autonomous to manage their own public interests (articles 137 and 142 CE). This self-government principle is effective

---

[8] STC *diputaciones catalanas* (32/1981, 28 July) [5].

[9] The most noticeable art 149, listing the general clauses to divide power in para 3, plus a long list of competences reserved in the hands of the state (para 1), and concurrent authority on cultural affairs (para 2).

[10] Federalism is taboo in Spain as it recalls the First Republic (1873), which did attempt to create a federation and ended in civil war.

[11] Jaime García Añoveros, public finance professor and Economics Minister with the UCD government in 1977–1982; quoted by L Moreno *The Federalization of Spain* (Frank Cass London 2001) 61, with some translation nuances introduced.

in the face of the state authorities, but also in the face of the new autonomous communities.[12]

The constitution also provided legal mechanisms to adhere to the then European Communities. Article 93 CE allows 'the conclusion of treaties by which powers derived from the constitution are vested in an international organization or institution'. This constitutional provision was soon to be used, when in 1985 Spain joined (what is now) the European Union. The decentralization of Spanish government cannot be understood without the European dimension: all Spaniards, even those who feel themselves only Catalonian or belonging to any other nationality, agree with the *regeneracionismo* opinion: 'Spain is the problem, Europe the solution'.[13]

B. The creation of the autonomous communities

The end result of the procedures provided in title VIII of the constitution is a new map of power in Spain. Seventeen autonomous communities were created between 1979 and 1983, covering all the territory of the country.[14] They differ wildly: there are large communities (like Andalucía), densely populated (Madrid) or sparsely (Castilla y León), heavily industrialized (Basque Country, Catalonia) and rural (Extremadura), large (Andalucía, Castillas) and small (Asturias, La Rioja). The so-called 'generalization' of the autonomies means there are three levels of government throughout Spain: local, 'autonomic', and 'general', 'national' or statewide. All the communities have a similar institutional structure, with a great variation in the names: there is a parliament, an executive body, and a president.

The parliaments of the autonomous communities are single chambers of between 40 and 110 members. They are elected every four years directly by the Spanish nationals with residence in the territory of each autonomous community. Every citizen has freedom to take up residence anywhere without legal restraints, and there are no minimum stay requirements to vote. Voting rights are governed by state legislation, autonomic legislation devoted to fixing the number of seats and some ancillary matters.

[12] Local governments do not belong to the autonomous communities, but have a dual dependence: from the respective autonomic body and from the national government: STC *transferencias locales* (84/1982) [4].

[13] On 'regeneracionism' see R Carr (ed) *Spain. A history* (Oxford University Press Oxford 2000) 224; JL Abellán *Historia crítica del pensamiento español* (Espasa Calpe Madrid 1988); J Costa *Reconstitución y Europeización de España* (Instituto de Estudios de Administración Local, Madrid 1900 edition of 1981). Quote from J Ortega y Gasset 'La pedagogía social como programa político' (1910) in *Obras completas* (n 5); see also 'De Europa meditatio quaedam'.

[14] The autonomous communities are: Basque Country; Catalonia; Galicia; Andalucía; Principality of Asturias; Cantabria; La Rioja; Region of Murcia; Community of Valencia; Aragon; Castile-La Mancha; The Canary Islands; Navarre; Extremadura; Community of the Balearic Islands; Community of Madrid; Community of Castile and Leon. That last of all the statutes creating a complete state of autonomies was, as history would have it, that of Castile and Leon (Organic Act 4/1983, 25 February). Ceuta and Melilla, Spanish cities in North Africa, were granted status of autonomous Cities in 1995.

The executive institutions of the autonomous communities are presided over by the president of the community, and formed by 'councillors'. The president of each autonomous community is a key figure. He is elected by the legislative assembly of the autonomous community and appointed by the King.[15] The president has a dual role: representative and executive. He represents the autonomous community and, at the same time, he offers 'the state's ordinary representation' in the community (article 152.1 CE). He is the head of the autonomous executive council, and generally has the authority to nominate and dismiss its members.

C. The statutes of autonomy

The legal framework of the 'state of autonomies' is formed by an assorted number of legal instruments. The main elements are the constitution itself and the statutes of autonomy (*estatutos de autonomía*) governing each of the 17 autonomous communities. Also of importance are other general state laws, governing the judiciary, the police, taxation and other financial arrangements, and fundamental rights (including voting and residence rights). The state can transfer some of its authority to some or all autonomous communities. Both the statutes of autonomy and these pieces of general legislation (enumerated in the constitution itself)[16] are adopted as basic laws (*ley orgánica*), so they need an absolute majority vote in the lower house of the Spanish parliament.

Together these instruments form the so-called 'block of constitutionality' (*bloque de la constitucionalidad*) because they are binding in relation to ordinary legislation. Legislation and regulations passed by the autonomous communities and by the general institutions of Spain must respect the rules and limits laid down by the constitution, the respective statutes of autonomy and those general laws on some key powers (judiciary, police), rights (residence, voting), and public budget arrangements (tax and other sources of public revenue, appropriations, accounting, and levelling financing).

The 'state of autonomies' has been legally created in two waves of 'deconstitutionalization' and 'reconstitutionalization'. First, different territories (nationalities or regions, as they choose to label themselves) drafted statutes of autonomy. Those drafts were presented to the Spanish parliament (*Cortes Generales*), which discussed them with representatives from the territories (elected local officials and the deputies and senators elected to national parliament from those autonomous communities). The *Cortes Generales* had the power to amend the proposed statute of autonomy, but with restrictions, in some cases

---

[15] The royal decree nominating the autonomous community president is countersigned by the Spanish prime minister. The Basque attempt to have the president of the autonomous parliament sign the nomination ended in constitutional court, STC *Lehendakari* (5/1987, 27 January).

[16] Arts 152.1 (judiciary); 104.2, 149.1.29 (police forces); 157.3 (taxation and treasury); 81, 139, and 149.1.1 (fundamental rights); 19 (freedom to cirulate); 23.1 (voting rights). On transfer legislation: art 150 CE.

very significant. Finally, the statutes of autonomy were made as organic laws. And, in most cases, they were ratified in a territorial referendum.

The statutes of autonomy have a dual aspect: they have the legal status of general state legislation (as *ley orgánica*) and, at the same time, they are at the head of the autonomous communities' legal orders. Article 147.1 CE specifies the statutes of autonomy 'shall be the basic institutional rule of each autonomous community and the state shall recognize them and protect them as an integral part of its legal system'. In general terms, they cannot be amended (nor indeed abrogated) unilaterally: an agreement has to be reached between the majority of both the Spanish parliament and the parliament of the autonomous community. In many cases, a territorial referendum is also required to amend statutes of autonomy, giving them a rigidity more extreme than that of the constitution itself. Only through a total revision of the constitution (which requires a general election to be called and a national referendum to be held) could all the statutes of autonomy be repealed or be subject to general amendments.

It is for each statute of autonomy to define the essential elements of each autonomous communities, including: the name of the community which best corresponds to its historical identity; the delimitation of its territory; the name, organization, and seat of its own autonomous institutions; and the powers assumed within the framework of the constitution (article 147.2 CE).

The procedures followed in adopting the 17 statutes of autonomy varied widely. Those territories that had enjoyed autonomy in the past could follow a simplified process (transitional provision 2): so Catalonia, the Basque Country and Galicia rushed forward. The remaining territories were supposed to go along a slow path (article 143 CE). Most of them did, but early on Andalusia decided to follow the difficult procedure provided by article 151 CE, and formed an autonomous community with the highest degree of powers. Referendums were held in early 1980, and their positive result meant that, from their inception, several autonomous communities also achieved a high degree of devolved powers: Andalusia, Valencia and Canary Islands.

Later, in 1981, a political agreement was reached between the two main national parties (Centrist Coalition and Socialist Party) which lead to the generalization of autonomy statutes to all the remaining territories, all of them endowed with legislative authority, and the creation of a general framework of co-ordination procedures and committees and several 'harmonization' principles to rule intergovernmental relations. Most of these rules, drafted as a basic law (*ley orgánica*) were declared unconstitutional by the constitutional court in 1983, the same year all the new autonomic bodies were created.

A second political agreement between the main national parties (then the socialists and the populars) was reached in 1992 so that all autonomous communities should expand their powers, so as to legislate in all fields and manage all public services not reserved to the general government by the constitution itself (mainly article 149 CE). Therefore, the statutes of autonomy of the 'slow' or 'gradual' autonomous communities have been amended between 1994 and 1999, to reach the present situation.

D. The 'block of constitutionality'

The 'deconstitutionalization' carried out by the different statutes of autonomy does not mean the Spanish legal system is in anarchy. First, some key constitutional clauses provide for an 'order of competences', as we shall see later. Secondly, the constitution has entrusted some organic laws (*ley orgánica*) made by the Spanish parliament to regulate essential elements of the decentralized state of autonomies:[17]

- organic law on the Judicial Power (1985), which governs all courts of law;
- organic law on security forces and bodies (1986), providing basic rules to all state (*policía nacional* and *guardia civil*), autonomic and local police forces;
- organic law to finance autonomous communities (1980), which is the cornerstone for taxation, budgeting, public accounting and borrowing, as well as coordination of state and autonomic authorities; only the Basque Country and Navarre enjoy a special status;
- organic law regulating the exercise of fundamental rights, notably those regulating elections (1985) and political parties (2002).

The Spanish parliament also retains some general powers to be exercised as the need may arise. Some relate to the creation of the autonomous communities, and have actually been exercised to solve the many problems facing the definition of Castile within the new governmental structure.[18] Others have to do with the definition of areas of jurisdiction entrusted to the self-governing bodies and the general state institutions. According to article 150 CE, the national parliament is empowered to enact legislation broadening the scope of authority granted to one, several or all of the autonomous communities: this provision has been used several times to grant competences which were later written into the statutes of autonomy themselves (but not always, as is the case of traffic policing in Catalonia). On the other hand, article 150 CE also empowers the general parliament to adopt laws in fields subject to autonomic legislation in order to harmonize conflicting legislation. Only once has such legislation been adopted, in 1982, and the constitutional court struck it down because the rules adopted were 'preventive': the national parliament may harmonize existing autonomic rules, not future legislation.[19]

---

[17] ibid. See F Rubio Llorente 'El bloque de constitucionalidad' in *La forma del poder (Estudios sobre la Constitución)* (CEPC Madrid 1993) 99 onwards.

[18] Art 144 CE allows the *Cortes Generales* to adopt specific decisions in the national interest, eg to initiate the creation of autonomous communities in the face of local inactivity or opposition, and derogate some of the general requirements to create an autonomous community or to enlarge it. See Organic Acts 13/1980, 16 December, on Almería; 6/1982, 7 July, on Madrid; 5/1983, 1 March, on Segovia; 1/1995 and 2/1995, 13 March, on Ceuta and Melilla.

[19] STC *LOAPA* (76/1983, 5 August).

The constitution, the statutes of autonomy, plus those organic laws defining boundaries in the powers of general and autonomic institutions form the so-called 'constitutionality block' (*bloque de constitucionalidad*). As a matter of fact, this set of legislative instruments is a far cry from forming a 'block' in any strict sense: it is a loose arrangement of different rules, often amended several times. Nevertheless, the idea is clear that all those rules enjoy supra-legal status: the constitution, of course, but also statutes of autonomy and organic laws must be complied with. All legislators, be it the Spanish parliament or any of the parliaments of the autonomous communities, must legislate within the subject matters entrusted to their jurisdiction by the block; and they cannot alter some key rules in the fields of justice and police, taxation and public expenditures, and fundamental rights and freedoms. It is the duty of the constitutional court to make sure that this constitutionality block is observed by the political institutions.

E. The constitutional order of competences

Once an autonomous community is created, a new legal order is established. In that territory, national law coexists with those laws adopted by the parliament of that autonomous community, which have the full force of law.

Those laws are enacted by the president of each autonomous community 'in the name of the King'. National authorities have no powers of political veto over autonomous communities' legislation. That possibility, which exists in Italy, was considered and rejected while drafting the constitution. As for legal controls, only the constitutional court has jurisdiction to hear direct challenges against the legislation of autonomous communities, on an equal footing with national legislation (article 153 CE). The only difference is that, if the national government starts proceedings for an autonomous community's law to be declared unconstitutional, it can have the operation of the challenged provisions suspended. This automatic freezing of the contested legislation cannot last more than five months; within that time limit, it is for the court to decide whether the legislation should be in force while judgment is pending or remain suspended until the end of the constitutional proceedings (article 161.2 CE). State legislation, on the contrary, is never suspended while a constitutional case is pending.

There is no hierarchy between state law and the laws adopted by autonomous communities. Each has the same legal force, each within its own realm. Legislation adopted by the autonomous communities must respect the procedures and subject matter defined in the statute of autonomy. On the other hand, state legislation cannot amend or abrogate autonomous communities legislation.

The organizing principle is, thus, that of 'competence'—the extent of power granted to the general institutions and the autonomic institutions of the Spanish state. Article 149(3) CE provides the key clauses:

- Matters not expressly vested upon the state by the constitution may fall under the jurisdiction of the autonomous communities by virtue of their respective 'statute of autonomy' (assumption of power clause).
- Authority over matters not assumed by the 'statutes of autonomy' shall fall within the jurisdiction of the state (residual or general competence clause).
- In case of conflict, state norms shall prevail over those of the autonomous communities in everything not granted to their exclusive power (prevalence clause).
- The law of the state shall in any case supplement the law of the autonomous communities (supplementarity clause).

The combination of those basic rules creates the 'constitutional order of competences'. Autonomous communities can and do legislate in many fields, those subject to their authority according to the long and detailed lists of subject matters written in their 'statute of autonomy'. The state institutions legislate in those areas reserved by the constitution (essentially article 149 CE), as well as any other subject not entrusted to the autonomous communities.

As for administration, the general rule is that the state implements national legislation, and the bureaucracies of the autonomous communities enforce autonomic laws.[20] Nevertheless, there are several important areas where national legislation is implemented by autonomous communities, including labour law and protection of the environment. Since 2002, all the autonomous communities are responsible for running education and public health services and now constitute, in practical terms, the main administration.[21]

The division of authority in relation to the administration of justice is worth noting. All the judicial courts are created and subject to national legislation: the Organic Act on the Judicial Power and procedural legislation. The career judges[22] are civil servants of the state, whose selection, status, professional career and discipline rest in the hands of the Judges Council (*Consejo General del Poder Judicial*, article 122 CE).[23] Autonomous communities, however, play an increasing administrative role at the expense of the national Ministry of Justice. The Catalonian and Basque statutes of autonomy, adopted in 1979,

---

[20] Although the court has denied the existence of an 'execution principle' in favour of autonomus communities, as in the German model: STC *transporte de fondos* (104/1989, 8 June) [3].

[21] The state administration employs 563,989 public servants, while 1,101,999 work for the autonomous communities (and 447,945 for local governments); thus half of the public employees work at the autonomic level, as opposed to 1 in 4 at the state level. The state institutions manage 48.7% of public expenditure, while autonomous communities spend 35.5% (and local government 15.8%); in 2002, autonomous communities' budgets amounted to €90.850 million. Sources: Ministro de Administraciones Públicas en las Cortes Generales (Congreso, Comisión de régimen de las Administraciones públicas, 1 October 2002); <www.map.es/po-autonomica/paginas/Princ_presinigas.htm> (14 April 2003).

[22] The terms 'career' judges and 'judicial' courts are used here to distinguish all other judicial courts from the constitutional court itself. On the relationship between the constitutional court and other courts, see bibliographical note below.

[23] The *Consejo General del Poder Judicial* is an independent body representing judicial power in the state, established by the constitution.

granted those governments responsibilities for allocating material means to the courts: buildings, office material, budgetary means; as well as the management of the judicial personnel (secretarial and executive staff). The Judiciary Act of 1985 generalized this arrangement throughout the other autonomous communities, which left only a minimum competence reserved to the state: the judges themselves. Those arrangements were declared valid by the constitutional court,[24] and further enlarged in the 1994 reformation of the Judiciary Act.[25] The resulting situation is that judicial courts are part of the state but their daily functioning is the responsibility of the autonomous community where they have their seat, with some transitory exceptions.[26] Only the National Court, the Supreme Court, and the constitutional court are fully integrated into the state structure.

5. THE ROLE OF THE CONSTITUTIONAL COURT IN THE 'STATE OF AUTONOMIES'

It should come as no surprise that the constitutional court plays a vital role in the equilibriums established by the constitution to decentralize public power. The ambiguity and inner instability of the political consensus reached in 1978, required an umpire to preserve the balance agreed upon by all the political forces. The detailed provisions of title VIII CE, additional and transitory provisions, the 17 statutes of autonomy finally adopted, and the many organic laws, which have some imprint into the 'constitutional order of competences', make conflicts of jurisdiction likely to occur and difficult to solve on a legal basis.

It should be mentioned that the senate has failed to represent autonomous communities. The constitution defines the upper house of the Spanish parliament as a chamber for 'territorial representation' (article 69 CE). But it provided for a provincial electoral system making the senate a duplicate of the lower house Congress of Deputies. This failure to integrate the autonomous communities' interests and political forces into the general fabric of the state has many perturbing consequences. One of them, not the least, is the overload of the constitutional court with conflicts that in other systems may be solved at the federal chambers (the US Senate or the German *Bundesrat*).

A. The constitutional court

A constitutional court (*Tribunal constitucional*) was created to be a guardian of the constitution. Its model was not the Tribunal of Constitutional Guarantees

---

[24] STC *poder judicial* (56/1990, 29 March).
[25] Subject to a correcting interpretation by STC *poder judicial II* (105/2000, 13 April).
[26] Ten autonomous communities have not yet assumed authority on judicial services, but they will in the foreseeable future; it is the Basque Government, Catalonian Generalitat, Galician Xunta, Andalousian Junta, Valencian Generalitat, Canarian Government, and Madrid Government that now run justice administration with state judges and legislation.

that had briefly existed in the Spanish Second Republic (1931–1939), following the Czech and Austrian examples. The 1978 court was defined following the experience of the German and the Italian constitutional courts created after the Second World War.

The constitutional court is composed of 12 judges (*magistrados*). They must be jurists of recognized competence, with at least 15 years' experience in the legal professions. In practice, most are appointed from the ranks of law professors and Supreme Court judges. They are formally appointed by royal decree issued by the King, under a proposal by all other institutions of the state. Most of the judges are elected by the national parliament: four by the lower chamber (*Congreso de los diputados*) and four by the upper chamber (*Senado*). It is significant that to select a candidate, a qualified majority is required: three-fifths of the members in the relevant chamber of parliament. This means an agreement must be reached by the two main political parties; until the round of appointments in 2001, political consensus was also reached with Catalonian nationalists and other minorities. Of the remaining four judges, two are nominated by national government and two by the Judges Council (*Consejo General del Poder Judicial*). The latter two are always Supreme Court judges, although there is no express written provision to that effect.

The judges are appointed for a term of nine years, with no possibility of reappointment: a third are appointed every three years. Therefore, the composition of the court has partially changed every three years since 1980, in the following order (established by lot in the first round of new appointments in 1983): congress of deputies; national government and Judges Council; senate. In July 1992 the first full change of personnel took place, the second full change was accomplished in December 2001.

Those elected to serve at the court are debarred from holding any other representative office or public post; from playing a leading role in a political party or a trade union (but not to belong to any of them, although in practice that is very rare); or from undertaking any other professional or commercial activity. The judges are independent, and only the court itself can dismiss them from office. The court elects its president and vice-president from among its judges every three years. It also appoints a secretary-general.

The court is funded by the state, but with full authority over its own budget (approximately €15 million). It is also empowered to decide on its own organization and functioning. The judges are assisted by 40 staff attorneys (*letrados, referendaires*), five registrars, a manager (*Gerente*) and around 120 auxiliary personnel.

Formally, the constitutional court is not part of the judiciary. The constitution establishes and regulates courts of justice, the status of career judges and the Judges Council in title VI (articles 117–127), under the heading 'Of the judicial power'. The constitutional court is created and defined in title IX (articles 159–165), 'Of the constitutional court'.

B. Principal powers of the constitutional court

An organic law passed in 1979 regulates in detail the functioning and procedures of the constitutional court (*Ley Orgánica del Tribunal Constitucional*, LOTC). The constitutional court is defined as the supreme interpreter of the constitution (article 1 LOTC). It is independent from all other constitutional bodies, and is subject only to the Constitution and to its own organic law (article 1.1 LOTC). The role of the court is to ensure that laws and governmental actions conform to the Constitution. Therefore, it can be said that the court performs three main functions, as follows.

First, to guarantee the supremacy of the constitution, even over the legislatures. Any law adopted by the national parliament or by any of the 17 parliaments of the autonomous communities that contradicts the constitution is null and void, but the only court empowered to make such a declaration is the constitutional court. Secondly, to adjudicate on the distribution of power between the national government and the autonomous communities, or between the autonomous communities themselves. Thirdly, to protect fundamental rights and freedoms of individuals. The Spanish constitution not only enumerates a list of rights and freedoms (articles 14–38 CE), but is also concerned with the effective protection of those rights and freedoms (articles 9, 53, 54, 55, 161, and 168 CE). Therefore, the constitution proclaims it has direct effect, and provides for judicial protection of fundamental rights, that is entrusted in the last resort to the constitutional court.

C. Types of proceedings

The constitutional court exercises jurisdiction in several fields, through a variety of proceedings. All of them are simple, flexible and, in the practice of the court, written. The most important of these procedures are: abstract review of legislation, conflicts of authority, and individual complaints on fundamental rights.

1. Abstract review of legislation

Abstract review of legislation takes place either by a direct challenge to the validity of laws (and governmental decrees having the force of laws) or by means of a preliminary reference from a judicial court (articles 161 and 163 CE). The constitutional court only reviews the validity of legislative acts;[27] it does not review the validity of lesser rules (the vast amount of regulations adopted by governmental and administrative authorities, subject to the review of administrative courts), except in two procedures—when protecting fundamental

---

[27] Those adopted by the national parliament and the legislative bodies of the autonmous communities, or those regulations adopted by the executive with the legal force of an Act (legislative decrees, in the execution of a legislative delegation, or law decrees, when an urgent need arises: arts 82, 86 CE).

rights in individual complaints and when solving conflicts of authority (on which, see below).

An 'appeal of unconstitutionality' (*recurso de inconstitucionalidad*) can only be lodged by public institutions—the president of the national government, the autonomous communities, the ombudsman (*Defensor del Pueblo*)—or by members of the national parliament (50 deputies or 50 senators: article 162 CE). Proceedings must be started within three months of the official publication of the law in question.

A 'question of unconstitutionality' (*cuestión de inconstitucionalidad*) may be referred to the constitutional court by any court of law, though not by administrative tribunals. The question is limited to a legislative act (never a regulation) relevant to a case pending before the court certifying it. It may be brought before the court adopts a final decision, after hearing the parties to the judicial proceedings.

The constitutional court has only limited powers to review legislation *before* it is enacted. The national government or either of the houses of the national parliament may refer any international agreement to the constitutional court, before ratification, to declare whether the text is compatible with the constitution (article 95 CE). This procedure has been employed only once, in relation to the Maastricht Treaty.[28] In the past, there was another procedure for challenging the constitutionality of legislation prior to the completion of the legislative process in the national parliament. It was possible for members of either house to challenge an organic law adopted by the Spanish parliament. This procedure for 'prior appeal of unconstitutionality' (*recurso previo de inconstitucionalidad*) was abolished in 1986. It was significant that most of the socialist government's legislative measures were challenged by the conservative minority in parliament. The organic law abolishing this prior appeal was itself reviewed by the constitutional court.[29]

2. Conflicts of authority

The constitutional court also hears cases about conflicts of authority, usually between the national government and one or more of the governments of the autonomous communities. Conflicts between the different national institutions are also possible, though to date only two have arisen, one relating to the Judges Council (*Consejo General del Poder Judicial*) against the national parliament, and in the other the national government against the senate.[30]

Conflicts over authority may also arise between different autonomous communities. An outstanding example is *Diputación Foral de Navarra contra el País Vasco*,[31] when the constitutional court declared that the constitution protects

---

[28] Declaration 1 July 1992.　　　[29] STC (85/1986, 25 June).

[30] STC (108/1986, 29 July), and STC (234/2000, 3 October).

[31] STC (94/1985, 29 July). In the case, the Basque government could not use the chains identifying the official seal of Navarre, even if Basque nationalists claim Navarre (and several French departments) as belonging to their homeland.

symbols identifying governmental entities. The great majority of conflict of authority cases, though, arise between the national government and the governments of autonomous communities.

'Conflict of authority or competence' (*conflicto positivo de competencias*) litigation may only be instigated by the national government or the government of an autonomous community. No other public authority may vindicate its powers before the constitutional court. Any regulation, decision, or act, including the refusal to act, may lead to a conflict. The purpose of the procedure is only to declare which of the contending authorities have jurisdiction to issue the regulation or decision in question, but the constitutional court may adopt any other measure to restore the constitutional distribution of authority, usually to declare null and void any regulation or decision found to be ultra vires.

The national government can demand certain remedies against any autonomous community (but not vice versa). First, if an autonomous government does not exercise its powers, the national government may commence proceedings before the constitutional court to compel the adoption of the missing regulation or decision (*conflicto negativo de competencias*: article 71 LOTC). This procedure has however never been used: all governments seem eager to exercise their competences. A second possibility open to the national government is to challenge the validity of autonomous community actions (article 76 LOTC). The procedure may be prompted by any regulation or administrative decision whatsoever and, as is the rule in conflicts of competence, for breach of the constitution. Whether the autonomous communities are acting within the confines of its authority is immaterial.[32] Therefore, the national government retains a general supervisory power over the activity of autonomous communities, though one limited to constitutionality. This power has been exercised in a number of occasions.[33]

The organic law of the constitutional court (*Ley Orgánica del Tribunal Constitucional*) provides for individuals to initiate conflicts proceedings, whenever national government or governments of autonomous communities refuse to act on the ground that each of them claims that jurisdiction belongs to the other. This 'negative conflict of authority' is of little significance, given the very restrictive scope afforded to it by the case law.[34]

3. Individual complaints relating to fundamental rights

Any person may seek redress of their fundamental rights: national and foreigners, individuals and companies or associations. Only fundamental rights and freedoms may sustain their claim (not any other breach of the constitution); and of them, only those rights and freedoms listed in articles 14–30 (article 53.2 CE, article 41 LOTC). In practice, this means most socio-economic rights (for

---

[32] Although it can be posed: STC (184/1996, 14 November).

[33] STC (54/1982, 26 July); STC (16/1984, 6 February); STC (44/1986, 17 April); STC (64/1990, 5 April); STC (66/1991, 22 March).

[34] STC (156/1990, 18 October).

example, the right to property and freedom to work) cannot be protected in individual appeals, but only in abstract review.

This 'appeal for protection' procedure (*recurso de amparo*) has proved to be more significant than intended when the constitutional court was established. The constitutional court reviews the validity of legislation in accordance with the Kelsen model: judicial courts apply the laws; the constitutional court guarantees that those laws conform to the constitution. The drafters of the constitution (and the *Ley Orgánica del Tribunal Constitucional*) placed most importance in the procedures to review the validity of the legislation: the 'appeal of unconstitutionality' and the 'reference or question of unconstitutionality' can only be decided by the full court; and the rules governing those procedures are more developed. As a rule, individual complaints (*recursos de amparo*) are to be adjudicated by chambers of six judges; only in special cases will the full court render judgment.

In fact, the constitutional court seldom rules on the validity of legislation. They are indeed very important decisions, especially in some controversial cases (dealing with for example, abortion, police powers, internment of foreigners, and the taking of a business conglomerate). But most of the judgments of the constitutional court are protecting fundamental rights of people bringing individual complaints. Many of those decisions have been of utmost importance, both for their general impact on the legal system and for the significance of the individual controversy decided upon. A respected author has declared that the Spanish constitutional court is better explained as a protector of fundamental rights and freedoms than as a jurisdiction to review the validity of legislation.[35] And the constitutional decisions allocating powers between the central government, on the one hand, and the 17 autonomous communities, on the other, were essential to affirm the validity of the 1978 constitution, and are still today one of the main sources of legitimacy and controversy for the court.

6. CONSTITUTIONAL JURISDICTION IN GENERAL

The constitutional court is not the only court of law devoted to constitutional adjudication in Spain. It is important to stress this because even in Spain cultural stereotypes blind many people, even lawyers, to reality. Spanish judicial power is organized in sets of specialized courts, not dissimilar to the French and German systems with some Anglo-Saxon influences. There are civil courts, dealing with private law matters: family, contract, property, land, and tort. There are criminal courts, devoted to crimes and misdemeanours. There are administrative courts, solving conflicts against public authorities under public law: taxation, immigration, civil service, licensing, urban planning, compulsory purchase, public contracts, and government liability. There are social courts for labour law and

---

[35] F Rubio Llorente 'Tendencias actuales de la jurisdicción constitucional en Europa' in F Rubio Llorente and J Jiménez Campo *Estudios sobre jurisdicción constitucional* (McGraw Hill Madrid 1998) 170.

social security claims. Moreover, there are military courts, dealing with army discipline and crime.

These courts work in isolation at every level of the judicial pyramid: civil, criminal, administrative, social, and military courts do not intersect or collaborate with one another, so it is fair to say in Spain there are five sets of independent courts. From the civil trial court (*Juzgado de Primera Instancia*) lies an appeal to the civil division of the provincial court (*Audiencia Provincial*), and in some cases an appeal in points of law (*recurso de casación*) to the Civil Chamber of the Supreme Court. Similar arrangements can be found in the other 'jurisdictional orders' (*órdenes jurisdiccionales*), all of them starting in single judge courts (*Juzgados*), with some sort of intermediate appeal level (located either at one of the 50 provincial courts or at one of the 17 high courts, *Tribunal Superior de Justicia*), and final appeal is to one of the five Chambers of the Supreme Court: First Civil Chamber, Second Criminal Chamber, Third Administrative Chamber, Fourth Social Chamber, and Fifth Military Chamber.

The constitutional jurisdiction exercised by the constitutional court is no more than another specialized jurisdiction. It is special in the sense that it only applies the constitution; any other legislation is construed and applied only to the extent necessary to implement the constitution itself. On the other hand, the constitutional court is a court of general jurisdiction in the sense that the court is concerned in any case affecting the constitution: be it the exercise of constitutional rights and freedoms by citizens or the separation and territorial division of public powers.[36] So all the specialized jurisdictions of the ordinary courts end up at the central jurisdiction exercised by the constitutional court, as far as any provision of the 1978 constitution is concerned. This role explains why the court is said to be 'unique in its jurisdictional order'; no other court can challenge the extent or exercise of its jurisdiction (articles 1 and 4 LOTC). There is no court superior to the constitutional court in the legal hierarchy: the constitutional court is beyond the system of courts (titles IX and VI CE).

Yet all courts of law construe and apply the constitution. Whenever they have to adjudicate any criminal, administrative or military case or any civil, administrative or social controversy, courts of law have to comply first and foremost with the constitution. The main difference is that only the constitutional court is empowered to declare legislation null and void (though laws made before the constitution was adopted can be dismissed by ordinary courts as unconstitutional).[37] Besides this central position enjoyed by the constitutional court, there

---

[36] See STC (26/1981, 17 July) [14]; STC (24/1990, 15 February) [2.9]; STC (245/1991, 16 December) [3].

[37] STC *régimen local* (4/1981, 2 February) [1]. Any judicial ruling that sets aside legislation adopted after 1978, on the ground that it is unconstitutional, is a judgment null and void: STC *Ureta Diezma* (23/1988, 22 February). This also applies to autonomous community legislation: judges must give it full effect, and cannot disregard it on constitutional grounds or for reasons unjustified: STC *Generalidad de Cataluña contra Martínez Calderón* (173/2002, 9 October).

is no essential difference between the 'constitutional jurisdiction' it exercises and the 'judicial jurisdiction' exercised by the ordinary courts.

To understand the work of the constitutional court the best way is to divide it into two different aspects: constitutional review of legislation, on the one part, and review of administrative action, on the other. In these two fields of its jurisdictional activities, the constitutional court adopts a very different position vis-à-vis parliament, the executive, and judicial courts.

7. CONSTITUTIONAL REVIEW OF LEGISLATION

The constitution of 1978 has not altered one basic tenet of Spanish law: courts must apply the law; and the law is adopted by parliaments (the national *Cortes Generales* and the parliaments of the autonomous communities) and by government when authorized to enact subordinate legislation or regulations with the force of law. It is not in the power of judicial courts to enjoin the execution of legislation; they can review only administrative regulations and rules of a lesser degree (though these ministerial orders, independent agencies instructions, etc are very important in practical life).

Therefore, as we have seen, only the constitutional court can free judicial courts from enforcing legislation passed by parliament because it is contrary to the constitution. A structural distinction has been introduced in relation to European Union law. When giving effect to European Community treaties and legislation, Spanish courts can deny effect to Spanish legislation on their own authority, following the European Court of Justice case law.[38] This has been accepted in Spanish law.[39]

Autonomous communities legislation is bound to comply with the constitution, the corresponding statute of autonomy and any legislation which belongs to the 'block of constitutionality', as we already know. Any legislative provision contrary to constitutional limits is null and void. And the constitutional court will declare it so, as it has done since 1981.[40]

On the other hand, it is very important to underline that national legislation is also bound to comply with the constitutional order of competences. Any law passed by the *Cortes Generales,* or any royal decree with the force of law adopted by the general cabinet, in fields reserved to the exclusive authority of one or more autonomous community, will be declared unconstitutional. Nevertheless, national legislation overstepping the jurisdiction of autonomous communities is not null and void. Different territories exercise only those powers granted by

[38] Case 106/77 *Amministrazione delle Finanze dello Stato v Simmenthal SpA (No 2)* [1978] ECR 629.

[39] Constitutional court STC *circunscripción europea* (28/1991, 14 February) [6]; STC *Apesco* (64/1991, 22 March) [4].

[40] In the seminal judgments STC *diputaciones catalanas* (32/1981, 28 July); STC *centro de contratación de cargas* (37/1981, 26 November).

each individual statute of autonomy, which give different degrees of jurisdiction. In addition, the constitution provides that national law is supplementary to autonomic law (article 149.3.3 CE). Therefore, those general laws that infringe the competence granted to one or several autonomous communities (those bringing suit to the constitutional court) will be declared 'inapplicable' within the territory of those governments. As a rule, the constitutional court will declare null and void only specific administrative acts adopted by the general authorities within the boundaries of the offended autonomous community.[41] But national legislation is valid and has effect in the territory of other autonomous communities with no jurisdiction on the subject matter in dispute.

Nevertheless, as we have seen, since 1983 the whole of Spain has been organized in autonomous communities. All of them are vested with jurisdiction in some areas, normally those matters listed as possible areas for political self-government in article 148 of the constitution: public works, social assistance, promotion of economic and cultural life, and so on. The most substantive of these grants of authority had to do with public and private transportation within the community boundaries and urban and regional planning. So it is not a surprise that in those fields the case law came to declare something which was felt to be a revolution in the 'state of autonomies': that national legislation adopted by the *Cortes Generales* is null and void when trespassing the limits of autonomous communities authority. That declaration was issued in the *transportes terrestres* judgment[42] and in the *suelo* judgment.[43] This last opinion made the point with some dramatic effect: most of the legislation governing urban planning was declared unconstitutional and void as a result.

Invalidity of state legislation is a direct consequence of the development of the 'state of autonomies'. When a given subject matter is under the authority of all the 17 autonomous communities, the inevitable deduction is that the general institutions of the state cannot act in that field any more. It is left to the parliaments of the autonomous communities to legislate on the field, or not to legislate, which is also a policy decision left to the discretion of the self-governing political institutions.[44] It is fit to say that it was the adoption of the last of the autonomy statutes in 1983 that took away from the national state all those powers assumed by all the 17 autonomous communities in the whole of the Spanish territory.

The constitutional court reviews the validity of national and autonomic legislation when deciding any remedy within in its jurisdiction. In any proceedings before the court, the issue of validity of legislation can be raised (specific provisions in regard to individual complaints and conflicts of authority: articles 55.2 and 67 LOTC). In regard to the territorial distribution of powers, two procedures have special significance: 'appeals for unconstitutionality' (*recuso de*

---

[41] As it was the case with inspection records on cinemas in Catalonia in STC (143/1985, 24 October).

[42] STC (118/1996, 27 June) especially [6] and holding.

[43] STC (61/1997, 20 March) [12] and holding.　　[44] STC *pesca de cerco* (147/1991, 4 July) [7].

inconstitucionalidad) and 'positive conflicts of competences' (*conficto positivo de competancias*). Doubts have arisen as to the scope of those two forms of proceedings. Early on, the constitutional court declared that the difference was strictly formal, and therefore clear and easy to implement: if a law of the national parliament or parliament of an autonomous community is challenged, an 'appeal for constitutionality' must be lodged; no 'positive conflict of competence' proceedings may be initiated against legislation, or government regulations having the force of law.[45] The grounds of the appeal may be lack of competence (ultra vires), substantive grounds (constitutional principles or fundamental rights) or, as it is often the case, both kinds of argument may be raised against the autonomic and the national legislation challenged. Several consequences flow from this clarification.

A. Time limits for lodging appeals for unconstitutionality

The 'appeal for unconstitutionality' against any legislation must be commenced within three months of its official publication (article 33 LOTC), though a reform was adopted in 2000 to alleviate the large number of constitutional appeals brought to the constitutional court.[46] The reform has provided that whenever national and autonomic officials are discussing the content and validity of legislation on competence grounds, the time limits may be extended up to a total of nine months. This provision has been used on a number of occasions.

B. Standing

As for standing to lodge an appeal against legislation, there are no limits for state authorities, deputies, or senators in the national parliament. But the standing of autonomous communities to challenge the validity of national legislation is limited to those laws that 'might affect their field of autonomy' (article 32.2 LOTC). Initially the constitutional court read this clause in restrictive terms.[47] Very soon, however, it accepted that any nexus between the public interests relevant to an autonomous community and the purposes or effect of the contested legislation is enough to grant standing.[48] Therefore, in today's case law there are no significant limits to the standing of autonomous communities.

   In relation to international treaties, only the national government or parliament can demand that the constitutional court review their validity prior to ratification (article 95 CE). But autonomous communities may challenge any international agreement in an 'appeal of unconstitutionality' (if having the force

---

[45] STC *diputaciones catalanas* (32/1981, 28 July) [1], confirmed and developed in STC *películas X* (49/1984) [1], [2].
[46] Organic Law 1/2000, 7 January, inserting new art 33.2 LOTC.
[47] STC *antiterrorista I* (25/1981, 14 July).
[48] STC *transferencias locales* (84/1982, 23 December) and STC *antiterrorista II* (199/1987, 16 December).

of law), or in 'conflict of competence' proceedings (if the agreement does not have the force of law but is merely regulatory in status). An example *mutatis mutandi* is offered by the judgment *circunscripción europea*,[49] solving the appeal made by the Basque cabinet against the organic law amending the electoral legislation to provide for direct elections to the European Parliament, in pursuance of the Act Concerning the Election of the Representatives of the European Parliament by Direct Universal Suffrage of 20 September 1976, attached to the European Communities Council Decision 76/787.

C. Scope of review

Finally, a mention should be made on the scope of review. The constitutional court has adopted a very wide approach: it reviews the compatibility of national and autonomic laws using those legal instruments which form the 'block of constitutionality'. The constitutional court has also accepted jurisdiction to solve collisions between national and autonomic legislation, something that is open to doubt. The conflict between the mandate of a law passed by the national institutions and the rule laid down by an autonomous community does not affect directly the constitution itself. The theory espoused by the court is that such a conflict between legal rules poses constitutional issues 'indirectly'.[50] Either the law made by the autonomous community has overstepped the boundaries of the autonomous community's powers, so the law is unconstitutional; or the national law should be declared 'inapplicable', or even null and void, so as not to be an obstacle to the effective application of autonomic legislation.[51] Judicial courts, in contrast, regularly solve conflicts of national and autonomic legislation—and, as far as they do not declare any of the two conflicting rules unconstitutional or void, there is no problem.[52] Only recently, a minority of judges have declared their willingness to refine the constitutional case law, accepting a more developed role for judicial courts in the field of conflicts of general and autonomic laws.[53]

8. REVIEW OF ADMINISTRATIVE ACTION

The constitutional court defines in practice the extent of the powers granted by the 'block of constitutionality'. Not only legislation, but any act, proceeding, administrative regulation or even omission to act from the part of a public official can be challenged as ultra vires of the constitutional order of competences (article 161.1.c CE, article 61 LOTC). Both the state general administration and the executive bodies of the 17 autonomous communities must comply with

---

[49] STC (28/1991).
[50] ie 'remote or indirect unconstitutionality': STC *interinos de Canarias* (151/1992, 19 October) [1].
[51] See further STC *espacios naturales en Andalucía* (163/1995, 8 November) [4].
[52] As can be seen in STC *Tapia Fernández* (236/2000, 16 October).
[53] Dissenting vote to STC *excedencias extremeñas* (1/2003, 16 January).

the limits of their power. All public officers must act within the spheres defined
by the 'block of constitutionality'. Those limits also affect administrative agencies and even public corporations acting under the colour of private law.[54]

'Conflict of authority' proceedings may be brought only by the highest executive bodies (*Gobierno de la Nación* or *Consejos Ejecutivos*). Proceedings may
not be commenced before the constitutional court until an official intimation has
been addressed to the offending government: the challenged executive council
must answer within one month, explaining the jurisdictional grounds to support
its action or regulation. Once the answer has been given, or the month has
passed, it is possible to ask the court for a declaration as to who has the authority
to act (articles 62 and 63 LOTC).

There is some asymmetry relating to powers for commencing proceedings.
The National Council of Ministers (*Consejo de Ministros*) may challenge action
by an autonomous community directly, without prior intimation to the autonomous government, although in practice it seldom uses this power. There are also
some differences in relation to interim relief: the contested administrative regulation or action is rendered ineffective when the Spanish government so
demands; on the other hand, when the government of an autonomous community challenges national or other autonomous community actions, it is for the
constitutional court to decide whether to suspend the operation of the administrative action or not. Interim relief is very important as the constitutional court
suffers from delays. Nevertheless the difference between the national government and the executive bodies of the autonomous communities when demanding
the suspension of challenged administrative action is not so extreme, given the
fact that in five months the court must review the automatic suspension achieved
by the national government, so as to ratify or to lift it (articles 62, 64(2)–(3), and
65(2) LOTC). The court has applied the same approach on the interim relief,
whether it is demanded by the national government against autonomous community action or vice versa. A minority of judges have recently has espoused the
view that the position of the national government should be reinforced.[55]

The final judgment declares which of the contending executive bodies has
jurisdiction on the contested action, regulation, or omission. In addition, the
court may adopt any other remedy, such as declaring null and void any official
action adopted ultra vires (article 66 LOTC). In practice, this is very rare, given
the long time it takes nowadays to solve authority conflicts.

The main question in regard to conflicts of authority has to do with the role
played by the judicial courts. The legislation only provides that constitutional
proceedings take precedence over any ordinary judicial proceeding that might be
pending upon the contested administrative action: any case pending must
be suspended until the constitutional judgment is rendered (article 61.2
LOTC). In order to safeguard this precedence, the constitutional court gives

---

[54] STC *La Almoraima* (52/1994, 24 February) [5].
[55] Dissenting vote to decision STC (3/2003, 30 January).

notice of any new conflict registered to competent courts, and has it published in the *Official Gazette*. This has not, however, proved to be a good solution. First, the delays suffered by the constitutional court affect judicial proceedings; it would be much better if judicial courts could alleviate the work of the constitutional court.

Secondly, precedence is declared on proceedings where the contested administrative action is the same. However, judicial courts hear many cases that rely on the same jurisdictional issue but originating in different administrative acts. Therefore, in practical terms, while the constitutional court is determining a 'conflict of competences' case, administrative and social courts are adjudicating hundreds if not thousands of equivalent cases, before any constitutional judgment is rendered. This is because in Spain alternative forums have been created, those offered by the constitutional court and by judicial courts. The former hears conflicts of authority confronting central and autonomous governments. The latter hear cases confronting individuals and companies to public administrations. In addition, judicial courts hear many cases brought by municipal bodies (having no access to 'constitutional conflicts' proceedings) and they also hear cases confronting the central and autonomous executives. Judicial courts adjudicate inter-administrative litigation in two cases. First, whenever the disagreement between national authorities and autonomous communities is substantial, not jurisdictional, for example on tax assessments.[56] However, is not unusual that public administration chooses the judicial forum in cases where a constitutional conflict of authority would be possible. This is for many reasons: political factors, estimated length of the procedure, the subject matter of the conflict.

The result of this situation is a little bit anarchic, but only to a point. Judicial courts of law must adjudicate on any constitutional or legal issue presented in cases subject to their jurisdiction; the constitutional authority of national or autonomous communities officers involved in litigation is but one of them. Therefore, it is inevitable that ordinary courts are active in helping to define the case law defining the constitutional order of competences. There is the risk of diverging interpretations of the constitutional limits placed on national and autonomous communities' administrative officials. And, indeed, there is the reality of too many cases pending before the constitutional court. Maybe a better system could be devised: the judicial courts would always adjudicate conflicts of authority; and the constitutional court could be left as a last resort, on appeal from judicial rulings grounded on the constitutional order of competences.

9. THE PROBLEM OF DELAY

This general picture of the constitutional court as umpire of the Spanish decentralized state of autonomies would not be complete without some factual data.

---

[56] See STC *Comunidad de Madrid contra Meneu Garrido* (176/2002, 9 October).

Statistics can give a clearer understanding of the role played by the court and of its greatest single problem—delay.

The court is flooded with individual complaints on fundamental rights. Of the 7,456 new cases registered in 2002, 7,285 were *recursos de amparo*. The general perception is that the court plenarium (which reviews the validity of legislation and conflicts of authority) 'only' received 171 new cases, but this number of cases represents a significant level of constitutional litigation on any scale of measurement. There were 61 appeals of unconstitutionality, most of them presented by autonomous communities against general state laws (35) and by the state against autonomic legislation (17). The largest number of cases were questions of unconstitutionality referred by judicial courts on state and autonomous community legislation (99), although a large number of those referrals dealt with similar issues. The number of cases is very high. A comparison with Germany reveals the different roles played by the Spanish senate and the German *Bundesrat*.[57]

Comparison with previous years (see Table 7.1) indicates that the absolute majority of seats in the national parliament obtained by the Socialist Party at the 1982 and 1986 elections, and by the Popular Party in the 2000 general election, increased the level of challenge to legislation.

The number of conflicts of authority, though, is not very high. A comparison with the very high level of conflicts introduced in the 1980s is revealing (Table 7.1). The constitutional case law has drawn fairly clear rules to divide the fields of authority of the national and autonomic goverments in relation to most subjects, with the resulting reduction in litigation.

Generally, however, the court is unable to deliver judgment in all the cases registered every year. In 2002, it delivered 10 judgments solving 12 appeals of unconstitutionality, and three judgments solving six conflicts of competences.

Table 7.1: Number of cases registered

General elections	1982	1986	1989	1993	1996	1999	2000	2001	2002
Abstract review of legislation (*recurso de inconstituionalidad* and *cuestión de inconstitucionalidad*)	17	20	47	31	14	23	35	26	61
Conflicts of authority (*conflicto positivo de competencias*)	49	96	32	10	5	13	16	13	10

[57] See ch 8.

Obviously this was not enough to finish the 71 new cases introduced that same year (61 appeals of constitutionality plus 10 conflicts of authority), not to mention the proceedings pending from previous years. Most of the work of the court, therefore, is devoted to protecting fundamental rights in individual complaints (221 judgments on 231 cases in 2002).

Even if the court could render more judgments, as it did in previous years,[58] and taking into account those cases dismissed without judgment (applications struck out for procedural reasons, agreement of the parties, or any other justified reason),[59] the number of new cases is higher than the output of the court. The result is that the large number of cases awaiting judgment is very worrying. At the end of 2002, the court had to deliver 175 judgments on appeals of unconstitutionality and 62 on conflicts of authority;[60] not to mention 203 questions referred by judicial courts, and 357 individual complaints. Were the court to render the same number of judgments as in 2002, it would need more than 18 years to solve the appeals and conflicts already pending, not to mention future cases.

The end result of this situation is chronic delay. The court takes between three and 10 years to deliver judgment in plenary cases. When this affects judicial proceedings, as it does in the case of questions of unconstitutionality referred by other courts of law, those delays violate the right of private litigants to a trial without undue delay within a reasonable time.[61] There are good reasons to consider that public institution litigation has a longer time span, but the court is at the limit of acceptable delay, especially in regard to appeals challenging legislation that meanwhile is in operation or, worse still, suspended in its effect pending judgment. Some far-reaching reform is needed by the court together with more collaboration with judicial courts of law and lawyers. The key reform needed, however, is reform of the senate so that it fulfils its role of territorial chamber in the Spanish parliament.

10. FINAL REMARKS

The constitutional court of Spain plays an essential role in assessing the conflicting claims of general and autonomic institutions of a state which offers the paradox typical in all federal or decentralized structures of goverment:

---

[58] In 1998, for example, the court adjudicated 21 unconstitutionality appeals in 14 judgments, and 13 conflicts of authority in eight opinions; the figures for 2000 were 11 appeals in eight judgments, and seven conflicts in six judgments. The highest numbers were achieved in 1993: 36 judgments on appeals and 27 on conflicts, a record total of 63.

[59] In 2002, 23 appeals were dismissed without judgment (most of them for autonomous communities withdrawal of appeals against state legislation on income tax revenue-sharing); in 2001 there were three; in 2000, eight; in 1999, six; etc.

[60] With joined cases, the numbers are 205 appeals and 74 conflicts: *Tribunal Constitucional Memoria 2002* (2003).

[61] Art 24 CE, Art 6 ECHR, and (A/262) *Ruiz Mateos v España* (1993) 16 EHRR 505.

indivisible unified (national or general) government, with indestructible diverse (regional or national) goverments. Some results have been very positive. Indeed, it is doubtful whether the experiment in self-government launched in the 1978 constitution would have been possible, had the constitutional court not been in place and had it not rendered some of the basic judgments regulating Spain today. On the other hand, problems are visible. Calibrating jurisdiction over constitutional matters with that of the judicial courts is an important task, and some inefficiencies have arisen. A national parliament where autonomic institutions do not participate enough, increases constitutional litigation on territorial grounds to a level which cannot be sustained and may have some negative side-effects when appointing judges to the constitutional court. There is a need to provide legitimate autonomic interests with a say in selecting constitutional judges; it is the role of the senate to provide for such a political input; and political practices—including nationalist minority parties in the bargaining between the two main national political forces—have worked until the last round of appointments to the constitutional court, but the problems faced in 2001 might be repeated, and institutional reform of the senate is better in the long run. But that is another matter.

Bibliographical note

The two basic legal studies on the state of the autonomous communities are Eduardo García de Enterría *Estudios sobre autonomías territoriales* (Civitas Madrid 1985) and Santiago Muñoz Machado *Derecho público de las Comunidades Autónomas* (2 vols Civitas Madrid 1982, 1984). See also Juan José Solozábal Echevarría *Las bases constitucionales del Estado autonómico* (McGraw Hill Madrid 1998); Juan Fernando López Aguilar *Estado autonómico y hechos diferenciales* (CEPC Madrid 1998); Eliseo Aja *El Estado autonómico, federalismo y hechos diferenciales* (Alianza Editorial Madrid 1999). A good general introduction is Ignacio Torres Muro *Los Estatutos de Autonomía* (CEPC Madrid 2000); in English, L Morreno *The Federalization of Spain* (Frank Cass London 2001).

The annual surveys carried out by the Instituto de Derecho Público/Institut de Dret Public (Barcelona) under the name of *Informe de las Comunidades Autónomas* are very useful, as well as those compiled by Fundació Carles Pii Sunyer *Informe Pii Sunyer sobre Comunidades Autónomas* (Barcelona). See also statistics and studies compiled by the Ministerio de Administraciones Públicas, in print and at <http://www.map.es>.

On Spanish courts, see Luis María Díez-Picazo *Régimen constitucional del Poder Judicial* (Civitas Madrid 1991); F Rubio Llorente 'Sobre la relación entre Tribunal Constitucional y Poder Judicial en el ejercicio de la jurisdicción constitucional' op cit n 17; Pablo Pérez Tremps *Tribunal Constitucional y Poder Judicial* (CEC Madrid 1985). Also of interest is Rosario Serra Cristóbal *La guerra de las Cortes* (Tecnos Madrid 1999).

TOP-LEVEL NATIONAL COURTS
IN THE WIDER EUROPE

8

The German Federal Constitutional Court: Present State, Future Challenges

1. INTRODUCTION

The UK government's plans to establish a new supreme court made clear that this did not entail any significant change in the power of the judges in relation to Acts of Parliament. The basic constitutional arrangement contained in the Human Rights Act 1998—whereby the higher courts lack the power to strike down primary legislation that violates Convention rights—will remain in place. The UK will not have any 'constitutional review' of legislation as a result of these reforms. Since its foundation in May 1949, the Federal Republic of Germany has taken a dramatically different path.

Its constitution, the *Grundgesetz*[1] (the Basic Law or 'GG'), has made it unmistakably clear that the basic rights and freedoms there established bind all powers, including the parliament. Article 1(3) GG states: 'The following basic rights are binding on legislature, executive, and judiciary as directly enforceable law'. The *Grundgesetz* also created an institution, the *Bundesverfassungsgericht* (Federal Constitutional Court or FCC), which was designed to be the final safeguard and primary interpreter of the constitution, initially only with respect to the balance of powers between the institutions, and later also with respect to the basic rights and freedoms laid down in the *Grundgesetz*. As a result of the constitutional arrangement, the FCC, though often criticized, became one of the most powerful and most respected constitutional institutions in Germany.

This essay discusses the ways in which the Federal Republic and its constitutional court managed the difficult problem of how to organize human rights and civil rights adjudication and constitutional adjudication in general. The

---

* Assistant professor at the Wilhelm-Merton-Centre for Global Governance, Institute for Public Law, Johann Wolfgang Goethe-University, Frankfurt am Main. Legal Advisor at the German Federal Constitutional Court 1998–2001.

[1] An official translation of the constitution is available on the website of the Bundestag <http://www.bundestag.de/htdocs_e/info/gg.pdf>. Unfortunately, the text is already outdated; it does not include some substantial changes in 2001 and 2002 (art 12a GG now allows armed military service of women, and another amendment from 2002 added the protection of animals to the goals included in art 20a GG).

status and function of the Federal Government and of the FCC come under pressure from two different levels. Those that arise from a strong federal system, on the one hand, demand a clear concept of constitutional federalism. The challenges connected with the 'ever closer Union' and with the growing role of European human rights adjudication, on the other hand, threaten the function of the FCC as an integrative social factor.

This essay consists of three parts. The first part sketches the legal federal framework of constitutional adjudication in Germany, and the particular role and function of the FCC within this framework. The second part describes the relation between the FCC and the constitutional courts of the 16 *Länder*[2] that form the Federal Republic. The third part analyses the challenges arising from international and supra-national law above the level of the constitution, namely the European Convention on Human Rights (ECHR) and EU law. More precisely, the chapter focuses on how the human rights adjudication of the European Court of Human Rights (ECtHR) influences the status and function of the FCC, and scrutinizes how the European Court of Justice's (ECJ) adjudication on European Community law affects the position of the FCC. Finally, the question of constitutional adjudication in the era of 'Europeanization' is addressed.

2. The German court system

A. Federalism and unified court system

Germany is a federal republic[3] but the distinctive and complex relationship between state sovereignty and federal government regulation creates a federalism that is significantly different from that of the USA. Although the German constitution stresses the importance of the 16 *Länder* within the federal structure of Germany in articles 20 and 28 GG, they in reality do not play as prominent a role as the text of the constitution suggests.[4] This is especially true in the field of

---

[2] There are 16 states but only 15 states have constitutional courts or comparable institutions; the state of Schleswig-Holstein has used the opportunity art 99 GG offers and assigned constitutional disputes within the state to the FCC.

[3] Art 20 GG expressly states: 'The Federal Republic of Germany is a democratic and social federal state'. According to art 79(3) GG, the federalist structure cannot even be reversed by constitutional amendment. This *Ewigkeitsgarantie* ['guarantee for all times'] reads as follows: 'Amendments of this constitution affecting the division of the Federation into Länder [states], their participation on principle in the legislative process, or the principles laid down in arts 1 and 20 shall be inadmissible.' From a logical point of view, this provision contains a paradox: it denies the people constitutional powers, ie the status of a *pouvoir constituant*.

[4] This is, of course, a very simplified description; the real powers of the states lie *within the procedures* of federal legislation. Many federal laws need approval by the second chamber of the federal legislative system, the state council (*Bundesrat*). The *Bundesrat* consists of representatives of the governments of the 16 states. As a result, the federal government and the *Bundestag* need the support of the majority of the state representatives in order to bring forward a proposed legislation touching the interest of the states. Through this mechanism the influence of the *Bundesrat* becomes

legislation. Article 70(1) GG, for example, grants the power of legislation to the states 'insofar as the constitution does not confer legislative power on the federal state'. If one reads article 71 GG and the following provisions, it becomes clear that almost all main fields of legislation lie within the power of the *Bundestag* (federal parliament), although the text of the constitution suggests otherwise. Especially misleading is the text of article 74 GG. It contains a catalogue of matters in which the states have legislative powers 'as long as and to the extent that the federal state does not exercise its right to legislate by statute' (article 72(1) GG). In reality, the federal parliament has used its powers to extend its legislation to almost all the fields mentioned in article 74 GG. The catalogue laid down in this article covers all major areas of legislation: civil law, criminal law, business law, labour law, social security law, and so on. Because article 31 GG establishes that, as a rule, federal law takes precedence over state law, there are, in effect, only very limited areas in which state law stands alone and rules alone.

Moreover, the German court system reflects the dominant position of federal legislation by putting federal courts at the top of the judicial system. Article 92 GG states: 'The judicial power is entrusted to the judges; it is executed through the Federal Constitutional Court, through the federal courts established by this constitution, and through the courts of the states'. In Germany jurisdictions are not only divided by geographical districts but also by areas of law. Accordingly, there are currently five supreme federal courts: the Federal Court of Administrative Law in Leipzig; the Federal Court of Civil and Criminal Law in Karlsruhe; the Federal Court of Labour Law in Erfurt; the Federal Court of Tax Law in Munich; and the Federal Court of Social Security Law in Kassel.[5] On the next, intermediate, level in the hierarchical ranking, the highest state courts are found, which usually function as appellate courts. Below that level there are district and magistrates courts as courts of first instance in all 16 states.

The basic structure of the court system, then, has three tiers: a civil law suit is filed with the *Amtsgericht* (magistrate court) or *Landgericht* (regional court),[6]

---

very strong, and it can even lead to a situation where partisan politics produces a legislative 'standstill'. The last years of the Kohl government were characterized by a lack of a conservative majority in the *Bundesrat* (and subsequent blockades of many legislative projects), and the present Schröder government also has to deal with changing majorities within the *Bundesrat*. In December 2002, the government launched a new initiative addressing the shortcomings of the present constitutional system of federalism, see Hans-Günter Henneke 'Föderalismusreform kommt in Fahrt' [Reform of Federalism gains pace] [2003] *Deutsches Verwaltungsblatt* 845. The instalment of an all-party commission on constitutional reform is imminent; see *Frankfurter Rundschau*, 9 July 2003.

[5] There is a sixth federal court, the Federal Court of Patents in Munich, which is functioning as the first instance court in the field of patent law, and a seventh federal court, the Federal Disciplinary Court, also situated in Munich, which deals which disciplinary questions (proceedings against federal public service officers).

[6] Claims worth up to €5,000 are filed with the *Amtsgericht*, above this sum with the *Landgericht*. Some other groups of cases are exclusively handed over to the *Amtsgericht*, eg family law matters. The details are of no interest here.

and the judgment of the small claims court or regional court can be appealed. For the former, the *Landgericht* is the appellate court, for the latter it is the *Oberlandesgericht* (higher regional court). A restricted category of cases can then be brought in front of the *Bundesgerichtshof* (Federal Court of Justice) in Karlsruhe for final review. The appeal must meet strict admissibility criteria and only the legal findings of the appellate court, not the facts, must be in question. Since federal courts, as courts of last resort, do not hear evidence, they decide solely on the correct interpretation of statutes. This appellate remedy is called *Revision*.

The same three-tier structure exists in administrative law with the *Bundesverwaltungsgericht* at the top (Administrative Court, Higher State Administrative Court, Federal Administrative Court). So too in labour law with the *Bundesarbeitsgericht* at the top (Regional Court of Labour, Higher Regional Court of Labour, Federal Court of Labour), and in social security law with the *Bundessozialgericht* at the apex (Regional Court of Social Security, Higher Regional Court of Social Security, Federal Court of Social Security). Only in the field of tax law is there no intermediate level court; appeals against decisions of tax courts go directly to the *Bundesfinanzhof* (Federal Tax Court).

B. Federal courts as safeguards of unified adjudication

The federal courts at the top of each field of law serve different purposes. Their tasks are to make sure that important legal matters are settled in a final way, that new legal questions are answered, and that a uniform interpretation and application of law is guaranteed. This latter function ensures that there are no conflicting judgments in the same matter in different state jurisdictions, and it guarantees a certain degree of consistency of case law in the federation. Because the parallel structure of the top-level courts allows for differing views among the top federal courts, and even within the courts themselves, the cautious formula of a 'certain degree' is necessary.[7]

Questions relating to all fields of law, especially procedural questions such as the right to file an action by fax or email, for example, can be brought to the attention of the general senate of the highest federal courts of justice (*Gemeinsamer Senat der Obersten Gerichtshöfe des Bundes*). This top institution of adjudication consists of members of each of the federal supreme courts. It is worth mentioning, though, that the possibility to call upon the federal senate is used only on very rare occasions (ie once every 10 years).

Federal courts deal with a significant caseload. Table 8.1 shows the number of new cases in 2002 and the number of decisions rendered by the five major federal courts.

---

[7] eg in the 1980s two senates of the *Bundesgerichtshof* held completely different views in the so-called *Bürgschaftsfälle* ('suretyship cases'); the legal problem was later subject of a famous decision of the FCC on private autonomy and fundamental rights, BVerfGE 89, 214.

Table 8.1: *Number of new cases in federal courts, 2002*

Court	Number of new cases 2002	Decisions rendered in 2002
Bundesgerichtshof (Federal Court of Justice)	6,547*	6,135
Bundesverwaltungsgericht (Federal Administrative Court)	2,982	2,686
Bundesarbeitsgericht (Federal Labour Court)	1,770	1,956
Bundessozialgericht (Federal Social Security Court)	2,337	2,255
Bundesfinanzhof (Federal Tax Court)	3,512	3,425
Total	17,148	16,457

* Among these were 4,595 cases in criminal law and 1,952 in civil law matters.

Thus, in total, the five major federal supreme courts[8] rendered almost 16,500 decisions in 2002. Although many cases are dismissed for formal reasons, the courts still deliver a huge number of important 'material' decisions each year, adding another 'layer' on the written statute law. Major parts of civil, criminal, and administrative law are structured and formed this way, with some fields of law such as collective labour law being formed almost exclusively through case law.

3. The FCC: constitutional adjudication

A huge caseload is also one of the major problems pressing the FCC. The court is accessible by constitutional complaint for every (not only German) person affected by a decision or measure of the German public authorities. This wide definition of the court's jurisdiction has led to a constant rise in the number of cases since the court's foundation in 1951. For almost a decade now the number has stabilized around the figure of 5,000 cases per year.[9] The FCC has a very specific status within the German court system. The clarification within the already mentioned clause in article 92 GG ('Judicial power [. . .] is exercised by the Federal Constitutional Court, by the federal courts provided for in this constitution, and by the courts of the states') suggests that it is simply a supreme

[8] All five courts can be found on the internet: <www.bundesgerichtshof.de>, <www.bundesverwaltungsgericht.de>, <www.bundesarbeitsgericht.de>, <www.bundessozialgericht.de>, <www.bundesfinanzhof.de>. Unfortunately, all websites are available in German only.

[9] For more details concerning the last five years, see the online reports on <www.bundesverfassungsgericht.de> (under *Aufgaben, Verfahren und Organisation*).

court like those found in many other legal systems, ie a court which decides important legal questions and matters in all legal fields as the last instance for review. But this is not true; the FCC decides *only constitutional questions*.

First of all, the FCC is not a 'regular' but a *constitutional* court. The primary source of its caseload is the right to lodge a constitutional complaint. Since 1951, the right to lodge a constitutional complaint has been provided by the statute that established the court and its procedures, the *Bundesverfassungsgerichtsgesetz* (Federal Constitutional Court Act or BVerfGG). In 1969, this individual right to petition the court was incorporated into the GG (article 93(1)(4a) GG). Since then, everyone has a *constitutional right* to lodge a constitutional complaint with the FCC if she or he thinks that a court ruling, an administrative action or a law—federal or state—violates his or her constitutional rights. Approximately 99% of the 5,000 cases filed with the FCC each year are constitutional complaints. But a constitutional complaint is not a regular legal remedy against 'wrong' decisions of the lower courts and therefore no regular remedy at all; it is characterized by the court itself as an *extraordinary* remedy[10] because of its focus on the violation of constitutional rights.

Secondly, in theory the FCC does not control the inferior court's decisions on the grounds that a statute was interpreted rightly or wrongly. But of course it is sometimes not easy to draw a distinction between the interpretation of 'ordinary statutes' (the FCC calls them *einfaches Recht*—'simple law') and constitutional review. Distinguishing constitutional questions from 'simple' judicial review is especially difficult when civil law questions are at issue. One of the leading cases of the court, the *Lüth* decision,[11] stated that the basic rights and freedoms do not only constitute individual rights which are directed against the state and its institutions; the Court found that the Basic Law also established a system of objective values (*objektive Wertordnung*) that penetrates the whole legal system. This 'objective dimension' of the basic rights and freedoms extends their impact on all fields of law. As a consequence, the FCC made clear that the courts have to take the basic rights and freedoms of the Constitution into account when interpreting civil law statutes. Since the *Lüth* ruling, all fields of civil law have come under scrutiny of the FCC, sometimes with a remarkable degree of detailed

---

[10] BVerfGE 78, 58 <68> (BVerfGE = *Entscheidungen des Bundesverfassungsgerichts*, 'decisions of the FCC', cited by volume, first page and <page of the cited passage>): 'The concept of the constitutional complaint is one of an extraordinary remedy, and it should question the finality of judgments only in exceptional cases'. This self-description has not stopped the ECtHR viewing the FCC as something like a national court of last instance—with the consequence that in some cases the ECtHR has found a violation of Art 6(1) ECHR where constitutional complaints have been pending awaiting determination by the FCC for more than four years.

[11] In this 1958 case, the FCC held that an injunction by a civil law court against a Hamburg politician named Lüth violated his freedom of speech. Lüth had publicly demanded the boycott of a film which was made by Veit Harlan, a director who shot Nazi propaganda films during the Nazi era. The lower courts had found that the call for a boycott violated civil law. The FCC stressed that Lüth's actions were covered by art 5 GG which guarantees freedom of speech: BVerfGE 7, 198 <204ff>.

supervision on the lower courts' jurisprudence.[12] A wave of decisions on land-lord and tenant law in the late 1980s, for example, reformed the landlord–tenant relation of the civil law code (*Bürgerliches Gesetzbuch* or BGB) from a constitutional law perspective.[13] Judicial activism of this kind has made some critics mock that the FCC, in this respect, has become the 'nation's magistrate court'.

A. Jurisdiction of the FCC

The constitution extends the FCC's jurisdiction to 12 categories of disputes and 'such other cases as are assigned to it by federal legislation' (article 93(2) GG). Originally, the 1949 constitution ruled that the court's jurisdiction could only be invoked by federal and state governments (the chancellor/prime minister and his or her cabinet), parliamentary political parties and, in certain circumstances, courts of law. The constitution's framers rejected the proposal to confer on private parties the constitutional right to petition the FCC, a decision in line with the general practice of constitutional review in Weimar Germany and in Austria.[14] But the first elected federal parliament voted in favour of an individual complaint. As mentioned above, an individual right to lodge a constitutional complaint was first created by statute in 1951 and then incorporated into the GG in 1969.

The FCC's jurisdiction, established by the constitution itself, includes: forfeit-ure of basic rights (article 1); constitutionality of political parties (article 21(2));[15] review of election results (article 41(2)); impeachment of the federal president (article 61); disputes between high state organs (article 93(1)); abstract

[12] For recent and comprehensive discussions about the pros and cons of the FCC's constitutional adjudication see B Guggenberger and T Würtenberger (eds) *Hüter der Verfassung oder Lenker der Politik? Das Bundesverfassungsgericht im Widerstreit* [Guardian of the Constitution or Ruler of Politics? The FCC in dispute] (Nomos Baden-Baden 1998); Gunnar-Folke Schuppert *Bundesverfas-sungsgericht und gesellschaftlicher Grundkonsens* [The FCC and the basic social consensus] (Nomos Baden-Baden 2000).

[13] See for example BVerfGE 68, 361 (1985); BVerfGE 71, 230 (1985); BVerfGE 79, 80 (1988); BVerfGE 79, 283 (1988); BVerfGE 79, 292 (1988); BVerfGE 80, 48 (1989). Additionally, there was a remarkably large number of chamber decisions refining the judgments of the senate.

[14] DP Kommers 'An Introduction to the Federal Constitutional Court' (2001) 2:9 *German Law Journal* <www.germanlawjournal.com>. Kommers is the author of one of the most comprehensive books on German constitutionalism in the English language: DP Kommers *The Constitutional Jurisprudence of the Federal Republic of Germany* (2nd edn Duke University Press Durham NC 1997).

[15] In the year 2000, the federal government, the *Bundestag*, and the *Bundesrat* initialized party-banning proceedings before the FCC, seeking the ban of the extreme right-wing 'National Democratic Party of Germany'. After recognizing that the motions in the party-banning proceedings against the NPD were partly based on evidence provided by secret informants (members of the party who were supervised and paid by the secret services of the states and the federal government), and after suspending the decision to hold the substantive hearing because of this information, the FCC finally rejected the party-banning proceedings in March 2003. A number of judges stated that the surveil-lance methods of the secret services put into doubt whether there still was a possibility for the NPD to enjoy a fair trial according to Art 6(1) ECHR. As a result, it had become impossible to reach the

judicial review (article 93(1)); federal–state conflicts (article 93(1) and 84(4)); concrete judicial review (article 100(1)); removal of judges (article 98); intra-state constitutional disputes (article 99); public international law actions (article 100(2)); applicability of federal law (article 126); and constitutional complaints (article 93(1)). All these jurisdictions are also enumerated in the Federal Constitutional Court Act (BVerfGG or FCC Act).

B. Constitutional complaints—procedure and consequences

Of the FCC's various competences, the constitutional complaint is the most frequently invoked and the most visible.[16] A former president of the FCC once remarked that the 'administration of justice in the Federal Republic of Germany would be unthinkable without the complaint of unconstitutionality'.[17] According to article 93(1)(4a) GG, any person may file a complaint of unconstitutionality if one of his or her fundamental substantive or procedural rights under the constitution has been violated by 'public authority,' including judicial decisions, administrative decrees, and legislative acts. Before filing a constitutional complaint, all other available means to find relief in the ordinary courts must be exhausted. Constitutional complaints must be lodged within a certain time, identifying the offending action or omission and the agency responsible. The complaint must also specify the constitutional right that has been violated. The FCC Act requires the court to accept any complaint if it is constitutionally significant or if the failure to accept it would work a grave hardship on the complainant. The procedure for filing complaints in the FCC is relatively easy and inexpensive. No filing fees or formal papers are required. Some complaints are even handwritten, and a significant number are prepared without the aid of a lawyer. No legal assistance is required at any stage of the complaint proceeding.[18]

As a consequence of these rather permissive 'standing' rules, the FCC has been flooded with complaints—from 452 in the court's first year to almost 5,000 in latter years. However, the number of successful complaints is very small: in the last five years, only approximately 3% of the complaints were upheld. This figure also reflects the strict standards of subsidiarity applied by the FCC; complaints are quickly dismissed if they do not pass the strict scrutiny tests of 'substantiality' and 'subsidiarity'.

two-thirds majority of judges necessary for a decision banning the NPD: decision of 18 March 2003, cases no 2 BvB 01/03, 02/03 and 03/03, <www.bundesverfassungsgericht.de>. It was the first time since the 1950s, when the Court declared two political parties unconstitutional (the Neo-Nazi Party SRP and the German Communist Party KPD), that the federal government had initiated such a proceeding (attempts to ban right-wing groups in 1990 failed because these groups were not 'political parties' in the sense of art 21), and it was the first time ever that the *Bundestag* and the *Bundesrat* also took part in the proceedings.

[16] Kommers (n 14). Justice Wolfgang Zeidler 'Public Address' noted in *The Constitutional Jurisprudence of the Federal Republic of Germany* (n 14) 14 fn 60.

[17] Zeidler (n 16).   [18] See art 90ff FCC Act.

C. Structure and procedures of the FCC

The FCC Act codifies and fleshes out the Basic Law's provisions relating to the court's organization, powers, and procedures.[19] The Act, inter alia, lays down the qualifications and tenure of the court's members; specifies the procedures of judicial selection; provides for the two, eight-judge senates (with each of them being 'the' FCC); and enumerates the jurisdiction of each senate.

The most important structural feature of the FCC is its division into two, eight-judge senates with mutually exclusive jurisdiction and personnel. Jurisdiction over constitutional complaints and the judicial review of laws is shared by the two senates, with special jurisdiction assigned to each senate.[20] In all other proceedings the second senate has exclusive jurisdiction.

The judges of each senate are assigned to the senate's three to four chambers, each of which is staffed by three judges. The court's president, Professor Hans-Joachim Papier (a member of the first senate), and the vice-president, Professor Winfried Hassemer (a member of the second senate), participate in the work of two of their senate's chambers. The chambers' main task is to determine whether a constitutional complaint is to be accepted for adjudication. A chamber may dismiss a complaint if all three of its members consider it to be 'inadmissible or to offer no prospect of success for other reasons'. If one of the three judges votes to accept the complaint, the case is then registered with the full senate. The chambers may also rule on the merits of a constitutional complaint if all three judges agree with the result and the decision clearly lies within standards already laid down in a case decided by the full senate. Thus, the chambers dispose of 95% of all complaints, relieving the senates of what would otherwise be 'an impossible task'.[21]

D. Status and recruitment of judges and personnel

The recruitment of the judges of the FCC is basically a political process. Half of the judges are elected by the federal parliament (*Bundestag*) and the other half by the state council (*Bundesrat*): article 94(1) GG. The federal parliament elects an electoral committee, and the committee elects the judges with a majority of two-thirds of the votes. The same majority is needed in the state council where judges are elected by all members of the council. As a consequence of this election system, the two leading political parties, the Christian Democrats and the Social Democrats, have to reach a consensus over the candidates to be elected. There are no public hearings, and the outcome of an election is mostly a result of 'package deals' and negotiations behind closed doors. Consequently, each justice has entered the court on a 'party ticket'. However, this does not mean that the

---

[19] Kommers (n 14). Also <www.bverfg.de>.
[20] For the present *Geschäftsverteilung*, see <www.bverfg.de> (sv '*Verfahren*').
[21] Kommers (n 14) para 16.

elected candidate is actually a party member, or even an affiliate to one of the major political parties. In fact, even if justices were clearly sympathetic to one or the other political party before they were elected, many of them turned out to be rather independent from party lines, and in some cases party politicians deeply regretted their choice afterwards.

The judges are appointed for one 12-year term, with an absolute age limit of 68 and a minimum age requirement of 40 years. Justices in office may not be members of the federal parliament, the state council, the federal government, or of any of the corresponding bodies of a state. Except for teaching at a law school, they are not allowed to exercise an additional occupation. At least three of the eight judges of each senate have to be selected from one of the federal supreme courts. The majority of the other five judges consist of legal scholars, and some of the judges are former politicians.[22] As at 2003, there are three former federal supreme court judges, four law professors and one former politician in each senate; there are five women among the 16 judges serving as FCC Justices. There is no gender quota, and no regional or *Länder* quota is laid down by procedural rules.

Each Justice is assisted by three legal advisors (*wissenschaftliche Mitarbeiter*). Most of these legal advisors are practising judges who leave their bench for two or three years and return to their court at the end of their term. It is generally believed that the fact that they have served some time at the FCC is in no way harmful to their career. A smaller group of *wissenschaftliche Mitarbeiter* consists of district attorneys, lawyers and public servants from federal or state ministries, and some of the *Mitarbeiter* were assistant professors at university law schools. Although this is of course not a typical career, some *Mitarbeiter* later become judges of the FCC; five out of the 16 judges currently serving at the Court formerly worked as *wissenschaftliche Mitarbeiter*.[23] The group of *Mitarbeiter* as a whole is frequently referred to as the 'third senate' of the court. In the FCC Act, the *wissenschaftliche Mitarbeiter* are not mentioned at all. Only the court's own standing orders (*Geschäftsordnung des Bundesverfassungsgerichts*) describe in rather vague terms that the judges can select their *Mitarbeiter* at their own discretion and that they assist the judges 'with the execution of their duty of office' (article 13 of the standing orders). Some commentators are critical of the fact that the invisible, but supposedly actual, influence of the *Mitarbeiter* on the outcome of the decisions of the FCC is far too great, taking into account that they are not elected but only selected.[24] On the other hand, without them the court would probably soon collapse under the huge caseload.

---

[22] Most politicians appointed to the FCC in the last 50 years were former ministers of justice in one of the *Länder*.

[23] In the first senate: Haas, Jaeger; in the second senate: Sommer, Broß, Mellinghoff.

[24] See R Lamprecht 'Ist das BVerfG noch gesetzlicher Richter?' 2001 *Neue Juristische Wochenschrift* 419 for further references.

4. STATUS AND FUNCTION OF THE FCC WITHIN THE GERMAN COURT SYSTEM

A. The FCC as the 'guardian of the constitution' and 'highest organ of the constitution'

The FCC is a court, but it is also more than a court. Immediately after its foundation 50 years ago, debates started concerning its legal status, its relation to the government and other political bodies of the Federal Republic, its funding, and so on. The FCC Act was very vague about the status of the FCC. Therefore, in 1952 the Court issued a memorandum stating the following: 'The FCC as the highest guardian of the constitution is, according to the text and the meaning of the Constitution and the Federal Constitutional Court Act, at the same time an organ of the Constitution provided with highest authority'; as a court, it belongs 'to a completely different level than all the other courts'.[25]

The FCC's power to enact its own standing orders reflects its outstanding position as a federal constitutional body. The standing orders are published in the same way as federal laws—a privilege which belongs only to the other highest federal constitutional bodies, especially the *Bundestag* and the *Bundesrat*. Additionally, the FCC has its own budget and the president of the court is the principal (though not the employer) of the court's staff.

Since its foundation in 1951, the FCC plays a prominent role not only among the federal constitutional bodies, but also within German society as a whole. It is said to be an important factor of social integration; the fact that the FCC, as an institution, leads the polls when citizens are asked for institutions they trust the most, illustrates that beyond all criticism the adjudication of the Court is widely accepted and approved.[26] In these past 50 years the FCC has created a case law that literally breathed life into the *Grundgesetz* (GG). More than 100 volumes of its decisions, collected in the printed volumes of the BVerfGE and edited by the respective members of the court, have become the bedrock of constitutional interpretation and adjudication in Germany. All public powers, the legislative organs, the governments and the courts, are directly bound by the fundamental rights: 'The following basic rights shall bind the legislature, the executive, and the judiciary as directly applicable law' (article 1(3) GG). For this reason, all public powers are directly bound also by the decisions of the court interpreting the rights outlined in the constitution. Article 31 of the FCC Act repeats that obligation, adding at 31(2) that in certain cases the findings of the court have *statutory force*. If a court ruling declares a federal or state law to be void or unconstitutional it even has to be published in the official *Federal Law Gazette* (corresponding to the UK's Statutes of the Realm). This mechanism has led to an omnipresence of the fundamental rights and freedoms in the process of creating, interpreting, and applying ordinary statute law.

---

[25] See *Jahrbuch des öffentlichen Rechts* Vol 6 (1957) 144ff, 198ff; BVerfGE 6, 300, 304.
[26] J Limbach *Im Namen des Volkes* (Deutsche Verlags-Anstalt Stuttgart 1999) 153–154.

B. The FCC and the federal supreme courts

The relation between the FCC and the federal supreme courts can be described as rather distant and relaxed. Apart from occasional cases of direct confrontation or even resistance from lower courts,[27] all courts silently adopt the FCC's constitutional points of view, or even openly welcome its rulings. This is especially true for the federal supreme courts which usually follow the FCC's rulings and apply them without any public dispute. The FCC itself has rather distant relationships with the federal supreme courts. Due to the fact that only one of the federal supreme courts is situated in Karlsruhe with the FCC, personal contact between judges of the FCC and justices of the federal supreme courts is not routine. Of course, the FCC is criticized from time to time for allegedly blurring the limits of constitutional review and interfering with the sphere of judicial review in general. But this criticism can be found almost exclusively in law journals, and its authors are lawyers and legal scholars, not federal supreme court judges.

C. The FCC: a success story?

The FCC plays a central role in German jurisprudence and politics alike. A brief look at recent cases and recent public discussions involving the FCC illustrates best the role of the court and its influence within the German society than a long academic description. Within four weeks in June and July 2001, judgments were handed down in the following cases.

On 19 June 2001 the court held an oral hearing on the topic of the new NATO strategy. The *Bundestag* fraction of the PDS (Party of Democratic Socialism)[28] claimed that the federal government's assent to the new NATO Strategic Concept in April 1999 violated the constitutional rights of the *Bundestag* because the federal government did not first consult with and obtain the consent of the federal parliament. For almost three hours, the Foreign Minister Joschka Fischer and the Defence Minister Rudolf Scharping defended the governments' actions, characterizing the new NATO strategy paper as a mere political document and distinguishing it from an international treaty. Many constitutional and international law scholars gave statements for both sides and discussed the subject with the judges. The hearing was heavily covered by all major newspapers and television stations.[29]

---

[27] Recently, a North Rhine-Westphalia Higher Regional Administrative Court openly criticized an FCC ruling as being wrong, and applied its own constitutional opinion to a case concerning art 8 GG (freedom of assembly). The immediately following constitutional complaint against the Higher Regional Administrative Court's ruling was successful, and finally the lower court gave up its position.

[28] The PDS is the successor of the SED, the former ruling party of the GDR.

[29] For an English-language report on the NATO Strategic Concept hearing in the FCC, see 'Merely a Landmark or a Change of Course: The Federal Constitutional Court Hears Arguments in the Strategic Concept Case' (2001) 2(11) *German Law Journal* <www.germanlawjournal.com>.

On 26 June 2001, the court heard arguments concerning a provision of the state of Brandenburg which eliminated religion as a compulsory subject in state schools. Instead of religion, the state introduced a subject called 'Lebenskunde/ Erziehung/Religion' (LER) where religion was one of the topics but not the only topic. The Catholic Church and Protestant churches in Brandenburg, as well as the Christian Democratic opposition in Brandenburg, claimed that the Brandenburg law violated article 7(3) GG, which states that religion has to be 'an ordinary subject' in state schools.[30] In response, Brandenburg claimed that its statute was covered by article 141 GG, which, under certain conditions, permits exceptions to article 7(3) GG. Like the NATO strategy case, the *LER* case drew strong public attention with all major papers reporting and television stations sending reporters to Karlsruhe. More than 10 renowned public and constitutional law scholars attended the hearing, giving statements about their view of the relation between religion and public education.[31]

On 11 July 2001, the court held an oral hearing on the new federal Partnership for Life statute which grants lesbian and gay couples the right to form a 'registered partnership.' The Bavarian government claimed that these provisions constituted a lesbian and gay marriage and therefore violated article 6 GG, which they argued granted 'special protection' to the traditional, heterosexual marital institution and forbids an equal or comparably strong legal protection to lesbian and gay partnerships. As the statute was meant to come into force on 1 August 2001, the Bavarian and Saxon state governments sought a temporary injunction postponing its entry into force. The eight judges of the first senate of the FCC delivered their judgment on 18 July 2001.[32] By a majority of 5:3, they rejected the request for a temporary injunction, again heavily covered by the news media.

Many other recent cases could be mentioned here to underline the hypothesis that the FCC has taken both the position of an additional arena for the self-reflection of German society and the position of a legal authority ending (but not finishing) controversial political and legal debates. The political, legal, and ethical question, for example, whether and to what extent Prenatal Implementation Diagnostics (PID) should be allowed and/or practised is one of the biggest political issues in Germany. The existing laws prohibit the production and use of embryos for research purposes but leave a loophole for the import of embryos.

---

[30] There are only few private schools in Germany; the overwhelming majority of pupils attend state schools.

[31] Additionally, F Merz, the leader of the Christian Democratic faction in the federal parliament (and a possible candidate for prime minister in the next federal elections), came to Karlsruhe and delivered a statement.

[32] Recent judgments of the Court and further information about the Court can be found at its website: <www.bverfg.de> or <www.bundesverfassungsgericht.de>—unfortunately only in German. For an English-language report on the FCC's hearing on the request for a temporary injunction in the *Lifetime Partnership Act* case, see A Maurer 'Federal Constitutional Court to Decide Whether to Issue a Temporary Injunction Against Germany's New Lifetime Partnerships Law for Homosexual Couples' (2001) 2(12) *German Law Journal* <www.germanlawjournal.com>.

For several months debates in the news media and political debates in the federal parliament examined this issue from all possible angles. What is striking, though, is that all participants of the discussion referred to article 1 GG ('human dignity is inviolable') and to the constitutional jurisdiction of the FCC as 'their' authority and reference point. The judgments of the FCC have become a political weapon *and* a moral and legal argument within this debate. Everyone takes for granted that the questions of PID and medical research on mature human cells will be brought before the court: 'sooner or later Karlsruhe is going to decide'.

These examples show the strong political impact of the FCC's constitutional power and its case law, and they illustrate that there can be no doubt about the fact that the FCC is a crucial factor in the political process. But this outstanding position of the court at the same time causes irritations within the political system itself. At a very early stage of public and political debates, participants refer to the case law of the FCC to strengthen their arguments, a strategy that is of course legitimate. But this 'constitutionalizing' of the political process has had the effect that the public and law-makers alike, depending on their political point of view, fear or threaten with forthcoming decisions of the FCC. At this early stage of legislation, then, political parties represented in the federal parliament engage lawyers and scholars to interpret the relevant decisions in detail and to predict—like the Delphic oracle—the possible outcome of a dispute before the court. Thus, there is a danger of anticipatory obedience too often guiding the political and law-making process. Professor Jutta Limbach, the former president of the court, comments on this chilling effect:

We judges could be proud about this omnipresence of the federal Constitutional Court if the political debate indicated a sensitivity towards fundamental rights on the part of politicians. But that is only true to a limited extent. In the Federal Parliament and the State Council, and among the public, political arguments are daily spiced up by using the accusation of the alleged unconstitutionality of a planned decision. The threat of taking the road to Karlsruhe is now part of the ritual stock-in-trade of politics in Germany. This anticipation of a constitutional risk leads to risk-aversion and lack of innovation. Anticipatory obedience is harmful to the social imagination and tends to cripple the legislator's delight in deciding.[33]

Although this criticism of too much self-obedience of law-makers is convincing, there is also the other side of the coin. To a certain degree, the court's chilling effect on the creative powers of parliament is self-made. Its broad interpretation of the status and function of the fundamental rights as an 'objective order of values' has initiated some very detailed interventions[34] by the Court in the first

---

[33] J Limbach 'The Effects of the Jurisdiction of the German Federal Constitutional Court' (EUI Working Paper LAW 99/5 European University Institute Florence 1999) 21.

[34] A perfect example of strong judicial activism is the second decision of the FCC on abortion, BVerfGE 88, 203. In it the court declared void a statute that was a result of a complex compromise between MPs of all factions of the *Bundestag*. Additionally, using its powers under art 35 FCC, the court handed down a temporary injunction with a list of detailed provisions for pre-abortion counselling, thus acting like an *Ersatzgesetzgeber* ('ersatz law-maker').

place. A prominent former Justice of the Court, Ernst-Wolfgang Böckenförde, correctly warns that there is a danger of a transition from a parliamentary system of law-making to a *'verfassungsgerichtlicher Jurisdiktionsstaat'*, a legal system dominated by constitutional court decisions.[35] Thus, by following a stricter concept of judicial self-restraint the court itself could loosen the chain it has imposed on the law-makers. Recent decisions in the field of social security law and tax law imposing even stricter constitutional scrutiny, however, suggest that the Court's constitutional policy heads into the opposite direction.

5. HIERARCHICAL DOMINANCE: THE FCC, THE STATE CONSTITUTIONS, AND THE STATE CONSTITUTIONAL COURTS

A. Competences and conflicts: the flexible tools of 'Selbständige Verfassungsräume', and 'Homogenität'

Of the 16 *Länder* that form the Federal Republic, each *Land* has its own constitution, and 15 out of the 16 *Länder* have set up a state constitutional court in their respective constitutions, most of which have been established even before the foundation of the Federal Republic in 1949.[36] The institutional and procedural design of the courts varies greatly: in many *Länder*, the constitutional court can only decide about matters related to the balance of powers, and the court can only be addressed by the *Länder* parliament, political parties represented in the *Länder* parliament, or the government, whereas in some *Länder* the citizens are entitled to lodge a constitutional complaint similar to the complaint on the federal level.[37] In the latter cases, the courts are entitled to decide about violations of fundamental rights as laid down in the respective state constitution. As the courts are state courts, their jurisdiction is in principle restricted to decisions of state courts (or legislative measures of the state parliament, if the respective procedures Act allows these to be addressed by an individual's complaint).

In its major decisions on the relationship between the state constitutions and the Basic Law, the FCC had to define the connection between the constitutional sphere of the states and federal power. The task was to find a balance between two conflicting principles: autonomy and coherence. The court held in several decisions, on the one hand, that the constitutional order of a state creates an independent and autonomous 'constitutional zone', a *'selbständiger*

---

[35] Ernst-Wolfgang Böckenförde 'Grundrechte als Grundsatznormen' ('Fundamental rights as fundamental norms') (1990) *Der Staat* 1, 25.

[36] Hessen was the first state to introduce a new constitution after the fall of Nazi Germany; its constitution dates from 1946.

[37] A typical example for a 'balance of power'court is the *Verfassungsgerichtshof* in North Rhine-Westphalia, whereas in Hessen, art 131(3) of the constitution in connection with 43 of the statute on the state constitutional court allows for a Hessen citizen to lodge an individual complaint claiming an infringement of a fundamental right laid down in the Hessen constitution.

Verfassungsraum'.[38] This means that the states are entitled to create their own constitutional and legal order, and that federal institutions are not allowed to interfere with this state legal order. Article 28 GG, on the other hand, demands that the constitutional order in the *Länder* 'must conform to the principles of a republican, democratic, and social state governed by the rule of law, within the meaning of the Grundgesetz'.

This principle of homogeneity (*Homogenitätsprinzip*) proved to be a flexible tool in the hand of the FCC. In its highly debated 1990 decisions on *Länder* statutes granting local voting rights to non-German citizens,[39] the court held that the execution of local authority pursuant to article 28 GG demands an 'uninterrupted chain of legitimation' starting with the democratic sovereignty of the German people in article 20(1) GG.[40] Thus, the FCC found, state parliaments were forbidden to grant voting rights to non-German citizens without a *Grundgesetz* provision expressly allowing this transfer of sovereignty to non-Germans, because these persons are not part of the (German) *Volk* according to article 20 GG. As a consequence, non-EU citizens are still excluded from state voting rights, whereas since 1993 article 28 GG allows for EU citizens to take part in local elections.

The recent decision of the FCC on the new Immigration Act represents the latest example of a flexible use of conflicting *Grundgesetz* principles and standards.[41] In this decision the court balanced the principles of autonomy and homogeneity in a rather dubious way:[42] It had to decide, among other questions, whether a *Land* prime minister is entitled to vote for the whole group of *Land* representatives in the state council (*Bundesrat*) in case of conflict between the respective representatives of the *Land*. According to the relevant constitution of Brandenburg, its prime minister Manfred Stolpe actually was the head of the government so that one might conclude that in case of conflict (this was what happened here) the prime minister had the final word. The FCC, however, found otherwise. It emphasized that the respective constitutional provisions of the *Land* Brandenburg and the hierarchical order between the prime minister and the other members of his government did not play any role in the procedure. In the *Bundesrat*, the FCC found, the prime minister of Brandenburg had no right

---

[38] BVerfGE 99, 1, 11 onwards with further references.

[39] BVerfGE 83, 37 (concerning a Schleswig-Holstein statute) and 60 (concerning a Hamburg statute).

[40] For a detailed and sharp critique of this concept see B-O Bryde, 'Die bundesrepublikanische Volksdemokratie als Irrweg des Demokratietheorie' [Democratic theory on a wrong track—the concept of a German people's democracy'] (1994) *Staatswissenschaften und Staatspraxis* 330 (discussing the *Maastricht* decision and the *Kommunalwahlrecht* decision). In 2001, Professor Bryde himself became Justice of the first senate of the FCC.

[41] Case 2 BvF 1/02, judgment of 18 December 2002 <www.bverfg.de> (sv '*Entscheidungen*'). For a comprehensive English summary of this judgment, and information about its background, see N Arndt, R Nickel 'Federalism Revisited: Constitutional Court Strikes Down New Immigration Act for Formal Reasons' (2003) 4(2) *German Law Journal* <www.germanlawjournal.com>.

[42] For a detailed critique of this decision see N Arndt, R Nickel (n 41).

to overrule the voting of his fellow Brandenburg ministers, and from the point of view of the *Grundgesetz* he lacked legal authority over their conduct in the voting process. In its reasoning the court used the principle of the '*selbständige Verfassungsräume*' to underline the superior position of the *Bundesrat* provisions in the *Grundgesetz*—although article 51(3) GG clearly allows for orders of the state cabinet to bind its *Bundesrat* representatives. Thus, the court failed to deliver a sound reason why Brandenburg's constitution was irrelevant and why its prime minister was not entitled to use his constitutional powers to override a dissenting vote of another Brandenburg representative.[43]

B. Distributing the caseload burden: strategies

The consistently overwhelming caseload of the FCC—with almost 5,000 cases submitted each year—inspired the FCC in the 1990s to revive the role of state constitutional courts. A number of FCC decisions recognized the exclusive jurisdiction of these courts in several matters, eg regarding state parliament and municipal elections if election principles are at stake.[44] Reversing its former judgments in this respect, the court held that the principle of homogeneity in article 28 GG expressly demands that 'the people shall be represented by a body chosen in general, direct, free, equal, and secret elections in the States and municipalities' but does *not* constitute a federal constitutional *right of individuals* to lodge a complaint with the FCC. Thus, it is the task of state constitutional courts to safeguard the election principles laid down in article 28 GG.[45] In other cases the FCC demanded that complainants address certain legal aspects, especially concerning due process, first to the respective state constitutional courts before a constitutional complaint could be lodged with the FCC, given that the state constitutional court is accessible for individuals.[46] Although meant to ease the caseload burden of the Court, these measures have not been very successful as the overall number of constitutional complaints did not drop significantly.

Furthermore, the FCC assumes jurisdiction over state elections when it considers it to be appropriate. The court's recent decision in the *Hessen election* case[47] is a good example for a back and forth of positions that some commentators call an arbitrary handling of self-written rules by the court, and others praise as a safeguard for constitutional coherence in a federal system. In this respect, there are no great differences between the FCC and the US Supreme Court.

---

[43] N Arndt, R Nickel (n 41) paras 45–48.   [44] BVerfGE 99, 1, 11 onwards.
[45] BVerfGE 99, 1, 17 onwards.
[46] The execution of this power seems to lead to the effect that state constitutional courts measure federal law on state constitutions thus violating art 31 GG, which states that federal law shall take precedence over state law. However, state constitutional courts can be invoked in federal law cases (for example, in civil law cases) only if the respective state constitution contains provisions equivalent to the respective GG provision. A state constitutional court is not entitled to declare that federal law violates state constitutional law.
[47] BVerfGE 103, 111.

In conclusion, although German federalism is strong when it comes to the mechanisms of federal legislation, due to the fact that there is only little room for state legislation, the influence of state constitutional courts is rather small. In addition, the *Grundrechte* (civil, political, and social rights) laid down in the *Grundgesetz* are binding for all local, state and federal legislative bodies, courts and authorities. State law and actions of state or local authorities, thus, can be subject of a constitutional complaint lodged with the FCC if the *Grundrechte* are affected. As a consequence, there is only a limited number of fields left where state constitutional courts have exclusive jurisdiction over state affairs. And in the fields of shared jurisdiction the FCC can always overrule state constitutional court decisions if it finds that the Federal Constitution was violated, and in this respect the vague principle of homogeneity in article 28 GG is also a flexible and useful instrument. The limits of the FCC's discretion to decide state matters are, of course, highly debated. But as the decisions of the FCC are irreversible, the final word always belongs to the Court: Karlsruhe *locuta, causa finita*.

6. Leaving the nation state behind: the FCC and the European courts[48]

Apart from inevitable criticism on the FCC's structural defects and on disturbing effects of its adjudication, the Court's high reputation in the German public opinion shows that its creation 50 years ago marked the beginning of a success story. Donald P Kommers praises the Court:

Owing to its record in defending the principles of democracy and constitutionalism, not to mention the volume and sophistication of its jurisprudence, the Federal Constitutional Court has blossomed into one of the world's most prestigious constitutional tribunals. The Court has served as a leading model for the creation of judicial review in the new democracies of Eastern Europe as well as in many other countries around the world. In addition, national courts of constitutional review routinely consult its decisions when deciding cases and disputes under their respective national constitutions. In short, the Federal Constitutional Court's influence around the globe is now fully the equal, if not more so, to that of the United States Supreme Court.[49]

The success of the FCC has been embedded within the framework of the nation state of West Germany, and since 1990, of the unified Germany. But with the rise of the epoch of 'Europeanization' in the 1990s, the political and legal framework has dramatically changed. The court's role as a comprehensive 'guardian of the Constitution' is in danger. First, since the Treaties of Maastricht, Amsterdam, and Nice, European Community law covers or may cover an increasing number of subjects that were previously reserved to the member states' national sovereignty

---

[48] This part is a summary of a lecture I gave at a conference at the FCC in 2000. It was later published as R Nickel 'Zur Zukunft des Bundesverfassungsgerichts im Zeitalter der Europäisierung' ['On the Future of the FCC in the Era of "Europeanization"'] (2001) *Juristenzeitung* 625.

[49] Kommers (n 14) fn 18.

(such as laws relating to political asylum). In addition, the Charter of Fundamental Rights of the European Union may also grant the European Court of Justice (ECJ) a new broadly defined tool to further European Union human rights jurisdiction.[50]

Secondly, although less threatening, the European Court of Human Rights (ECtHR) also plays an important role in all fields of law, particularly since the ECtHR has become permanent, thus significantly increasing its production of case law. The greater density of ECtHR case law may lead to conflicting decisions in similar cases and/or to conflicting interpretations of similar civil, political and social rights.

Both courts—the ECJ and the ECtHR—threaten the key role of the FCC as a guardian of the German constitution and its traditional function as a force of social integration.

A. The ECtHR: a 'deficiency guarantor' rather than a competitive constitutional court

The European Convention on Human Rights (ECHR) was for a long time only an additional instrument of human rights protection in Germany. Due to the comprehensive jurisdiction and the detailed adjudication of the FCC, the ECHR had only very limited significance in Germany. Only since the intensifying of the European integration in the 1990s and the introduction of a 'new' ECtHR through Protocol 11 ECHR, the Convention has gained more importance in the national context. Three particular reasons can be identified for this development: access to the ECtHR is much easier now than before 1998 when admissibility applications were considered by the European Commission on Human Rights; a public relations offensive in 1998 increased awareness about the ECtHR within the German population; and finally, the number of contracting states of the Council of Europe has risen dramatically, so that nowadays 45 countries have signed the Convention, and the ECtHR's 43 judges have to deal with tens of thousands of applications.

The ECtHR's jurisprudence is a constant flow of decisions that interpret the contents and range of the fundamental rights of the ECHR in a more and more detailed manner. Although the *Grundgesetz* contains more fundamental rights than the ECHR, there are already overlapping subjects of adjudication. This is so not only with respect to procedural rights, but also for a number of fields where the range of 'substantial' human rights (the right to privacy or freedom of expression, for example) is at stake.[51]

The most prominent example in Germany is probably the case of Dorothea Voigt, a school teacher who was once affiliated with the *Deutsche*

---

[50] Although still only a political document, the Charter has already been used by the Advocate-General, and it has become part II of the new Draft of an EU Constitutional Treaty.

[51] For some examples from the German legal context, see Nickel (n 48) 627.

Kommunistische Partei (DKP).[52] In 1986, Mrs Voigt was temporarily suspended by the *Land* of Lower Saxony, and later laid off, on the ground that she was an active DKP party member and therefore had 'failed to comply with the duty of loyalty to the Constitution'. The duty of political loyalty, which admittedly restricts civil servants' fundamental rights, was one of the traditional principles of the civil service and has constitutional status by virtue of article 33(5) GG. The administrative court deciding the matter stated that this duty should take precedence over the provisions of international instruments such as the ECHR. In 1990, a chamber of the FCC declined to admit the constitutional complaint for review, on the ground that it had insufficient prospects of success. In an earlier decision in 1975, the second senate of the FCC had declared that the practice of the *Länder* to screen their civil servants regarding political loyalty, and to lay off active DKP members, does not violate the freedom of expression (article 5(1) GG) or the freedom of association (article 9(1) GG).[53] In contrast, the Grand Chamber of the ECtHR, by a slim majority of 10 to 9, held that the action taken by the state of Lower Saxony constituted a violation of Article 10 ECHR (freedom of expression) and Article 11 ECHR (freedom of association). It cautiously started with the following statement: 'The Court's task, in exercising its supervisory jurisdiction, is not to take the place of the competent national authorities but rather to review under Article 10 the decisions they delivered pursuant to their power of appreciation.' Nevertheless the ECtHR came to the conclusion that under the given circumstances there was no adequate justification for the dismissal of Mrs Voigt, and awarded her compensation under Article 50 ECHR.

Another important field of conflicting jurisdictions is criminal law. Some commentators have already concluded that the ECtHR plays a more active and effective role regarding the defence of individual rights of defendants against the 'ever wider and more intense encroachment powers of police forces and public prosecutors', than the German FCC does in its decisions.[54] Additionally, recent decisions of the ECtHR in the field of family law have raised public attention in Germany.[55]

In the end, however, the ECtHR is hardly a serious threat to the FCC's dominant position in the field of fundamental rights and their interpretation and application. The ECtHR is still 'only' an instrument of international law. Its judgments cannot be formally enforced against the contracting states and it has no power to quash a decision of a court within a Council of Europe contracting state. Although an active human rights court, the ECtHR basically protects only a minimum standard of rights, and apart from rather timely conflicts in the fields

---

[52] (App 17851/91) *Vogt v Germany* (1996) 21 EHRR 205 <www.echr.coe.int>.

[53] BVerfGE 39, 334. For a sharp (and excellent) critique of this decision and its methodical flaws, see J Esser [1975] *Juristenzeitung* 555.

[54] Kühne and Nash [2000] *Juristenzeitung* 996.

[55] See the 'parental rights' and 'family life' cases concerning Art 8 ECHR: (App 30943/96) *Sahin v Germany* (2003) 36 EHRR 43; (App 46544/99) *Kutzner v Germany* (2002) 35 EHRR 25; (App 25735/94) *Elsholz v Germany* (2002) 34 EHRR 58.

of criminal law and family law, there are only very limited areas where the ECtHR ensures a clearly higher standard of protection than the FCC. Finally, the ECHR does not deliver a 'constitutional framework for Europe', but rather an additional safety net in case the domestic legal institutions fail to protect basic human rights. The ECtHR is currently not another constitutional guardian, but only a 'deficiency guarantor' for the protection of fundamental human rights.

B. Multi-level constitutional adjudication: a pacified relationship between the FCC and the ECJ

For a long time, the institutional relationship between the FCC and the European Court of Justice (ECJ) seemed to have been clarified. After the first 'as long as' decision of the FCC,[56] reserving the FCC a right to constitutional scrutiny over European Community law, the ECJ in numerous decisions stated (a) that there are—mostly unwritten—fundamental rights within the Community legal order, and (b) that it is the task of the ECJ to protect these rights against violations through Community legal acts. Subsequently, the FCC delivered its second 'as long as' decision,[57] analysing the ECJ's fundamental rights adjudication and stating that *as long as* the ECJ generally protects fundamental rights on an essentially similar level as the FCC, constitutional complaints concerning Community law are inadmissible.

However, this apparently clear vertical division of two parallel legal orders was obscured by the famous 1993 Maastricht decision. In it, the FCC made some strong remarks on the legitimacy of Community law and the relation between German constitutionalism and the emerging EU legal order. It was the first time that a constitutional court of an EU Member State seriously challenged the legal construction of the EU and its democratic legitimacy. Many commentators criticized the FCC as a defender of a backward nation state ideology,[58] and some saw the EU again under supervision of the FCC.[59] A misleading quotation, and a seemingly general scepticism towards a further democratization of the EU expressed within the decision, fuelled fears that the FCC was seeking to redefine the limits of Europeanization.

In the following years, the *Banana market* cases (concerning import restrictions on non-EU bananas) became a focus point for the hopes for (and the fears of) a new FCC regime on Community law.[60] The FCC's *Banana market* decision

---

[56] BVerfGE 37, 271 (1974), and stating that *as long as* there is no equivalent fundamental rights protection on the Community level, the FCC is entitled to scrutinize whether Community legal acts violate the fundamental rights laid down in the *Grundgesetz*.

[57] BVerfGE 73, 339 (1986).

[58] See especially JHH Weiler 'The State *'über alles'*, Demos, Telos, and the German Maastricht decision' in *Festschrift für Ulrich Everling* (Nomos Baden-Baden 1996) vol 1, 1651.

[59] C Tomuschat 'Die Europäische Union unter der Aufsicht des Bundesverfassungsgerichts' (1993) *Europäische Grundrechte-Zeitschrift* 489.

[60] See CU Schmidt 'All bark and no bite: Notes on the FCC's "Banana-Decision"' (2001) 7 *European Law Journal* 95.

in 2000, however, disappointed those who expected a serious turn.[61] The FCC fully confirmed the findings of the second 'as long as' decision, stating that the Maastricht decision had been 'misunderstood', and declaring that it did not contain any shift in constitutional scrutiny with regard to fundamental rights.

Indeed, the real meaning of the Maastricht decision has to be located somewhere else. In a central passage of the judgment, the FCC vigorously addresses the topic of competences and states that legal acts of the EU overstepping the limits of EU competences ('*ausbrechende Rechtsakte*') were not binding for German authorities.[62] Who defines which EU/Community legal acts lie within the limits of EC competences, and which ones overstep the limits, are issues which remain open today. In this regard, the latest ECJ judgment on the tobacco advertisement directive can be interpreted as one possible answer to this question.[63] In its tobacco ruling the ECJ clearly rejects the Commission's attempt to interpret the respective articles of the EC Treaty in a too flexible manner, thus signalling to the public and the constitutional courts of the EU Member States alike that it is taking its duties as a 'competence court of the EU' seriously.

In conclusion, the political influence of the FCC's Maastricht decision has been strong, but the *legal* impact has been rather limited. There was not even a single case where the FCC had to decide whether a legal act of the EU oversteps the limits of competences laid down in the EC Treaty. Thus, the FCC and the ECJ have returned to business as usual, and the ever growing law production of the EU will slowly but certainly erode the central position of the FCC as *the* fundamental rights court of Germany. At the same time, the ECJ moves into the position of an additional constitutional court. Whether the ECJ is also able to supplement the function of the FCC as a factor of social integration remains to be seen. The 'Brussels regime' and 'Luxembourg findings' are still too distant, it seems, to replace a home-grown institution deeply rooted both in the legal tradition and social practice of the Federal Republic.

7. Outlook

Although many voices claim that there is already an EU/EC constitution,[64] the European Union still seems to be in search of its 'real' constitution. Fulfilling the Laeken Council mandate from 2001, which took the work of the Charter Convention as a good example and asked for a Constitutional Convention, the Presidency of the European Convention delivered a Draft Treaty for the

---

[61] BVerfGE 102, 147 (2000).

[62] BVerfGE 89, 155, 188.

[63] Case C-376/98 *Germany v European Parliament* [2000] ECR I-8419.

[64] I Pernice calls it *Europäischer Verfassungsverbund* ('European Constitutional Union') see (2000) 40 *Jahrbuch des öffentlichen Rechts der Gegenwart* 205; A v Bogdandy describes it as *Supranationaler Föderalismus* ('Supranational Federalism') (Nomos Baden-Baden 1999); see also N Walker 'The Idea of Constitutional Pluralism' (EUI Working Paper Law 1/02 European University Institute Florence 2002), about constitutionalism under the condition of a plurality of legal orders.

European Union on 18 July 2003 to the European Council.[65] This event sets another milestone in the process of Europeanization towards an 'ever closer Union', a process that hat been vigorously pushed forward in the 1980s with the European Single Act, and in the 1990s with the Treaties of Maastricht, Amsterdam, and Nice. If the European Council in 2004, and subsequently the Member States according to their legal systems, finally decide to engage in the project of a European Constitution, national constitutional courts such as the FCC will have to deal with a written and clearly shaped superior European constitutional order. Their future may be that they will shrink to courts in the second row.

[65] CONV 850/03 (Draft Treaty) and CONV 851/03 (Report from the Presidency of the Convention to the President of the European Council) <http://european-convention.eu.int>.

9

The Law Lords and the European Courts

DAVID ANDERSON*

1. Introduction

This chapter[1] is concerned with relations between the House of Lords, the Court of Justice of the European Communities (ECJ) in Luxembourg[2] and the European Court of Human Rights (ECtHR) in Strasbourg.[3] It does not address the respective places of those courts, and the legal orders over which they preside, in the European constitutional hierarchy.[4] The focus is, rather, upon the practical interaction between the House of Lords on the one hand and the two European Courts on the other, and upon any recommendations that can be drawn from that experience for the future supreme court of the UK.

There is a degree of overlap between the judicial activities of the House of Lords and of the two European Courts. Neither European Court claims the power to apply the law of the UK (though their judgments may have the practical effect of declaring it incompatible with, respectively, EU law and the ECHR). However, the House of Lords, together with other UK courts, routinely applies the law of both the EU and the ECHR. Furthermore, although there is no system of appeals from the House of Lords to either of the European Courts, both those

* QC at Brick Court Chambers, London; visiting professor of law, King's College London.

[1] I am grateful to David Edward, Nicholas Forwood, and John Vaux for their comments on a draft of this chapter.

[2] The ECJ is the ultimate judicial authority of the European Union, whose 15 Member States are scheduled to become 25 in 2004. The principal powers of the ECJ and its Court of First Instance (CFI) are set out in Arts 220–245 of the Treaty Establishing the European Community, as amended most recently by the Treaty of Nice, in force since 1 February 2003. The distinction between European Community and European Union, which is significant in other contexts but which would be removed by the new draft Constitutional Treaty is ignored for the purposes of this chapter, 'EU' being used throughout.

[3] The ECtHR determines complaints against the 45 Contracting States which have undertaken to secure the rights and freedoms set out in the Convention for the Protection of Human Rights and Fundamental Freedoms (European Convention on Human Rights or ECHR) and to abide by its judgments. The powers of the ECtHR are set out in Arts 19–51 ECHR, as amended by Protocol No 11, in force since 1 November 1998.

[4] The writer's thoughts on this intractable but intriguing subject are to be found in D Anderson 'Shifting the Grundnorm (and other tales)' in D O'Keeffe (ed) *Judicial Review in European Union Law, Liber Amicorum in Honour of Lord Slynn of Hadley* (Kluwer The Hague 2000) 343.

courts have occasion, from time to time, to review the application of 'their' law by the courts of the UK.

Judicial citation by the House of Lords of European Court judgments began in the 1970s, following the introduction of the right of individual petition to Strasbourg in 1966[5] and UK accession to the EEC in 1973. Both types of European law were increasingly relied upon by advocates during the 1970s and 1980s, though the relevance of the ECHR to domestic law was often difficult to establish, and the impact of both types of law was uneven as between different courts and different subject areas.[6]

Since the late 1980s, there has been explosive growth in the practice first of EU and then of human rights law in the UK. Professional interest in EU law was raised by political controversy over the Single European Act and Maastricht Treaties, by the litigation involving the Spanish fishermen,[7] which brought home the implications of the supremacy of Community law to the English legal establishment, and by the single market or '1992' programme, made possible by the Single European Act and driven through by UK Commissioner Lord Cockfield in conjunction with Commission President Jacques Delors.

After the election of the Labour Government in 1997 it was the turn of human rights law to emerge from relative obscurity, fuelled this time by the Scotland Act and Human Rights Act, both of 1998, and by a vast and unprecedented programme of judicial education. Human rights advocacy and adjudication were brought home from Strasbourg and into the mainstream. Though fewer cases than had initially been expected are exclusively attributable to the Human Rights Act,[8] recourse to human rights arguments has been widespread and has influenced the law in fields ranging from crime and judicial review to family law, immigration, and civil procedure.

A full analysis of relations between the House of Lords on the one hand and the Luxembourg and Strasbourg courts on the other would be a substantial

---

[5] The first judgment of the ECtHR in a case against the United Kingdom was *Golder* (1975) 1 EHRR 524. Judicial reference to the ECHR had begun a few years earlier: *Broome v Cassell & Co Ltd* [1972] AC 1027, 1133A (Lord Kilbrandon).

[6] Thus, it is noticeable that EU law made significantly less headway in the criminal courts and Patents Court than it did, for example, in the Administrative Court (formerly the Crown Office) and Commercial Court. On the greater readiness of English courts in contexts other than that of administrative law to give effect to the presumption of conformity with the ECHR when interpreting statutes, see M Hunt *Using Human Rights Law in the English Courts* (Hart Oxford 1997) 140. The half-dozen purposes for which the ECHR was used by the English courts in advance of the HRA were summarized by Lord Bingham of Cornhill in his maiden speech in the House of Lords: Hansard HL vol 573 cols 1466–7 (3 July 1996).

[7] See, in particular the first of the three rulings of the ECJ in that litigation (Case C–213/89 *R v Secretary of State for Transport, ex p Factortame Ltd* [1990] ECR I-2433), and the judgments of the HL that preceded and followed that ruling ([1990] 2 AC 85 and [1991] 1 AC 603). The true legal pioneers were however the Divisional Court judges (Neill LJ and Hodgson J) who, in defiance of accepted UK constitutional principle, had already suspended the operation of an Act of Parliament: [1989] 2 CMLR 353.

[8] Joint Committee of Human Rights Minutes of Evidence taken on 19 March 2001, HL 66–ii/HC 332–iii Q49 (Lord Irvine of Lairg LC).

exercise in the legal history of the past 30 years.[9] No such exercise is attempted here. This chapter provides, rather, a snapshot of current relations and a few recommendations. The most ambitious of those—the eventual repeal of Article 234(3) of the EC Treaty—would materially change the competence of the UK's supreme court where EU law is concerned.

2. The Law Lords and Luxembourg

A. Legal framework for the relationship

Like all national courts in the EU, the House of Lords is obliged to apply the law of the EU alongside domestic law and, where there is conflict, in precedence to it. That is a consequence of the wise decision, by the framers of the original treaties, not to restrict the application of EU law to a dedicated system of EU courts but rather to deposit it, cuckoo-like, in the existing courts of the Member States. This has enabled those courts both to nurture it, under the guiding influence of the ECJ, and to learn its habits.

Equally wise was the decision not to provide for a system of appeals from national top courts to the ECJ on matters of EU law. In the early years, such a solution could easily have provoked resentment towards the new legal order on the part of national courts which were not accustomed to playing a subordinate role. Instead, national courts were given the power to request preliminary (ie pre-judgment) rulings from the ECJ, pursuant to what is now Article 234 (ex 177) EC. This was good psychology. The eventual ruling of the ECJ enables the national court to give an authoritative judgment on the relevant points of Community law, without diminishing the jurisdiction of the national court or requiring it to give a judgment which might subsequently be overruled.

The preliminary ruling procedure is the basis for relations between all national courts and the ECJ. Its influence in fostering the generally harmonious relations between national courts and the ECJ would be difficult to overestimate. It has enabled the ECJ to describe that relationship as co-operative rather than hierarchical,[10] based on the recognition that each court has a different function[11] and on mutual goodwill and respect.[12] From the perspective of the national court, as explained extra-judicially by Lord Bingham of Cornhill when he was Master of the Rolls, references are made:

---

[9] Such an exercise has already been partly performed: see as regards EU law L Collins *European Law in the United Kingdom* (4th edn Butterworths London 1990) and as regards ECHR law *Using Human Rights Law in the English Courts* (n 6) ch 4.

[10] Case 244/80 *Foglia v Novello (2)* [1981] ECR 3045 [14].

[11] Case 338/85 *Pardini Fratelli SpA v Ministero del Commercio del'Estero* [1988] ECR 2041 [8].

[12] Case 44/65 *Hessische Knappschaft v Maison Singer et Fils* [1965] ECR 965, 975 (Gand AG).

rather as an architect is willing to seek advice of a consulting engineer or a quantity surveyor as a source of specialised expertise, needed by the architect to enable him to perform his task.[13]

The harmonious functioning of the relationship is enhanced by the fact that most national courts enjoy an unfettered discretion, with few exceptions, over whether to make references. Where guidance is received from the ECJ, therefore, it is as a consequence of a deliberate decision by the referring court to request it.[14]

It is open to a national court to express its own opinion on an issue of Community law when referring it to the ECJ for decision. However, the ECJ does not solicit such opinions;[15] and experience at least in the UK suggests that, with rare exceptions,[16] courts are unlikely to invest the time and effort necessary to arrive at and express such a conclusion in circumstances where that conclusion will not be determinative and indeed risks being contradicted by the ECJ.

In the case of courts from whose decisions there is no judicial remedy (including the House of Lords, at least on the final hearing of an appeal), the position is somewhat different.[17] The third paragraph of Article 234 EC (henceforth, Article 234(3)) *requires*, rather than permits, such courts to refer questions of EU law to the ECJ. They must do so without regard to the interests of the parties in the expeditious resolution of the case.[18]

The severity of that requirement has been mitigated, to an extent, by the doctrines of *acte éclairé* (which excuses a top court from the duty to refer when a question is 'materially identical to a question which has already been the subject of a preliminary ruling in a similar case')[19] and *acte clair* (which

[13] M Andenas (ed) *Article 177 References to the European Court: Policy and Practice* (Butterworths London 1994) 45.

[14] D Anderson and M Demetriou *References to the European Court* (2nd edn Sweet & Maxwell London 2002) ch 5.

[15] The ECJ's Information Note on references by national courts for preliminary rulings, para 6, specifies the matters that must be included in a decision to refer but makes no reference to the opinion of the referring court on the point at issue.

[16] The most celebrated exceptions are the judgments of the Patents Court, effectively challenging established lines of ECJ authority, which accompanied the references in Joined Cases C–267/95 and C–268/95 *Merck v Primecrown* [1996] ECR I-6285 (Jacob J) and Joined Cases C–414/99 and C–416/99 *Zino Davidoff SA v A&G Imports Ltd* [2001] ECR I-8691; [2002] 2 WLR 321 (Laddie J). Neither was effective in persuading the ECJ: but such dialogue can only be healthy.

[17] (n 14) ch 6. The HL is the final court of appeal even in circumstances where permission to appeal could previously have been sought from the Court of Appeal: *Chiron v Murex* [1995] All ER (EC) 88; Case C–99/00 *Lyckeskog* [2002] ECR I-4839. Recognition of this fact has recently prompted the HL to announce its intention to give reasons for the refusal of leave in cases raising issues of Community law: HL 89, Appeal Committee 38th Report of Session 2002–03. See further ch 12.

[18] Thus, the HL in *R v Secretary of State for Transport, ex p Factortame* [1990] 2 AC 85 was obliged to refer the question of whether Community law obliged it to make available an interim injunction against the Crown. It did so, notwithstanding that the time occupied by the reference (though kept to a minimum by the ECJ: Case C–213/89 [1990] ECR I-2433) substantially reduced the protection that the eventual injunction was able to give, resulting in a huge claim for damages.

[19] Joined Cases 28–30/62 *Da Costa en Schaake NV v Nederlandse Belastingsadministratie* [1963] ECR 31, 38.

excuses a top court from the duty to refer when the answer to a question is sufficiently obvious, even if there is no decision of the ECJ directly in point).[20] The scope for top courts to decide points of EU law for themselves however remains strictly limited. The ECJ has warned that it is only open to a top court to apply the *acte clair* doctrine if it is 'convinced that the matter is equally obvious to the courts of the other Member States and to the Court of Justice'.[21] This is an exacting standard. The ECJ has not felt able to relax any further its interpretation of the mandatory words of Article 234(3), despite invitations from, among others, a serving Advocate General,[22] a former Judge[23] and, in the case of *Lyckeskog*, a senior national court.[24]

The purpose of the obligation to refer in Article 234(3) is:

... to ensur[e] the proper application and uniform interpretation of Community law in all the Member States ... and ... to prevent a body of national case-law that is not in accordance with the rules of Community law from being established in any member State.[25]

The importance of that objective is not in doubt. It may however be questioned whether Article 234(3) is an effective way of achieving it. Top courts in nearly all Member States have from time to time tacitly defied Article 234(3) by deciding, without a reference, issues which were far from plain and obvious.[26] In a few cases, top courts have even decided issues of Community law notwithstanding a minority on the court which would have decided them the other way.[27] Furthermore, courts which have disobeyed the Article 234(3) duty to refer have so far done so with impunity.

Two recent cases before the ECJ address possible mechanisms for deterring national top courts from the wrong application of EU law. In Case C–129/00 *Commission v Italy*, the ECJ was asked to decide whether (and if so, when) the Commission may bring infringement proceedings under Article 226 EC against a Member State in respect of national jurisprudence that is inconsistent with EU law. In Case C–224/01 *Köbler*, it was asked to decide whether claims for damages must be available against national top courts in respect of their decisions on EU law. The respective Advocates General advised the Court to answer each of these questions in the affirmative.[28] In *Köbler*, the Court has agreed.

---

[20] Case 283/81 *CILFIT v Ministry of Health* [1982] ECR 3415. [21] ibid [16].

[22] Case C–338/95 *Wiener v Hauptzollamt Emmerich* [1997] ECR I-6495 [64] (Jacobs AG).

[23] Lord Slynn of Hadley 'Foreword' in *References to the European Court* (n 14) vi–vii.

[24] The Swedish Court of Appeal, by its second question in Case C–99/00 *Lyckeskog* [2002] ECR I-4839; [2003] 1 WLR 9.

[25] Case C–393/98 *Gomes Valente* [2001] ECR I-1327 [17].

[26] A number of examples (from France, Greece, Germany, the Netherlands, Sweden and Spain as well as the UK) are cited in *References to the European Court* (n 14) [6–052]–[6–059].

[27] See eg judgments 815/84, 2807/1997 and 3457/1998 of the Greek Council of State. That tendency is not uniquely Greek: see the speeches of Lords Hoffmann and Millett in *R v Secretary of State for Health, ex p Imperial Tobacco* [2001] 1 WLR 127 (although, by the time of the judgment, the issue had become moot).

[28] Opinions of Léger AG in *Köbler* (8 April 2003; see the Judgment of 30 September 2003) and Geelhoed AG in *Commission v Italy* (3 June 2003).

It remains to be seen whether these constitutionally delicate remedies will be extensively used in practice. But they are, in any event, directed not towards the enforcement of the procedural Article 234(3) duty to refer, but rather towards enforcement of a distinct and substantive duty that has not hitherto been enforceable: the duty of top courts not to make significant or inexcusable errors of EU law.[29] It is unlikely that these remedies could be used to target a refusal by a top court to refer, whether in damages or infringement proceedings, if the court then reached a legally correct answer, or even if it made an excusable error with limited consequences for the effectiveness of EU law. Their purpose is, rather, to deter national courts from establishing significant 'rogue' bodies of case law. They would do little to improve the enforceability of the Article 234(3) duty to refer: but they could arguably reduce the need for such a duty, by substituting more effective sanctions for judicial error.

B. Influence of the ECJ on the Law Lords

The UK is not widely noted for the *communautaire* tendencies of either its political class or its public. Yet the attitude of the Law Lords to the ECJ over the first 30 years of UK membership of the European Union has for the most part been one of loyal and uncritical compliance with all those rulings from which they have been able (in accordance with common law principles of *stare decisis*) to extract a legal rule applicable to the case before them. If the Law Lords have found occasional judgments of the ECJ to be obscure or difficult to apply, they have—in the manner of High Court judges who experience such difficulties with judgments of the Court of Appeal—been too polite to say so.

A good example is the reaction of the House of Lords when asked to apply the apparently irreconcilable judgments of the ECJ in three cases concerning Sunday trading.[30] The mixed messages coming out of Luxembourg had by that stage almost paralysed the enforcement of Sunday trading law in England and Wales: but their Lordships resisted the temptation to criticize or to strike out on their own, referred to the ECJ a number of questions aimed at clarifying the position and eventually received an answer which (though it avoided most of their specific questions) was sensible and wholly clear.[31]

As a matter of UK law, such loyal compliance is mandated by section 3(1) of the European Communities Act, which requires that questions of EU law:

---

[29] 'Excusability' was said to be the litmus test for liability by Légér AG in *Köbler* [139]. Geelhoed AG in *Commission v Italy* [62]–[67] stressed that not every error by national courts will justify infringement proceedings, citing impact on the effectiveness of EU law as the most important of a number of criteria for determing whether judicial error should engage the liability of a Member State.

[30] Case C–145/88 *Torfaen BC v B&Q plc* [1989] ECR 3851, Case C–312/89 *Conforama* [1991] ECR I-997 and Case C–332/89 *Marchandise* [1991] ECR I-1027.

[31] Case C–169/91 *Stoke-on-Trent City Council v B&Q plc* [1992] ECR I-6635. For an illuminating account of the Sunday trading saga from a legal and political perspective, see M Sunkin and A Le Sueur *Public Law* (Longman London 1997) chs 9 and 30.

be treated as a question of law and, if not referred to the European Court, be for determination as such in accordance with the principles laid down by and any relevant decision of the European Court or any court attached thereto.

It has been said of section 3(1) that it:

appears to extend to relevant decisions of the European Court, followed in United Kingdom law, the rule of strict precedent applied by United Kingdom courts in respect of decisions made originally by those courts.[32]

To this it might be added that section 3(1) appears to resolve, in the EU's favour, any question that there might otherwise have been about the constitutional propriety of English courts taking instructions from the ECJ.

The reception of the authority of the ECJ in some other Member States has been less straightforward. This is in part a question of legal cultural differences: in particular, the much reduced emphasis placed by civilian legal systems on the principles of binding authority or *stare decisis* that are applied with such notable strictness in the UK. Most national courts are less accustomed than their English counterparts to extracting broad legal rules from the judgments of higher courts and regarding themselves as bound by them. It would not be surprising, therefore, if such courts were less likely to consider themselves bound by ECJ rulings reached in different factual contexts, or on the basis of different (though materially similar) legislative provisions.[33]

Difficulties in the reception of EU law cannot, however, all be put down to the unconscious influence of different legal cultures. They have in part been a consequence of national constitutional provisions which, as interpreted by national courts, have been held to reserve to those courts the power to declare that the EU law has stepped outside the competences attributed to it by Treaty.[34] It may be no coincidence that the Netherlands and UK, two Member States without constitutional courts of their own, have experienced no serious difficulty in accepting the supremacy of EU law.

The acknowledgment in recent years of 'constitutional' principles underlying UK law, notwithstanding the absence of a written constitution, has brought with it a recognition that UK judges might some day be asked to reject a provision of EU law which the ECJ considers to be valid. As Laws LJ stated in the *Metric Martyrs* case:

---

[32] EH Wall *European Communities Act 1972* (Butterworths London 1973) 29.

[33] This under-researched but important subject is touched upon in D Anderson and M Demetriou *References to the European Court* (n 14) [14–032]–[14–055].

[34] The judgment of the Federal Constitutional Court in the German Maastricht case, *Brunner v European Union Treaty* [1994] 1 CMLR 57 (on which see ch 8), amounts to a repudiation of the ECJ's decision in Case 314/85 *Foto-Frost* [1987] ECR 4199, which provides that only the ECJ is competent to declare acts of the EU institutions invalid. A similar position was taken by the Danish Constitutional Court in *Carlsen v Rasmussen* [1999] 3 CMLR 854. Further examples (eg from France and Italy) are given in the illuminating comparative study of the reception of EU law by seven national jurisdictions in A-M Slaughter, A Sweet and JHH Weiler (eds) *The European Courts and National Courts: Doctrine and Jurisprudence* (Hart Oxford 1998). See further T Hartley *Constitutional Problems of the European Union* (Hart Oxford 1999) 157; D Anderson (n 4).

In the event, which would no doubt never happen in the real world, that a European measure was seen to be repugnant to a fundamental or constitutional right guaranteed by the law of England, a question would arise whether the general words of the ECA were sufficient to incorporate the measure and give it overriding effect in domestic law.[35]

For the moment, however, the possibility remains hypothetical. Parliament has decreed that EU law is supreme:[36] until it decides otherwise, the subjection of the UK courts to the sovereignty of Parliament subjects them also to the dictates of the European Union and of its highest court.

C. Influence of the Law Lords on the ECJ

Judgments of the House of Lords are from time to time cited to the ECJ, at least in UK cases, and are no doubt read more frequently by some of the members and staff of that Court. It is however difficult to identify even a single House of Lords judgment that has materially influenced the development of Community law, in over 30 years of UK membership.

The expression by a national court of willingness to contemplate a particular development in EU law may, perhaps, reassure the ECJ—whose authority after all rests on the acceptance of its rulings by national courts—that the time is ripe for such a development. Thus, the decision of the House of Lords in *Garden Cottage Foods v Milk Marketing Board*,[37] refusing an interim injunction on the basis that damages were probably available for breach of the EU competition rules, was cited during the debate during the 1990s on the circumstances in which damages should be available for breach of EU law.[38] It is, however, impossible to think of any other judgment of the House of Lords which has enjoyed even this modest degree of prominence.

Three explanations may be suggested for this lack of influence.

The first explanation, which has already been addressed, is Article 234(3), which inhibits national top courts from developing or expressing any worthwhile expertise in substantive EU law by requiring them to refer to the ECJ any question the answer to which is not completely obvious.

The second, and paradoxical, explanation is the exemplary loyalty of the UK courts towards the ECJ. Such influence as national top courts have exerted on the development of ECJ jurisprudence tends to have resulted not from co-operation but from confrontation on the constitutional borderline between EU and Member State. The best-known example is the series of judgments of the German Federal Constitutional Court declaring the acceptance of Community

---

[35] *Thoburn v Sunderland City Council* [2002] EWHC Admin 195; [2002] 3 WLR 247 (HC) [69].

[36] *R v Secretary of State for Transport, ex p Factortame Ltd* [1990] 2 AC 85, 140 B-D; *R v Secretary of State for Employment, ex p EOC* [1995] 1 AC 1 at 27 D-E; Sir J Laws 'Law and Democracy' [1995] *Public Law* 72, 89.

[37] [1984] AC 130.

[38] See eg Case C–5/94 *R v MAFF, ex p Hedley Lomas (Ireland) Limited* [1996] ECR I-2553 (Léger A-G [98]).

law in Germany to be dependent upon its compliance with certain features of the German constitution, judgments which are credited with provoking a number of legal developments including, principally, the discovery by the ECJ of fundamental rights.[39] The House of Lords, by contrast, has never challenged the supremacy of EU law, or the competence of the ECJ to delimit the boundaries of EU power.

The third explanation for the lack of influence is less tangible. It may be expressed as the feeling still shared by most UK judges that EU law is a technical subject, founded on barely familiar civil law notions, which they may be competent to understand and to use, but not to declare with authority. Members of the House of Lords have been distinguished international lawyers, and their opinions on matters of international law (as in the *Pinochet* case) command universal attention and respect. Few of them would however claim equivalent expertise in the law of the European Union. This self-perception is captured by Lord Bingham's image of the English judge seeking guidance on EU law as an architect consulting a civil engineer.

3. THE LAW LORDS AND STRASBOURG

A. Legal framework of the relationship

Relations between the English courts and Strasbourg are governed by two legal constraints, one at domestic and one at international level.

The domestic constraint is section 2 of the Human Rights Act 1998, which requires national courts and tribunals determining questions which have arisen in connection with Convention rights to 'take into account' judgments and decisions of the ECtHR. Judgments and decisions of the ECtHR are thereby given special status, over and above that given to other foreign and international courts. They are however not given binding authority, on the analogy of EU law as given effect by means of section 3(1) of the European Communities Act 1972.

The international constraint is imposed by the right of individual petition to the Strasbourg court (coupled with the rarely used possibility of inter-state application). Although individual petitions are brought against the UK, communicated to the UK government, and defended by lawyers employed or instructed by the Foreign Office, it is common for the subject matter of such applications to be an alleged failure of the judicial branch to provide sufficient safeguards for Convention rights.

The Strasbourg court has the power not only to make a finding of violation but to award just satisfaction to the applicant against the government concerned.[40] The procedure for enforcement of ECtHR judgments by the Committee of

---

[39] This case law is discussed in *The European Courts and National Courts: Doctrine and Jurisprudence* (n 34) ch 3.
[40] Art 41 ECHR.

Ministers of the Council of Europe, though political in nature, is generally effective.[41] It is supplemented by monitoring procedures operated by the Parliamentary Assembly and by the Secretary-General.[42]

The flexibility suggested by the fact that UK courts have only to take judgments of the ECtHR into account is thus limited. The limit lies in the possibility that a rebellious judgment of the higher UK courts will eventually be contradicted by the ECtHR itself.

B. Influence of the ECtHR on the Law Lords

It is an impressive fact that in a country with such a long tradition of individual freedom as the UK, the legal debate over civil and political rights should to a large extent be conducted by reference to the case law of an international regional court which has been in existence for barely 50 years, and whose judges are drawn from 45 states of western Europe, eastern Europe, the Balkans, Anatolia, and the former Soviet Union.

This state of affairs is a consequence partly of the absence of a catalogue of domestic constitutional rights in the UK, and partly of the moral and legal authority that the Strasbourg court, for all its structural problems, has earned and retained for itself. With occasional exceptions (notably, the 10:9 finding of violation in the Gibraltar shooting case),[43] the judgments of the Strasbourg court have in the past been well received by the media and general public in the UK. Judges appear to find the institution less alien than the ECJ, believing perhaps that as the UK played a major role in establishing the Council of Europe and drafting the Convention, the Court is more British in character than its Luxembourg counterpart.

The Strasbourg case law is much better known in the UK than it is in most other Contracting States, including established Council of Europe members such as Germany. This is explicable partly by the existence in other States' constitutional law of domestic human rights catalogues that tend to be applied in preference to the ECHR, and partly by the surprisingly limited availability of ECtHR case law in languages other than French and English, the working languages of the Court.

On a number of occasions the Strasbourg court has drawn from the House of Lords an acknowledgment that a previous ruling requires adjustment if it is to be properly ECHR-compliant. An example is the modification that was recently effected to the English legal test for apparent bias of a tribunal. The 20th century cases vacillated between two possible approaches to the question, based respectively on the existence of a 'reasonable suspicion' or 'real danger' of bias. A form of the 'real danger' test appeared to have prevailed when the matter came before

---

[41] Art 46 ECHR.

[42] See A Drzemczewski 'La prévention des violations des droits de l'homme: les mécanismes de suivi du Conseil de l'Europe' (2000) 43 *Revue Trimestrielle des Droits de l'Homme* 385.

[43] *McCann v UK* (1996) 21 EHRR 97.

the House of Lords in *R v Gough*.[44] That decision was criticized in a number of commonwealth jurisdictions and in Scotland, as paying insufficient regard to the principle that justice must be seen to be done. It was however the Strasbourg jurisprudence which compelled the Court of Appeal to reformulate the test, in terms more redolent of 'reasonable suspicion', after the entry into force of the Human Rights Act 1998.[45] This 'modest adjustment of the test in *R v Gough*' was gracefully accepted by the House of Lords in the subsequent case of *Porter v Magill*.[46]

Correction from Strasbourg has in general been well received by UK courts. It was in the past rendered more palatable by the fact that those courts had not been empowered to apply the ECHR themselves, and could not therefore have been blamed for inconsistencies with it. Now that this excuse is not available (save possibly in relation to Article 13, which was, anomalously, not included in the catalogue of Convention rights scheduled to the Human Rights Act 1998), it will be interesting to see if correction from Strasbourg continues to be taken in such a well-mannered way.

Although the ECHR provides a mandatory minimum standard of human rights protection, Member States are expressly permitted to exceed that standard in their own courts. The higher courts of the UK have occasionally expressed themselves willing to do so,[47] acceding in one case to an argument founded on Article 10 which had already been dismissed by a Committee of the Strasbourg Court, pursuant to Article 35(3) ECHR, as 'manifestly ill-founded'.[48]

C. Influence of the Law Lords on the ECtHR

Incorporation of the ECHR into English law by means of the Human Rights Act 1998 was welcomed in Strasbourg, not least for the opportunity that it gave the ECtHR to learn from informed judgments of the UK's higher courts. As the President of the ECtHR recalled in 2003:

Before the Convention was incorporated into United Kingdom law, we argued that incorporation when it came would greatly enrich the Convention jurisprudence, that British judges deciding directly on Convention issues would make a major contribution

---

[44] [1993] AC 646.

[45] *In re Medicaments and Related Classes of Goods (No 2)* [2001] 1 WLR 700 (CA) 711 B-C (Lord Phillips MR)

[46] [2001] UKHL 67; [2002] 2 AC 357 [100]–[103] (Lord Hope).

[47] *R (S) v Chief Constable of S Yorkshire Police* [2002] EWCA Civ 1275; [2002] 1 WLR 3223 [34] (Lord Woolf CJ).

[48] *R (Pro-Life Alliance) v BBC* [2002] 3 WLR 1080 (CA). The Administrative Court had considered the adverse decision in Strasbourg to sound 'the death knell' of the Art 10 ECHR claim: however the Court of Appeal, mindful that the decision was unreasoned, unpublished, and adopted pursuant to a procedure applied to several thousand other decisions in the same year, did 'not think it possesses any particular force whatever' [41] (Laws LJ). On appeal to the House of Lords, Lord Hoffmann (whose views conformed to those in the decision) however accorded it greater respect: [2003] 2 WLR 1403 [71]–[72].

to the development of Convention law. Just over two years after the entry into force of the Human Rights Act, that is indeed proving to be the case.[49]

His comments confirmed those of Lord Bingham of Cornhill, currently Senior Law Lord, who said in oral evidence to the Joint Committee on Human Rights:

I do myself think that one of the great advantages in having incorporated the Convention is that it makes it possible to have a dialogue with the Court in Strasbourg. Of course, we have a lot to learn from them but I venture to suggest that they have a great deal to learn from us, not least in areas which are unfamiliar to most Continental jurists, of which jury trial is the most pre-eminent example... They are now, for better or worse, getting our views on these questions and one would hope that they would treat those with the same serious respect with which we treat their judgments, though of course we have a duty ultimately to take account of their jurisprudence, whereas they have no duty to take account of ours.[50]

It is perhaps not surprising that the ECtHR should be more open to influence from national courts than the ECJ. The massive expansion in the Council of Europe after the fall of the Iron Curtain has vastly increased the number of applications, to the current level of some 44,000 per year. Oral hearings are an increasingly rare luxury: the Court's on-line diary reveals there to have been only 41 in the whole of 2002. It is not difficult to see why the ECtHR should welcome the assistance of well-disposed national courts which have the time to think deeply about the proper interpretation and application of the ECHR. That is so in particular where the Law Lords are concerned, with their grounding in the common law liberties respected across Europe, their English-language judgments and their Privy Council experience in applying ECHR-based catalogues of constitutional rights.

In response, and particularly since the passage of the Human Rights Act 1998, the House of Lords has shown itself unafraid to tackle difficult issues of human rights, even to the extent of suggesting innovative solutions to the Strasbourg court. Two recent examples, both in the context of Article 6 ECHR, are the *Alconbury* case and the *Osman* saga.

The issue in *R v Secretary of State for Transport and the Regions, ex p Alconbury*[51] was whether the Article 6(1) right to an independent and impartial tribunal was violated by a system whereby planning decisions were taken by planning inspectors or by the Secretary of State, and were then appealable to a court which could not review either the decision-makers' assessment of the facts or the Secretary of State's planning policy. The Divisional Court, applying Strasbourg case law, found that this system lacked the tribunal with 'full jurisdiction' that was required by Article 6(1). The House of Lords however applied

---

[49] Speech by Luzius Wildhaber at the opening of the judicial year, 23 January 2003 <http://www.echr.coe.int/ eng/Speeches/SpeechWildhaber.htm>.

[50] Minutes of Evidence taken on 26 March 2001, HL 66–ii/HC 332–iii) Q30 (Lord Bingham of Cornhill).

[51] [2001] UKHL 23; [2001] 2 WLR 1389 (HL).

the same authorities in a different and innovative way, interpreting the requirement as relating only to 'full jurisdiction to deal with the case as the nature of the decision requires', and concluding that there had been no violation of Article 6(1) since inspectors were independent as regards their factual determinations and were not required to be independent as regards matters of policy and planning judgment, which in a democracy were properly determined by the Secretary of State rather than the courts. It is possible to infer at least a measure of acceptance of the House of Lords' approach from the fact that a subsequent application to the ECtHR by a disappointed claimant was declared (albeit with limited reasoning) to be manifestly ill-founded.[52]

The contribution of the House of Lords in the *Osman* saga was more striking still, since rather than charting a novel course through difficult case law, as was the case in *Alconbury*, it confronted the ECtHR over one of its own recent decisions and caused it to back down. The issue was whether the Article 6(1) guarantee of 'access to court' required Contracting States to modify their substantive laws in order to remove statutory or common law 'immunities' that excluded liability where particular categories of claimants or defendants were involved. The jurisdictional significance of the issue lay in the fact that if Article 6(1) operated in such a way, every national exclusionary rule would have to be subject to scrutiny on the grounds of proportionality. The UK would have been accountable to the ECtHR for everything from statutory exclusions and limitations of liability to the boundaries of the tort of negligence and any plans to replace it by no-fault liability, irrespective of the fact that no substantive human rights were involved.

In *Osman v UK*,[53] a Grand Chamber of 20 judges (including the UK Judge, Sir John Freeland) held unanimously that Article 6(1) was violated by the operation of the substantive common law rule to the effect that it was not 'fair just and reasonable' to impose a duty of care upon the police in the investigation of crime. The reaction of the House of Lords was encapsulated in the speech of Lord Browne-Wilkinson, then Senior Law Lord, in *Barrett v Enfield*.[54] In that speech, Lord Browne-Wilkinson described the *Osman* judgment as 'extremely difficult to understand' and pointed out—in terms which by the restrained standards of the UK judiciary could be described as forthright—some of the inaccuracies and logical inconsistencies in what was indeed a poorly reasoned decision.[55] Speaking and then writing extra-judicially, Lord Hoffmann criticized the *Osman* decision in stronger terms still, concluding his remarks with a thinly coded call upon the UK government to withdraw the right of individual petition.[56]

The next Strasbourg case in which the issue was raised, *Z v UK*,[57] concerned the common law rule that local authorities owed no duty of care in relation to

[52] Application 2352/02 *Holding and Barnes plc v UK* admissibility decision of 13 March 2002.
[53] (1998) 29 EHRR 245.   [54] [2001] 2 AC 550.   [55] ibid 558–560.
[56] Lord Hoffmann 'Human Rights and the House of Lords' (1999) 62 *Modern Law Review* 159.
[57] (2002) 34 EHRR 3, an application arising from the first of the child-care cases in *X v Bedfordshire* [1995] 2 AC 633. The writer appeared for the government.

their decisions whether or not to take a child into care. The Government accepted that such decisions might constitute a violation of substantive Convention rights and so require a remedy under Article 3 or Article 8, but resisted the application of Article 6(1).

In its submissions to the Grand Chamber, the Government sought to convey to the Strasbourg court the degree of judicial incomprehension and disapproval with which the *Osman* case had been greeted by judges in England, including in particular the House of Lords. In its judgment, the ECtHR held by a majority of 11 to 6 that there had been no violation of Article 6, explaining its change of heart by the claim that its decision in *Osman* had been based upon a misunderstanding of the English law of negligence.[58] This remarkable retreat from a recent and unanimous decision of the full Court may have been facilitated by the fact that *Osman* was decided by the old part-time ECtHR, only a quarter of whose members were transferred to the new Court established under the 11th Protocol to the ECHR in 1998. It may also have been significant that Arden LJ, a member of the English Court of Appeal whose concurring opinion indicated her own difficulties with the line of authority that led to *Osman*, sat as ad hoc judge in Z.

Most recently, in 2003, the House of Lords in *Matthews v Ministry of Defence*[59] cemented the ruling in Z into English law, whilst taking the opportunity to identify and criticize what it perceived as some remaining inconsistencies in the Strasbourg case law. Though the *Osman* saga put relations between the English courts and Strasbourg under a degree of strain, it provides a textbook example of the advantages, for both sides, of a constructive exchange of views.

4. RECOMMENDATIONS FOR REFORM

This concluding section considers ways in which the example of the European courts, and the experience of UK courts in relating to them, could bear upon the composition and functioning of the UK's new supreme court.

A. Composition and procedure

1. Appointment of judges

The UK's judicial monoculture has in recent years been narrowing rather than broadening, as individual Law Lords have given up their legislative role and the judicial functions of the Lord Chancellor have become a thing of the past. That trend was motivated in part by 'European' notions of independence and impartiality.[60] There is thus irony in the fact that the judges of the European courts themselves vary not only in their nationality and gender but in the range of their

---

[58] ibid [100].   [59] [2003] 1 AC 1163.
[60] See eg *McGonnell v UK* (2000) 30 EHRR 209.

collective experience, which tends to encompass work in academe, politics, national civil services and international institutions as well as the practice of law and of judging.

The debate over the optimal range of experience and method of appointment of top court judges in the UK has been influenced by the fact that the UK's top court now has an important human rights jurisdiction. It is certainly arguable that decisions as to whether acts or measures were 'necessary in a democratic society' should be taken by a more diverse group than the current Law Lords, who share not only the same gender but the same professional training and career path. The inability of a group of 'elderly male judges' to second-guess a standard-setting decision, particularly when that decision was taken by a woman for the perceived benefit of women, has even been advanced by one member of the House of Lords as a reason for judicial reticence in applying the 'necessary in a democratic society' test.[61] However, the systems of appointment to both European courts are in varying degrees haphazard.[62] It is not suggested that the new Judicial Appointments Commission will have much to learn from them.

A number of national top courts have counted among their members former judges and Advocates General of the ECJ.[63] The presence in the new supreme court of such a figure could only strengthen its expertise in the often technical and complex subject of EU law: though for as long as top courts are forbidden by Article 234(3) from deciding difficult points of EU law, it will not be possible to make full use of such expertise. Whether or not the supreme court should necessarily include, by convention, a former member of the ECJ may therefore depend on the future of Article 234(3), discussed further below. Former Strasbourg judges would also bring distinctive knowledge and experience to the supreme court, though it is not suggested that their Strasbourg experience alone should entitle them to a place there.

2. Judicial assistance

There is not the same need for judicial assistance in the UK as there is in the European courts, multilingual bodies in which judges must develop some familiarity with the laws of other states, and in which the prevailing tradition is for the court rather than counsel to take primary responsibility for legal research. To the extent that the new supreme court makes increased use of law clerks or research assistants, however, the two European courts present contrasting models. The judges of the ECJ have their own private offices, with three *référendaires* assigned exclusively to each judge and Advocate General. In Strasbourg the

---

[61] *R v BBC, ex p ProLife Alliance* [2003] 2 WLR 1403 [80] (Lord Hoffmann).

[62] Judges of the ECJ are nominated by their governments, after whatever internal processes they choose to apply, and almost invariably accepted by the other Member States. Governments make three nominations for the post of judge at the ECtHR, stating their preference at the same time, and the Parliamentary Assembly of the Council of Europe chooses between them after interviewing the candidates.

[63] Member States which have appointed former members of the ECJ to one of their 'top courts' include Finland, Germany, Ireland, the Netherlands, Sweden, and the UK.

judges have no equivalent staff of their own: judgments are drafted by registry officials, who sit in on the deliberations of the court and seek to reflect those deliberations in their drafts.

It is unlikely that either of these models would be adopted by UK judges, who do not need large personal staffs and have the habit of drafting for themselves. Preferable, and closer to the existing use of judicial assistants, might be the system operated until recently in the EU's Court of First Instance, in which the judges' individual staff were supplemented by a small pool of law clerks with specialist expertise, available to be used by any judge requiring knowledge of that subject area.

3. Procedure

The UK's new supreme court has little to learn from the European courts at the level of procedure. The comparatively very limited caseload of the House of Lords allows it to provide both for detailed written cases from the parties, sequentially exchanged, and for oral hearings which are long enough to allow for a full dialogue between Bench and Bar. In contrast, the exchange of written observations at the merits stage of a Strasbourg case and in all references to the ECJ is simultaneous, with the result that pleadings can be less than fully respon-sive to one another; and oral hearings, rare in Strasbourg, seldom result in meaningful dialogue in either of the principal European courts.[64]

B. Judgments

The writer is among those who would like to see a 'judgment of the court' on the Strasbourg or US model, accompanied as necessary (in contrast, here, to the ECJ model) by concurring or dissenting opinions.[65] This would have the considerable advantages of rendering the *ratio* of supreme court judgments (and thus the law) more accessible and comprehensible to the reader, whether in the UK or abroad; avoiding the duplication inevitable in five separate and self-contained speeches; and encouraging, through the deliberation which is at the heart of the work of both European courts, a closer dialogue between judges, to the ultimate benefit of the quality of the majority's reasoning.

C. Relations with ECtHR

The relationship between the House of Lords and the ECtHR works well. Neither court is willing automatically to endorse the decisions of the other: but the resultant tension can be creative. The statutory duty to take Strasbourg

---

[64] The two senior courts are to be contrasted with the Court of First Instance of the EU, which by allocating more time to oral hearings and approaching them in a more interventionist way, makes optimum use of the hearing in what remains a predominantly written procedure.

[65] A less prosaic view is expressed by R Munday in his pair of articles 'All for One and One for All' [2002] *Cambridge Law Journal* 321 and 'Judicial Configurations' [2002] *Cambridge Law Journal* 612.

jurisprudence into account, together with the liberty to exceed Strasbourg standards of minimum protection, has so far combined well with the right of individual petition to ensure that the House of Lords shows respect and understanding towards the Strasbourg court, coupled with a willingness to suggest improvements to its jurisprudence. It seems that these suggestions are, in turn, received in a constructive spirit by the Strasbourg court.

In the event of any future strains between the two courts it is likely to be the right of individual petition to Strasbourg, rather than the statutory duty to take Strasbourg law into account, that comes under pressure. The removal of the right of individual petition was indeed seriously discussed in government legal circles after the judgment in the Gibraltar shooting case,[66] and the idea was revived in the wake of *Osman*.[67] To remove this right would, however, in current circumstances be a mistake. It would cut off the UK from the benevolent influence of the Strasbourg case law, whilst setting a dismal example to those east European, Balkan, and former Soviet states which have most to gain from an independent international court of human rights.

D. Relations with ECJ

The relationship between the House of Lords and the ECJ is, in jurisprudential terms, less satisfactory. Article 234(3) EC renders the House of Lords, in Vaughan and Randolph's striking phrase, a 'judicial postbox',[68] requiring it to refer any question the answer to which is not obvious, and so preventing it from contributing anything controversial or innovative to EU jurisprudence. After the ECJ's recent decision in *Lyckeskog*,[69] there seems little prospect in the short term of the ECJ watering down the obligation to a greater extent than has already been done in the *CILFIT* case. Indeed it is difficult to see how, consistently with Article 234(3), it could.[70]

The requirement that top courts not decide difficult issues of Community law for themselves is submitted to be unsatisfactory, for three main reasons.

First, as has already been explored, the obligation to refer is neither an enforceable nor a particularly effective means of achieving the objective of ensuring the proper application and uniform interpretation of Community law in all the Member States.

Secondly, it prevents top courts such as the House of Lords from adjudicating in a timely manner in the full range of cases affecting the lives and livelihood of

---

[66] *McCann v UK* (1996) 21 EHRR 97.

[67] (1998) 29 EHRR 245; see Lord Hoffmann 'Human Rights and the House of Lords' (1999) 62 *Modern Law Review* 159.

[68] D Vaughan and F Randolph, 'The Interface between Community Law and National Law: The United Kingdom Experience' in Curtin and O'Keeffe (eds) *Constitutional Adjudication in European Community and National Law, Essays for the Hon Mr Justice T F O'Higgins* 228.

[69] (n 17).

[70] cf the strict interpretation by the ECJ standing requirements for direct actions under Art 230 EC in Case C–50/00 *Unión de Pequeños Agricultores v Council* [2002] ECR I-6677.

those under their jurisdiction. The House of Lords will no doubt continue to make some references, even if it is no longer required to do so by Article 234. If it had a discretion to refer, however, it could legitimately take into account—as it currently cannot—such factors as the likely impact upon the parties of a further delay that now exceeds two years.[71] This will be particularly desirable as Community law extends its reach further into the field of justice, including criminal justice, and home affairs.

Thirdly, the obligation to refer will prevent the new supreme court from realizing its potential to contribute to the development of EU law, as the Appellate Committee already contributes to the development of ECHR law, and as the widely read reports of the House of Lords Select Committee on the European Communities contribute to the European political and policy debate. Lord Goff of Chieveley has stated:

Our judgments are read by lawyers all over the world. I have been informed by distinguished European lawyers, on more than one occasion, that the House of Lords is the only court in Europe whose judgments are cited all over Europe—despite the fact that the United Kingdom is (apart from the Irish Republic) the only common law country in Europe.[72]

Yet where EU law is concerned—a body of rules that is common to most of the courts of Europe, and that bears increasingly upon the lives of hundreds of millions of people—no such influence is possible: the House of Lords is discouraged from developing its legal expertise, and the 'dialogue' between the ECJ and national top courts remains resolutely one-way.

There are, in short, strong arguments for saying that just as the European Commission has had to acknowledge that it needs the assistance of national courts and authorities in applying EU competition policy,[73] so the time will come when national top courts must be trusted—subject to the ultimate review of the ECJ, however that is ensured—to assist meaningfully in the task of applying and developing EU law. This will require the repeal of Article 234(3), a possibility that was floated by the Due Group in its proposals for what became the Treaty of Nice, and which—despite its non-inclusion in the Treaty of Nice itself—should, in the opinion of the President of the Court of First Instance, continue to be discussed.[74]

It remains to ask what safeguards might be necessary to deter top courts from developing their own 'rogue' lines of case law. Two such safeguards, in

---

[71] The average time spent by a reference at the ECJ was 24.1 months in 2002, not counting the interval that elapses between the decision to refer and the registration of the reference in Luxembourg and the time between judgment in Luxembourg and the final ruling of the referring court, each of which can also be significant.

[72] Written evidence to Royal Commission on the Reform of the House of Lords; Report of the Royal Commission on Reform of the House of Lords (2000), Cm 4534.

[73] Council Regulation (EC) No 1/2003 of 16 December 2002 on the implementation of the rules on competition laid down in Arts 81 and 82 of the Treaty [2003] OJ L1/1.

[74] B Vesterdorf, 'The Community Court System Ten Years from Now and Beyond: Challenges and Possibilities' (2003) 28 *European Law Review* 303, 318.

the form of damages actions and infringement proceedings, have already been referred to. Further control mechanisms might include a power in the Commission to refer aberrant decisions, if sufficiently important, directly to the ECJ,[75] or a power in the ECJ itself to call in a case (in the same way that it will be able to undertake an 'exceptional review' of preliminary rulings by the CFI under Article 225A EC), such a power to be exercisable of its own motion or on petition by the Commission, a Member State or a disappointed litigant. Either of those powers would be a more substantial deterrent to the rogue line of authority than the unenforceable requirement in Article 234(3) has proved to be. Indeed such powers might even, in practice, provide a stronger incentive to refer in appropriate cases.

The repeal of Article 234(3) is likely to prove too radical to be contemplated until the 2004 enlargement of the EU has bedded down: an obligation on top courts to refer has, rightly or wrongly, been thought helpful in inculcating a 'reference culture' throughout the court systems of new Member States.[76] Longer term, however, it is submitted to represent the way forward. Once freed to contribute to the development of EU law, the evidence suggests that the new supreme court of the UK will do so with distinction.

[75] This solution was suggested by Lord Slynn of Hadley in (n 14) vii. Judge Edward of the ECJ has listed some of the decisions that would have to be made were this proposed *pourvoi dans l'intérêt de la loi* to be introduced, relating for example to the scope of permitted arguments, time limits, and the effect (if any) of the reference on the case at issue: 'Reform of Article 234 Procedure: The Limits of the Possible' in (n 4) 124–125.

[76] ECJ figures show that most references in most Member States come from lower courts, though a realization that a question will eventually have to be referred by the top court may act as an incentive to the lower court to refer in the exercise of its discretion. Similar incentives would however be given by the other safeguards touched upon in this chapter.

INTERMEDIATE COURTS
OF APPEAL AND TOP-LEVEL
NATIONAL COURTS

10

The Role of the Court of Appeal in England and Wales as an Intermediate Court

CHARLES BLAKE* AND GAVIN DREWRY†

1. Introduction

Any discussion of the role of intermediate courts in the legal system of England and Wales must begin with a historical record of the provenance and original purposes of the principal court operating at this level, the Court of Appeal. This essay deals for the most part with the civil division of that court in England, which operates quite separately from the criminal division, though there is a close relationship between them, both functionally and logistically. Both divisions operate in the same building and draw most of their judicial manpower from the ranks of the Lords Justices of Appeal (albeit augmented significantly, in the criminal division, by puisne judges from the High Court). Although the recent introduction of the new Civil Procedure Rules (CPR) that form part of the background to our discussion have not directly affected the criminal division, it should be noted that the latter has itself been the subject of important changes. One instance of this is that concern about wrongful convictions has led to the creation of a Criminal Cases Review Commission to replace the task previously performed by the executive in the form of the Home Office. This is to investigate and refer to the court if thought fit, cases of alleged wrongful conviction.

2. Work of the Court of Appeal

Compared to the work of the High Court, the county courts, the myriad administrative and other tribunals and more or less formal ombudsmen, the Court of

* Solicitor; former head of civil litigation at the Departments of Health and of Social Security; part-time immigration adjudicator.

† Professor of Public Administration; Director of the Centre for Political Studies at Royal Holloway, University of London.

The writers are engaged in a large study of the civil work of the Court of Appeal, supported by the Nuffield Foundation. Any findings reported in this paper and any conclusions drawn about the operation of the court should be regarded as provisional. The authors are grateful to the project research assistant, Suzanne Fullbrook, for her help in preparing this essay.

Appeal handles a minute number of cases. For the last available year (2000) the figures show that the Court disposed of about 351 full cases but some were settled and not all of the rest came to a full hearing. Looking upwards, the House of Lords had to deal with only 70 full cases so, by this comparison, the workload of the Court of Appeal is very considerable.

Looking at the courts below, the High Court issued about 100,000 proceedings of which only 2,800 came anywhere near a trial. The vast majority that did not come to trial were settled. At the risk of some simplification, we can say that some form of default or summary judgment usually resolves debt claims. The County Courts issued 1.7 million proceedings (the vast majority being debt claims) of which, again, only a very small proportion (about 3,000) came to a trial. Tribunals received about 150,000 appeals most of which came to some kind of hearing because, for various reasons, such litigation is rarely capable of being settled. These very basic and somewhat simplified figures show nothing of themselves about appeals but the fact is that the Court of Appeal is normally the final port of call for the minute proportion of cases that are first litigated and then appealed. It necessarily follows that the House of Lords must be performing a different appellate function from that of the Court of Appeal.

3. A SUPREME COURT?

It is a result of intensely fought debates at the end of the 19th century that the House of Lords survived as the supreme judicial body. It was by no means certain that this would be the result of a set of reforms to judicial procedure in the 1870s. The history of the reforms, the consequent question of a reduced or enhanced role for the Court of Appeal in both a civil and criminal jurisdiction and some later developments are traced by Stevens[1] and Blom-Cooper and Drewry.[2] A more current study of civil procedure generally, with a rich comparative account of contemporary institutional developments in various jurisdictions, is Jolowicz.[3] A recent change, dealt with in more detail below and occasioned by concerns about appellate overload, has diverted many appeals from courts or tribunals of first instance to the High Court and away from the Court of Appeal. We choose to begin a modern account of the work of intermediate courts with a managerial change introduced in 1934 and we trace further such changes that are still continuing.

---

[1] RB Stevens Law and Politics *The House of Lords as a Judicial Body 1800–1976* (Weidenfeld and Nicolson London 1979).
[2] L Blom-Cooper and G Drewry *Final Appeal: A Study of the House of Lords in its Judicial Capacity* (Oxford University Press Oxford 1972).
[3] JA Jolowicz *On Civil Procedure* (Cambridge University Press Cambridge 2000).

4. THE COURT OF APPEAL AS A GATEKEEPER: LEAVE/PERMISSION TO APPEAL

The change to which we refer was contained in the Administration of Justice (Appeals) Act 1934. This imposed a requirement of leave to appeal to the House of Lords in place of the absolute right of further and third appeal.[4] Leave was to be granted either by the Court of Appeal to which application had first be made or by the House of Lords itself. So, if both bodies refused leave, the Court of Appeal would become the final court for the parties in that case. This procedure remains. We are currently investigating the formal criteria and the less overt factors that determine whether cases can proceed upwards from the Court of Appeal. The origin of the leave requirement seems to have lain more in the workload of the Privy Council than that of the House of Lords, given that the membership of both bodies was, broadly speaking, the same—although the Privy Council contained some members from the dominions and what were then colonies. Again, Blom-Cooper and Drewry[5] trace the history of this development.

Those who supported the 1934 Act did so more out of concern to protect poor litigants who had won their cases in the lower courts from any further challenge than being actuated by arguments about the desired nature and form of the appellate process. It was felt that an unlimited right of appeal placed great power in the hands of large corporations and government departments even at a time when public law still remained undeveloped. Moreover, the Crown Proceedings Act (removing many anomalous and outdated procedural and substantive privileges and immunities of the state) had yet to be enacted. A multiplicity of appeals was also seen as a source of delay and of enabling one party, usually the stronger one, to force a settlement on the other. There was some discussion at that time about abolishing either the Court of Appeal or the judicial function of the House of Lords.[6] That did not happen but the process of obtaining leave to appeal further from the Court of Appeal to the House of Lords remains.

A major change in the operation of the means of turning an intermediate appeal into a final one has been to effectively remove an oral hearing from the process. If the Court of Appeal refuses leave to appeal (which it almost invariably does today even if the broad, unstated but generally recognized criterion of general public importance is met,) a renewed application to the House of Lords will normally be dealt with on the papers without a hearing before a three-person appeals committee. Only if the committee is divided will there be a hearing of such an application. If they are unanimous the application will be granted or refused. The committee first indicates a provisional view and invites written comments by the parties. It then reaches a final decision.

---

[4] See ch 12.
[5] *Final Appeal: A Study of the House of Lords in its Judicial Capacity* (n 2).
[6] *The House of Lords as a Judicial Body 1800–1976* (n 1) 191–192.

Since that time there has not been any serious discussion of abolishing either the Court of Appeal or the House of Lords (the judicial role of the Lords has hardly featured at all in recent discussions of the future of the second chamber). But there has also not been any examination of the relationship between the two courts. The fundamental reforms brought about by the interim and final reports of Lord Woolf[7] on civil litigation (shortly referred to as the Civil Procedure Rules (CPR) 1999) did not touch on appeals in their initial implementation.

A development that was first recommended by the Evershed Committee in 1953, the leapfrog appeal, enjoyed some popularity when it was first introduced in 1970[8] but is a rare event today. The House of Lords has only heard a handful of such cases in recent years. The procedure may be little known (or forgotten) by advocates and those who instruct them. The first instance court must certify that such an appeal is appropriate and that the criteria specified in the legislation are met (a point of law of general importance arising from the construction of legislation, a binding precedent in the Court of Appeal or the House of Lords and the House agrees to take the case). It seems unlikely that such an issue would be actively canvassed before the court has given judgment. We return to this issue later in the context of decisions on abstract or moot points outside the reference point of a specific case.

5. THE COURT OF APPEAL: PROCEDURAL CHANGES

The next point that arises in any consideration of intermediate courts is the changes that have occurred in recent years to the prospects of taking a case to the Court of Appeal at all. The development of the requirement of leave to appeal, restated in the CPR as 'permission to appeal', entailed not merely the extension of this requirement to almost all cases; the mechanisms and discretions by which permission can be obtained have also been made progressively more onerous. There has been little public discussion of this change, either in principle or relating to the way in which the criteria are applied in practice.

These changes can best be traced by briefly looking at the pre- and post-Bowman[9] position. There was normally a requirement for leave to appeal in what were called 'interlocutory appeals', broadly procedural issues and other matters arising during the course of litigation. This generated a vast amount of largely sterile case law about the distinction between such instances and 'final appeals'. It was always the case that appeals from lower courts were either limited in nature and scope (the prime example was challenges to decisions in

---

[7] Lord Woolf of Barnes *Access to Justice: Final Report to the Lord Chancellor on the Civil Justce System in England and Wales* (HMSO London 1996).

[8] G Drewry 'Leap Frogging and a Lord Justice's Eye View of the Final Appeal' (1973) 89 *Law Quarterly Review* 260.

[9] Sir J Bowman *Review of the Court of Appeal (Civil Division): A Report to the Lord Chancellor* (Lord Chancellor's Department London 1997).

small claims by district judges (the lowest tier of civil jurisdiction, tribunals apart) which were limited to serious errors of law. Further, appeals from the county courts always required permission if the amount at stake was less than an amount that varied from time to time. Appeals from the vast array of administrative and other tribunals (a review of this jurisdiction by Sir Andrew Leggatt, a retired member of the Court of Appeal, has now been published) were usually contained by second-tier, specialized bodies. There were also limitations on further appeals as of right from such bodies.

One enduring feature of the English system of civil litigation is that, despite the unification of the rules of civil procedure after and as a consequence of the Woolf report,[10] the county and High courts have not been combined into a unified civil court. The reasons for this are complex, ranging from differential roles and status for High and county court judges, an understandable wish to retain the local connection represented by the county courts, and a residual understanding that county courts are essentially small claims venues for consumer litigation or venues for resolving disputes about matrimonial finance and the separate but related care of children. In fact, most district judges in the county courts are, except in Greater London, also procedural judges in a localized structure of the High Court. This accentuates the anomaly of the retention of both High and county courts as separate jurisdictions. Unification is not, however, high on any reform agenda although a recent substantial reduction in litigation of all kinds (save for family and child care cases) may excite the interest of the Treasury in a unification programme designed to reduce expenditure. This is especially so because the Treasury strategy of charging the greater part of the cost of the courts to litigants by way of fees has not produced the anticipated return due to the reduction in the number of claims issued.

6. APPEALS TODAY

The distinction between interlocutory and final appeals has now been abolished. But a universal permission requirement has been created in its place. With little public attention or even informed legal debate, the operation of this requirement has been made progressively more demanding for appellants. Without tracing each procedural twist and turn in recent years, it may be noted that such changes may be made with very considerable ease (and lack of scrutiny) as a matter of technical rules which are a form of barely scrutinized delegated legislation. Beginning with where we now are, we see that the workload of the Court of Appeal had increased very considerably at the time of the creation of the Bowman Inquiry into the work of the court. All the undesirable features of litigation identified by Lord Woolf in his major report into civil litigation[11] were also observed in the workings of appellate courts. These were, set out

---

[10] *Access to Justice* (n 7).   [11] ibid.

here separately but closely related: delay; expense; complexity; excessive adversariality; a lack of court control and management of the acts of the parties to the litigation; and a lack of proportionality in the allocation of court resources devoted to the resolution of individual cases and later appeals.

Bowman[12] saw the most significant problem as delay. His principal solution was to reaffirm the necessity for appeal mechanisms so that a dissatisfied litigant could have his or her case reconsidered by a higher court, and, unstated but undoubtedly present in submissions made to Bowman, the need for a court that can both adapt the common law and, in practice, be a final appeal destination for the vast majority of litigants. But this would not necessarily be a task for the past and present Court of Appeal. The appeal system should not be seen as an automatic further stage. More than one level of appeal could not normally be justified. This sounds a reasonable principle but it has important implications in terms of the workload, the types of cases heard, and the functions of the Court of Appeal.

7. THE MULTIPLE PURPOSES OF APPEAL

Bowman[13] identified the purpose of an appeals system as not merely correcting wrong decisions as far as they concern the parties to the dispute. There is also a public purpose in ensuring confidence in the administration of justice and, where appropriate, to clarify the law, practice and procedure and to help maintain the standards of first instance courts and tribunals. This corresponds to the argument put by Blom-Cooper and Drewry[14] for the necessity of an appellate process. They argued that appeals serve two separate but related purposes. The first is best termed review. This is the means of correcting mistakes at first instance and of creating some kind of continuity, consistency, and certainty in the administration of justice. The second is termed supervision. This is the process of laying down fresh precedents and updating old ones for the guidance of lower courts in the hierarchy. In a small number of cases this also consists in resolving legal problems of a particularly high order both of difficulty and of public importance raised in a small percentage of cases.

Blom-Cooper and Drewry[15] also pointed out that there is a difference in emphasis between the two above functions. Review is principally to do with achieving justice in the instant case whereas supervision has primarily to do with solving legal problems in the wider public interest. They distinguished the role of the Court of Appeal from that of the House of Lords. The Law Lords primarily acted as a supervisory court having, at that time, most of its case load selected by the Court of Appeal. Since then the Court of Appeal so rarely grants leave to take a case further that it effectively picks the cases it wishes to hear

---

[12] *Review of the Court of Appeal (Civil Division)* (n 9).   [13] ibid.
[14] *Final Appeal: A Study of the House of Lords in its Judicial Capacity* (n 2).   [15] ibid.

itself. The role of the Court of Appeal is mainly one of review although, if the case stops there, as most do, the court is bound to act as a supervisory body in many instances, particularly on points of procedure where the House of Lords is normally reluctant to take appeals.

Because English law has no universal means of resolving points of law in the abstract, these two functions could not be separated. Since those two functions were identified, limited but significant means of resolving abstract issues have been developed. These take two forms. First, there is the possibility of any court referring an issue of interpretation or legality in EU law to the European Court of Justice. This is significant in a case that would otherwise give rise to European points of complexity, principle, or would otherwise be likely to go as far as the House of Lords. By obtaining an authoritative ruling on the applicable point of EU law, the Court of Appeal or even a lower court may be able to dispose of the case itself. A court from which there is no appeal must, if a decision on the point is necessary to resolve the case, refer the issue to the ECJ but the case may never be taken that far. (We will leave aside the arcane debate on whether the Court of Appeal is to be classified as such a court where it or the House of Lords refuses to allow a case to proceed from the Court of Appeal to the House of Lords). Secondly, there is the possibility of the Administrative Court (the specialist public law limb of the High Court) deciding an abstract point of public law by means of a declaration, as part of an application for judicial review. This development of such a jurisdiction is proceeding very slowly and is, at present, limited to public law including human rights.

8. PERMISSION TO APPEAL

The criteria established after Bowman[16] for permission to appeal to be granted do not explicitly recognize the above two purposes of an appeal. He did not further consider the twin purposes of appeals as we have identified them above. Bowman saw the advantage of permission being mandatory as saving time and also as providing an opportunity for judicial case management should permission be granted. He had in mind the giving of specific directions, determining the length of hearings and allocating a particular supervisory Lord Justice. In practice, as the appeal will normally be limited to an issue of law, the occasion for case management is generally limited. Bowman was silent on the criteria to be used for granting permission, which he left to the Rule Committee. Permission will only be given where the court granting it, which may include the lower court, '... considers that the appeal would have a real prospect of success or there is some other compelling reason why the appeal should be heard' (CPR, part 52.3).

Researching this area is difficult because, when granting or refusing permission, the Court of Appeal rarely uses the precise words of the rule embodying

---

[16] *Review of the Court of Appeal (Civil Division)* (n 9).

these criteria. It is, therefore, often difficult to say why permission has been granted or refused. The parties are required to lodge a skeleton argument with the application so, in many cases, the process and hearing of the application may be regarded as a truncated appeal. This is even more so in cases where the initial application is refused but is renewed by way of an oral hearing. Where a litigant is in person, an oral hearing is normally fixed as soon as the application for permission is made. The Lord Justice who hears the oral application may have been provided with a memorandum written by a research assistant summarizing the facts and the law. Such a document is not normally made available to the applicant. This use of research assistants is a novel development in the courts. The experiment seems to have been successful because it has been extended to the Law Lords.

Bowman[17] recommended that the application should be served on the respondent who might intervene by submitting a skeleton argument. This was not accepted although it is always possible that it will be seen as an attractive option in the future. The court has discretion to involve the respondent in the permission application and this will frequently be used where the applicant is asking for some interim remedy pending a full appeal. Permission may be limited to argument on certain issues. Security for costs may be ordered by the court at the permission stage, or later.

The effect of the above rule changes has been to considerably raise the threshold for permission in recent years. The majority of Lords Justice dealing with civil work, some 20 out of a total of 35, are, at any one time, more heavily engaged in deciding such applications than in hearing substantive cases. (Some of them—we are investigating the figures—sit with one or two High Court judges in the Administrative Court, hearing the more important applications for judicial review of the acts of public bodies.)

There is an oddity at work in the permission process. The Court of Appeal has said in a practice direction that pre-dated the CPR, but which still appears to be extant, that:

The court below is often in the best position to judge whether there should be an appeal. It should not leave the decision to the Court of Appeal. Courts below can help to minimise the delay and expense which an appeal involves. If the court below is in doubt whether an appeal would have a realistic prospect of success or involves a point of general principle, the safe course is to refuse permission to appeal. It is always open to the Court of Appeal to grant it.

This is not the approach the Court of Appeal adopts to applications for leave to appeal from itself to the House of Lords. It is very exceptional for such applications to be granted today although the House of Lords has not indicated (at least, not formally, what is spoken across the benchers' tables or elsewhere in the Inns of Court is not known) that it favours such a self-denying ordinance in the Court

---

[17] *Review of the Court of Appeal (Civil Division)* (n 9).

of Appeal. We accept that different considerations may apply to appeals to the highest court than to an intermediate court. But the work of the House of Lords was not subject to the scrutiny either of Woolf[18] or Bowman.[19] In consequence the principles that should inform the division of responsibility and jurisdiction between intermediate and final appellate courts have been neither fully articulated nor discussed.

9. Second appeals and appeals below the Court of Appeal

As recommended by Bowman,[20] but having a significance that has not been sufficiently recognized, the general rule is that appeals must stop at a second level of judge. A further related principle is that certain appeals, which previously reached the Court of Appeal, should normally be heard at a lower level. The almost universal requirement of permission has been achieved by changes to the CPR. The only exceptions are committal orders, a refusal to grant habeas corpus, and secure accommodation orders for children. Liberty is at stake in all of these cases but it may equally be at stake in others such as, for example, some asylum cases.

The questions of second appeals and the diversion of appeals from the Court of Appeal are complex. First, we will consider the manner in which the rules operate. The Access to Justice Act 1999 states that appeals to a county court judge or to the High Court (normally from a lower-level judge in either court) shall not normally lead to a further appeal to the Court of Appeal from that court. The exception is where the Court of Appeal considers that an important point of principle or practice is raised or there is some compelling other reason for the Court of Appeal to hear the further appeal. This appears to mean that the appellate court beneath the Court of Appeal cannot itself give permission to appeal in such a case or, if it can, the Court of Appeal must have the final word about whether it wishes to hear the case or not. It seems very doubtful whether a case could contain a compelling reason for it to be heard by the Court of Appeal if it did not raise an important point of principle or practice. This is best regarded as a rarely to be used exception to the principle that appeals are now to be contained at the lowest possible point. This is a principle reminiscent of Maastricht subsidiarity.

If there is a problem here it arises more from the irrational distinction between the county court and the High Court (now applying identical rules of procedure) than from being a necessary feature of the jurisdiction of the Court of Appeal. There is a further anomaly at work here. If an appeal is made to a tribunal a further appeal may lie to the relevant second-tier body. For example, an asylum appeal is heard by an immigration adjudicator with an appeal, itself with permission, to the

---

[18] *Access to Justice* (n 7).
[19] *Review of the Court of Appeal (Civil Division)* (n 9).   [20] ibid.

Immigration Appeal Tribunal. That is a second appeal but a further challenge to the Court of Appeal is not subject to the restrictive rules applicable to appeals passing through a second tier in the High or county courts. This has not been commented upon at all in any of the previous literature on higher courts.

Secondly, and in more detail, appeals from High Court Masters, district judges of the High Court and their deputies lie to a High Court Judge. Appeals from most cases heard in the county court lie to the High Court but if the decision is of a district judge (or deputy) of the county court the appeal lies to the county court judge. Certain appeals in the more important (in terms of money involved or length) cases heard in the county court lie to the Court of Appeal. The operation of these rules has already led to some administrative difficulties and misunder-standings in the Court of Appeal, particularly relating to second appeals. The absurdity of the present structure of the courts becomes plain when we see that a district judge in the county court will, outside London, almost invariably also be a district judge of the High Court. Appeals in similar cases proceeding before such a judge may go to the High Court or to the county court depending on which function the district judge is performing at the time. This does not appear rational. It may be that a further degree of limitation and diversion of appeals will occur once the present system has settled down and some conclusions can be drawn about the existing effect of limiting and diverting appeals.

The limitation on double appeals has a particular effect in our system of administrative and other tribunals. Many of these have an inbuilt tier of appeal. For example, immigration adjudicators, a very hard-pressed jurisdiction at present, have above them an Immigration Appeal Tribunal. An appeal to this tier already has to satisfy a permission stage, which can only be granted by the Tribunal and not by the adjudicator. The test for permission is 'a real prospect of success or some other compelling reason for the appeal to be heard'. This is identical to the criteria for permission to appeal to the Court of Appeal. Once the appeal has reached the Tribunal it can proceed further to the Court of Appeal with the permission of either the Tribunal or the Court of Appeal using the above criteria applied to all cases intended for the Court of Appeal.

There is one complexity at work here and one anomaly at work in the case of other tribunals. If the tribunal refuses leave to appeal to itself, that decision cannot itself be appealed to the Court of Appeal or, indeed, anywhere else. But judicial review can be used to challenge the decision refusing leave to appeal on the basis that the underlying decision of the adjudicator contains an error of law. The recently appointed President of the Immigration Appeal Tribunal has said that there are far too many applications for judicial review in such cases leading to great delay in the hearing of immigration appeals generally. It is fair to say that for the first 20 or so years of its existence the Immigration Appeal Tribunal was not the most illustrious star in the legal firmament. This has changed and it has now considerably improved in quality. It is difficult to see the purpose of permit-ting the possibility of interposition of an application for judicial review between two stages in an appellate process. This creates a distortion between appellate systems with two tiers and those where there is only an appeal to the High Court as is the case for tax tribunals and leasehold valuation/rent level tribunals. In such instances the 'double appeal' rule (explained above) will apply but this does not bite upon the possibility of judicial review of the decision of a second-tier body refusing leave to appeal to itself. This has arisen because our tribunal system is haphazard and bewildering in its complexity and effect.

The effect of these procedures on the work of the Court of Appeal is uncertain and requires further research. At this time it is enough to point to the issue and to stress that a more rational system of appeals would enable more meaningful comparisons to be made between the function of the Court of Appeal in, say, immigration and in consumer law.

10. THE EVERSHED REPORT

It is instructive to compare the position of access to the Court of Appeal today and as considered by the Evershed Committee in 1953.[21] Their emphasis was then, as now, on the cost of litigation and the possibility of the ultimate loser having to pay as many as three sets of costs, or four where there was an initial hearing before some kind of tribunal. The successful litigant would also have incurred substantial but irrecoverable costs, possibly out of proportion to the amount of damages recovered. They also pointed to cases growing in size and importance as they proceed from one appellate body to another. Fresh minds are brought to bear, new arguments are advanced, and further points arise for consideration. This added further to the costs.

At that time appeals to the Court of Appeal were only limited by a permission requirement in the case of interlocutory appeals and, of course, by a leave requirement from that court to the House of Lords (this having been introduced in 1934 as explained above). But there were also some substantive limitations. An appeal on fact did not lie from the county court. Evershed realized that to abolish all appeals was unrealistic and unjust. But some limitation was essential to limit costs. They first considered whether the multiplicity of appeals could be limited. This might be done by eliminating one tier of appeals. They considered whether some appeals might be funded at public expense in addition to the provision of legal aid. They were also prepared to consider changes to the jurisdiction of the House of Lords even though its functions were outside the immediate terms of reference. This is very typical of the systems of management and organization of the courts. The Court of Appeal and the House of Lords are considered and administered as separate and very watertight compartments within the system of justice. That they are both part of a composite whole is often overlooked. For example, the Woolf reforms took no account of the

---

[21] Lord Evershed MR 'Final Report of the Committee on Supreme Court Practice and Procedure' (1953) Cmd 8878.

judicial work of the House of Lords.[22] The House of Lords very rarely considers civil cases with procedural dimensions.

The distinction between interlocutory and final appeals produced a vast amount of obscure and impenetrable case law. What appears to be a straightforward distinction led to very many cases about the distinction between, for example, an application for summary judgment for damages to be assessed at a later stage and for a specific debt claimed to be due from the defendant. The Committee was opposed to a restriction on appeals on a point of fact from the High Court. The reasons advanced were that this would represent a retrograde step and was not supported in any quarter: hardly reasons and more akin to lists of assertions. A suggestion of a universal leave requirement from the High Court in the case of final orders fared no better.

The Committee agreed that such a step would limit costs in appeals that had little or no prospect of success. But they said that it would be difficult to formulate any principle in accordance with which leave to appeal might be granted or refused. This is in contrast to the Bowman report[23] which was prepared to leave the precise criteria to the Rules Committee. We wonder if what troubled Evershed was the difficulty not only of formulating the criteria but also of ensuring that they were followed in practice. We have drawn attention to this point above when discussing the present requirement for permission. The Evershed Committee said that the leave requirement worked in interlocutory appeals because most of these turned on a procedural point or points and leave would be granted if a point of principle were involved. By contrast, decisions on points of fact may depend on many variable considerations. The veracity of particular witnesses, their opportunities for observation, and the accuracy of their recollection were all problematic areas. Sometimes the result depended not so much on accurate observation as on inferences to be drawn. Sometimes large sums of money would be involved. Sometimes the result would interest a large number of people and in some they would interest only the immediate parties concerned. The Committee thought it was too difficult to devise one test to cover such a variety of cases. The Committee was correct in identifying a range of issues that were likely to arise in appeals. But why then did Bowman[24] not find these issues an inexorable stumbling-block to its proposal for a universal permission requirement?

The explanation seems to lie in the differing perceptions of a review team concerned with better management as compared with those of Evershed, a Committee dominated by lawyers and judges. Such members probably knew very well what they had grown up with and wanted to maintain but adjust such a system where necessary and, preferably, essential. A contemporary inquiry necessarily placed more emphasis on what has been called 'New Public Management' and its preoccupations with greater efficiency, effectiveness, and economy

---

[22] *Access to Justice* (n 7).
[23] *Review of the Court of Appeal (Civil Division)* (n 9).   [24] ibid.

in the delivery of public services. Whether for this reason or otherwise, Bowman[25] was prepared to take the risk that the criteria fixed for the grant of permission would be followed in practice.

As we have said above, our research shows that this issue may be rather more problematic than Bowman seemed to think. The discussion by Evershed of the possibility of increased rights of appeal from the county court comes from a past era. The Committee also considered the possibility of machines becoming available that would enable the proceedings to be recorded! They were also unhappy about too great a change to the traditions of hearing appeals orally from beginning to end and the reading aloud of the transcripts of evidence in the court below and they also were hostile to the introduction of an American system of written briefs. The Court of Appeal was opposed to it as was everyone else who gave evidence to the Committee. Unrestricted oral argument was seen as the best way of testing every point raised by each party. The oral argument would be conducted in the presence of all members of the court, there would be a greater likelihood of agreement between all such members and the US system tended to lead to many and varying dissents. Working as a team was seen as indispensable to reaching a fair decision. The court would be more likely to be able to deliver an oral judgment at the conclusion of the oral argument rather than having to put up with limited oral argument and the need to take away and study the briefs. Further, the division of the legal profession into barristers and solicitors meant that counsel would inevitably be instructed to draft the brief. In any event solicitors would have neither the time nor the capacity to undertake the drafting. In short, the introduction of what was seen as a foreign innovation was perceived to be unsuitable for a system that, being dominated by the interests of the Bar, could change only very slowly if it had to change at all.

By contrast, the present system of hearings in the Court of Appeal places great emphasis on written skeleton arguments, the limitation of oral argument and the use of reserved judgments only where it is thought essential to postpone a decision. We have seen some signs that judgments, or the greater part of them, have been written by one Lord Justice before the oral hearing begins. We understand the pressure to produce results speedily and it may be that in many cases oral argument, contrary to what Evershed thought, adds little or nothing to what the court has before it. But litigants may see such a method or approach to deciding appeals as less than fair.

11. A NOTE ON STATISTICS

The consequence of rules about permission to appeal, and the limitations on double appeals, combine to reinforce a tendency that existed before recent reforms. The vast majority of cases that come before the Court of Appeal end

---

[25] ibid.

in that court. It may be designated and perceived as an intermediate court but the reality is otherwise. In order to verify this proposition, we undertook a small study to examine the actual numbers of cases that ended in the Court of Appeal, as opposed to those which progressed to the House of Lords.

We wanted to examine two groups for comparative analysis, to see how many cases in a given period were heard in the Court of Appeal. Our sample consisted of all cases where a party asked the Court of Appeal for leave to petition the House of Lords and were either granted or refused leave. (Consistent with our perception of the separate administration of each court, the language of 'permission' in place of 'leave' and 'application' in place of 'petition' has not found its way into the rules of the House of Lords.) Our study periods were of three months' duration each: from 9 February to 9 May, in the year 2000, and again in 2001. Having listed those cases we went to the House of Lords and recorded those cases where people had petitioned the House for leave despite having had their leave applications refused, orally or on paper, by the Court of Appeal.

Of these groups we wanted to establish how many of the cases were substantive appeals and how many were applications for permission to appeal. We asked the following questions: how many parties are given leave to take their case to the House of Lords; how many parties, if refused leave by the Court of Appeal, still went anyway to petition the House of Lords? Unfortunately, the data required for the group in 2001 was not available from the House of Lords in terms of outcome—we could only establish how many parties had brought their cases before the Lords. We therefore concentrated our efforts on the data from the group of 2000, and traced the journey through the House of Lords to a final conclusion. The results of our research are described in Table 10.1.

The rules say that a petition to the House of Lords cannot be brought to challenge an unsuccessful application to the Court of Appeal for permission to appeal. There is some recent case law that confirms this cut-off for further appeals. In 10% of the total cases before the Court of Appeal in our sample in 2000, and 11% in 2001, petitions were presented to the House of Lords. But in the class where such a further appeal is prohibited the numbers were much higher, 29.5% in 2000 and 23% in 2001.

Of these numbers in 2000, permission to seek leave to petition the Lords was sought in 137 cases, and in 2001, 121 cases. This represents 10.9% in 2000 and 11.01% in 2001. We can go further and break the figures down to distinguish between those who attempt, hopelessly, to take an application for permission to appeal further and those who want to challenge a substantive decision against

Table 10.1: *Number of cases heard by the Court of Appeal*

	Substantive cases	Permission to appeal only
2000	408	949
2001	351	748

them. The outcome is that many unsuccessful parties in the Court of Appeal wish to take their cases further, however hopeless such a venture may be.

In the year 2000 group no applications to the Court of Appeal for leave to proceed to the House of Lords were granted. Of those who went further and petitioned the House of Lords for leave (a small number, 38% of a total sub-sample of 102), only two cases (c.5%) were given leave to proceed and both had their cases dismissed.

In conclusion, our small study revealed that a large number of litigants, represented or in person, will ask to go to the House of Lords should their case be unsuccessful in the Court of Appeal. Of those whose application for permission to appeal to the Court of Appeal has been refused, a number will ask anyway for leave even though there is no possibility in law of such an application succeeding. Of those who are granted a substantive hearing of their case, a large proportion will not accept the view of the Court of Appeal but will petition the Lords in any event. Very few of these will have their case heard and only a tiny number will be successful.

These findings support the proposition that whereas from a constitutional and legal perspective the Court of Appeal is an intermediate court with the Lords acting to review and or supervise litigation, in reality the Court of Appeal is the final court for the vast majority of cases. This is either because of statutory and common law rules or because the court itself will not grant permission to petition the Lords and the Lords themselves will rarely grant leave.

Finally, we are undertaking more work on a very concealed set of statistics. These relate to cases where appeals have been brought in the Court of Appeal but which are compromised, usually in private between the parties, after the appeal has been lodged. These raise some interesting issues. How many of these appeals were brought for tactical reasons to reduce an award of damages or for some other purpose? Are there any mechanisms for identifying such cases and ensuring that, by their very existence, they are not occupying too great a share of the resources available to the court? Should there be a 'good faith' or reverse security for costs requirement in the prosecution of an appeal? Should there be some reverse security for costs requirement in cases that do not appear to be a proper use of the court's time? How could such cases be identified? We hope soon to have some answers to these questions.

11

Intermediate Courts of Appeals and Their Relations with Top-level Courts: the US Federal Judicial Experience

RUSSELL R. WHEELER*

1. INTRODUCTION

This essay describes aspects of the relationship between the Supreme Court and the federal courts of appeal in the US, particularly structural and procedural changes proposed since the mid-1960s. Such discussion allows coverage, from the US federal perspective, of the following questions of likely interest to those considering changes in the UK's appellate judicial system, particularly the top courts.

First, what is the nature of the relationships between different levels of courts? The US Supreme Court and the courts of appeals are part of a national appellate system. The Supreme Court relies on the courts of appeals to correct errors, freeing it to decide a small number of cases each year that it believes present issues that most need national judicial resolution.

Secondly, how does the work (and reform) of intermediate courts of appeals affect top-level courts? Because the Supreme Court has almost total control over its docket, it is not greatly affected by changes in the work of the intermediate appellate courts. Those courts, for example, dispose of a majority of their cases without a published opinion explaining the decision. This would create a problem if the Supreme Court were obliged to review all courts of appeals decisions. In fact, the cases in which the courts of appeals provide less than the full panoply of appellate procedures are usually not likely to be candidates for the exercise of the Supreme Court's broad discretionary jurisdiction.

Thirdly, how (if at all) are changes in the caseload of intermediate courts reflected in the caseload of final courts of appeals? The greater output of the

* Deputy Director of the Federal Judicial Center, Washington DC. Opinions expressed in this paper are those of the author, not the Center's.

courts of appeals helps account for the increase in petitions for review in the Supreme Court, but that Court's discretionary docket has let it in fact reduce the number of cases it decides even as the number of merits decisions by the courts of appeals has increased. The reduction in Supreme Court decisions, combined with the increase in reviewable terminations in the appellate courts, may retard the total number of requests for review that would be otherwise presented, given the decreased likelihood of success.

Fourthly, to what extent should intermediate courts of appeals be involved in regulating access to a final court of appeals? Controlling access to the Supreme Court is the job of the Court itself.

Fifthly, are there any circumstances when litigation should jump from first instance trial courts directly to the final court of appeals, bypassing the intermediate appellate court? Very few: the Supreme Court benefits from analysis of legal issues by several appellate courts.

Sixthly, why does the Supreme Court take so few cases on certification from the courts of appeals? The rules permit certification only of pure law questions, which arise rarely. More important, the Court looks with disfavour on certification, which is inconsistent with the Court's discretionary control over its docket.

Lastly, should a period of prior service on the bench of an intermediate court of appeals be regarded as the normal career background of judges of the final court of appeals? Currently, there appears to be a strong presumption that Supreme Court justices should have served previously on an appellate court.

A caveat about the data: this essay, in tables and text, compares various aspects of the work of federal courts, with a brief reference to state courts. These data come from different sources, which use different time frames. Much federal court data are reported on a calendar year basis, but some on a fiscal year basis (1 October to 30 September), which is roughly comparable to the October Term of the Supreme Court. While quantitative comparisons are thus slightly but necessarily imprecise, I am confident that they accurately display the phenomena at issue.

Today there is no significant support for structural or procedural overhaul of the US federal appellate system. By contrast, a commentator at various points during the previous 40 years would necessarily have reported that many proposals for major change were under serious consideration, prompted by the effects of an appellate caseload that began vigorous escalation in the 1960s.[1]

---

[1] Summaries of the many analyses and proposals put forth in that period are available in J McKenna *Structural and Other Alternatives for the Federal Courts of Appeals* (Federal Judicial Center Washington DC 1993) and TE Baker *Rationing Justice on Appeal: the Problems of the US Courts of Appeal* (West Publishing St Paul 1994).

Soon thereafter, judges and scholars questioned the workability of the statutory framework of the national appellate system,[2] and claimed that 'the Supreme Court does not have the capacity to perform [its] tasks adequately'.[3] In 1985, Judge Richard Posner published *The Federal Courts: Crisis and Reform*.[4] The 1990 report of the statutory Federal Courts Study Committee warned that 'the long-expected crisis of the federal courts, caused by unabated rapid growth in case filings, is at last upon us' and included a chapter entitled 'Dealing with the Appellate Caseload Crisis'.[5]

There has been little crisis talk since the mid-1990s—the subtitle of Posner's revised 1996 edition substituted 'Challenge' for 'Crisis'[6]—and little clamour for major changes, even though federal appellate caseloads continue to increase faster than judgeships; structural changes have been quite modest, and procedural changes only somewhat more extensive.

The lessons that the US experience offers the UK's examination of the appellate courts may lie more in the debate over rejected proposals than in the impact of changes made.

2. OVERVIEW OF THE US APPELLATE SYSTEM

Article III of the US Constitution vests the 'judicial Power of the United States . . . in one supreme Court, and in such inferior Courts as the Congress may from time to time ordain and establish.' Table 11.1 summarizes federal court structure, personnel, and workload. It is a structure of one supreme court, 13 intermediate courts of appeals in 12 geographic 'circuits' and one subject-matter circuit, and, within each geographic circuit, from one to 15 districts, each with two trial courts—a district court (the major trial court) and a bankruptcy court (a unit of the district court). (In addition, within the executive branch are judicial bodies to enforce laws and administrative rules, such as the federal immigration courts, the US tax court, and administrative law judges.)

---

[2] PD Carrington 'Crowded Dockets and the Courts of Appeals: The Threat to the Function of Review and the National Law' (1969) 82 *Harvard Law Review* 542.

[3] Testimony of Judge Shirley Huftstedler (Ninth Circuit) before US Senate Committee on the Judiciary 94th Cong 2nd sess (1976). Hearings on s 2762 and s 3423, 40.

[4] RA Posner *The Federal Courts: Crisis and Reform* (Harvard University Press Cambridge 1985).

[5] Federal Courts Study Committee *Report of the Federal Courts Study Committee* (1990) 6 and ch 6.

[6] RA Posner *The Federal Courts: Challenge and Reform* (Harvard University Press 1996).

Table 11.1: The judicial branch of the United States—2002[7]

```
                    SUPREME COURT
                       9 justices
             Cases: 8,000+/−   Decisions: 80+/−
        Appointment: President, Senate   Term: Life
```

```
                    COURTS OF APPEALS
    179 judges in 12 geographic and one subject-matter circuit
          from 6 to 28 judges/circuit   Cases: 57,000+/−
           Appointment: President, Senate   Term: Life
```

```
                      DISTRICT COURTS
   663 judges in 94 geographic 'districts'—from 2 to 28 judges/district
              Cases: civil 250,000+/− criminal 63,000+/−
             Appointment: President, Senate   Term: Life
Bankruptcy judges (326), appointed by the courts of appeals; 14-year terms
 Magistrate judges (533), appointed by the district courts; 8-year terms
```

Judicial branch	Budget $5,000,000,000+/−	Employees: 30,000+/−
Congress	$2,700,000,000+/−	
Executive branch	$1,600,000,000,000+/−	

As Figure 11.1[8] indicates, Congress uses state boundaries as the bases for the geographic units of the federal judicial system.

The US judicial systems include that of the national government (the 'federal' system) and those of the 50 states, the District of Columbia and Puerto Rico, and hybrid systems in Guam, the Northern Mariana Islands, and the Virgin Islands. There are roughly 1,500 federal judges and about 30,000 state judges.

Table 11.2 compares the federal and state appellate judiciaries. I will not be examining state appellate courts here, although the states, especially the larger states, may provide fruitful comparative data for analyses of other countries' top and intermediate appellate courts.

---

[7] Sources: Judgeships, Supreme Court, 28 USC s 1, courts of appeals, 28 USC s 44(a), district courts, 28 USC s 133(a), bankruptcy courts, 28 USC s 152(a)(2), magistrate judge, Table 14, Administrative Office of the United States Courts, *Judicial Business of the US Courts, 2001* (hereafter cited as *Judicial Business*) <www.uscourts.gov> (6 August 2003). Case data, Supreme Court, *Judicial Business* (Table A-1), court of appeals, district, and bankruptcy courts, *Judicial Business* at 16.

[8] From R Wheeler and C Harrison *Creating the Federal Judicial System* (2nd edn Federal Judicial Center Washington DC 1994) 26 <http://www.fjc.gov> (6 August 2003); this material is publicly available.

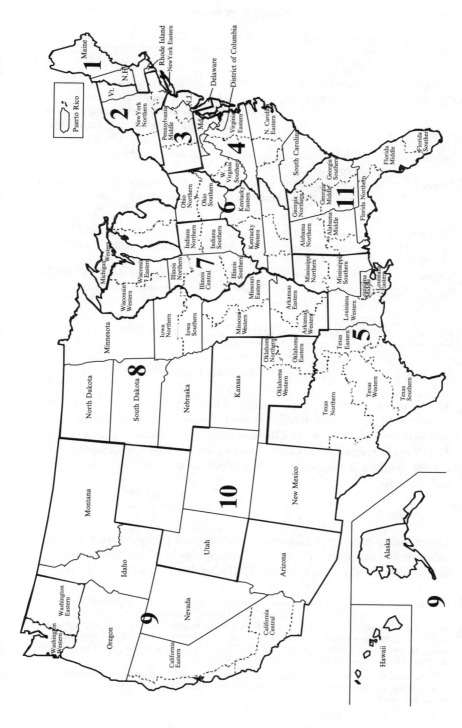

Figure 11.1: *Geographical units of the federal judicial system*

Table 11.2: Elements of appellate systems in the USA[9]

	Federal	State
HIGHEST COURT	US Supreme Court	State supreme court (except on federal questions) (called 'court of appeals' in a few states, e.g. New York); (Okla. and Tex. have separate civil and criminal high courts)
Judges	9 (Chief Justice and 8 associate justices)	Between 5 and 9
Filings	8,023 filings, 2001 88 cases disposed with full hearing and opinion	96,616 filings in 1999 (mandatory appeals 34,138; discretionary petitions 62,478)
INTERMED. APPELLATE COURTS	12 regional and one national jurisdiction courts	In 40 of the 52 states and territories—usually 'court of appeals'
Judges	179 judgeships (from 6 to 28; as of May 2002, 151 active judges, 28 vacancies, and 105 senior judges)	995 judgeships (from 3 to 93; 25 of 40 have over 10 judgeships)
Filings	57,464 (fiscal year 2001)	295,738 in 1999

3. THE US SUPREME COURT[10]

The Court, six members when established in 1789, grew to 10 in 1863 and has been at nine since 1870. It was the only federal court with mainly appellate jurisdiction until 1891, when Congress created intermediate courts of appeals. The Court has almost total control over its docket, which has enabled it to stay current despite a significant increase in appellate cases and requests for Supreme Court review.

A. Personnel

The president nominates and Senate confirms, and then the president appoints, members of the Court, as is true for federal appellate and district judges. The membership of the Court of the 2003 October Term (from October 2003

---

[9] Major data sources: **Federal**: United States Code provisions (n 7); *Judicial Business* (n 7) 1 <www.uscourts.gov> (6 August 2003) and 'The Statistics,' Table II (2002) 116 *Harvard Law Review* 460; Administrative Office of the United States Courts, internal 'Statistical Report' (monthly fact sheet); **State**: Bureau of Justice Statistics *State Court Organization 1998* (2000) table 2; Bureau of Justice Statistics *State Court Organization 1998* (2000); National Center for State Courts *Examining the Work of State Courts, 1999–2000* (2001) 77–78 (2001).

[10] Most of the historical information reported here is from *Creating the Federal Judicial System* (n 8) and sources cited there. (Unless otherwise noted, 'Court' (with a capital 'C') refers to the US Supreme Court.)

through late June or early July 2004) has been the same since Justice Breyer's appointment in 1994, one of the longest periods without a change in the Court's history.[11] The president appoints the Chief Justice as such.

As with all life-tenured federal judges, there are no statutory age, education, or previous service requirements. There are some fairly strong informal requirements. No non-lawyer has ever served on the Court, and both the administration and the Senate Judiciary Committee, with assistance and independent investigation by the bar, the press, and interest groups, analyse nominees' professional and personal qualifications. The process became raucous for some Supreme Court nominations in the 1980s, and may become so again. Presidents have typically nominated persons who are at least nominal members of his political party and appear likely to decide cases as the president would wish (a likelihood that has been frustratingly hard for presidents to predict). Another general expectation is that various demographic groups will be represented on the Court. Geography was a major consideration in the 19th century but is less so today. Unlike in earlier years, all but one of the justices in the 2003–04 term had served on a lower appellate court.

Justices have the same retirement provisions as other federal judges and can move from 'active' to 'senior' status based on their age and years of service but still draw the salary of the office if they perform some judicial work. Retired justices, like other federal judges, may sit temporarily on the courts of appeals or district courts, but not on the Supreme Court.[12]

Each justice is entitled to four law clerks—young lawyers who assist them for a year or two in research and preliminary drafting (Chief Justice Rehnquist hires only three).[13] A three-person staff attorney office provides non-case-related legal work and some assistance on cases in special circumstances. Congress appropriates funds for the Court separately from other judicial branch appropriations. In fiscal year 2003, the Court operated with a budget of almost US$50 million (plus additional funds for the Architect of the Capitol to maintain the building and grounds, and, over the next several years, to undertake a major renovation of the building) and a staff of over 400.[14]

B. Jurisdiction

The history of the Court's jurisdiction has been one of expanding discretion. The 1891 statute creating the courts of appeals vested the Court with limited discretion over its docket.[15] The 1925 'Judges Bill,' so called because Chief Justice Taft and his colleagues drafted the bill and pressed its passage, significantly reduced

---

[11] As of 14 Nov 2003.
[12] 28 USC s 371 (retirement); 28 USC s 294 (a) (assignment of retired justices).
[13] T Mauro 'Clerks Follow New Path to High Court' *Legal Times*, 21 October 2002.
[14] Senate Report 108–144, 'Departments of Commerce, Justice, and State, the Judiciary, and Related Agencies Appropriation Bill, 2004' 108th Cong 1st sess 114 (2003).
[15] An Act to establish Circuit Courts of Appeals 8 March 1891 26 Stat 826 (1891) 828, s 6.

the categories of cases that were appealable as of right,[16] and subsequent legislation whittled down that category. By 1971, appeals as of right were less than 10% of the docket (370 of 4,371 filings).[17] In 1988, Congress eliminated almost all appeals as of right.[18] Of the almost 8,000 cases presented to the Court in 2002, it rejected over 98%. (This figure calls into question the accuracy of characterizing the US Supreme Court as the country's 'final court of appeal.' In almost all cases, that term better applies to the federal intermediate appellate courts and the state supreme courts.)

The Court's discretionary docket reflects two premises: first, the Court's primary role is not to correct other courts' errors but to provide national resolution of important legal questions, and, second, the Court itself should determine which questions need such resolution.

A case may come to the Court by one of six means:

1. *Writs of certiorari*

All but a handful of cases are presented pursuant to writs of certiorari. Congress has specified that litigants may petition the Court to issue a writ of certiorari in cases from the federal courts of appeals or from the highest court of a state in cases involving federal law.[19] The Court denies almost all certiorari petitions filed, almost always without comment.[20] Unlike some courts with discretionary review, the Court's decision not to review a case does not imply that it thinks the case is meritless. Denial has no precedential value. Justices will occasionally dissent from certiorari denials.[21] The Court has long operated under a 'rule of 4': the votes of four of the nine justices are necessary to grant a petition for certiorari (or decide a case on appeal, although five are necessary to grant a writ of habeas corpus, discussed below).[22]

---

[16] See An Act to amend the Judicial Code 13 February 1925 43 Stat 936 (1925) s 237.

[17] Study Group on the Case Load of the Supreme Court (Freund Commission) *Report of the Study Group on the Case Load of the Supreme Court* (Federal Judicial Center Washington DC 1972) A-8.

[18] Public Law 100–352 102 Stat 662 (1988).

[19] 28 USC ss 1254(1), courts of appeals, and 1257, state courts. Although s 1254(1) permits the Court to grant a writ in a federal appellate case prior to judgment, the Court's rules discourage it (Rule 11), and it almost never occurs.

[20] A recent order reads, for example '*Rivera-Becera v US*, No. 00–8792, April 2, 2001. Case below, 243 F 3d 6551. Petition for writ of certiorari to the United States Court of Appeals for the Ninth Circuit denied.' 121 S Ct 1503 (2001).

[21] For example, an excerpt from a recent dissent reads: 'I believe that the Second Circuit's [court of appeals'] approach is very likely correct, and that the decision below leaves victims of egregious prosecutorial misconduct without a remedy. In any event, even if I did not have serious doubts as to the correctness of the decision below, I would grant certiorari to resolve the conflict among the Courts of Appeals on this important issue.' *Michaels v McGrath* 121 S Ct 873 at 874 (2001) (Justice Thomas dissenting).

[22] RL Stern and others *Supreme Court Practice: for Practice in the Supreme Court of the United States* (8th edn Bureau of National Affairs Washington DC 2002) s 5.4 ('Granting Certiorari on Four Votes'). For an analysis of the Court's internal practices requiring different numbers to grant certiorari as opposed to habeas corpus writs, see I Robbins 'Justice by the Numbers: The Supreme Court and the Rule of Four—Or Is It Five?' (2000) 36 *Suffolk University Law Review* 1.

The Court's Rule 10, 'Considerations Governing Review on Certiorari,' states that review on certiorari 'is not a matter of right, but of judicial discretion [, which] will be granted only for compelling reasons.' Rule 10 does not provide an objective list of reasons that will compel the Court to grant certiorari. Instead, it offers as examples decisions of courts of appeals or state supreme courts that conflict with decisions of other such courts and decisions implicating important federal questions that the Supreme Court should decide. In a typical passage, illustrating the first principle, the Court said in a 2001 case about federalism, 'We granted certiorari . . . to resolve a split among the courts of appeals on the question of whether an individual may sue a State for money damages in federal court under the' Americans with Disabilities Act.[23] Illustrating the second, it said the same year, in a challenge to a state law authorizing the medical use of marijuana, 'Because the decision [of the court of appeals] raises significant questions as to the ability of the US to enforce the Nation's drug laws, we granted certiorari.'[24] The Court usually grants certiorari on only some of the questions presented in the petition. Again in 2001, for example, it decided that prison authorities could regulate an inmate's providing legal advice to another inmate as long as the regulation was 'reasonably related to legitimate penological interests,' but declined to decide whether the regulations in the instant case were so related 'because we granted certiorari only to decide whether inmates possess a special right to provide legal assistance to fellow inmates.'[25]

Why the Court in fact grants certiorari has been the subject of extensive and multi-theme social science research that suggests, at the least, that the motivation of successive Supreme Courts for accepting cases is not necessarily described solely by the criteria contained in the Court's rules.[26]

'A petition for a writ of certiorari', Rule 10 continues, 'is rarely granted when the asserted error consists of erroneous factual findings or the misapplication of a properly stated rule of law.' On the rare occasions that the Court grants certiorari to consider the assertion of such an error, the purpose of review is usually to rein in courts that the justices believe need reminding of some basic proposition. In these situations, the disposition is often by per curium opinion and without oral argument. In 2001, for example, the Court reversed a court of appeals for ignoring 'courts' limited role in reviewing the merits of arbitration awards . . . To be sure, the Court of Appeals here recited [the correct] principles, but its application of them is nothing short of baffling.'[27]

---

[23] *Board of Trustees of the University of Alabama v Garrett et al* (2001) 121 S Ct 955, 961.

[24] *US v Oakland Cannabis Buyers' Cooperative and Jeffrey Jones* 532 US 483, 489 (2001).

[25] *Shaw v Murphy* 532 US 223, 232 (2001).

[26] A summary of this literature is in HW Perry *Deciding to Decide, Agenda Setting in the United States Supreme Court* (Harvard University Press Cambridge 1991) and K Smith 'Certiorari and the Supreme Court Agenda: An Empirical Analysis' (2002) 54 *Oklahoma Law Review* 727.

[27] *Major League Baseball Players Association v Steve Garvey* 532 US 504 (2001).

2. Other writs

Congress has authorized all federal courts, including the Supreme Court, to issue other writs,[28] such as habeas corpus and mandamus, but the Court has made clear that doing so is a matter 'of discretion sparingly exercised.' Petitioners, says the Court's rules, must show that the writ will aid the Court's appellate jurisdiction, that exceptional circumstances demand granting it, and that relief in no other form and from no other court is available.[29]

3. Appeals from three-judge district courts

The term refers not to judicial districts with three judges, but rather to ad hoc panels of two district judges and one circuit judge, specially convened when authorized by statute. Today, the major use of such courts is hearing suits challenging the size and configuration of federal or state legislative districts. Appeals from three-judge courts go directly to the Supreme Court,[30] which the Court may, in its discretion, decide. In the 2001 October Term, one of the Court's plenary decisions was an appeal from three-judge courts.[31]

4. Legislatively authorized direct and expedited appeals

These are quite rare. Congress writes such authorizations into statutes when it believes a quick, binding ruling on constitutionality is particularly important. For example, a 2002 statute sought to make significant changes in how politicians, political parties, interest groups, and individuals contribute to and and spend money in political campaigns. Members of Congress did not want to function any longer than necessary in legal limbo while challenges to the statute's constitutionality worked their way from district courts, to the courts of appeals, and finally to the Supreme Court. Thus the statute provided that any challenge to the statute was to be brought in the District of Columbia and heard by a three-judge court, convened pursuant to statute, with direct appeal to the Supreme Court.[32]

5. Certification

When it created the courts of appeals, Congress authorized them to certify to the Court 'questions of law in any civil or criminal case as to which instructions are desired.' Court action is discretionary.[33] Although once fairly common, deci-

---

[28] 28 USC s 1651.

[29] Rules of the Supreme Court 20(1).

[30] 28 USC s 1253. Provisions governing these courts' jurisdiction are 28 USC s 2284. 42 USC ss 1973b(a), 1973(c), 1973h(c), which authorize three-judge courts to hear legislative districting cases. 42 USC ss 2000a-5(b) and 2000e-6(b) authorize them in cases involving the public accommodations sections of civil rights laws, but such cases from three-judge courts have not been before the Court for some time.

[31] (2002) 116 *Harvard Law Review* 461, Table II (E).

[32] An Act to amend the Federal Election Campaign Act of 1971 to provide bipartisan campaign reform, Public Law 107–155, 116 Stat 81 (2002) s 403(a) . For the statute and the briefs filed in the litigation <http://www.law.stanford.edu/library/campaign finance>.

[33] 28 USC s 1254(2) and Supreme Court Rule 19.

sions on certification have been so rare in the last 50 years that one observer suspected 'there are few lawyers (and perhaps few circuit judges) who even know it remains an option.'[34] The scant use is a function in part of the requirement that courts of appeals not certify mixed questions of fact and law, but only questions of law (which occur rarely). Also, though, the Court simply disfavours certification. A robust use of certification would weaken the Court's control over its docket. In the 1970s, the Court agreed to decide on certification whether a semi-retired judge ('senior judge') could vote whether to rehear a case en banc, but refused to accept a question involving disqualification of judges to hear a case asserting judicial salary claims; different panels of the same court of appeals had decided the question differently. Said the Supreme Court, resolving such conflicts is a job for the court of appeals, and 'not...the occasion for invoking so exceptional a jurisdiction of this Court as that on certification'.[35]

6. Original jurisdiction

The Constitution vests the Court with original jurisdiction over cases involving diplomatic officials and those 'in which a State shall be a Party.' Congress has drawn distinctions here that limit original jurisdiction cases to suits between states.[36] In the 2000 Term, of the Court's 7,713 dispositions, two were original jurisdiction cases, and both received a full opinion; in the 2001 Term, of the 8,023 dispositions, only one was an original jurisdiction case, and it received a full opinion.[37] Original jurisdiction cases are usually disputes over boundaries, as when New Jersey sued New York over ownership of the island in New York harbour on which sits the Statue of Liberty.[38] The Court does not try these cases; it appoints a master to make recommended findings of fact.

C. Operations

The Court's annual term begins the first Monday in October[39] and is referred to as the 'October Term' for the particular year, even though there are no other regular terms during the year. The Court adjourns when it has announced its decisions in all cases argued that term, usually late June. The Court hears arguments Monday through Wednesday (two cases or less per day, 30 minutes per side), in two-week 'sittings', followed by two or more weeks of non-sittings. For the October Term 2002, the Court scheduled 39 days for oral argument, the last day being 30 April 2003.[40] Upon adjournment each June or early July, most

---

[34] E Hartnett 'Deciding What to Decide, The Judges' Bill at 75' (2000) 84 *Judicature* 120, 124

[35] *Supreme Court Practice* (n 22) s 9.2 ('Form and Content of Certificate').

[36] 28 USC s 1251.

[37] 'The Statistics' (2001) 115 *Harvard Law Review* 545 and (2002) 116 *Harvard Law Review* 459, 462. Summary information on the Court's work in the previous term appears at the end of the first number of each volume of the *Harvard Law Review*; some of the data are provided by the Supreme Court Clerk's Office.

[38] *New Jersey v New York* 523 US 767 (1998).   [39] 28 USC s 2.

[40] 'Court Schedule' at 'Oral Argument' <http://www.supremecourtus.gov> (6 August 2003).

justices leave Washington for lectures or vacation and return in September to prepare for the new term. Petitions for review come to the Court in a steady stream, even over the summer.

The Court does not sit in panels. Each justice, however, serves as 'circuit justice' for one or more circuits,[41] primarily to act on emergency petitions from litigants in that circuit (a petition for a habeas corpus writ to stay an execution, for example), deciding whether to preserve the matter until the entire Court can consider it.

The Court disposes of cases in one of four ways. Of the October Term 2001's 8,023 case dispositions, 7,865 were denials of requests for review, dismissals or withdrawn requests. Of the 158 other cases, 88 were decided on the merits after oral argument and with a signed opinion for the Court, and 70 were summarily decided.[42] A signed opinion is a written explanation of the decision. The Chief Justice or the most senior justice in the majority in any particular case assigns opinion-writing responsibilities in that case.

D. Administrative responsibilities

Except for the Chief Justice, the members of the Court have only minor responsibilities for the administrative superintendence of the federal courts. Instead, that is the task of the Judicial Conference of the US, which the Chief Justice chairs, and which includes the chief circuit judges and a district court judge elected from each regional circuit, plus the chief judge of the Court of International Trade.[43] The Conference has no administrative competence over the Supreme Court.

4. THE INTERMEDIATE COURTS OF APPEALS

Congress created nine intermediate federal appellate courts in 1891, after decades of debate about how to structure the federal judicial system to deal with the influx of cases created by industrialization, geographic expansion, and an enlarged federal jurisdiction. The Supreme Court, with its mandatory jurisdiction, was overwhelmed with cases. The major trial courts (then called 'circuit courts'), over which the justices were expected to preside along with district judges, were also heavily backlogged, both with trials and a limited appellate jurisdiction for cases from the district courts.

---

[41] 28 USC s 42.

[42] 'The Statistics' (2002) 116 *Harvard Law Review* 460, Table II (c). 'Summary decisions' are those made without oral argument and by per curiam opinion. For example, the Court might accept the case, vacate the decision of the court of appeals, and remand it to that court to reconsider in light of a Supreme Court case decided after the petition for review was filed. Also, cases of the type referred to at note 27 (reversal for error correction by per curium opinion) are summary decisions.

[43] 28 USC s 331. For a summary description of federal judicial administration, see R Wheeler 'The Administration of the Federal Courts: Understanding the Entities and Interrelationships that make Federal Courts Work' in GM Griller and EK Stott (eds) *The Improvement of the Administration of Justice* (American Bar Association Chicago 2002) 51–66.

Congress considered enlarging the Court or having it sit in panels, or restricting federal jurisdiction in favour of greater reliance on state courts. It decided instead to abolish the circuit courts and create three-member courts of appeals in each of the then nine judicial circuits to hear most appeals from the district courts in the respective circuits. Today, size and number of authorized judgeships vary considerably within the intermediate appellate system, as shown in Table 11.3. The courts of appeals have almost no control over their dockets and have faced a major increase in appeals since the 1960s. Appellate judgeships have increased much less than the number of cases. The courts of appeals have dealt with their increased workload primarily by creating alternative procedural tracks for different types of cases.

A. Personnel

As with the Supreme Court and the district courts, the president appoints courts of appeals judges ('circuit judges') after Senate confirmation of his nominees. The only formal requirement for appointment is that the nominee resides in the circuit (except for the District of Columbia circuit), and that every state in a circuit be represented on its appellate court.[44] There is less attention to ideology than in Supreme Court appointments (but more than in district court appointments). Senators, especially members of the president's political party who represent states in the circuit (particularly states in line for an appointment), have considerable sway in determining the nominee (or at least in blocking

Table 11.3: Size, judgeships, filings, filings/judgeship for regional federal courts of appeals—2002[45]

Circuit	Pop. (1998)	Sq. miles	Circuit J'ships	Filings (fy 2001)	Filings per Cir. J'p	Districts	Dist. J'ships
First	13,337,709	52,144	6	1,762	294	5	26
Second	21,996,062	61,318	13	4,519	347	6	65
Third	20,901,091	54,328	14	3,860	276	6	59
Fourth	24,829,436	152,289	15	5,303	354	9	55
Fifth	26,521,607	352,394	17	8,682	508	9	82
Sixth	30,236,545	178,714	16	4,853	303	9	62
Seventh	22,929,634	145,777	11	3,455	314	7	47
Eighth	18,498,575	478,233	11	3,034	276	10	41
Ninth	51,453,880	1,347,498	28	10,342	369	15	107
Tenth	14,073,217	554,869	12	2,758	230	8	50
Eleventh	26,459,341	162,606	12	7,535	628	9	543
DC	528,964	61	12	1,401	117	1	15
TOTAL	271,766,061	3,540,231	167	57,504	4,016	94	1,152

---

[44] 28 USC s 44(c).

[45] Adapted and updated from *Final Report of the Commission on Structural Alternatives for the Federal Courts of Appeals* (1998) table 2–9, 27; caseload data from *Judicial Business* (n 7) <http://www.library.unt.edu/gpo/csafca/CSAFCA.html>.

unacceptable nominees). The whole process of nomination and appointment of circuit judges has become much more rancorous in recent years.

Each active circuit judge is entitled to three law clerks plus two secretaries. Each court of appeals also has an office of from roughly 10 to 50 staff attorneys[46] and most have one or two 'conferencing attorneys,' who help parties settle cases prior to oral argument. Overall, the courts of appeals collectively employ about 2,700 staff (in addition to some 260 active, semi-retired, and retired judges) and operate on an annual budget of about US$470 million.[47] The chief judge is selected by a statutory formula based on a combination of age and seniority.[48]

B. Jurisdiction

Unlike the Supreme Court, the courts of appeals decide all cases properly presented to them.[49] Cases come from, and are binding only on, the federal district courts in the respective circuits. Statutes also provide for direct review of some administrative agency decisions. The courts of appeals caseload grew modestly from 1891 until the 1960s, when it shot up, due in part to judicial decisions and statutes expanding remedies available to prisoners and criminal defendants, and in part to various economic regulatory statutes. Table 11.4 shows the increase since 1940 for the courts of appeals, and for comparison, with the district courts and the Supreme Court.[50] Between 1970 and 2001, filings in the courts of appeals increased 394%, compared with 146% in the district courts. By contrast, filings per circuit judgeship increased by 187%, but district court per-judgeship filings increased only 48%. One reason is that the circuit judges themselves have generally urged Congress not to provide commensurate increases in their numbers. ('Per-judgeship' figures provide an imprecise measure of individual work, because at any one time, all judgeships are not filled while at the same time courts are using senior and visiting judges to help with their work. Capturing these subtleties, however, is an arithmetically daunting task, and thus judgeships serve as an acceptable surrogate for total available judges.)

There is a relationship between filings in the courts of appeals and in the Supreme Court. A majority of petitions for review come from federal appellate

---

[46] J McKenna, L Hooper and M Clark *Case Management Procedures in the Federal Courts of Appeals* (Federal Judicial Centre Washington DC 2000) 6 <http://www.fjc.gov> (6 August 2003). The allocations are based on caseload.

[47] Administrative Office of the United States Courts *The Judiciary, Budget Estimates for Fiscal Year 2003* Congressional Submission [5.7], [5.10].

[48] 28 USC s 45.   [49] 28 USC ss 1291.

[50] Case data are drawn, for district courts, from tables C-1 and D-1; for courts of appeals, from table B-1, for the Supreme Court, from table A-1, *Annual Report of the Director of the Administrative Office of the US Courts* (more recently titled *Judicial Business of the United States Courts* (n 7)). Judgeship data are primarily from Administrative Office of the US Courts *History of the Authorization of Federal Judgeships* (Analysis and Reports Branch of the Administrative Office of the US Courts Washington DC 1999) (relevant tables not available online).

Table 11.4: Filings over time in district courts, courts of appeals, Supreme Court[51]

	District courts		Courts of Appeals		Supreme Court	
	Filings	Per Judge	Filings	Per Judge	Filings	Per Judge
1940	68,135	362	3,446	60	981	109
1950	91,005	429	2,830	44	1,270	141
1960	89,112	370	3,899	57	1,862	207
1970	127,280	322	11,622	120	3,408	379
1980	197,710	388	23,200	176	4,959	551
1990	265,841	412	40,898	245	5,727	636
1995	294,123	456	50,072	300	7,551	839
2001	313,615	478	57,464	344	8,023	891
% increase since 1940	360%	32%	1,567%	473%	718%	718%
% increase since 1970	146%	48%	394%	187%	135%	135%

courts, not state supreme courts.[52] (The great majority of plenary dispositions are in cases from the lower federal courts.)[53] As to petitions for review, however, Judge Posner has noted a decline in the percentage of reviewable courts of appeals decisions from which litigants actually seek Supreme Court review, from 15% in 1960 to 1.1% in 1993.[54] He suggests that the increase in reviewable decisions, combined with the decrease in the cases that the Court accepts for review,[55] discourages litigants from seeking review because of the very low likelihood of success.[56] Thus, while the raw number of petitions is increasing, Posner's economic analysis suggests that the increase in reviewable decisions retards an even greater increase.

C. Operations

Unlike the Supreme Court, the courts of appeals work almost exclusively in panels.[57] Each court, administratively, generates three-judge panels at random for periodic 'sittings,' and then, in a separate process, generates dockets of appeals to assign to each panel. Some circuits adjust the dockets to provide panels an even distribution of different case types. The judges on the panels read the briefs, hear oral argument in cases they think merit it, and prepare judgments and opinions or

[51] See (n 50).
[52] The most recent readily available figures indicate less than half the requests came from federal courts in 1960 but by 1993, the figure was over 66%. *The Federal Courts: Challenge and Reform* (n 6) 121–22.
[53] Seventy-one of the 80 cases disposed of by full opinion in the 2001 Term. 'The Statistics' (2002) 116 *Harvard Law Review* 461, Table II (E).
[54] *The Federal Courts: Challenge and Reform* (n 6) 82–83.   [55] See Table 11.6.
[56] *The Federal Courts: Challenge and Reform* (n 6) 82–83.   [57] 28 USC s 46.

other statements explaining (or at least stating) the judgment. Oral argument, when a panel permits it, usually ranges from 10 to 20 minutes per side.[58]

A panel's decision is a decision for the entire court. By statute, each court of appeals may decide cases en banc, either originally or by rehearing a case decided by a panel.[59] The Federal Rules of Appellate Procedure look with disfavour on en banc hearings except when necessary to maintain consistency in the law of the circuit or to decide exceptionally important cases.[60] Between 1994 and 1998, the highest number of en bancs in any year was 110 nationally.[61] Despite the increase in per-judge caseload, the courts of appeals have stayed relatively current. The number of pending cases in 1997 was 76% of the number of filings, and 70% of filings in 2001.[62]

D. Administrative responsibilities

Regional administrative governance of the federal courts is the responsibility of circuit judicial councils, consisting of the chief judge of the circuit, ie the chief judge of circuit's court of appeals (who chairs the council), plus an equal number of circuit and district judges.[63]

E. Differences among circuits and their courts of appeals

Although the courts of appeals operate under a common statutory framework and the Federal Rules of Appellate Procedure, there are noticeable differences among them. The circuits themselves are the product of history more than logic; they were created originally as a means of allocating Supreme Court justices' trial court duties, not to demarcate the geographic jurisdiction of intermediate appellate courts.[64] Table 11.3, above, shows that the circuits, and their courts of appeals, differ greatly in size. They differ also in culture. The small First Circuit, for example, comprising most of New England—plus, due to historic trading patterns, the district of Puerto Rico, in the un-New Englandish Caribbean Sea—is a different judicial place than, say the Fifth Circuit, which embraces the Gulf Coast and Texas, or the Tenth, which occupies most of the inter-mountain west. The courts of appeals differ as well; each has, for example, its own set of local rules, supplementing the national rules, and practices and procedures can differ considerably.[65] So can their decisions. This is not the place to analyse different decisional patterns in the courts of appeals. However, for one simple measure, see Table 11.7 below, showing the difference in Supreme Court reversal rates of the Ninth Circuit's court of appeals and the other courts, including that of the Fourth Circuit, which is generally regarded as more in tune with the Supreme Court.

---

[58] *Case Management Procedures in the Federal Courts of Appeals* (n 46) 17.
[59] 28 USC s 46(c).   [60] Federal Rule of Appellate Procedure 35(a).
[61] *Case Management Procedures in the Federal Courts of Appeals* (n 46) 22.
[62] Calculated from figures in Table 1 *Judicial Business* (n 7).
[63] 28 USC s 332. See Wheeler (n 43).
[64] An Act to establish the Judicial Courts of the United States 1 Stat 73, s 4 (24 September 1789).
[65] *Case Management Procedures in the Federal Courts of Appeals* (n 46).

5. THE SUPREME COURT AND THE COURTS OF APPEALS PLAY DIFFERENT BUT OVERLAPPING ROLES

Having now described the federal appellate system in outline, we may move on to analyse the relationship between the Supreme Court and the courts of appeals. We do this, first, by examining a proposition that most observers believe does exist and should exist, namely that the Supreme Court and courts of appeals play different but overlapping roles. (A further proposition, that the courts of appeals assist the Supreme Court, is considered in part 6, below.)

A. The Supreme Court has one role: resolution of important federal legal questions

The Court's role is to provide national judicial resolution of federal legal questions that are unsettled because of conflicting interpretations in lower appellate courts or because of the lack of resolution by the Court or Congress. The Court's function is not to correct errors in individual cases except in the course of exercising its national law-declaring role. This view rests on the principle that litigants have a right to one mandatory appellate review—but not two. More than the country needs a second federal level of error correction, it needs a single authoritative judicial body to provide guidance to state and federal courts on the proper interpretation of federal law. As one justice put it recently, the courts of appeals decide 'cases', but the Supreme Court decides 'issues' (albeit as framed in individual cases).

Some have complained that the Court's almost total freedom to set its own course within the framework of broad jurisdictional statutes makes it more of a legislature than a court.[66] Contributing to that view is the difficulty in identifying the criteria that guide the justices' decisions about what cases to decide. Thirty years ago, Justice Brennan favourably invoked Justice Harlan's observation that '[f]requently the question whether a case is "certworthy" is more a matter of "feel" than of precisely ascertainable rules.'[67] The ability to set its own course certainly makes it a very unusual court. As a practical matter, though, if the Court were not to decide which cases to decide, someone else would have to do it. Alternatively, Congress could require the Court to decide a far greater number of cases than it now does, which might lead the Court to stick more closely to the mix of cases occurring naturally in the courts of appeals and state supreme courts. But, putting aside what good, if any, would come from such an arrangement, requiring the Court to decide a much greater number of cases would run into the problems described below.

1. The court should not sit in panels

The courts of appeals increase their decision-making capacity substantially by letting panels of three judges decide cases for the entire court. It would

---

[66] Hartnett (n 34) 125–26.

[67] WJ Brennan 'The National Court of Appeals: Another Dissent' (1973) 40 *University of Chicago Law Review* 473, 479. See the analysis in *Deciding to Decide, Agenda Setting in the United States Supreme Court* (n 26) especially ch 9.

be inconsistent, however, with the Supreme Court's role as national law declarer to have panels of the Court make decisions for the entire Court. Panel decisions might be inconsistent with the constitutional prescription for 'one Supreme Court'. Furthermore, use of randomly appointed panels could increase the Court's workload. Some litigants who would not seek review based on a prediction of how the full Court would decide the case might be willing to take their chances of drawing a sympathetic panel. And, because of the higher stakes, the Court would be under pressure to grant en banc reconsideration of panel decisions. Alternatively, the Court could, like other supreme courts, decide cases by subject-matter panels. That, however, would also run into the same 'one Supreme Court' argument. Furthermore, determining the membership of the panels could itself become contentious, unless that were done randomly as well. In any event, none of these options has been much considered, because there is no obvious pressure for the Court to increase the number of cases it decides each year.

2. The court must be small enough to allow collegial deliberation among its members

Similarly, although all the federal courts of appeals but one have more than nine judges, it is settled wisdom that nine justices is the right number for the Court. Expanding it to a larger size, without provisions for panel decisions, would not decrease the decisional burden on the justices (but might decrease their opinion-writing burdens). President Roosevelt's 1937 proposal to expand the Court by one member for every justice over the age of 70 was really an effort to change the Court's anti-New Deal decisions, and few took seriously his claim that the nine-member Court was unable to keep up with its work. What has lasted from that debate is Chief Justice Hughes's rebuttal, cited favourably in 1972 by the Study Group on the Case Load of the Supreme Court: 'more judges to hear, more to consult, more to be convinced'.[68]

3. Although the court cannot and should not decide every case presented to it, Congress should not create other national appellate bodies to decide some of the cases that the Supreme Court does not decide

Debate over proposals in the 1970s and 1980s to create a level of review between the intermediate appellate courts and the Supreme Court provides a context for analysing the Court's role as the 'top court'. The proposals were grounded on the assumption that the Court had more work to do than any nine-member en banc court could do. In particular, change proponents argued that the Court was unable to resolve all the intercircuit conflicts that needed resolution.

In 1972, the Study Group on the Case Load of the Supreme Court (the 'Freund Commission'), which Chief Justice Burger appointed in 1971, proposed a National Court of Appeals of seven judges drawn for three-year terms from the federal courts of appeals. This National Court would screen all petitions for Supreme Court review and refer 400 or 450 each term to the Supreme Court,

---

[68] *Report of the Study Group on the Case Load of the Supreme Court* (n 17) 7.

which would, in its discretion, decide, deny, or refer them to the National Court for decision. The National Court could also decide intercircuit conflicts that it elected not to refer to the Supreme Court.[69] In 1975, the statutory Commission on Revision of the Federal Court Appellate System proposed a National Court of Appeals of seven permanent judges. The Supreme Court could refer cases from its docket to the National Court for decision or dismissal. Likewise, the courts of appeals could transfer cases, particularly intercircuit conflicts, to the National Court for decision or dismissal, in either case subject to review by the Supreme Court on certiorari.[70] Variations on these proposals appeared into the 1990s, such as the 'intercircuit panel of the courts of appeals,' the 'In Banc Intercircuit Conference' and the 'Central Division of the United States Courts of Appeals'.[71] The only structural change enacted was the 1982 creation of the Court of Appeals for the Federal Circuit, with a national jurisdiction over appeals from certain trial courts and administrative bodies (eg the Court of Federal Claims and Court of International Trade) and from district courts in certain areas (mainly patent infringement suits).[72] The court does not resolve conflicts among the regional courts of appeals, although it eliminates intercircuit conflicts in areas over which it has exclusive jurisdiction. Its decisions are subject to Supreme Court review in the normal course.

The rejection of a new tier of review over the intermediate appellate courts reflected several arguments. First, opponents claimed that vesting some national appellate authority in another court would violate not only the constitutional mandate for 'one Supreme Court' but also the underlying concept that the members of the Supreme Court are the judges whom the president and Senate select to make nationally binding decisions, which carry the respect they do because the Supreme Court makes them. Second, opponents worried that inserting another appellate tier would diminish the status of the judges on the regional appellate courts. One circuit judge worried, 'the courts of appeals . . . will become mere "whistlestops" on the way to the Supreme Court or the national court of appeals.'[73] Third, opponents claimed good judges would not want to serve on the new tier, resolving intercircuit conflicts of insufficient gravity to engage the attention of the Supreme Court.

Finally, new analysis suggests that the problem of intercircuit conflicts may not be anywhere as great as perceived by many new-tier proponents. Professor Arthur Hellman has meticulously followed batches of intercircuit conflicts from creation to resolution, death, or unimportance and concluded that most conflicts, regardless of Supreme Court inaction, do not persist or do not cause the unequal treatment feared by those proposing structural measures to eliminate them.[74]

[69] ibid. 47.

[70] Commission on Revision of the Federal Court Appellate System *Structure and Internal Procedures: Recommendations for Change* (The Commission Washington DC 1975) vii.

[71] *Structural and Other Alternatives for the Federal Courts of Appeals* (n 1) analyses, at 75 and 108, the numerous proposals for new tiers as well as structural revisions of the appellate courts.

[72] Jurisdiction is set out primarily in 28 USC s 1295.

[73] Testimony of Judge Donald Lay (Eighth Circuit) to US Senate Committee on the Judiciary 94th Cong 2nd sess (1976). Hearings on s 2762 and s 3423, 131.

[74] AD Hellman 'Light on a Darkling Plain: Intercircuit Conflicts in the Perspective of Time and Experience' (1998) *Supreme Court Review* 247.

The decline in the number of cases to which the Supreme Court grants review
stands as a measure of the Court's view that the number of intolerable conflicts is
not a serious problem.

4. *Decisions of which cases the court should review should be made by the court itself*

As noted, the Court's virtual freedom to decide how many cases it will decide is
largely uncontested, and because of that, there is little support for structural
change to increase the country's national-level appellate capacity. To be sure,
some have argued that certain types of cases or categories of litigants—especially
political and racial minorities asserting denial of constitutional rights—need
statutorily protected access to the Court. The weight of opinion has come
down on the other side. Even Justice Thurgood Marshall, who was especially
alert to the need for judicial protection of minorities, argued that the only
'reason for retaining a significant group of cases that come to the Supreme
Court by right rather than by...certiorari...is to give the law reviews and
clerks interesting problems of jurisdiction to muse over.'[75]

Proposals to have lower appellate judges decide who may present issues to the
Supreme Court have attracted few adherents. The Freund Commission proposal
for a National Court of Appeals to screen petitions was perhaps the most
severely criticized. Opponents argued that only the Court itself is in a position
to know which of the many cases presented for its review provide the best vehicle
for clarifying the law or making new law. Former Justice Goldberg cited the well
known 1963 Supreme Court case of *Gideon v Wainwright*[76]—holding, contrary
to the Court's own precedents, that indigent defendants in state felony proceedings must be provided a lawyer—as the kind of petition that a national court
might be unlikely to send to the Supreme Court.[77] Furthermore, the justices have
said that the process of reviewing petitions itself is helpful to them.[78] Even now,
when eight of the justices participate in a 'cert pool', by which their law clerks
allocate the certiorari petitions for initial review and make recommendations to
the participating justices, the actual decisions to grant certiorari appear still to be
made by the justices themselves. Some have suggested that the 'cert. pool' has
reduced the number of certiorari grants, on the theory that law clerks, recommending dispositions to their own justice and seven others, may be reluctant to
recommend certiorari except in clearly compelling cases. Based on one justice's
papers, however, one scholar has concluded that cert. pool recommendations, at
least in the 1970s and 1980s, bore little relation to the Court's decision whether
to grant certiorari.[79]

---

[75] Statement authorized by Justice Marshall in *Structure and Internal Procedures: Recommendations for Change* (n 70) 183.
[76] 372 US 335 (1963).
[77] Testimony of Justice Goldberg to US Senate Committee on the Judiciary 94th Cong 2nd sess
(1976). Hearings on s 2762 and s 3423, 95.
[78] Brennan (n 67) 483.
[79] B Palmer '"The 'Bermuda Triangle?" The Cert Pool and Its Influence over the Supreme Court's
Agenda' (2001) 18 *Constitutional Commentary* 105.

5. *The court can police the courts of appeals even though it reviews a very small percentage of court of appeals decisions*

The number of cases the Court decides each term has declined over the last decade. A Rip Van Winkle who fell asleep in the 1970s amid complaints that the Court's 100 to 150 annual decisions were too few to guide the lower appellate courts would be surprised to awake today and find the Court deciding about 80 cases a term, with few complaints about the number of decisions. Table 11.5 shows that the annual requests for review have increased steadily, but the Court, in the last 10 years has reduced the number of cases to which it gives full review. Various reasons are offered for this change. Some argue that the courts of appeals need less 'policing' by the Supreme Court, either because the Court's opinions provide better guidance than in earlier years or because the courts of appeals consist mainly of judges with views similar to those of the current Court majority. Others say that the intercircuit conflicts that need resolution have either declined or there has been a reconsideration of which conflicts need resolution.[80]

To some, the increase in court of appeals decisions, combined with a steady or declining number of decisions by the Supreme Court, calls into question the Court's ability to supervise the courts of appeals. Table 11.6 shows that the percentage of courts of appeals merit decisions to which the Court gave plenary review has fallen from 3% in 1950 to 0.25% in 2001.

But the figures do not necessarily mean that Supreme Court supervision of the appellate courts is too limited. As McKenna notes, inasmuch as the Court's role

Table 11.5: Supreme Court petitions for review and cases disposed of by full written opinion[81]

Term	Cases filed	Cases with full written opinions	Written opinions per term as % of cases filed
1950	1,270	108	8.5
1960	1,862	110	5.9
1970	3,408	105	3.1
1980	4,959	155	3.1
1990	5,727	137	2.4
1995	7,551	95	1.3
2000	7,924	76	0.9
2001	8,023	88	1.1

[80] Hellman (n 74).

[81] Note: Comparing the written opinions in a term with the cases filed in the term is somewhat imprecise, in that the Court does not dispose, in any single term, of all cases filed in that term. Some decisions are in cases filed late in one term and scheduled for oral argument the next. Because the Court stays current with its docket, however, and because the change in filings from year to year is incremental, the imprecision is minor.

Sources: Table A-1, *Judicial Business* (n 7); Rehnquist '2002 Year-End Report on the Federal Judiciary' 8 <http://www.supremecourtus.gov> (14 November 2003) and 'The Statistics' (n 37). Sources for some years do not present filing data; for those years, I estimated filings as follows: Cases on docket *minus* cases carried over from previous term *plus* cases remaining on docket.

Table 11.6: Percentage of Federal Courts of Appeals meriting decisions receiving plenary review in Supreme Court[82]

Year	Supreme Court Plenary Decisions in cases from Courts of Appeals	Courts of Appeals decisions on the merits	% of merits decisions given Supreme Court plenary review
1950	70	2,355 (fiscal year)	3.0
(Oct. term)			
1978	101	8,850	1.1
1985	132	16,944	0.78
1990	90	20,943	0.43
1995	67	27,772	0.24
2001	70	28,840	0.24

is not error correction, 'the number of cases it declines to review is less important than the number of legal issues it leaves undecided despite a need for authoritative national resolution.'[83] Pegging that number is a real task. Even though the number of intolerable intercircuit conflicts is not (and may never have been) as great as once thought, there is no reliable measure of questions, if any, that the Court should decide but does not. That is true in part because of the elusiveness of agreement on what cases the Court 'should decide.' Again, though, although not dispositive, it is relevant that few observers are calling for a large increase in the number of cases that the Court decides.

6. The court also needs discretion as to its operations

The Court is afforded great discretion, not only about what cases it will decide, but about the process by which it decides them. For example, the Court announces a disproportionate number of decisions in the closing weeks of each term, often in the most contentious and difficult cases. On the final three days of the October Term 1999, for example (19, 26, 28 June 2000), the Court announced 12, or 16%, of its 77 fully decided cases, including eight blockbuster decisions.[84] This practice reflects the Court's insistence on disposing of all argued cases in any October Term before it adjourns for the summer. This insistence has been the object of chronic grumbling from the media and even a few comments by justices. Critics say the quality of the so-called 'June opinions' is sometimes sub par, given what appears to be the Court's sometimes frantic rush to clear its docket, and that it is difficult for the public and

---

[82] Adapted from Table 2–1 in Commission on Structural Alternatives for the Courts of Appeals (n 45) and updated from data from 'The Statistics' (n 37) and Table B-5, *Judicial Business* (n 7).

[83] *Structural and Other Alternatives for the Federal Courts of Appeals* (n 1) 56.

[84] The cases, with their pages numbers in vol 120 S Ct Reporter, are: *Santa Fe Ind. School Dist. v Doe* (school prayer) 2266; *Dickerson v US* (*Miranda* warnings) 2326; *Apprendi v NJ* (sentencing enhancements) 2348; *California Democratic Party v Jones* (blanket primary elections) 2402; *Boy Scouts v Dale* (excluding homosexuals) 2447; *Hill v Colorado* (abortion clinic demonstrations) 2480; *Mitchell v Helms* (parochial school aid) 2530; *Stenberg v Carhart* (partial birth abortion) 2597.

even other judges to absorb what the Court has done. (For example, the June 2000 decision in *Apprendi v New Jersey*, which threw into question many state and even federal criminal sentencing practices, was virtually hidden when announced along with a batch of higher-profile decisions.[85]) The justices, however, prize their summer respite. ('I soon learned', Justice Brandeis said in 1940, recalling his early days on the Court, 'that I could do twelve months' work in eleven months, but not in twelve.'[86]) There is no serious effort to change the schedule.

Likewise, a few legislators have begun to echo journalists' calls for the Court, like Congress and the courts of appeals, to allow video cameras to record its hearings for news broadcasts. Again, this is unlikely to happen until the justices support the idea, which now they do not.

B. The courts of appeals have two roles: error correction and law declaring

A judicial system must provide litigants some opportunity for review of decisions of its principal courts, the first instance courts. The courts of appeals provide that opportunity. And in the course of correcting errors, the courts of appeals, in the common law tradition, announce and clarify the law to guide federal trial courts in their respective circuits.

1. *To perform their functions, the courts of appeals must be relatively small, individually and collectively*

Intermediate appellate courts, especially those that permit panels to decide cases for the entire court, must be small enough to maintain *intra*-court consistency. One way to allow individual courts to remain small in the face of rising caseloads is to divide a court that has become too large into two or more smaller courts. Congress has twice divided a circuit on the belief that its court of appeals had grown too large. In 1929, it created the Eighth and Tenth Circuits out of the Eighth Circuit in order to reduce the size of the Eighth Circuit's court of appeals (then six judges). In 1980, it created the Fifth and Eleventh Circuits out of the Fifth Circuit in order to reduce the size of the Fifth Circuit's court of appeals (then 26 judges).[87] More courts, however, may increase the number of conflicting decisions that the Supreme Court must reconcile. A way to keep individual courts small *without* increasing the number of courts is to change procedures, but that may threaten procedural integrity and substantive justice. (A third way is to reduce jurisdiction, a source of regular discussion but not one I treat here.[88])

---

[85] ibid (n 84). Arguments for and against the current schedule are summarized in Editorial 'Promoting Public Understanding of the Supreme Court' (1992) 76 *Judicature* 4. (Disclosure: I chaired *Judicature*'s editorial committee at the time.)

[86] AT Mason *Brandeis: A Free Man's Life* (Viking Press New York 1946) 78.

[87] Summaries of both circuit splits, and references to literature about them, are in Commission on Structural Alternatives for the Federal Courts of Appeals *Final Report of the Commission on Structural Alternatives for the Federal Courts of Appeals* (The Commission Washington DC 1998) 17–21.

[88] See *Structural and Other Alternatives for the Federal Courts of Appeals* (n 1) 141.

a. The number of judges on a court of appeals must be small enough to maintain decisional consistency and adherence to Supreme Court precedent: The federal judiciary's official view is that the need for 'carefully controlled growth' in judgeships applies with special force to the courts of appeals.[89] The perceived proper size of a court of appeals has shifted. In 1964, a special Judicial Conference committee reported that 'nine is the maximum number of active judgeship positions which can be allotted to a court of appeals without impairing the efficiency of its operation and its unity as a judicial institution.'[90] In 1964, the largest court was nine and the modal size of the courts was nine. By 1997, three-fourths of the circuit judges said that the maximum size for a court of appeals to function effectively is between 10 and 18, which, as it happened, embodied all but two of the courts of appeals.[91] The optimal size of a court of appeals at any particular time may be clustered around the status quo.

The current debate centres on whether the Ninth Circuit's court of appeals, with 28 judgeships (which have never all been filled) is too big to function effectively and should be divided. Part of the debate is the claim that the court creates more work for the Supreme Court than two smaller courts would create. Table 11.7 shows that the Supreme Court reverses the Ninth Circuit's court more often than it reverses other courts (the table also shows the reversal rate for the Fourth Circuit's court of appeals, whose members are generally regarded as more in line with the majority of members of the Supreme Court).

The Ninth Circuit's critics attribute the greater reversal rate in part to what they see as the appellate court's inability to harmonize the decisions of its many three-judge panels. Two courts, each with fewer judges, they argue, would be more collegial, more respectful of colleagues' views, and better able to conform their decisions to the Supreme Court's jurisprudence. It would be difficult, for example, for the Ninth Circuit's court to circulate (as do seven other courts) draft

Table 11.7: Supreme Court reversals and vacated decisions for the Courts of Appeals[92]

	OT 97	OT 98	OT 99	OT 00	OT 01
Ninth Circuit	14 of 17 (82%)	14 of 18 (78%)	9 of 10 (90%)	13 of 17 (76%)	14 of 18 (78%)
Other Circuits	35 of 64 (55%)	32 of 48 (67%)	29 of 53 (55%)	29 of 49 (59%)	40 of 52 (77%)
Fourth Circuit	1 of 2	2 of 4	5 of 9	3 of 5	7 of 11

[89] Judicial Conference of the United States *Long Range Plan for the Federal Courts* (Judicial Conference of the United States Washington DC 1995) 44.

[90] *Report of the Special Committee on the Geographic Organization of the Courts* quoted in *Annual Report of the Proceedings of the Judicial Conference of the United States* (1964) 63.

[91] See Table 11.3.

[92] Source: 'Statistics,' in no 1 of volumes 112–116 of *Harvard Law Review* (n 37).

panel opinions to all judges of the court, at least opinions that would conflict with precedent in other courts.[93] Critics also complain that the court's size precludes effective use of en banc procedures as a means of keeping the circuit's law consistent with itself and with Supreme Court jurisprudence. Only the Ninth Circuit uses a statutory provision that permits courts with more than 15 judgeships to use en bancs of less than the full complement of judges.[94] An en banc in the Ninth Circuit consists of the chief judge plus 10 judges selected at random, with provision for rehearing by the full court. [95]

The Ninth Circuit's defenders say the differences in reversal rates are exaggerated and that what differences there exist are due mainly to the prevalence in the West of novel legal issues about which it is difficult to anticipate the Supreme Court's views. They argue that its en bancs are rarely closely divided and note that the whole court has never voted to have the full court rehear a case decided en banc.[96]

Congress created the Commission on Structural Alternatives for the Federal Courts of Appeals in 1997 as a way out of a legislative stalemate over what to do about the court of appeals. The Commission recommended dividing the court (but not the circuit itself) into three divisions, based largely on survey data and Commission members' perceptions to the effect that Ninth Circuit trial judges and lawyers had more difficulty discerning the law of their circuit than judges and lawyers in other circuits had in discerning theirs.[97] Prospects for legislative implementation of the Commission recommendations are dim.

b. The number of courts of appeals must be small enough to contain inter-court inconsistency: It is generally conceded that citizens in one part of the country should not have different federal legal rights and obligations from those in other parts. One of the arguments against dividing the Ninth Circuit to create a 13th regional intermediate appellate court was that 13 courts would make more intercircuit conflicts than would 12 courts for the Supreme Court to resolve. Proponents of division respond that conflicting interpretations of federal law need only a few courts to tease them out. There is, they say, no reason to assume that the number of conflicts will increase proportionately to the number of appellate courts.

---

[93] *Case Management Procedures in the Federal Courts of Appeals* (n 46) 36. At the time of that report, the Ninth Circuit's court of appeals was preparing a test of a project to notify the court, pre-publication, of opinions that would affect cases pending before other panels.

[94] Public Law 95–486, s6†/92 Stat 1629, 1633 (1978). The courts of the Fifth and Sixth Circuits are also eligible, with 17 and 16 judgeships respectively.

[95] *Final Report of the Commission on Structural Alternatives for the Federal Courts of Appeals* (n 45) 32.

[96] ibid (n 45) 35–36.

[97] ibid (n 45) 39–47. It did not recommend splitting the circuit itself, in part because circuit-splitting was not a precedent that would help much with other courts of appeals in circuits of three or four states.

2. *To perform their functions, the courts of appeals must be able to adapt*
   procedures that provide different types of cases with different levels
   of attention, depending on the nature of the cases

The types of cases that have been responsible for the increased caseload in the
courts of appeals are largely those that permit abbreviated procedures. As Table
11.8 shows, petitions by state and federal prisoners seeking review of their
convictions or changes in their conditions of confinement have increased much
more rapidly than the overall caseload. Such petitions (combining the categories
in the first and second rows) went from less than 20% of the appellate docket in
1985 to over 30% in 2000, and the trend over longer periods is even more
dramatic. Nevertheless, as the Commission on Structural Alternatives put it,
those cases 'generally do not involve as much work for judges as fully counselled
cases because they typically are controlled by well-settled precedent or require a
highly deferential standard of review.'[98]

Table 11.8: Changes in caseload composition[99]

Type of appeal	1985		1990		1995		2000*		1985–2000
US prisoner petitions	1,492	4.5%	2,246	5.5%	3,453	6.9%	4,955	9.1%	232.1%
Private prisoner petitions	5,052	15.1%	7,749	19.1%	11,527	23.0%	12,297	22.5%	143.4%
Criminal	4,998	14.9%	9,608	23.6%	10,147	20.3%	10,707	19.6%	114.2%
Administrative appeals	3,179	9.5%	2,532	6.2%	3,298	6.6%	3,237	5.9%	1.8%
Bankruptcy	1,051	3.1%	1,110	2.7%	1,662	3.3%	1,007	1.8%	−4.2%
Other private civil	11,935	35.7%	12,630	31.0%	14,749	29.5%	14,788	27.0%	23.9%
Other US civil	5,125	15.3%	4,213	10.4%	4,460	8.9%	3,740	6.8%	−27.0%
Original proceeding	618	1.8%	589	1.4%	740	1.5%	3,966	7.3%	541.7%*
Total	33,450		40,677		50,036		54,697		63.5%
Per authorized judgeship	199.1		242.1		279.5		305.6		53.5%

*The 2000 data include counts for types of original proceedings not previously counted as appeals.

Some of the changes that courts of appeals have adopted since the 1960s
to help accommodate more cases per judge are highlighted in Table 11.9,
showing changes over time in the types of dispositions used by the courts of
appeals. These changes have not been unanimously blessed. As the Federal
Courts Study Committee put it in 1990, 'the "crisis of volume'... has transformed [the federal appellate courts] from the institutions they were even a
generation ago.'[100]

[98] ibid (n 87) 16–17.
[99] Prepared from data in the Federal Judicial Center Integrated Data Base; the IDB uses Administrative Office data but cleans them in some respects, which accounts for the difference in per-judgeship
figures here and in Table 11.4. This table adapted from one prepared by Patricia Lombard of the
Federal Judicial Center for a different purpose; available from author.
[100] *Report of the Federal Courts Study Committee* (n 5) 109.

Table 11.9: Changing procedures in the US Courts of Appeals[101]

Type of disposition	1985		1990		1995		2000		1985–2000
All terminations	**32,536**		**38,790**		**49,805**		**56,512**		73.7%
By consolidation	2,888	8.9%	3,39	9.9%	3,177	6.4%	2,740	4.8%	−5.1%
Cross appeal	1,080		893		770		713		
Consolidated appeal	1,808		2,946		2,407		2,027		
Procedural termination	12,704	39.0%	14,008	36.1%	18,856	37.9%	26,256	46.5%	106.7%
By judge	5,076		5,581		6,817		12,330		
By staff	7,628		8,427		12,039		13,926		
Termination on the merits	16,944	52.1%	20,943	54.0%	27,772	55.8%	27,516	48.7%	62.4%
After oral hearing	9,537	56.3%	9,434	45.0%	11,080	39.9%	9,752	35.4%	
After briefs submitted	7,407		11,509		16,692		17,764		
Oral opinion	177		93		99		63		
Written published opinion	6,921	40.8%	6,690	31.9%	6,689	24.1%	5,558	20.2%	−19.7%
Written unpublished opinion	9,846		14,160		20,984		21,895		122.4%
All terminations	32,536		38,790		49,805		56,512		73.7%
Per authorized judgeship	193.7		230.9		278.2		315.7		63.0%
Termination on the merits	16,944		20,943		27,772		27,516		62.4%
Per authorized judgeship	100.9		124.7		155.2		153.7		52.4%

[101] Data drawn from sources cited (n 50), primarily B tables. This table adapted from one prepared by Patricia Lombard of the Federal Judicial Center for a different purpose.

These changes include:

a. Screening and central legal staffs: Courts of appeals 'screen' cases to determine the procedural course most appropriate—including which cases need to be argued orally. In nine of the 12 regional courts of appeals, a central legal staff screens cases.[102] The size of these staffs varies, based on filings, but in the largest court has around 50.[103]

b. Settlement: Most courts have instituted pre-argument conference procedures, whereby staff attorneys seek to identify cases that can be settled without being placed on one of the tracks to regular disposition. A study of this practice in one court of appeals determined that it settled enough cases to equal the work of one judge.[104]

c. No oral argument: Table 11.9 shows that in 1985 the courts of appeals heard oral argument in over half the cases that those courts terminated on the merits. By the end of the century, the figure was about one-third. The Federal Rules of Appellate Procedure prescribe oral argument in every case unless the panel agrees unanimously that the appeal is frivolous or the dispositive issues have been authoritatively decided or the briefs and records are such that oral argument would add nothing significant to the decisional process.[105]

d. Unpublished opinions: Similarly, cases announced with a written published opinion were about 40% of merits terminations in 1985 and are now about 20%. 'Unpublished' opinions, nomenclature notwithstanding, typically are published by the online reporting services. The courts have developed varying criteria for which opinions will be published and whether they will entertain citations to 'unpublished' opinions.[106] Electronic data bases, however, make it difficult to keep opinions 'unpublished' and thus accord advantages to law firms with sufficient resources to inventory such opinions and cite them where permitted. In 2002, the Judicial Conference's advisory committee on appellate rules

---

[102] *Case Management Procedures in the Federal Courts of Appeals* (n 46) 10.

[103] ibid (n 46) 6.

[104] ibid (n 46) 17, which updates information in R Niemic *Mediation and Conference Programs in the Federal Courts of Appeals* (Federal Judicial Center Washington DC 1997) <http://www.fjc.gov> (6 August 2003). The particular programme referenced above is described in J Eaglin *The Pre-Argument Conference Program in the Sixth Circuit Court of Appeals* (Federal Judicial Center Washington DC 1990).

[105] Federal Rule of Appellate Procedures 34(a)(2).

[106] *Case Management Procedures in the Federal Courts of Appeals* (n 46) 20–21, Table 18 'Criteria for Publication' 33–34, Table 19 'Circuit Rules of the Citability of "Unpublished" Opinions' 35–36.

proposed an amendment to the rules to require all courts of appeals to allow citation to those opinions.[107]

e. Visiting judges: One way that the courts of appeals have avoided asking Congress for large increases in permanent judgeships is by relying on temporary visiting judges to assist in their work. Visitors include both judges of the district courts in the circuit, as well as senior district and circuit judges from other circuits. Panels consisting of at least one visiting judge now hear about 20% of all appeals decided on the merits.[108]

6. THE COURTS OF APPEALS ASSIST THE SUPREME COURT

The previous part of this essay has considered the proposition that the Supreme Court and the courts of appeals play different but overlapping roles. I now move on to consider a second proposition relating to the relationship between the courts: that the courts of appeals assist the Supreme Court.

A. The courts of appeals relieve the Supreme Court of the error correction function

As discussed earlier, the courts of appeals make available to litigants the one appellate review as of right to which US judicial culture generally agrees they are entitled as a means of identifying error in the trial court. Because the courts of appeals provide litigants that review-for-error function, they free the Supreme Court to devote its energies almost exclusively to establishing national judicial policy.

B. The courts of appeals' analyses of common legal questions assist the Supreme Court

In addition to correcting errors and declaring the law for their circuits' trial courts, the courts of appeals assist the Court through the 'percolation' of issues. Professor Levin describes percolation as 'the examination of an issue in a number of circuits. We invite the independent views of numerous panels in order to give the Supreme Court the benefit of a variety of opinions in different factual contexts... A new and important doctrine of constitutional

---

[107] A Liptak 'Federal Appeals Court Decisions May Go Public' *The New York Times*, 25 December 2002; CW Tobias '*Anastasoff*, Unpublished Opinions, and Federal Appellate Justice' (2002) 25 *Harvard Journal of Law and Public Policy* 1171.

[108] *Case Management Procedures in the Federal Courts of Appeals* (n 46) 5.

[or non-constitutional] law does not emerge full-blown the very first case in which it is recognized.'[109] Judge Posner put it a little more bluntly:

Although Supreme Court justices are abler on average than district and circuit judges (because more carefully screened for appointment) and have better staff and a superior perspective for formulating legal doctrine, the courts of appeals alone have twenty times as many judges as the Supreme Court. These judges have in the aggregate an important contribution to make to the formulation of legal doctrine—especially when dealing with factual situations that have never been before the Supreme Court and therefore have never been considered by the Supreme Court justices except possibly in their imagination.[110]

This perceived value of intermediate appellate review explains the resistance to allowing litigants to take their cases straight from the district courts to the Supreme Court. Direct appeal was once common. The 1891 statute creating the intermediate appellate courts permitted writs of error from the trial courts directly to the Supreme Court in capital cases, cases involving the US Constitution, and in several other categories.[111] Then, in 1903, Congress authorized the three-judge district courts described above,[112] with direct appeal to the Supreme Court. The idea was that three judges would be less likely than one to throw out social and economic regulatory statutes, and, if they did, the Supreme Court could review the case right away.

Direct appeals from single judge trial courts were gradually eliminated. And in 1975, despite misgivings by some civil rights leaders,[113] Congress eliminated the jurisdictional basis for three-judge courts except in the narrow categories of cases described above.[114] Chief Justice Burger complained that appeals from these courts came to the Supreme Court in high numbers but 'without the benefit of intermediate review by a court of appeals.'[115] The Freund Committee noted that 'direct appeal means that the Supreme Court does not have the benefit of the preliminary screening and sharpening of issues that the courts of appeals ordinarily provide.'[116] Much of the debate over the three-judge courts involved the jurisdictional complexities that arose in satellite litigation over the grounds for seeking direct review and when the intermediate appellate courts could intervene.[117]

[109] AL Levin 'Uniformity of Federal Law,' in C Harrison and R Wheeler (eds) *The Federal Appellate Judiciary in the 21st Century* (Federal Judicial Center Washington DC 1989) 133–134.

[110] *The Federal Courts: Challenge and Reform* (n 6) 377.

[111] An Act to establish Circuit Courts of Appeals (n 15), s 5.

[112] Text at nn 30 and 31.

[113] See letter of Anthony Amsterdam to Congressman Robert Kastenmeier 13 December 1973 in Hearings on Three-Judge Courts and Six-Person Civil Juries before the House Subcommittee on Courts Civil Liberties and the Administration of Justice 93rd Cong 1st sess 123 and testimony of Nathaniel Jones, General Counsel NAACP 141.

[114] n 30.

[115] W Burger '1972 Report on the State of the Judiciary' (1972) 58 *American Bar Association Journal* 1049, 1053 (1972).

[116] Report of the Study Group on the Case Load of the Supreme Court (n 17) 30.

[117] See Senate Report 94–204, Revision of the Jurisdiction of Three-Judge Courts 94th Cong 1st sess (1975) 5.

C. Only to a limited degree do the courts of appeals assist the Supreme Court by limiting the number of conflicting interpretations of common legal questions and thus reducing the Court's obligation to resolve conflicts among the circuits

In a country as large as the USA, with different regional cultures, many see value in what Judge Henry Friendly called 'the law of the circuit', as a means of providing some flexibility in the application of national legal standards, as well as providing the benefits of 'percolation'. There have been, to be sure, many steps to encourage the courts of appeals themselves to promote uniformity. The Federal Rules of Appellate Procedure, for example, offer as one justification for seeking en banc rehearings that a three-judge panel has decided a case in conflict with the decision of another court of appeals.[118]

More ambitious proposals, however, have not been well received. The Judicial Conference opposed two Federal Courts Study Committee recommendations. One would have encouraged a court of appeals panel that was facing a question already decided in another court of appeals to give 'considerable respect' to that earlier decision and circulate the draft opinion in any conflict-creating decision to the entire court. The other rejected proposal was for a five-year pilot project by which the Supreme Court could randomly refer selected conflicts to a court of appeals not involved in the conflict for en banc resolution creating a national precedent.[119] Proposals to create some system of 'national *stare decisis*' at the intermediate appellate level have foundered partly because of the perceived benefits of percolation and various practical problems. [120]

D. The court of appeals can serve as a recruitment source for the Supreme Court

All but two of the Supreme Court justices of the 2002 October Term came to the Court from the US courts of appeals. Chief Justice Rehnquist had no judicial experience prior to his 1971 appointment as an associate justice, and Justice O'Connor had been a former state intermediate appellate judge. The conventional wisdom is that the next Supreme Court nominee will probably come from the federal, or perhaps state, appellate courts. Earlier courts, however, even in this century, had different mixes. In 1943, for example, only one justice (Rutledge) had served on the lower US courts (although two had served briefly as state trial judges). Table 11.10 provides thumbnail sketches of the backgrounds of the members of the Court in the 1942 and 2002 October Terms.

---

[118] Federal Rule of Appellate Procedure 35(b)(1)(B).

[119] The recommendations are at *Report of the Federal Courts Study Committee* (n 5) 125–30. The Judicial Conference opposition is at *Report of the Proceedings of the Judicial Conference of the United States* (Judicial Conference of the United States 1990) 88.

[120] *Structural and Other Alternatives for the Federal Courts of Appeals* (n 1) 66.

Table 11.10: Backgrounds of Supreme Court justices, OT 1942 and 2002[121]

	October Term 1942			October Term 2002	
Justice	*Age at year of app't*	*Career highlights*	*Justice*	*Age at year of app't*	*Career highlights*
Harlan Stone (Chief Justice)	68 ('41)	prof./dean; US attorney-general, assoc. justice, US Sup. Ct ('25–'41)	**William Rehnquist** (Chief Justice)	61 ('86)	Sup. Ct law clerk, practice, ass't US attorney-general, assoc. justice, US Sup. Ct ('71–'85)
Owen Roberts	55 ('30)	practice; prof; ass't state prosecutor; special federal prosecutor	**John Stevens**	55 ('75)	Sup. Ct law clerk; practice; law school lecturer; judge, US court of appeals, 7th circ.
Hugo Black	51 ('37)	police court judge; state prosecuting attorney; US senator	**Sandra O'Connor**	51 ('81)	state prosecutor; practice; state legislator; Arizona state trial and appellate judge
Stanley Reed	53 ('38)	practice; state legislator; gen. counsel of two fed. agencies; US solicitor general	**Antonin Scalia**	50 ('86)	practice; prof.; ch. US Admin. Conf.; ass't US attorney-general; judge, US court of appeals, DC circuit
Felix Frankfurter	54 ('39)	ass't federal prosecutor; gov't lawyer; professor	**Anthony Kennedy**	51 ('88)	practice; prof; judge, US court of appeals, 9th circuit
William Douglas	41 ('39)	prof.; member, chair, Sec. and Exchange Commission	**David Souter**	51 ('90)	ass't, then state attorney-general; state trial, then appellate judge; judge, US court of appeals, 1st circuit
Frank Murphy	49 ('40)	practice; prof.; state trial judge; mayor of Detroit; gov. commissioner, Philippine Is.; gov. Michigan; US attorney-general	**Clarence Thomas**	43 ('91)	ass't state prosecutor; aide to US senator; ass't sec., US Dept of Education; ch., Eq. Emp. Opp. Comm.; judge, US court of appeals, DC circuit

(cont.)

[121] Data drawn from Federal Judges Biographical Database, part of the History of the Federal Judiciary website available at <www.fjc.gov> (6 August 2003).

Table 11.10: Backgrounds of Supreme Court justices, OT 1942 and 2002
—Contd.

	October Term 1942			October Term 2002	
Robert Jackson	49 ('41)	practice; city atty; counsel to fed. agencies; US solicitor general; attorney-general	Ruth Ginsburg	59 ('93)	law clerk to a fed. dist. judge; prof.; counsel, American Civil Liberties Union; judge, US court of appeals, DC circuit
Wiley Rutledge	49 ('43)	prof./dean; US court of appeals, DC circuit	Stephen Breyer	56 ('94)	Sup. Ct law clerk; Dep't of Justice atty; prof.; counsel, Senate judiciary committee; judge, US court of appeals, 1st circuit

Table 11.11 illustrates variations in presidential inclinations to turn to sitting or former judges for Supreme Court candidates. (It also shows the decline in turnover of the Court.)

Table 11.11: Sources of Supreme Court appointments[122]

	Appointments	From state and/or fed. app. cts		From fed. app. cts	
1891–1920 (30 yrs)	16	10	(63%)	5	(31%)
1921–1950 (30 yrs)	20	6	(39%)	5	(25%)
1951–1970 (20 yrs)	11	7	(64%)	6	(55%)
1971–2002 (31 yrs)	10	8	(80%)	7	(70%)

The increased tendency to appoint sitting judges to the Court reflects in part presidents' desires to find individuals with established records with which to predict their behaviour on the Supreme Court. It also reflects presidents' desires to put before the Senate (and the press) nominees who bring no long history of statements made in the policy arenas, statements that could haunt them before hostile senators. Whether prior service on a lower appellate court generally enhances one's ability to serve well on the Supreme Court could be informed by a panel research design assessing the performance of justices with, and without, prior federal appellate service. There have been some complaints that the current Supreme Court, with experience heavily weighted to appellate judging, may lack familiarity with the diverse social, political, and legal currents implicated in cases before it.

[122] ibid (n 121).

The courts of appeals, moreover, have become the major pool for the justices' law clerks. Almost all of the clerks appointed nowadays spend a year clerking for judges on the courts of appeals, or occasionally on a state supreme court; an increasing number have also practised law for a year or two, usually after the appellate clerkship and before the Supreme Court clerkship.[123]

7. CONCLUSION

Although much of the debate over possible change in the US federal appellate system is cast in technical terms, the status quo and revisions to it also implicate important political questions about the distribution of power and government services. The debate over the division of the old Fifth Circuit and its court of appeals involved more than whether a large court could function effectively. It also involved whether the proposed allocation of judges would maintain the old court of appeals' commitment to protecting minority rights. The current debate over the Ninth Circuit's court of appeals sits within a debate over the role of courts in protecting the environment and economic growth. The opposition to new national tiers of appellate review was fuelled in part by disagreements over the proper limits of judicial activism in the Supreme Court. The truncated procedures adopted by most courts of appeals in an effort to maintain relatively small and collegial courts,[124] and proposals to limit the number of federal judges,[125] are seen by some as an effort to deny access to the federal courts by minorities who most need judicial protection, and by others as ways of preserving the federal courts as an effective forum to protect the right of all litigants, perhaps especially political and other minorities who do not fare well in the political process.

To identify any of these disagreements is not to credit either side. The point is simply to recognize that, at least in the US, many interests perceive themselves as having a stake in the outcomes of judicial branch changes. Still relevant is Frankfurter and Landis's 1928 observation about the 19th century effort to restructure federal appellate capacity as new demands threatened to overwhelm the Supreme Court:[126]

The reorganization of the federal judiciary did not involve merely technical questions of judicial organization, nor was it the concern only of lawyers. Beneath the surface of the controversy lay passionate issues of power as between the states and the Federal Government, involving sectional differences and sectional susceptibilities... Stubborn political convictions and strong interests were at stake which made the process of accommodation long and precarious.

---

[123] Mauro (n 13).   [124] Discussed at text nn 99–108.

[125] Arguments pro and con are laid out in W Bermant, W Schwarzer, E Sussman and R Wheeler *Imposing a Moratorium on the Number of Federal Judges* (Federal Judicial Center Washington DC 1993) <http://www.fjc.gov>.

[126] F Frankfurter and J Landis *The Business of the Supreme Court, A Study in the Federal Judicial System* (Macmillan New York 1928) 85.

12

Panning for Gold: Choosing Cases for Top-level Courts

ANDREW LE SUEUR

One of their Lordships told the author that it is not uncommon for members of the House of Lords going up in the lift to the committee room for an appeal hearing to look at each other with wild surmise and ask 'Who on earth gave leave in this case?'

> R Pattenden, *English Criminal Appeals 1844–1994*
> (Clarendon Press Oxford 1996), p.321

Your Lordships' House is only able, in any given year, to hear and determine a limited number of cases and it is important for the evolution of the law as a whole that those should be carefully chosen.

> *In re Wilson* [1985] AC 750, 756 (Lord Roskill)

1. INTRODUCTION

In common law legal systems, top-level appellate courts hear argument and give full judgments in only a relatively small proportion of cases brought to them. Rudimentary statistics for 2001 reveal the scale of the task of choosing cases. The House of Lords disposed of 269 petitions for leave to appeal,[1] allowing 68 to go forward to a full hearing (25%). The US Supreme Court was presented with 7,924 petitions for certiorari[2] and heard argument in 88 cases (1%). The Supreme Court of Canada had 658 applications for leave to appeal and 96 appeals were heard (14%).

The main argument advanced in this essay is that we must take the process and product of case selection seriously. Choosing cases is far more than merely a way

---

[1] In 1999 in England and Wales, the Civil Procedure Rules (CPR) made radical changes to the procedures for civil litigation, and its terminology. The term 'leave to appeal' was replaced by the 'permission to appeal' (see CPR Part 52). The House of Lords has an entirely distinct set of procedural rules and these still use the expression 'leave to appeal' (see n 23).

[2] See ch 11.

of limiting the workload of the court to a manageable size, though that is important. The main significance of case selection is that it enables a court to *define* its constitutional role and power. (A court with a broad jurisdiction that chooses to hear mainly commercial litigation appeals has a different role and status from one that focuses on human rights issues.) As such, it is vital that case selection be carried out in accordance with relevant constitutional principles, notably that it is a transparent procedure with opportunities for scrutinizing outcomes. For many years, case selection by the House of Lords has been carried out away from public gaze (academics pay little attention to the totality of the Lords' work in a given year, focusing instead on particular judgments) and the criteria used to select cases is opaque. The creation of a new supreme court presents an opportunity to reassess practices and expectations.

2. OF LEAVE/PERMISSION REQUIREMENTS GENERALLY

Generally, judicial 'filter mechanisms' are created where access to a higher court needs to be controlled on the basis of a preliminary view of a case, without a full hearing of the merits of the rival contentions. The justification for such controlling devices varies according to the contexts in which they operate.

In England and Wales, almost all appeals *to the Court of Appeal* from first instance decisions now require 'permission' from either the court that has already decided the case or the Court of Appeal.[3] The main rationalization for this filter here is that the aggrieved person has already had a 'day in court' and there is a public interest in finality of litigation[4]—but the system also acknowledges that from time to time judges at first instance make errors. The principal criterion for leave to appeal to the Court of Appeal seeks to capture this balance. The test is whether 'the court considers that the appeal would have a real prospect of success'.[5] The filter mechanism in this context is thus outcome-oriented, focusing on whether there is a risk of error and whether an individual litigant may be treated unfairly if an appeal does not take place.

The filter mechanism operated for access *to the Law Lords* is significantly different. The preliminary assessment of a case does not involve a prediction of whether a would-be appellant will succeed if a further full hearing takes place. It is not concerned with the outcome of the particular case, any unfairness to the individuals concerned, or even whether the court below applied the law correctly. In 1985, Lord Roskill 'emphatically' sought to correct what had appar-

---

[3] See ch 10.

[4] The fundamental right of 'access to court' guaranteed by Art 6 ECHR does not extend to appeals, though the Council of Europe expects opportunities for appeal to be provided within national legal systems. See further A Le Sueur 'Access to Justice in the United Kingdom' [2003] *European Human Rights Review* 457.

[5] CPR 52.3(6)(a), which also provides '(b) there is some other compelling reason why the appeal should be heard'.

ently become a widespread impression among the legal profession—that if the Law Lords refused leave in a case, 'this refusal indicated at least implied approval of the decision which it had been unsuccessfully sought to impugn'.[6] 'Conversely', he said, 'the fact that leave to appeal is given is not of itself an indication that the judgments below are thought to be wrong. It may well be that leave is given in order that the relevant law may be authoritatively restated in clearer terms'.[7] (Official statistics nevertheless record the success rates of appeals: in 2002, of the appeals dealt with by way of a full judgment in the House of Lords, 29 out of 72 were allowed—about 40%).[8]

The principal criterion for granting a petition for leave to the Lords is whether there is 'a point of law of general public importance'. Lord Roskill explained in the *Wilson* case that there was 'a multitude of reasons why, in a particular case, leave to appeal may be refused by an appeal committee'. These include that a case may not raise any 'general' point of law, or indeed any point of law; and 'the facts of the particular case are not suitable as a foundation for determining some question of general principles'.[9]

This reflects the principal function of a top-level court in common law systems: it ought to be concerned not with error correction but has the broader responsibility of clarifying and developing the law and exercising judicial 'management' over the whole legal system.[10] Other agencies, of course, share in these tasks. Law Commissions are expected to take a strategic approach in identifying legal problems and suggesting solutions. The legislature also attempts to tackle problems of lack of clarity or disconnection of the law from modern values (though most legislation is enacted to give effect to new social and economic policies proposed by government). The capacity of top-level courts to be strategic is more limited than these other law reform agencies as a court must rely on the 'invisible hand' of the litigious activities of tens of thousands of individuals to throw up the problems that need to be addressed.

3. THE CHANGING ROLE OF THE LEAVE REQUIREMENT IN THE HOUSE OF LORDS

Although it is possible to state, in the basic terms set out above, the main function of filter mechanisms for top-level courts, it needs to be recognized

---

[6] *In re Wilson* [1985] AC 750, 756.   [7] ibid.

[8] Lord Chancellor's Department *Judicial Statistics 2002* Table 1.4. In the intermediate courts of appeal, the Court of Appeal (Civil Division) gave 779 full judgments, allowing 344 (44%) and the Court of Appeal (Criminal Division) allowed 166 of the 485 appeals against conviction that it heard (34%) in 2002. These statistics give some support to a hypothesis that most appeal courts will tend to allow 30–40% of the cases they consider. Any more, and doubts would arise about the general competence of the court below; any less, might call into question the need for an appeal (especially a *second* appeal) mechanism.

[9] ibid.

[10] See A Le Sueur and R Cornes 'What Do the Top Courts Do?' (2000) 53 *Current Legal Problems* 53.

that perceptions of the purpose of the leave requirement for House of Lords appeals has changed over time. Originally introduced in 1934 as a way of *promoting access* to justice, by the 1960s the leave procedure was seen primarily as a *case management tool* to protect the House of Lords from a flood of cases. Today, I am suggesting, it should be recognized that the process of selecting cases is one of the main ways by which a *top-level court defines its role* in the constitutional system and *sets its agenda*. If this is accepted, there are implications for the design of the case selection process.

A. Access to justice in the 1930s

When the requirement of leave in civil appeals from the courts of appeal in England and Wales and Northern Ireland was introduced by the Administration of Justice (Appeals) Act 1934, it was expressly designed to promote access to justice.[11] Introducing the Bill in the House of Lords, Lord Sankey LC said:[12]

Some reforms are designed both in the interests of the State and of the individual, to ensure economy and expedition in the administration of the law; others are intended in the interests of the litigant himself. There present Bill is mainly intended for that object . . . The fact that there is an unrestricted right is not seldom held *in terrorem* over the heads of an intending litigant, especially in revenue cases . . . I do not prophesy that this Bill will mean a great saving in judicial time, but it will save great anxiety to many a litigant.

Lord Atkin spoke in support of the Bill:[13]

Speaking for myself after five or six years experience of this House, I may say that very few cases have, in fact, come before your Lordships' House which were not suitable for appeal and in which in all probability leave would have been given. There have been a few cases, but I agree with what has been said by the Lord Chancellor: the great importance of this reform is this, that a rich corporation—or perhaps I might say a strong Government Department—will not for the future be able in any way to terrorise the person with whom they may have a dispute by the threat that the case will certainly be taken to the House of Lords.

In 1972, Blom-Cooper and Drewry suggested that the 1934 Act 'took a statutory sledgehammer to crack a very tiny litigious nut'.[14] Thirty years on from that assessment, it seems more a case of a 1934 sledgehammer being used for completely different purpose from the one originally envisaged. Access to justice no longer provides a convincing rationale for the leave requirement. Times have changed: with the CPR in place in England and Wales, there are now new protections for claimants anxious about disproportionate and uncertain costs at the outset of litigation.

---

[11] For a fuller account in relation to civil appeals, see L Blom-Cooper and G Drewry *Final Appeal* (Clarendon Press Oxford 1972) ch 7.
[12] Hansard HL vol 92 col 789 (5 June 1934).
[13] ibid at col 794.   [14] Blom-Cooper and Drewry (n 11) 123.

B. Managerialism in the 1960s

The modern arrangements for criminal appeals to the House of Lords were put in place in 1960. They resulted from a decision to end the role of the Attorney-General in regulating appeals to the House of Lords.[15] Prior to the Administration of Justice Act 1960, a person convicted following a trial on indictment before a jury who wished to appeal from the Court of Criminal Appeal to the House of Lords required a certificate from the Attorney-General that the grounds of appeal involved 'a point of law of exceptional public importance' and that it was 'in the public interest that a further appeal should be brought'. There was dissatisfaction with the Attorney-General's dual role of being the prosecuting authority and gatekeeper for final appeals. The reforms were also prompted by a desire to create a second appeal for those criminal cases dealt with by the Divisional Court,[16] which heard appeals from magistrates' courts by way of case stated and (what we now call) judicial review. It was undesirable to extend the already problematic Attorney-General's fiat to a newly created appeal. Introducing the Bill into the Commons, the Solicitor-General (Sir Jocelyn Simon MP) in the then Conservative government explained for both a certificate and leave:[17]

we do not think that it would be possible to take the easy way out of allowing an appeal to be brought from the Court of Criminal Appeal or the Divisional Court simply with the leave either of that court or of the House of Lords. We are convinced that any such provision would lead to the House of Lords, or at any rate its Appeals Committee, being swamped with applications for leave to appeal.

In relation to the certificate, there was also a change from the criterion previously used by the Attorney-General ('a point of law of exceptional public importance') to one of 'general public importance'. In the House of Lords debate on the bill, Viscount Kilmuir LC echoed the concerns about caseload: 'clearly, some limitation must be imposed on the right of appeal if the House of Lords is to be flooded with criminal appeals to an unmanageable extent'.[18] This conception of the leave stage sees the requirement as being primarily a case management tool. If this is so, then the resources of the court devoted to the task should be kept in check and not be a diversion from the main task of hearing the chosen cases in full and giving judgment.

---

[15] For a fuller account, see R Pattenden *English Criminal Appeals 1844–1994* (Clarendon Press Oxford 1996) ch 9.

[16] ie a panel of two judges in the Queen's Bench Division of the High Court in England and Wales. Today, such cases fall within the jurisdiction of the Administrative Court. Radical reforms of the criminal appeal systems are planned which will remove such appeals from the QBD: see Sir Robin Auld *Review of the Criminal Courts of England and Wales* ch 12, para 30 and the White Paper *Justice for All* (Cm 5563, July 2002).

[17] Hansard HC vol 625 col 1695 (1 July 1960).

[18] Hansard HL vol 222 col 249 (24 March 1960).

C. A role-defining and agenda-setting function

A different, or further, purpose for case selection House of Lords (and the UK's new Supreme Court) is now apparent—and is likely to become more important when the UK's new supreme court begins to operate. The constitutional function of the leave filter is to enable the top-level court to define, for itself, its judicial role and how it is to exercise its power. To suggest that the new supreme court will (or ought to have) an 'agenda' is not to imply that it will be a court with a partisan political 'mission'—a criticism levelled at many top-level courts, including the European Court of Justice and the Supreme Court of Canada.[19] It is simply to recognize that a supreme court is an important public institution with discretion as to how to meet its responsibilities. The discretion begins at the point of deciding which cases to accept for full hearing. The Department for Constitutional Affairs' consultation paper on the UK's new supreme court acknowledged this in suggesting that there might be a presumption that the new supreme court itself decides which cases to hear:[20]

The advantage of switching to a system whereby the Court itself decided which cases it should hear, subject only to the special exception of rulings on competence under the Scotland, Northern Ireland and Government of Wales Acts 1998 is that such a general rule would give the Supreme Court the control it needs over its own caseload, and would enable it to develop its own policies and approach about the categories and importance of the cases on which it should rule. It would enable it to work out where it sees its greatest added value and concentrate on developing jurisprudence in the areas which most need it.

The cases selected should be the ones that provide the best raw material for the court to carry out is functions.[21] Like other public institutions, we should expect the court to make itself accountable to its service users (appellants) and to the informed public for the manner in which it exercises its powers—in the present context, that power to select cases. In many respects, at least until recently, the House of Lords has not been as transparent as it ought in explaining why some cases are selected for hearing but not others. Practitioners complain that the criteria for case selection are not clear; many are surprised by the outcome of petitions for leave.[22]

4. CURRENT METHODS FOR SELECTING CASES

Before going further, it is necessary to outline of the principal features of the current case selection arrangements operating for the House of Lords. A firm

---

[19] eg P Neill *The European Court of Justice: A Case Study in Judicial Activism* (European Policy Forum London 1995); Canada has seen the rise of the term 'the court party', a pejorative reference to law academics and special interest groups alleged to use the Supreme Court as a political tool for change: for discussion, see K Roach *The Supreme Court on Trial, Judicial Activism or Democratic Dialogue* (Irvine Law Toronto 2001).

[20] DCA *Constitutional Reform: A Supreme Court of the United Kingdom* (DCA London 2003) paras 54–55.

[21] Le Sueur and Cornes (n 10).   [22] See ch 14.

distinction is made between appeals in civil cases and those in 'criminal causes or matters'.[23] It is important to note at the outset that case selection is currently a task to some extent shared between the House of Lords and the intermediate courts of appeal in the UK.

A. Civil appeals in the House of Lords

In relation to civil appeals, a litigant who loses in the Court of Appeal of England and Wales, or the Northern Ireland Court of Appeal, may ask that court for leave to appeal to the House of Lords. As Blake and Drewry show, it has become markedly less common than it once was for the courts of appeal to grant leave.[24] From time to time, this does however happen, as in *Nadezda Anufrijeva v Secretary of State for the Home Department*, in which the Court of Appeal dismissed an appeal (it was bound by a previous decision of the Court of Appeal on refugees' entitlement to income support) but granted leave to appeal to the House of Lords. Sedley LJ said:[25]

It seems to us that the facts of this case present no unique or unusual features; that they pose the same question as their Lordships considered deserving of their attention in *Salem*; and that the answer to the question will determine the legal rights of a finite but significant number of similarly placed individuals. In these circumstances, the case seems to us to be one of the rare instances in which we ourselves should grant leave to appeal to the House of Lords.

In *R v Secretary of State for the Home Department, ex p Salem* the House of Lords had declined to consider a question which had become moot by reason of the appellant being granted refugee status.[26]

When the Court of Appeal refuses leave, the unsuccessful litigant may petition an Appeal Committee of the House of Lords for leave to bring an appeal.[27]

In Scotland, a requirement of leave is the exception rather than the rule. No leave is necessary to appeal to the House of Lords from final judgments of the Inner House of the Court of Session which dispose of an action; nor is leave required to appeal against interlocutory judgments which dispose of some part

---

[23] There are two sets of rules. The Practice Directions and Standing Orders relating to Civil Appeals is known as the 'Blue Book'; the Practice Directions and Standing Orders relating to Criminal Appeals as the 'Red Book'. Whether this bifurcation is necessary or desirable is open to question. A challenge to a public authority by way of a claim for judicial review in the Administrative Court may be either a criminal or civil matter.

[24] See ch 10.

[25] [2002] EWCA Civ 399. On 26 June 2003 the House of Lords allowed the appeal, Lord Bingham dissenting: [2003] UKHL 36. Clearly their Lordships found the case a difficult one. Lord Millett, allowing the appeal, said: 'I have had the advantage of reading in draft the powerful speech of my noble and learned friend, Lord Steyn. Until then I was of the opinion that the appeal should be dismissed; but I have been persuaded to change my mind'. The case turned on the legal status of an uncommunicated decision terminating an asylum seeker's right to income support, and whether this offended against principles of legality and access to justice.

[26] [1999] 1 AC 450.

[27] Administration of Justice (Appeals) Act 1934, s 1.

of the action if the judges are not unanimous or where the interlocutory judgment sustained a dilatory defence and dismissed the action.[28] Instead, there is a requirement that two counsel certify that a case raises points fit for appeal. In other cases, leave to appeal to the House of Lords is necessary, and where this is so it is entirely a matter for the Court of Session to grant or refuse leave; there is no further petition to an Appeal Committee.[29] Looking back at the parliamentary debates in 1934 on the Administration of Justice Bill, it seems likely that Scottish civil litigation was excluded from the leave requirement not for any reason of principle, but through oversight or lack of parliamentary time.[30]

B. Criminal appeals in the House of Lords

The House of Lords' jurisdiction to hear criminal appeals is comparatively recent: the first such appeal in modern times was heard in 1911. The House of Lords does not hear appeals from the Scottish criminal courts.[31] In criminal causes or matters, a would-be appellant has two hurdles to jump.[32]

First, as a prerequisite for seeking leave, court that has determined the matter must certify that the grounds of appeal involve a 'point of law of general public importance'.[33] Without such a certificate, a putative appellant may not seek leave to appeal from the Divisional Court, Court of Appeal, or the House of Lords. The matter is at an end: it is not possible to appeal against the refusal of a certificate.[34] A recently published practitioners' text warns that 'in the light of practice of the Court of Appeal in not giving reasons for its refusal to certify a point it is somewhat difficult to try and define the criteria applied. Even when reasons are given it is difficult to discern any trend.'[35]

Secondly, a certificate having been granted, leave must be obtained either from the court that has determined the matter or, if this is refused, by petitioning the House of Lords directly. The criterion for leave is that the court considers

---

[28] DM Walker *The Scottish Legal System: An Introduction to the Study of Scots Law* (7th edn W Green/Sweet & Maxwell Edinburgh 1997).

[29] Court of Session Act 1988, s 40. There are a few other specific statutory requirements to obtain leave, eg no appeal is allowed to the House of Lords against a decision of the Court of Session on an appeal relating to estate duty except with leave.

[30] Hansard HC vol 291 cols 1531–1533. Mr Milne, a Scottish MP, said: ' . . . I scan the Bill and scan it vain to find any reference whatever to the Court of Session in Scotland. The compelling reasons which constrained the Committee [presided over by the Master of the Rolls] to make their recommendations apply with fourfold force to the case of the Court of Session'. The Solicitor-General indicated that the matter would be considered, but it is not clear whether this was done and if so to what effect.

[31] Though note that most of the 'devolution issues' that have reached the Privy Council under the Scotland Act 1998 relate to the alleged violation by the Scottish Executive of defendants' rights in criminal prosecutions. See ch 1.

[32] See further P Taylor *Taylor on Appeals* (Sweet & Maxwell London 2000) ch 14 and R Pattenden (n 15).

[33] Criminal Appeal Act 1968, s 33(1).

[34] *Geldberg v Miller* [1961] 1 WLR 456 (HL).

[35] Taylor (n 32) para 14–027.

the appeal that is 'one that ought to be considered by the House'. It is quite common for the Court of Appeal to refuse leave, having immediately before granted a certificate that a point of law of public importance arises. Taylor comments that[36]

It is somewhat difficult to see the logic behind the statutory framework which allows the Court of Appeal or Divisional Court to state that a point is of 'general public importance' but, in refusing to grant leave, stating that it is not one which ought to be considered by the House.

Perhaps one justification is that these arrangements enable there to be an effective division of expertise between the criminal appeal courts and the House of Lords. The former may have a greater awareness of the legal issues that vex trial courts and the first-tier criminal appeal courts, whereas the Law Lords need discretion to be able to balance the demands of judicial management of the field of criminal law with all other areas of law within their jurisdiction.

C. Work of the Appeal Committees in the House of Lords

An Appeal Committee of three Law Lords determines petitions for leave. Since 1988 this has been done mainly on the basis of the documents; an oral hearing is the exception rather than the norm. The House of Lords does not have jurisdiction over some matters and petitions for leave seeking to raise such matters are refused as inadmissible. Where there are doubts about the jurisdiction of the House of Lords to entertain an appeal, on occasion leave has been granted so that a full judgment may be given explaining the reasons.[37] There are four other possible outcomes to a petition:

(a) The Appeal Committee may be unanimous that leave should be refused and the parties are notified of the result.
(b) The Appeal Committee may be of the provisional view that leave ought to be given, but invite the respondent to lodge written objections to the petition briefly setting out reasons why the petition should not be allowed or making other relevant submissions as to the terms upon which leave should be granted. This occurred in 53 of the 236 petitions (20%) presented during the calendar year 2000. If the Appeal Committee requires further argument, the petition will be referred for oral hearing (as happened in 29, or 12%, of the petitions in 2000). Curiously, the rules provide that 'authorities should not normally be cited before the Appeal Committee' (para 4.15).

---

[36] ibid para 13–028.
[37] eg *R v Secretary of State for Trade and Industry, ex p Eastaway* [2000] 1 WLR 2222 (House of Lords cannot hear appeals against the refusal of permission to apply for judicial review). The Privy Council also provides full reasons where doubts arise as to the admissibility of a petition for special leave on the ground that there is not a 'devolution issue': see eg *Hoekstra and others v HM Advocate* [2001] 1 AC 216 and *Follen v HM Advocate* [2001] UKPC D2; [2001] 1 WLR 1668.

(c) The Appeal Committee may be unanimously of the view that leave should be granted, but subject to terms. Terms are very rarely imposed on leave to appeal, perhaps to no more than four petitions a year. The most common terms are to restrict argument to a particular point or points, or to impose a costs order in advance, for example that the appellant pay the respondent's cost in any event. Even when terms are imposed, they do not bind the Appellate Committee that hears the full appeal.

(d) The Appeal Committee may be unanimously of the view that leave is granted.

In the selection process, the Appeal Committees are helped by four judicial assistants, posts first created on an experimental basis in September 2000. They write memoranda to accompany each petition, setting out the main points and drawing attention to the passages in the judgment of the court below which are relevant to each of the points the petitioner seeks to make. Petitions for leave are generally referred to Appeal Committees in batches of six. Typically, a Law Lord expects to spend about 30 minutes reading each petition. The aim is to obtain a provisional view from the Appeal Committee within 10 days, which means that in addition to his other work, a Law Lord will need to find an extra three to four hours in some weeks for reading petitions and, where necessary, meeting with colleagues to discuss them.

D. UK appeals in the Privy Council

This essay concerns the House of Lords, but as the Law Lords spend approximately half their time sitting as the Privy Council a few comments are needed about this court, especially as it is proposed to amalgamate some of the Privy Council's jurisdiction into the work of the new supreme court.

Until recently, about 10% of the Privy Council's time—or approximately 20 cases a year—was taken up with appeals brought by aggrieved doctors, dentists, and other health care professionals against disciplinary decisions made by their professional bodies (such as the General Medical Council). Such appeals could be made as of right without any preliminary screening of the merits of the arguments or any need for the parties to demonstrate that a point of law of general public importance was involved. Such cases constituted a grave misapplication of scarce judicial resources. They were abolished by the Part II of the National Health Service Reform and Health Care Professions Act 2002, under which this appellate jurisdiction was transferred to the High Court and comparable courts in Scotland and Northern Ireland.

The Privy Council does still, however, have two areas of mandatory jurisdiction, where it has no discretion but to consider a case.[38] Under the devolution

---

[38] I leave aside any consideration of the Privy Council's overseas appellate jurisdiction, on which see my analysis in A Le Sueur and R Cornes *The Future of the United Kingdom's Highest Courts* (UCL Constitution Unit London 2002) ch 11.

Acts, while appeals from the intermediate courts of appeal raising devolution issues are subject to a leave requirement, the Privy Council appears to have no choice but to accept for decision *references* of devolution issues from those courts[39] (and the Appellate Committee of the House of Lords) or direct references in relation to Bills of the Scottish Parliament and Northern Ireland Assembly from the Law Officers.[40] There is also section 4 of the Judicial Committee Act 1833, which is so rarely invoked as to have fallen into disuse, which provides that:

It shall be lawful for his Majesty to refer to the said judicial committee for hearing and consideration any such other matters whatsoever as his Majesty shall think fit; and such committee shall thereupon hear and consider the same, and shall advise his Majesty thereon in the manner aforesaid.

5. POTENTIAL FOR LESSON LEARNING ABOUT CASE SELECTION

The final part of this essay considers what scope exists for lesson learning about the process of case selection in top-level courts, especially in relation to the two main challenges facing the UK. The first of these is the need to cope with a growing number of petitions for leave. Brice Dickson, in his analysis of the work of the House of Lords between 1967 and 1996, states:[41]

It is obvious that, in terms of the number of cases considered, the workload of the Appeal Committee has increased dramatically during the thirty-year period under review: by 1996 there were over three times as many petitions being considered *per annum* as there were in 1967 (196 compared with 62)...The rise in the number of petitions must be partly explained by the rise in the number of lower court decisions eligible to be appealed against.

Since then, the number of petitions for leave presented has continued to rise—though the impact of the Human Rights Act 1998 on the number of cases has not been as great as some feared.

A second challenge for the UK's case selection process will be a growing awareness of the constitutional role the new UK supreme court. Brice Dickson has noted that petitions for leave have 'low-profile status' and that they 'tend not to attract much attention beyond the particular parties and lawyers involved'.[42] This will, and should, change.

Like many aspects of a court's work, case selection arrangements are the product of rules made at different levels:

---

[39] eg Scotland Act 1998, sch 10 paras 10–11. See ch 2.
[40] ibid, paras 33–35. See ch 2.
[41] B Dickson in B Dickson and P Carmichael (eds) *The House of Lords: its Parliamentary and Judicial Roles* (Hart Publishing Oxford 1999) 139.
[42] ibid 138.

(a) the enactment and amendment of primary legislation (for instance specifying that a leave requirement exists and *perhaps* setting out the basic criteria for case selection);

(b) a court's formal rule-making and decisional powers including the issue of practice directions;

(c) informal working methods achieved by 'intra-mural' administrative action taken by the judges of the court in conjunction with the court's administrative officers.

I sketch out the beginnings of one possible strategy for the future. The general aim is to extend the discretionary power of the Law Lords to choose their caseload—but to balance that with a structuring of the discretion and increased transparency and accountability for the choice of cases. The shift requires a reconceptualization of choosing cases from being merely a managerial task to a central one by which the court defines its role. There are at least seven main points of lesson learning.

A. Lesson 1—enabling the UK supreme court to decide for itself which cases it hears

In redesigning the UK's top-level court, two main questions arise in relation to the processes by which cases are selected. The first is whether the UK supreme court should decide for itself which cases to hear, rather than having leave to appeal granted by lower courts or appeals as of right. This issue was canvassed in the Department for Constitutional Affairs' consultation paper on the new UK supreme court, which 'welcomed views' on whether there should be a presumption that the supreme court itself decides which cases to hear.[43] The main argument in favour is that this would enable the new supreme court 'to work out where it sees its greatest added value and concentrate on developing jurisprudence in the areas which most needed it'.[44] The main counter-arguments are that (a) it would require changes in relation to Scottish civil appeals—appeals as of right are 'long established' and 'there is no evidence that change is needed'; (b) 'in all respects it would mean that more of the work of the Court would be absorbed in deciding what cases to hear, rather than hearing them'; and (c) 'it would mean that all those seeking the judgment of the court would have to incur the cost of petitioning for the right of appeal'.[45]

To a considerable extent, the tide has already turned towards enabling the Law Lords to have greater control over the content of their caseload than once was the case. In civil and criminal cases alike, the Court of Appeal's practice is now rarely to grant leave to appeal to the House of Lords, preferring instead to leave the decision to the Law Lords. The burden of hearing mandatory appeals from the medical professional bodies has also been removed from the Law Lords sitting as the Privy Council.

---

[43] See (n 20).   [44] ibid para 55.   [45] ibid para 56.

The DCA consultation paper states that allowing the new UK supreme court to have control over the selection of its cases 'would also bring the Court broadly into line with other English-speaking Supreme Courts'.[46] This is not in and of itself a weighty argument in favour of change, though comparisons may provide reassurance to policy-makers. The trend towards top court autonomy to determine which cases to hear is evident in the USA and Canada.

In the USA, by a series of enactments from the Judiciary Acts 1925 to 1988, Congress has removed appeals as of right to the US Supreme Court and conferred on the court ever-greater discretionary control over the kinds of cases it hears on the merits.[47] The 1925 Act is often referred to as 'the Judges' Bill' because the initiative for change came from the court itself. Explaining the reason for this development, Boskey and Gressman say:[48]

For the last 100 years or so, the litigation explosion in the United States has almost constantly augmented the flow of cases into the Supreme Court. But the Court is a unitary body, finite in membership, time, and energy. It simply cannot function efficiently or properly if it must decide on the merits all cases that parties seek to bring before it. Moreover, to the extent that mandatory appeals involve issues of somewhat less than national significance—and at times the issues might border on the trivial—the Court is required to divert its energies and resources away from its prime duty of setting the nation's important constitutional and legal agenda.

The procedure by which intermediate courts of appeal may certify for the US Supreme Court 'questions of law in any civil or criminal case as to which instructions are desired' has also fallen into disuse.[49]

A process of replacing mandatory appeals with discretionary choice has also occurred in the Canadian Supreme Court. Chief Justice Dickson explained:[50]

In 1975, the centennial year of the Supreme Court of Canada, the Supreme Court Act was amended to give the Court almost complete control of the cases that appear on its docket. Rights of appeal in civil cases concerning sums over $10,000 were abolished and the 'public importance' of the legal issues raised in a given case was established as the criterion for the court granting leave to appeal . . . The importance of the 1975 amendments cannot be overestimated. The Court was freed of its responsibility as a court of error, that function being left to the various courts of appeal, and was able to get on with the task of supervising the growth and development of Canadian jurisprudence.

In Canada, the Criminal Code still provides appeals as of right to the Supreme Court on a point of law where a judge of a provincial court of appeal dissents. As

---

[46] ibid para 55.

[47] See ch 11. For a detailed account of this point see EA Hartnett 'Questioning Certiorari: Some Reflections Seventy-five Years After the Judges' Bill' (2000) 100 *Columbia Law Review* 1643.

[48] B Boskey and E Gressman 'The Supreme Court Bids Farewell to Mandatory Appeals' 121 *Federal Rules Decisions* 81, 83.

[49] See ch 11.

[50] Chief Justice Dickson, Address to the University of Ottawa Conference on the Supreme Court of Canada, 4 October 1985, quoted in *Supreme Court of Canada Practice* 7.

the Court of Appeal (Criminal Division) in England and Wales gives a single judgment of the court, this has no application in any process of lesson learning.

As to the specific question of imposing leave requirements on Scottish civil appeals, the number of such cases is small and as such they do not have a major impact on the Law Lords' work.[51] In the final analysis, the decision on reform of Scottish appeals will be one of principle based on a vision of the role of the UK supreme court in relation to the UK's three legal systems—and it will be the vision of the Scottish Parliament, for questions relating to access for to the Supreme Court from the Scottish courts are devolved issues.[52]

As to the 'reference' jurisdiction that the UK's new supreme court is likely to inherit from the Privy Council, there may be a little scope for lesson learning from Canada, where the Supreme Court also has a reference jurisdiction. Like that of the UK, though, it is not one that is frequently invoked. Therein, perhaps, is the justification for permitting reference procedures to be created despite the fact that they impinge upon a top level court's discretion to choose cases: the number of such references are likely to be so small as not to appreciably hinder the court in its role of determining for itself the constitutional and legal agenda. On the contrary, an occasionally used reference process may provide the court with opportunities to determine vital constitutional law questions.

B. Lesson 2—the role of the intermediate courts of appeal

The relationship between top-level courts and intermediate courts of appeal has been considered in other essays,[53] but a few further comments may be made about the specific question of the role of intermediate appellate courts in regulating access to a supreme court. First, as a matter of principle, it is regarded as important in the USA and Canada that the supreme courts decide for themselves what cases to hear. If it is desirable for top-level courts to have institutional autonomy—meaning they enjoy an appropriate degree of self-governance over their methods of work, caseload, administrative practices as well as, of course, the judicial decisions they reach in particular cases[54]—it is doubtful whether sharing the task of case selection with other courts is compatible with this ideal.

Set against this, however, are two pragmatic considerations. First, resource issues: many would-be appellants may simply want to 'have a go' at obtaining leave. At present in civil and criminal cases in England and Wales, they ask the Court of Appeal. When they are refused leave, for most of them, that is the end of the matter and they do not go on to petition the House of Lords. If the Court of Appeal no longer had the power to grant or refuse leave to appeal,

---

[51] During 2002 the House of Lords gave judgment in four appeals from the Court of Session, allowing the appeal in three of them. This constituted 5.5% of the total number of judgments in 2002 (72).

[52] See discussion in ch 1 on 'National perspectives'.

[53] See chs 10 and 11.

[54] Le Sueur and Cornes (n 38) para. 3.2.

the number of petitions to the House of Lords may rise, perhaps considerably—as the DCA consultation paper on the new supreme court recognizes. I suggest below that greater precision in the criteria used for determining leave would assist in encouraging would-be appellants and their lawyers to exercise self-restraint. Secondly, some have questioned whether it is necessary and desirable for the Court of Appeal (Criminal Division) to have the ultimate power of gate-keeping by certifying whether or not points of law of general public importance are involved, in addition to the power to determine leave. The Runciman Royal Commission on Criminal Justice in 1993 thought that the certification require-ment was 'unduly restrictive'.[55] It may, however, be argued that the Law Lords lack sufficient expertise in criminal matters (compared with the Court of Appeal) to select appropriate cases for the development of this field of law.

Lesson learning from other jurisdictions is more helpful in identifying the factors to be considered in redesigning a court procedure, then in suggesting how to weigh up the competing considerations. On balance, I believe that the UK's new supreme court ought to be given control over case selection.

C. Lesson 3—encouraging increased accountability for case selection

If the UK's new supreme court acquires control over its caseload, this ought to be accompanied by requirements that the process of case selection be transparent and subject to accountability. The notion of calling an independent court to account raises constitutionally sensitive issues, but given the 'accountability revolution' that has affected almost all other public authorities, there are good reasons why a top-level national court should be expected to explain and justify itself.[56] One method for ensuring accountability is the practice of reason giving. All final judgments of the Law Lords are, of course, based on detailed written reasons. Writing several years ago, Brice Dickson argued in favour of an obliga-tion to give reasons for refusing leave:[57]

reasons for decisions are never made public, even in summary form. This is surely unfortunate, even though the European Commission for Human Rights, no less, has said that, in appropriate circumstances, it sees nothing wrong with the practice. If reasons were made public it would help lawyers to know what legal points might be ones which the Lords would want to examine in future.

On 3 April 2003, an announcement was made by a Select Committee on Appeal, a body consisting of all 12 Lords of Appeal in Ordinary, that 'we have taken the opportunity to amend our procedure in order to provide for the giving of express reasons when leave to appeal is to be refused'.[58] The impetus for change came

---

[55] *Royal Commission on Criminal Justice Report* (1993) Cd 2263 para 10.79.

[56] See further A Le Sueur 'Developing mechanisms for judicial accountability in the UK' (2004) 24 *Legal Studies*, forthcoming.

[57] (n 41) 138, he cites *Webb v UK* (1997) 24 EHRR CD 73.

[58] Appeal Committee 'Petitions for Leave to Appeal: Reasons for the Refusal of Leave' 38th Report 2002–03 session, HL 89 para 6.

from concerns of the House of Lords to comply with requirements of the
EC Treaty and judgments of the European Court of Justice in Case 283/81
CILFIT v Ministry of Health[59] and Case C–99/00 *Criminal proceedings against
Lyckeskog*.[60] But significantly, 'so as not to discriminate between petitions
which raise a question of Community law and those which do not, the Appeal
will briefly indicate their reasons for refusing any petition for leave to appeal.'[61]
This new practice of giving reasons is welcome, though its utility in providing a
basis for the elaboration of what constitutes a 'House of Lords point' will depend
on the quality of the reasons given and whether or not they are published. The
custom of reason giving at the leave stage differentiates the Law Lords from the
US Supreme court, where only in exceptional cases have reasons been given for
the denial of certiorari.

There is a range of further activities which could make the case selection
process even more transparent. Some of the practices adopted in the USA and
Canada in relation to the case selection process could usefully be incorporated
into the UK.

(a) The American Bar Association produces a regular bulletin, *Preview of the
United States Supreme Court Cases,* which provides 'comprehensive, accurate, unbiased, and timely information' about the cases pending before the
court. It includes details of the amicus briefs filed. A publication of this sort
in the UK could help inform public debate about the issues at stake in the
forthcoming cases in the new supreme court.

(b) The US Supreme Court website allows users to track the progress of petitions. Similarly, the Supreme Court of Canada website publishes information about pending cases in the form of summaries of the issues.

(c) In both the USA and Canada, there is far more literature for academics and
practitioners on the certiorari/leave process. In Boskey's three-volume *West's
Federal Forms* on the US Supreme Court practically the whole of one volume
is given over to discussion of certiorari and there is a rich stream of academic
literature on the topic.[62] In Canada, Crane and Brown's *Supreme Court of
Canada Practice* devotes a chapter to the subject.[63] In the UK, in contrast,
there is little commentary or authoritative guidance. Detailed comment of a
practical kind in book form is confined to a chapter in a scholarly historical
study,[64] and a chapter in the recently published *Taylor on Appeals*.[65] Both
deal only with criminal cases. There is little UK journal literature.

(d) In the USA, there is a strong emphasis both by the US Supreme Court itself
and by commentators on the fact that the court works on an annual basis
(the 'term'). The cycle runs from the first Monday in October to the summer
recess in late June or early July. All cases in which argument is heard have

---

[59] [1982] ECR 3415.   [60] [2002] ECR I-4839.   [61] HL 89 para 8.
[62] B Boskey *West's Federal Forms: Supreme Court* (West Group St Paul 1998) vol 1.
[63] B Crane and H Brown *Supreme Court of Canada Practice 2000* (Carswell Toronto 2000) ch 3.
[64] R Pattenden (n 15).   [65] Taylor (n 32) ch 14.

judgments delivered within the same term. This leads to something of a flurry of judgments towards the end of the term, but if anything this increases public awareness of the court's work. Journalists and law review articles survey the US Supreme Court's work on a yearly basis. This helps emphasize accountability and the agenda-setting power of the case selection process. In the UK, by contrast, commentators tend to deal with the output of the House of Lords on an isolated case-by-case basis.

Initiatives such as these, adapted for use in the UK, could assist in increasing awareness and accountability of the court's selection of cases.

D. Lesson 4—stipulating the criteria with more precision?

In the UK, the main criterion set out in legislation is that an appeal involves a point of law of general public importance. The House of Lords' rules do little to amplify this. They state that 'the particular facts and circumstances of each petition will be taken into account' by the Appeal Committee. In time, the reasons given for refusing petitions for leave (if they are systematically published) may assist in building up an understanding of what the criteria are. As has been noted, many practitioners are frankly at a loss to know what they are.[66] In their seminal book *Final Appeal*, Blom-Cooper and Drewry argued that:[67]

Given a system which stipulates that leave is necessary, it is probably more desirable that the flexible criteria should be applied impressionistically from case to case rather than that rigid rules should be drawn up. The fetish of 'certainty' is not the ultimate virtue here.

Thirty years on, this should be revisited. The question is whether it is now desirable to flesh out this criterion to give some sort of guide to its application. Although both the US Supreme Court and the Supreme Court of Canada have been guarded about structuring their broad discretion in the case selection process with too much precision, both have gone far further than the House of Lords in setting out, either in rules or public statements by justices, what is regarded as important about the cases to be selected.

In the Supreme Court of Canada, section 40(1) of the Supreme Court Act provides that to grant leave, the court must be of the opinion that the question is

by reason of its public importance or the importance of any issue of law or any issue of mixed law and fact involved in such question, one that ought to be decided by the Supreme Court or is, for any other reason, of such a nature or significance as to warrant decision by it . . .

In their *Supreme Court of Canada Practice 2000*, Brian Crane QC and Henry Brown QC set out in some detail extracts from extra-judicial speeches by justices

---

[66] Taylor (n 32).   [67] (n 11) 146–149.

of the court which have sought to exemplify and discuss the nature of that criterion.[68]

In the US Supreme Court, some guidance as to what makes a case 'cert worthy' (ie worth granting certiorari) is found in the rules of the court:

Rule 10. Considerations Governing Review on Certiorari

Review on a writ of certiorari is not a matter of right, but of judicial discretion. A petition for a writ of certiorari will be granted only for compelling reasons. The following, although neither controlling nor fully measuring the Court's discretion, indicate the character of the reasons the Court considers:

(a) a United States court of appeals has entered a decision in conflict with the decision of another United States court of appeals on the same important matter; has decided an important federal question in a way that conflicts with a decision by a state court of last resort; or has so far departed from the accepted and usual course of judicial proceedings, or sanctioned such a departure by a lower court, as to call for an exercise of this Court's supervisory power;

(b) a state court of last resort has decided an important federal question in a way that conflicts with the decision of another state court of last resort or of a United States court of appeals;

(c) a state court or a United States court of appeals has decided an important question of federal law that has not been, but should be, settled by this Court, or has decided an important federal question in a way that conflicts with relevant decisions of this Court.

A petition for a writ of certiorari is rarely granted when the asserted error consists of erroneous factual findings or the misapplication of a properly stated rule of law.

In spite of this, commentators remain dissatisfied. Hartnett argues that the US Supreme Court defines what is 'cert worthy' in a tautologous way: 'that which makes a case important enough to be certworthy is a case that we consider to be important enough to be certworthy'.[69]

A fetish for certainty is not necessarily a healthy thing to have, but in any remodelling of the UK's case selection processes a little more precision could be useful to both the court and would-be appellants. If, under the new arrangements in the UK, appellants will no longer seek leave from the intermediate appellate courts but be required to go directly to the top-level court for leave, greater clarity about the criteria for leave is likely to help appellants and their lawyers make properly informed judgements about the likelihood of success in seeking leave.

E. Lesson 5—selecting 'issues' rather than 'cases'?

When considering petitions for leave in criminal matters, the Appeal Committees of the House of Lords benefit from the certificates granted by the Court of Appeal (Criminal Division) or the Divisional Court identifying the point of law of general public importance on which the appeal will be based.

---

[68] Crane and Brown (n 63) ch 3.   [69] (n 47) 1721.

In civil cases, the legal question may be far less clearly identified. This is certainly so where appeals of right are brought from the Court of Session. One extreme illustration is provided by *Governor and Company of the Bank of Scotland v Brunswick Development (1987) Ltd*,[70] in which Lord Clyde commented:

It is often found that during the history of a case through successive appeals the arguments become narrowed and refined. The present proceedings are an exception to that. The various presentations appear to have lurched from one argument to another so as to give rise to a suspicion about the basic stability of the case. While some subsidiary points do seem to have fallen away, the issues remained, to use the Lord President's words, still remarkably fluid even during the second reclaiming motion. This characteristic was not lost when the matter reached this House.

Even where a petition for appeal is more specific, Appeal Committees rarely exercise power to grant leave to argue only one or some of the grounds of appeal advanced in a petition. In the UK, the Law Lords seem to select cases rather than issues.

The process of lesson learning may suggest the desirability of change to these practices. In the US Supreme Court, there is a very strict requirement that a question of law be presented as the first item of a petition: Rule 14.1(a) of the court rules states that:

The questions presented for review, expressed concisely in relation to the circumstances of the case, without unnecessary detail. The questions should be short and should not be argumentative or repetitive ... The questions shall be set out on the first page following the cover [of the booklet], and no other information may appear on that page. The statement of any question presented is deemed to comprise every subsidiary question fairly included therein.

West's Federal Forms: Supreme Court gives numerous examples of questions, including:

Whether the filing of a suit by the United States to condemn mining claims in public lands deprives the Secretary of the Interior of his authority to conduct a subsequently-instituted administrative proceeding to determine the validity of such claims.

And:

As a result of a car accident more than five years ago, Nancy Curzan is an incompetent person in a persistent vegetative state without hope of ever recovering cogitative inter-action with the world around her. She can live indefinitely in this state. She is kept alive by means of a surgically implanted gastronomy tube which artificially provides her fluid and nutrition. The question presented is: Whether a state's interest in life, codified in the state 'living will act', can override all constitutional privacy, liberty and equal protection rights of an incompetent person to reject medical treatment.

It is also common practice for the US Supreme Court to grant certiorari in relation to one but not other questions of law in a petition.

---

[70] 1999 SC (HL) 53.

F. Lesson 6—internal working methods

Lord Goff of Chieveley has written: 'Consideration of petitions for leave is burdensome, and occupies a significant part of our time'.[71] The extent to which diversion of judges' time from deciding appeals to choosing cases is a misapplication of resources obviously depends in part on the view taken of the relative importance of the two activities. A theme of this essay has been that determining petitions for leave ought to be regarded as more important than it has been in the past. The justices of the US Supreme Court estimate that 20% of their time is spent on the case selection process—and the view is taken there that this is an entirely appropriate allocation of time.[72]

If the number of petitions for leave continues to increase, it will be necessary to consider how the UK's top court can cope. Some suggested reforms, such as abolishing the role of the intermediate courts of appeal in choosing cases for the Law Lords, might also lead to greater pressure.

Detailed consideration of the internal decision-making organization of the UK's top court has to fall outside the scope of this essay, except to highlight briefly two related matters. The first is whether it is appropriate for the task of choosing cases to be delegated to committees of three Law Lords, rather than being done by the whole court. In the US Supreme Court it is seen as important that all the justices are involved in the selection process.

A second, related, matter is the resource of the court. In both the US Supreme Court and the Supreme Court of Canada the justices each receive considerable assistance in the case selection process. In the US, as is well known, each justice has a team of law clerks who serve for a year and who are involved in writing memoranda and discussing petitions for certiorari with the Justice. In Canada, the temporary justices' law clerks now play no role in leave applications.[73] These are now handled by 18 or 19 staff lawyers (the number has grown from eight over the past five years). The idea to use staff lawyers came from the justices themselves in the mid-1990s. The impetus for change was to deal with delays in the court. One advantage of using staff lawyers rather than law clerks on leave applications is that the former are more mature and more ready to refuse leave. The court aims to appoint staff lawyers with a view to their staying in post for the mid to long term. They are recruited from academic backgrounds, private practice, and legal publishing—but the majority have previously worked as lawyers in the public service. When staff lawyers first began to be used, they specialized either in working on leave applications or on preparing judgments. Now the idea is that each lawyer will work on both types of task, ideally following a case through the system. On leave applications, staff lawyers prepare two documents. One is an objective summary of the case; this is a public

---

[71] Written evidence to the Royal Commission on the Reform of the House of Lords *A House for the Future* (2000) Cm 4534.

[72] Private communication with the author from a justice of the US Supreme Court.

[73] The following account is based interviews with staff of the Supreme Court of Canada in 2001.

document. It is planned to place these on the internet. The news media and also groups wishing to intervene in cases find these summaries useful. The second document, printed on green paper, is a strictly confidential recommendation by the staff lawyer as to whether the leave application should be granted or refused. A more senior lawyer reads every memo written by a staff lawyer before being placed before the justices. Leave applications are still considered by committees of three justices—as they were when there were oral hearings. The justices view the work of staff lawyers as useful, but insist that they do not feel bound in any way to accept the recommendations. In more than 80% of applications, though, it is absolutely clear whether leave should be granted or, more usually, refused.

G. Lesson 7—selecting fewer appeals?

One final lesson from the US Supreme Court is the insight that it is possible for a top-level court to achieve a shrinking caseload. The number of cases granted certiorari has declined significantly over the past 10 years. This appears not to be the consequence of a conscious strategy by the court and has been the subject of much academic speculation. The most plausible explanation is that there are fewer divergent decisions among the courts of appeals, which is one of the main factors for the grant of certiorari (see Rule 10(a) of the court's rules set out above).

Concern about the growing caseload has clearly been an important anxiety within the UK's highest courts. In 2000, the Appellate Committee, was a court under considerable pressure:

The backlog of appeals awaiting determination has grown to 94 (including 19 awaiting judgment). This backlog can only be reduced when both Appellate Committees sit at once, something rarely possible as the ten available Lords of Appeal in Ordinary sit daily in both the Judicial Committee of the Privy Council and the Appellate Committee.[74]

A year before the coming into force of the Human Rights Act 1998,[75] the then Senior Law Lord, Lord Browne-Wilkinson, told *The Times*:

With the Human Rights Act just around the corner, and devolution appeals . . . there will be a crisis of judge-power. 'We will see a doubling of our workload. And nobody has worked out how we are going to find the judge-power to deal with it all'.[76]

---

[74] House of Lords Annual Report 1998–1999.
[75] The main parts of the Act came into force on 2 October 2000.
[76] Interview with F Gibb *The Times* (Law Section), 19 October 1999. The impact has, perhaps, been less than expected. See V Bondy *The Impact of the Human Rights Act on Judicial Review: An Empirical Research Study* (Public Law Project London 2003). The capacity of a court is obviously related to the number of judges at its disposal—since January 1997, a year after becoming a Law Lord, Lord Saville has been engaged more or less full time chairing the Bloody Sunday inquiry and in July 2003 Lord Hutton was appointed to chair an inquiry into the circumstances surrounding the suicide of Dr David Kelly, a government scientist.

Is it unthinkable that the solution lies in the Law Lords' own hands and that they, simply, allow fewer petitions for leave? One of the defining characteristics of a top-level court is that it has rather more leisure to consider questions of law than hard-pressed intermediate courts of appeal. Only rarely can it be said that it is *essential* for the Law Lords to given judgment in a particular case.

JUDGES

13

Selecting Judges in the Era of Devolution and Human Rights

KATE MALLESON*

1. INTRODUCTION

One of the few points of agreement about the long-term implications of devolution and the Human Rights Act 1998 is that they will lead to greater scrutiny of the judicial appointments process of the UK's highest courts. Whether the senior judges take a more or less activist approach to the cases which they are asked to consider as a result of these new jurisdictions, there is little doubt that politically and morally sensitive questions are more frequently coming before the courts. In carrying out the function of adjudicating between competing rights claims and setting constitutional boundaries the judges will increasingly come to be recognized as the third branch of government. The inevitable result of this change is to raise questions about how the judges of the highest courts should be chosen and what qualifications are needed for their role.

The answer to these questions is dependent on the particular functions which the judiciary is understood to fulfil. The arrangements for selecting judges who undertake decision-making which impacts upon government policy, constitutional arrangements or fundamental rights are different from those which are applicable for judges who fulfil the more conventional adjudicative role of dispute resolution. The greater the political importance of the courts decision-making (in common with all public bodies) the greater the requirement of accountability and transparency in its selection process and the need for those chosen to be representative to some degree. By contrast, the more traditional the judicial role, the greater the requirement for technical legal expertise and the less significant the judges make-up, background, or values.

Two problems flow from the recognition that the requirements of the judicial appointments process are dependent on the nature of the judicial function. First, the division between the different judicial roles is not a neat one. Extremely technical tax law cases, for example, can have significant implications for public finances. Equally, highly political human rights cases such as the *Pinochet*[1] case

---

* Senior Lecturer in Law, London School of Economics.

[1] See *R v Bow Street Metropolitan Stipendiary Magistrate, ex p Pinochet Ugarte (no 1)* [2000] 1 AC 61; *R v Bow Street Metropolitan Stipendiary Magistrate, ex p Pinochet Ugarte (no 2)* [2000] 1 AC 119; *R v Bow Street Metropolitan Stipendiary Magistrate, ex p Pinochet Ugarte (no 3)* [2000] 1 AC 149.

often involve complex legal questions. The allocation of decision-making into one type of function or another can only be a rough approximation. Second, senior judges in the UK regularly undertake both types of adjudication. While the House of Lords and the Privy Council have always been required to decide cases concerning rights and constitutional questions, they have also spent much of their time on relatively narrow legal issues which affect only a small proportion of society. Nor is this situation unique to the UK. Many supreme courts and constitutional courts around the world spend only a small proportion of their time on decision-making which has an overtly political content. Even the US Supreme Court has a substantial diet of 'lawyers law' cases which have no constitutional significance.

The effect of the Human Rights Act and devolution will be to change the balance between the different functions carried out by the senior judges. To date, the process for appointment to the highest courts in the UK has been based on the assumption that the senior judges are fulfilling traditional adjudicative roles, differing only in their function from the lower ranks of the judiciary by the fact that they deal with an almost exclusive diet of difficult legal questions. In consequence of this interpretation of the judicial function, the judicial appointments process of the senior judges has prioritized the appointment of candidates who are insulated from political life and who are drawn from a relatively closed and homogeneous community of elite practitioners who have succeeded in acquiring a high level of specialized legal skills and knowledge. If the senior judges come to spend a greater proportion of their time deciding more politically sensitive cases this will necessitate a reconsideration of the judicial selection process. The increasing mismatch between the priorities and assumptions of the judicial appointments process and the current (and future) functions of the senior judiciary is producing a legitimacy gap. Three particular areas can be identified in which problems of legitimacy arise; these are the nature of political involvement in the system, the transparency of the selection procedure, and the make-up of the judges appointed.

These problems are not unique to the UK, but are evident in many other jurisdictions. In particular, countries such as Canada, Australia, New Zealand, and South Africa have all in recent years been grappling with the issue of increasing judicialization and its implications for legitimacy of their judicial appointments process. Even the civil law jurisdictions in Europe with their very different legal cultures have been confronting similar problems of how to ensure high intellectual and ethical standards in their judiciaries and to strike an appropriate balance between accountability and judicial independence in the judicial appointments process in an era of increasing judicial power.

2. POLITICAL INVOLVEMENT

The tension arising from the dual functions of senior judges is particularly obvious in the debate around the appropriate nature of political involvement in the judicial appointments process. On the one hand, it can be argued that there is too much politics in the system, with the process open to the danger of party patronage; on the other, that the system is unacceptably divorced from the electoral process and suffering from a 'democratic deficit'.

A. Excessive political interference

On paper, the current appointments process for the senior judiciary looks highly politicized. The head of the judiciary, the Lord Chancellor, is a direct party political appointment to the senior bench. All other appointments above the High Court are, constitutionally, made by the Queen on the recommendation of the Prime Minister on the advice of the Lord Chancellor. Since, in practice, the Queen has no active involvement in the process, the decision is solely in the hands of two politicians, one of whom is a direct political appointment of the other.

In the 19th century, it was clearly the case that this arrangement gave rise to a high degree of party political influence in the system. The senior judicial posts were regularly handed out as a reward for party service and it was not uncommon for competence to take second place to a candidate's political record. By the 1930s, however, party politics had been almost completely removed from the system.[2] As the role of the House of Lords in matters of public law and constitutional issues declined, the political views or experience of a candidate ceased to be a consideration.[3] The last generally accepted example of party political interference in the appointments process was the failure by the Labour Lord Chancellor, Lord Elwyn Jones, to promote Sir John Donaldson from the High Court to the Court of Appeal in the 1970s because of his role as President of the Industrial Relations Court set up by the Conservative government of Edward Heath. It was not until Lord Hailsham came to the Woolsack that Sir John finally received the promotion he was widely regarded as deserving on merit, going on to become Master of the Rolls.

During the last 20 years, despite the renewed involvement of the senior judges in policy-making through the development of judicial review, the tradition of non-party appointments has held. The extent of this convention is most clearly demonstrated in the appointments of Lord Irvine and his predecessor. Lord Mackay, a Conservative, appointed a number of noted liberals to the upper ranks, while the first two appointments to the House of Lords made by the Labour Lord Chancellor, Lord Irvine, were Lords Millet and Hobhouse,

---

[2] R Stevens 'A Loss of Innocence: Judicial Independence and the Separation of Powers' (1999) 19 *Oxford Journal of Legal Studies* 390.
[3] By 1953 the Appellate Committee heard only half the cases it had heard in 1939 and half of those concerned tax law. R Stevens 'The British Constitution in the Twentieth Century: Government and the Judiciary', British Academy Millennium Lecture (1999) 11–12, to be published in updated form as R Stevens 'Government and the Judiciary' in V Bogdanor *The British Government in the Twentieth Century* (Oxford University Press Oxford 2003).

both commercial lawyers with reputations as conservatives. Lord Irvine clearly followed the tradition of non-party appointments, despite being a much more party political Lord Chancellor than Lord Mackay. The effect of this de-politicization process has been to drive up the intellectual quality, and so the reputation, of the higher bench.

The degree of confidence in the current immunity of the system from political control was recently evidenced by Lord Nolan:

In some countries, less happy than ours, it may need great courage for a judge to decide a case against the government. In this marvellous country, all that happens if you decide a case against the government is that you get rather a good press and very possibly promoted.[4]

Such a sanguine approach, however, needs to be treated with some caution. The fact that, as clearly happens, Lord Chancellors appoint to the Court of Appeal and above individuals who have decided against the government in the High Court does not mean that the present system is completely free from political control. The role of the Prime Minister, in particular, is open to question. In 1996, the Home Affairs Select Committee when taking evidence about judicial appointments heard that Margaret Thatcher, when Prime Minister, had not always accepted the preferred candidate of her Lord Chancellor. Lord Mackay's characteristically diplomatic evidence to the Committee indicated that she had exercised discretion in her choice:

Chairman: I think you answered, just to confirm to Peter Butler, that all your recommendations [to the Prime Minister] had been accepted?

Lord Mackay: I was careful not to say that. What I did say was that I make these recommendations in confidence to the Prime Minister. I have never been disappointed by any recommendation that the Prime Minister has made to Her Majesty during my time—neither surprised nor disappointed.[5]

On the basis of such evidence the Committee concluded that it was left with 'some qualms' about the role of the Prime Minister in the appointments process and questioned whether he or she should continue to play a part in the system.[6]

While it may be the case that recent Prime Ministers have chosen to have only a limited input into judicial appointments, it is arguable that the convention of non-political involvement at this point in the system is not so clearly defined or firmly established that it might not be eroded. While 20 or 30 years ago there was very little incentive for the Prime Minister to take the time or trouble to intervene over appointments to the senior judiciary, this is less the case today and may be even less so in the near future. The senior judges in the UK may never have the

---

[4] Lord Nolan and S Sedley *The Making and Remaking of the British Constitution: The Radcliffe Lectures at the University of Warwick 1996–1997* (Blackstone Press London 1997) 75.

[5] Home Affairs Select Committee *Judicial Appointments Procedures: Minutes of Evidence and Appendices* (HC Paper (1996) 52ii) vol 2 [459].

[6] Home Affairs Select Committee *Judicial Appointments Procedures: Report* (HC Paper (1996) 52i) vol 1 [128].

policy-making power of their US counterparts, but as the potential for judicial decision-making to impact on government policy increases, the temptation to seek to affect the overall political outlook of the bench on the part of future Prime Ministers will grow.

Most observers would regard such a change as a wholly retrograde move which would run the risk of a return to the pre-war patronage system which undermined the integrity, competence, and legitimacy of the highest courts. The successful removal of patronage in the UK is viewed in many other jurisdictions as one of the most successful aspects of the system and one which should be jealously guarded. In the US the decision of the Bush administration to remove the role of the American Bar Association in assessing the qualifications of candidates for judicial office has been widely greeted with dismay as a step back in the long, slow process of reducing party patronage and increasing competence and integrity on the federal bench. Similarly, in Canada, research by Peter Russell and Jacob Ziegel in 1991 on federal appointments concluded that continuing party patronage adversely affected the competence of the judiciary.[7] Nor is there any evidence in the intervening 10 years that the struggle to remove such patronage, widely supported by Canadian judges, lawyers, academics, and the media, has made much progress. The usefulness to politicians of having this valuable reward in their gift has proved too great to readily abandon, despite the fact that a recent study found that while 80% of the public supported the Charter of Rights, only 8% approved of judicial appointment by the Prime Minister.[8]

In Canada, awareness of the role of the Prime Minister in the appointments process may be somewhat higher than in the UK, where the focus of concern about political patronage has, to date, largely been limited to the office of the Lord Chancellor. The multiple constitutional functions of the Lord Chancellor have long been a source of amazement to observers in countries with a stricter application of the separation of powers. Most English commentators have, however, traditionally considered the involvement of the Lord Chancellor in all three branches of government as a quirk which on paper offends constitutional niceties but works in practice. However, in recent years the claim that the Lord Chancellor can fulfil his multiple roles without any conflict of interest has attracted growing scepticism. Criticism of his control of judicial appointments has emerged as part of this wider attack on his role.[9] An example being Lord Irvine's role in 2001 in seeking donations to a fund-raising dinner for the Labour Party from senior members of the legal profession—the pool from which

[7] P Russell and J Ziegel 'Federal Judicial Appointments: An Appraisal of the First Mulroney Governments Appointments and the New Judiciary Advisory Committees' (1991) 41 *University of Toronto Law Journal* 4.

[8] J Fletcher and P Howe 'Canadian Attitudes towards the Charter and the Courts in Comparative Perspective' (2000) 6(3) *Choices* 22 (Institute for Research on Public Policy Montreal).

[9] In 1998, for example, an attempt was made in the House of Lords to pass an amendment to the Scotland Bill to prevent the Lord Chancellor sitting as a Law Lord in devolution cases or in case where the Government had a direct interest.

applicants to judicial office are drawn. Although there was no serious suggestion that those individuals who had not contributed might have had their chances of silk or judicial appointment affected, there was a widespread concern that such political activity is incompatible with a system which prioritizes the need to avoid even the appearance of patronage.[10]

The strength of feeling which that incident generated is evidence of the degree of support for keeping party patronage out of the judicial appointments process. This is not, however, to conclude that the judicial appointments process for the senior judiciary should be entirely removed from the political process. There are sound arguments for saying that far from being depoliticized, the appointments process needs to be drawn more closely into the democratic process.

B. The democratic deficit

Once it is accepted that judges in the highest courts exercise a significant political role, even if only as one part of their judicial work, the need to retain a direct link with the electoral system in the way they are appointed becomes a pressing necessity. Although the Prime Minister and the Lord Chancellor are both politicians, the level of electoral accountability in the current system is negated by the fact that the Lord Chancellor is unelected. In most parliamentary systems in which judges are appointed by the executive, this function is carried out by a Minister of Justice who is also an elected member of the legislature and so directly accountable for his decisions. In practice, it might be very unlikely that such a minister would fail to be re-elected because of her or his decisions on judicial appointments, but the possibility of such is a vital element of a parliamentary system. The potential effect of this democratic deficit on the legitimacy of the appointments process has only just started to be a subject of debate, but the experience of Canada after the implementation of the Charter of Rights suggests that this issue will soon find its way onto a wider political agenda. There, the question of how to reinforce the link between the electorate and the judicial appointments process has received a considerable amount of attention in recent years.

3. TRANSPARENCY

Closely linked to the problem of accountability is the issue of openness in the judicial appointments process. In contrast to the lower ranks, which have undergone substantial increases in transparency through the introduction of the advertising of posts, application forms, and interviews, the process of selecting the top judges remains more like that of co-opting members onto a board or a club. In 1976 Lord Justice Scarman wrote that: 'In the English

---

[10] 'Too Big for His Wig' *The Sunday Times*, 25 February 2001.

practice of judicial appointment there is no systematised plan'.[11] While this is no longer true of the lower ranks which are now considerably professionalized and formalized, it can still be said of the process of appointment to the highest courts. Individuals are not able to apply for vacancies but must wait to be invited to join by the Lord Chancellor who makes his decision for approval by the Prime Minister after consultation with other senior judges who are canvassed about the suitability of possible candidates. It is this aspect of the system, sometimes described as 'secret soundings', that has attracted increasing public criticism. Although Lord Irvine has repeatedly claimed that the term is a misnomer in that the names of all those consulted are known, the impression that the senior posts are distributed during private chats over a glass of port remains. While the system may be less informal than is sometimes suggested, the equal opportunities implications of this type of process are obvious. The danger of self-replication is increased when the appointment decision depends primarily on the confidential opinions of the existing job-holders.

By comparison with the processes now used for appointing other public figures, such as senior civil servants or university professors, the current arrangements are a throwback to an earlier age. While there is clearly an argument for retaining a degree of confidentiality in the system in order to allow free and frank discussion between the Lord Chancellor and the Prime Minister and between the Lord Chancellor and the senior judges, the degree to which the nature of the decision-making process is closed to any public scrutiny is increasingly indefensible in a democratic society. Moreover, the low level of visibility makes it more difficult to scrutinize the risk of improper political manipulation discussed above. Because Lords Chancellors have been reluctant to discuss the nature of the decision-making process it is very difficult to identify whether, for example, the balance of power between the judges and the Prime Minister has changed. Nor is it possible to assess the appropriateness of the mechanics by which a person is chosen. Since we do not even know what information the Prime Minister is given in order to make his or her decision, whether a formal short-list of names is drawn up by the Lord Chancellor, whether these are placed in rank order of preference and if so, applying what criteria, it is not possible to judge whether the system is sufficiently objective and fair. While the current system is removed from public scrutiny, any changes will be implemented without any public debate about their advantages and disadvantages.

In the past, the lack of transparency in the system did not significantly dent public confidence in the judicial process for the simple reason that very few people knew or perhaps cared about how senior judges were appointed. Until recently, the appointment of a new Law Lord was not a newsworthy event. With the advent of the Human Rights Act the media began for the first time to turn its attention to the Law Lords. In 1998, before the Act even came into force, both

---

[11] L Scarman 'Foreword' to S Shetreet *Judges on Trial: A Study of the Appointment and Accountability of the English Judiciary* (North-Holland Amsterdam 1976).

The Guardian and *The Sun* newspapers published articles on the appointment of Lords Hobhouse and Millett. Both newspapers, although representing opposite ends of the political spectrum, chose to highlight the lack of openness in the appointments process. This link between the increasing political role of the senior judges and the level of secrecy in the way senior judges are chosen is now regularly made in press coverage of judicial decision-making under the Human Rights Act as a way of challenging the legitimacy of judgments which are controversial or unpopular.

4. THE COMPOSITION OF THE COURTS

Concern about lack of accountability, possible political manipulation, and transparency have only recently started to surface in the public debate on the judicial appointments process. In contrast, the lack of diversity in the composition of the top courts is an issue which has received widespread attention for many years. The one fact which most people claim to know about the senior judges is that they are elderly white men appointed from amongst barristers and educated at public school and Oxbridge. With the exception of a few state school and non-Oxbridge-educated judges, this picture remains an accurate description of all the 27 judges who are eligible to sit in the Appellate Committee of the House of Lords.[12] The composition of the Judicial Committee of the Privy Council is essentially the same, although the inclusion of Court of Appeal judges as eligible to sit very slightly diversifies the composition, in particular by including three women. There is no doubt therefore that the courts lack diversity in their make-up; the question relevant for the judicial appointments process is, does it matter? Does it affect the competence, integrity, or legitimacy of the courts?

According to the conventional approach to the judicial function, the answer is no on all counts. The make-up of the judges should be irrelevant because of the overriding principle of judicial impartiality. Since all judges must decide cases without prejudice or bias, the personal background of the judge can have no effect on the way she or he determines a case. This approach therefore rejects the argument that the judiciary is unrepresentative as misplaced, since it implies that judges can 'represent' the interests of individuals or groups; an idea which is incompatible with the terms of the judicial oath which requires judges to decide cases 'without fear or favour, affection or ill-will'.

However, such an unqualified dismissal of the concerns about the composition of the judiciary on the grounds of impartiality is very rarely argued any longer because it is dependent on an assumption that a judge can function as a remote and Delphic arbitrator fulfilling the role of a neutral conduit through which the

---

[12] Those eligible to sit in the House of Lords Appellate Committee are Lords of Appeal in Ordinary; other Lords of Appeal (those holding or who have held high judicial office) and the Lord Chancellor. (Appellate Jurisdiction Act 1876, s 5).

law is passed to the people. This model of adjudication is no longer seriously proposed by even the most die-hard traditionalist. The fact that senior judges exercise a wide discretion which often involves taking into account the policy implications of their decision-making means that their judgments are inevitably informed by their underlying beliefs.[13] Accepting that judges do not come to court washed free of all values does not inevitably lead to the conclusion that their decision-making is determined by their backgrounds. To date, the courts have consistently denied that a judge's background can undermine the impartiality of her or his decision-making. In the seminal case of *Locabail* in which the Court of Appeal set down guidelines on judicial bias in response to the rush of bias claims which followed *Pinochet,* the Court held that it 'could not conceive of circumstances' in which background factors such as gender, ethnicity or religious beliefs would give rise to an arguable case of bias.[14]

The court in *Locabail* chose not to open a potential Pandora's box by examining the empirical evidence on the impact of the background of the judges on their decision-making. Had it done so, it would have found a great deal of conflicting and inconclusive findings from both the UK and elsewhere. The largest number of studies relevant to this issue in recent years, particularly in the USA, has been on the effect of gender on judicial decision-making. Despite a strong degree of enthusiasm for difference theory amongst many academic carrying out the research, few have found any reliable significant differences. Nevertheless, the idea that women judges adjudicate differently from men appears to be attracting increasing numbers of supporters, including senior judges. For example, in New Zealand in 1993, the then President of the Court of Appeal, Justice Robin Cooke, made the following comment on a recently decided case:

The six judges who have sat on this case in the two courts are all men, most of us of more than middle age. This is a type of case suggesting that a woman's insight would be helpful on a least one of the Benches in assessing the claims, personality and situation of a litigant woman and arriving at justice between man and woman.[15]

In March 2001, this issue was raised in the UK courts for the first time when a submission was made to the House of Lords in a case concerning the 'rape shield' law that its all-male composition in such a case was a breach of the guarantee of an impartial tribunal under Article 6 of the European Convention on Human Rights.[16] The claim was turned down by the Law Lords on paper and without giving reasons so it is not possible to know whether they rejected its empirical

---

[13] D Robertson *Judicial Discretion in the House of Lords* (Oxford University Press Oxford 1998).

[14] *Locabail (UK) Ltd v Bayfield Properties Ltd* [2000] QB 451 (CA).

[15] G Gatfield *Without Prejudice: Women in the Law* (Brookers Wellington 1996) 260.

[16] *R v A (no 2)* [2001] UKHL 25; [2002] 1 AC 45. The case was put by the Fawcett Society, which promotes the equal rights of women in the UK. The Society sought permission to be joined as Interveners in a case reviewing the compatibility of the rape shield provisions of the Youth Justice and Criminal Evidence Act 1999 with the right to a fair trial under Article 6 of the European Convention on Human Rights. It argued that the issue of the relevance to a charge of rape of the existence of a previous sexual relationship between a female complainant and a male defendant was one on which there was a marked divergence of male and female perspectives.

basis or the point of principle that a competent court requires a measure of gender diversity when hearing cases involving gender issues.

Although the case was always unlikely to succeed, the fact that it was brought at all is indicative of the increasing concern over the homogeneous make-up of the judges, particularly in relation to cases dealing with sensitive moral, social, or political issues. While there may be little firm evidence which suggests that the particular background of judges in terms of such factors as gender and ethnicity has any significant impact upon the courts' decision-making, it is increasingly clear that the continuing lack of diversity in the make-up of the judges is having a damaging effect on public confidence and so the courts' legitimacy. This suggestion is supported by recent large-scale survey research by Hazel Genn which looked at people's attitudes to justice. The study found that 66% of respondents agreed or strongly agreed with the statement, 'Most judges are out of touch with ordinary people's lives'. In interviews, respondents, most of whom had never had contact with a judge, expressed strongly held views on the subject of the judiciary which clustered around the themes of age, values, bias, and consistency. The perception of the judges as old, white males out of touch with reality appeared to have an impact on the level of confidence which the respondents had in the courts. In questionnaires, only a bare majority of respondents (53%) agreed with the statement, 'If I went to court with a problem I am confident that I would get a fair hearing'. There was also a significant difference between men and women, with more men agreeing or strongly agreeing with the statement than women. Genn suggested that 'women's relatively lower confidence may be a reflection of the dominance of the courts by men'.[17] In general the findings led her to conclude that 'although the public regard the courts as important, there is some lack of confidence in the fairness of hearings, a belief that the courts serve the interests of the wealthy, and that the judiciary are remote and out of touch'.[18]

Even if the fears that the homogeneous make-up will lead to less fairness revealed by this study are wholly unjustified, the damage to the legitimacy of the court by these views remains. Moreover, even if it could be shown that male, elderly, white judges consistently decided in favour of the interests of young, black women, the legitimacy gap would not be closed. Arguments about the need for the appointment of a more 'representative' or 'reflective' judiciary are not essentially about the decision-making of the courts, they are about the need for a minimum level of inclusion of certain groups in public life. The fact that a body which makes significant political, moral, or policy decisions should be drawn exclusively from one very small section not just of society but of the legal profession is incompatible with the requirements of a liberal democracy.

---

[17] H Genn *Paths to Justice: What People Do and Think about Going to Law* (Hart Oxford 1999) 229.
[18] ibid 249.

5. POSSIBLE ALTERNATIVE PROCESSES

The challenge which the judicial appointments process faces in the light of the weaknesses outlined above is to create a more open and accountable system which promotes greater diversity in the composition of the highest courts and yet avoids the dangers of partisan political manipulation and patronage. A key question is whether reform can be carried out within the existing structure or whether more substantive change to the system is required.

A. Reform of the existing system

Over the last two decades or so a gap has opened up between the appointments process to the highest courts and the rest of the judiciary. For the lower ranks, a highly informal and relatively small system has undergone a dramatic process of expansion and professionalization. Approximately 800 appointments are made each year, most of which are publicly advertised in an annual appointments round. Candidates apply using standardized application forms and, if short-listed, are called for interview. In the recent review of the judicial appointments process by the outgoing Commissioner for Public Appointments, Sir Leonard Peach, a number of detailed proposals for extending this professionalization process were made, such as the use of assessment centres and psychometric testing, many of which are currently being implemented. Very few of his recommendations, however, related to the upper judiciary and no mention at all was made of the appointment process to the House of Lords and the Privy Council.[19] Likewise, the remit of the Commission for Judicial Appointments, the new scrutiny body established as a result of the Peach recommendations, does not include the highest courts.

The justification for excluding the top posts from the reform process has been that they are few in number and that selection is made, in practice, from a small pool of judges in the court below who are known to the Lord Chancellor. However, the fact that the pool of eligible candidates is limited does not invalidate the argument for using a transparent and fair procedure for deciding between the candidates who are considered. The viability of reform to the upper ranks was shown by the adoption of a more formal and open selection process for the nomination to the Council of Europe Parliamentary Assembly of three candidates for the position of the British judge in the European Court of Human Rights in 1998. The job was advertised, applications were received and candidates were interviewed by a three-person panel. The new system was not

---

[19] He recommended that there should be a more systematization of the procedure for appointment of High Court and Court of Appeal judges with regular formal meetings between the Lord Chancellor and senior judges to discuss past and future vacancies and review potential candidates, L Peach *An Independent Scrutiny of the Appointment Processes of Judges and Queen's Counsel in England and Wales* (Lord Chancellor's Department London 1999) <http://www.lcd.gov.uk/judicial/peach/indexfr.htm>.

adopted in order to improve the quality of the candidates selected, which had not been the subject of criticism, but to enhance the legitimacy of the selection process for the European Court of Human Rights. There is no reason why a similar more open system could not be extended to all senior appointments generally. If the political will existed, the Lord Chancellor could include in his Department's annual report on the judicial appointments process a detailed description of the process adopted for appointment to the highest courts and he could obtain the permission of the Prime Minister fully to answer questions put to him by the Home Affairs Select Committee on the subject.

Likewise, action to diversify the composition of the highest courts could also be taken within the existing process. The statutory eligibility rules are flexible enough to allow for a much wider pool of potential candidates to be considered, for example from senior judges in other jurisdictions, academe, employed barristers, those with paper practices, or solicitors.[20] If diversification were a priority, the rigid career pattern by which judges have traditionally reached the Lords could be modified so that excellent candidates from non-traditional career backgrounds could be identified and promoted. Those who fulfilled the intellectual and other selection criteria but lacked court experience could be appointed to the High Court to gain experience and test their powers on the bench for a few years before being appointed directly to the Lords. In addition, the rigid application of the convention that judges will not return to legal practice after appointment has served to push up the age at which successful lawyers are willing to undertake higher judicial office, with the cut in income which that often entails. If this rule were applied more flexibly so that it were acceptable to undertake a period of time on the bench as a stage in a person's career, then a few highly talented people in their thirties and early forties might be able to be brought into the Court of Appeal and House of Lords and help to counter the impression of the courts as staffed by aged and out of touch judges.

As Lady Justice Hale has recently argued, the skewed composition of the current courts is largely a result of a limited interpretation of the term 'merit', which is defined as successful practice at the bar and which carries many implicit assumptions about what skills and characteristics are required of a judge.[21] Changes to these assumptions require a change of political culture rather than structural reform of the system. Where greater diversity has been achieved in courts in other jurisdictions this has almost always been the consequence of an explicit political commitment to diversity. In Canada, for example, the improved gender mix on the higher courts has partly been achieved by widening the pool of potential candidates. Justice Bertha Wilson, the first woman appointed to the Supreme Court, has said that when she was on the Ontario Court of Appeal

---

[20] Precedents for some of these categories already exist. Lord Cooke came from the New Zealand Court of Appeal; Lady Justice Hale came to the High Court from an academic career, and two former solicitors have now been appointed to the High Court.

[21] B Hale 'Equality and the Judiciary: Why Should We Want More Women Judges?' [2001] *Public Law* 489–504.

there was 'a quite prevalent view that appointments to the Court should alternate between judges elevated from the trial division and candidates appointed directly from the profession or the academic community'.[22]

To date, the suggestion of introducing any form of quota in the courts in relation to background such as sex or ethnicity is generally considered to be an anathema and yet this has long been in place in relation to regional representation. By convention the Law Lords always include two judges from Scotland (currently Lords Clyde and Hope). Although this is sometimes explained on the grounds that they are required for their legal knowledge to assist the court with the interpretation of appeals from Scotland, there is, in fact, no requirement that they sit on such cases. In truth, the inclusion of Scottish judges is as much a political as a legal prerogative.[23] If the concept of inclusive participation is acceptable in principle in relation to a geographical area of the UK, there is no reason why an equivalent convention should not be developed in relation to other groups as their presence becomes an equal political necessity.

All these changes are structurally possible within the existing system since ultimately, much change, particularly in terms of composition, is dependent on political will. In the USA for example, President Carter and President Clinton's commitment to improving the gender and ethnicity balance on the federal bench resulted in a large increase in the number of nominations of women and minority candidates compared with those of President Reagan. In the UK, however, the key role played by the judiciary through the consultations process limits the extent to which a change of culture amongst elected politicians will translate into reform in the appointments process. Even if the political will existed in Parliament or the Government to prioritize change, its implementation is unlikely to be effective while the judges retain their role in the current system. For this reason alone, it is necessary to consider more root and branch change to the system.

B. A career judiciary

One option is to institute a career judiciary as exists in most European civil law systems whereby judges join the bench as graduates and are specifically trained for the bench.[24] The advantages of this system are that it is more transparent and clearly merit based since it is not dependent on whether a candidate belongs to an inner elite at the bar. The system generally results in the appointment of much younger judges with a greater diversity of background. The limitations of the system, however, are that it is has developed in countries in which judges have

[22] Quoted in R Devlin, W MacKay and N Kim 'Reducing the Democratic Deficit: Representation, Diversity and the Canadian Judiciary, or Towards a 'Triple P' Judiciary' (1999) 38(3) *Alberta Law Review* 794.

[23] In the same way that in Canada it is a statutory requirement that three justices on the Supreme Court should come from Quebec. This is not because their French speaking skills are required, but as a political necessity.

[24] See K Ewing 'A Theory of Democratic Adjudication: Towards a Representative, Accountable and Independent Judiciary' (1999) 38 *Alberta Law Review* 720.

less power and status and therefore do not necessarily attract the highest calibre lawyers. Nor do judges who are appointed to a career judiciary generally have the same reputation for judicial independence. One reason why judges in the UK have periodically been prepared to rule against the government is precisely because they are older and more established, with the security of a successful career behind them and are not necessarily looking to move up the judicial hierarchy, since the majority of those in the High Court and the Court of Appeal are not going to be promoted further.

The essential objection to the creation of a career judiciary in the UK is that it is the product of a different historical tradition. It is designed to limit the political power of judges by constructing the judiciary as part of the civil service rather than a branch of government. Some in the UK may prefer the reduced role which this implies, but the reality is that the current changes needed to the judicial appointments process are those which can accommodate a judiciary with greater power not less. Thus, adopting a career judiciary arguably might create the worst of both worlds; a weaker and more manipulable judiciary with less democratic accountability at a time when more politically sensitive cases are coming before the courts to be decided. Instead, there are stronger arguments for exploring options which increase democratic control of the higher courts.

C. Election

The most radical way to achieve this democratization of the judicial appointments process would be to move to an elected judiciary. Although this is generally regarded as being on the lunatic fringes of political arrangements by many in the UK, there are in fact a number of examples of the use of election amongst reputable jurisdictions. The most well known, of course, is the use of elections at state level in the USA. This leftover of Jacksonian democratization introduced in the mid-1880s has relatively few supporters outside the USA and in many states has been replaced by an appointments system in recent decades.[25] However, the use of indirect election of the judiciary by an elected assembly is much more widespread and popular, particularly as a method of selecting Constitutional and Supreme Courts. The judges of the European Court of Human Rights, the International Court of Justice, the Swiss Federal Supreme Court and the German Constitutional Court are all examples of judiciaries elected by the governing assembly. The advantage of elections is obvious, in that it provides a very direct form of accountability and for this reason it is most suitable for the most politically powerful courts. The disadvantage of the system is that the assembly members may not necessarily know much about the skills and characteristics of the individuals whom they select. For this reason, a better

---

[25] See K Malleson *The Use of Judicial Appointments Commissions: A Review of the US and Canadian Models* (LCD Research Paper No 6 Lord Chancellor's Department London 1997).

compromise between the need for democratic input and the need for a professional assessment of the merits of candidates may be the use of a parliamentary confirmation procedure.

D. Parliamentary confirmation

Since the highly politicized US Senate confirmation hearings of candidates Robert Bork and Clarence Thomas the use of confirmations has become almost as distasteful in the UK as judicial elections. The damage done to the reputation of confirmations by those two hearings is regrettable because it obscures the fact that the great majority of such proceedings are uncontroversial and conducted with professionalism and restraint. Moreover, the very different political culture of the UK makes it very unlikely that an unacceptable scrutiny of judges would occur; the danger would be more likely to be of excessive restraint and deference on the part of the MPs than invasive or inappropriate questioning. Despite the shadow cast by the Bork and Thomas hearings, the suggestion that judges should appear before a Parliamentary Committee at the point of recruitment and promotion, as a way of increasing openness and legitimacy, is one which has begun to attract some support in the debate on the implications of the increasing power of the judges.[26] This development mirrors the situation in Canada where the arguments in favour of similar change have increased in recent years and now have the public support of one former Supreme Court justice, Gerald La Forest.[27]

Critics of the proposal in Canada claim that it would expose the appointments process to an increase in ideological bias and lead to a situation where a candidate's personal philosophy becomes a condition of appointment.[28] Similar objections are heard in the UK debate. However, it is arguably that the injection of an element of scrutiny of the ideological beliefs of those appointed is precisely what is lacking in the present system. We currently leave the Lord Chancellor and Prime Minister to appoint a group of people on our behalf to make important ideological choices without knowing anything about the values which they bring with them and which will inform that decision-making. The use of a confirmation system need not undermine judicial independence but could at least provide some information about the people appointed to the highest courts. A more persuasive concern is, in fact, that the affirmation process is too limited, being restricted to the choice of affirming or rejecting and so to weeding out unacceptable candidates rather than actively selecting those with the positive characteristics in terms either of competence or of composition which Parliament wishes to see promoted in the judiciary.

---

[26] Ewing (n 24) 722.

[27] J Ziegel 'Merit Selection and Democratization of Appointments to the Supreme Court of Canada' (1999) 5(2) *Choices* 14 (Institute for Research on Public Policy Montreal).

[28] R Devlin, W MacKay and N Kim (n 22) 826.

E. Appointment commissions

Fears that a direct link with the electoral system would lead to the erosion of judicial independence and an unacceptable politicization of the bench seem sufficiently strong at present that neither parliamentary elections nor confirmations are likely options for reform. Instead, there is much greater support for the use of a judicial appointments commission as a means of promoting greater openness, a more diverse composition and a more open process while at the same time reducing the danger of improper political control. The UK is not alone in turning to the use of a commission to reconcile some of the conflicting demands of the judicial appointments process. Commissions have been established in a number of different jurisdictions including Canada, the USA, Ireland, South Africa, Israel, and many continental European jurisdictions. These commissions differ in their size, membership, and powers. They range from five to 25 members drawn from amongst judges, lawyers, members of the legislature, the executive, lay people, and academics. In most cases the final decision on appointments still rests with a minister who makes the selection from a list of qualified candidates provided by the commission. The range of different types of commission is one of the system's great strengths as it can be tailor-made to suit the practical, legal, and political needs of each country.[29]

In general they have a reputation for improving openness and instituting a culture of transparency. In South Africa, for example, the Judicial Service Commission has gone so far as to hold the interviews of all candidates in public. Although the introduction of this system caused great controversy at the bar and the judiciary at first—it was claimed that good candidates would not put themselves through such an ordeal—the process has proved itself to be successful and generally very well regarded both by observers and by those who have been interviewed with an appropriate balance of demanding but restrained questioning.[30] The public interviews have also had the unexpected advantage of allowing judges to reveal certain information about themselves in a controlled environment. In 1999, Justice Edwin Cameron, an openly gay member of the South African High Court and a highly respected judge, informed the Commission that he had AIDS at his interview for a post on the Constitutional Court. His subsequent appointment undoubtedly reinforced the Judicial Service Commission's reputation for making non-discriminatory appointments on the grounds of merit alone.

The evidence also suggests that judges appointed by commissions are equally as competent as those selected by the executive alone while also encouraging the appointment of a more diverse bench. In Canada, for example between 1989 and 1994 there was a rise in the number of female applications for federal appoint-

---

[29] Malleson (n 25).
[30] K Malleson 'Assessing the Performance of the Judicial Service Commission' (1999) 116 *South African Law Journal* 41–45.

ments from 12% to 26%.[31] The establishment of the judicial appointments committee in Ontario resulted in a dramatic rise in the number of women appointed: between 1989 and 1992, 41% of new appointees were women.[32] But perhaps the greatest strength of commissions is that they tend to generate increased public confidence in the appointments process and, in turn, the judiciary.[33] If the primary goal of reform to the system is to bolster its levels of legitimacy, this benefit is very significant.

Commissions are not, however, without their critics. In Ireland and some US states it has been claimed that they are unacceptably politicized. Two factors seem to be present in those jurisdictions where this claim is made. First, an excessive degree of control of the membership of the commission by elected politicians, such as the governor in some US states and, second, a strong culture of partisan politics within the judicial system generally. Those that work best in other countries appear to be the ones which have a wide range of participation, so that no one faction or interest group dominates the process. The great advantage of the system is that the model adopted can be chosen to suit the particular legal and political context of each country and can be adapted according to whether the judges are being appointed to trial courts or the higher courts with the different range of functions which these jobs entail.

It is now likely that a commission will be set up in the UK at some point. Although Lord Irvine has recently opted for a more limited scrutiny commission, he has indicated that his mind is still open to the creation of a full commission. Scotland has established one, and Northern Ireland is expected to do the same. In England and Wales, Lord Steyn is the first senior judge to have publicly supported the creation of a commission, though others have expressed sympathy for the idea privately. While it is not a cure-all, a well-structured commission staffed by highly competent members from a range of different backgrounds could provide the new cultural climate necessary to create the changes needed to the appointments process.

6. CONCLUSION

The quality of the judges in the UK's top courts in terms of intellectual ability and integrity is probably higher now than at any time in the 20th century, yet the judicial appointments process is facing an unprecedented challenge to its legitimacy. The increasing power of the senior judges is placing new pressures on the system. In the long term, it has no choice but to adapt if the judiciary is to continue to enjoy the public confidence on which its legitimacy ultimately rests. Moreover, the speed of change must accelerate. The judicial appointments

---

[31] M Friedland *A Place Apart: Judicial Independence and Accountability in Canada* (Canadian Judicial Council Toronto 1995) 242.
[32] K Malleson (n 25) 72.　　　[33] ibid 52.

process is increasingly anomalous with the selection processes for other areas of public life. Unless a conscious effort is made to reform, confidence will erode and legitimacy will be undermined.

Those who object to change do so on the grounds that moving from the traditional to a more open and accountable system which places a higher value on transparency and diversity in the make-up of the judges will inevitably undermine the qualities of legal expertise and independence. But much of the evidence from other countries which have engaged with these issues more proactively suggests that these different demands are not irreconcilable. Opening up the process, for example, and actively seeking ways of drawing in candidates from a broader pool can actually increase the quality of the judiciary since there are many highly talented lawyers who are currently excluded from judicial office by the narrow and closed system.

Nevertheless, it is important to acknowledge that the changes proposed are likely to expose the appointments process to greater public attention. It will no longer enjoy the freedom from scrutiny of the past. There is no reason to suppose, however, that the system is too fragile to meet this challenge. Given the relatively high levels of respect and authority which judges still generally command and the continuing high quality of the candidates coming forward for judicial office, the creation of a system more appropriate for the selection of members of the third branch of government is both a realistic and achievable goal.

7. Postscript

Many of the issues examined in this essay have moved rather dramatically from the realms of academic discussion to the top of the policy agenda since the announcement in June 2003 of the establishment of a new supreme court for the UK and a judicial appointments commission for England and Wales. The composition, powers, and procedures of the commission have yet to be decided. In particular, it is not currently known whether it will have responsibility for selecting judges to the new supreme court and, if so, what appointment procedures will be used.

Constitutionally, the idea of a commission for England and Wales appointing judges to the supreme court of the UK is unlikely to be acceptable. One option being considered is the creation of a sub-commission composed of the three chairs of the UK judicial appointments commissions (Scotland, Northern Ireland, and England and Wales). Whatever form the commission takes (assuming that the new UK supreme court is indeed appointed in this way) the question remains of whether the commission should be given ultimate responsibility for appointing the top judges or whether it should recommend candidates to the executive.

It seems likely that the requirements of democratic accountability will necessitate the involvement of the Secretary of State for Constitutional Affairs and possibly the Prime Minister. It remains to be seen whether that political involvement will be substantive or merely formal. One clear consensus which seems to have emerged in the short period since the changes were announced is that satisfying the requirements of accountability should not lead to the reintroduction of partisan political influences in the process. Achieving this balance requires careful attention to detail. Assuming that the commission takes the form of a recommending body it is likely that it will be required to provide a short-list from which the Secretary of State or Prime Minister will choose. How long that list should be, whether it should be ranked, and whether the political appointers will need to give reasons for their choices are critical questions. The answers to these, and similar questions will shape the appointments process and so influence the make-up of the UK supreme court in the years ahead.

14

The Relationship between the Bar and the House of Lords

RICHARD GORDON*

1. Introduction

Inevitably, consideration of a relationship by only one of the parties to it runs the risk of either souring that relationship for ever or distorting it in a way that Heisenberg—when formulating his famous uncertainty principle—would have well understood. For a mere barrister to suggest improvements that could be made to the structure of litigation before their Lordships' House may be thought to come close to lese-majesty. The reason for embarking upon so perilous a venture, however, is that if it is ever to be undertaken it should be now. Although the Human Rights Act 1998 came in with a relative whimper on 2 October 2000, it is emerging into the forensic daylight with increasing thunder. The most important cases, those with the most far-reaching constitutional effects, are likely to come before the House of Lords.[1] Indeed, this is already happening. Cases such as *Alconbury*,[2] *Daly*[3] and *Lambert*[4] each raise issues that are gradually shifting the tectonic plates of modern judicial review. They are all human rights cases. Each of them has an important constitutional dimension.

In this essay I query, amongst other things, an imagined premise that the current system of litigating cases in the House of Lords—and its successor the new UK supreme court—is the most suitable method of determining legal issues in the new constitutional litigation likely to be engendered by the Human Rights Act. I advance, and seek to answer, a series of questions designed to test that premise in order to sketch a number of alternatives to the present system. The starting point is, however, the present system and it is that to which I turn first.

---

* QC; Barrister at Brick Court Chambers, London.

[1] In fact the case load of the House of Lords is, significantly, a public law one: see A Le Sueur 'The Influence of the House of Lords on the Administrative Court and Vice Versa' in R Gordon (ed) *Judicial Review in the New Millennium* (Sweet & Maxwell London 2003).

[2] *R (Alconbury Developments Ltd) v Secretary of State for the Environment Transport and the Regions* [2001] UKHL 23; [2001] 2 WLR 1389.

[3] *R(Daly) v Secretary of State for the Home Department* [2001] UKHL 26; [2001] 2 AC 532.

[4] *R v Lambert* [2001] UKHL 37; [2002] 2 AC 545.

2. THE ADVOCATE'S ART: THE STRENGTH OF ORAL ARGUMENT

The advocate's voice may be but an echo. It is, though, an echo that has resonated in judges' minds long before the invention of the skeleton argument or the stylized syntax of the pleaded case. The idea that oratory can swing cases and that the mark of the truly distinguished barrister is to persuade judges and juries to decide issues against their better judgment has been around since, at least, the time of Cicero. Outcome in adversarial combat has, of course, been far from predictable. As Megarry J observed in *John v Rees*:[5]

As everybody who has anything to do with the law well knows, the path of the law is strewn with examples of open and shut cases which, somehow, were not; of unanswerable charges which, in the event, were completely answered; of inexplicable conduct which was fully explained; of fixed and unalterable determinations that, by discussion, suffered a change . . .

But reversal of outcome is a double-edged sword. In a case that depends in large measure upon the facts, the skill of the advocate can, perhaps, be seen as reflecting the right to fair process. In *Maltez v Lewis*,[6] Neuberger J emphasized the fundamental right of citizens to be represented by counsel or solicitors of their own choice. Where, however, issues of law—especially issues that affect the wider public interest—are in play it is by no means obvious that the same scope for greater forensic ability to prevail should be accorded. Both the European Court of Human Rights in Strasbourg and the European Court of Justice in Luxembourg have implicitly evaluated the limitations of oral argument. Less than 1% of cases now proceed to an oral hearing in Strasbourg. In Luxembourg time limits are imposed at the outset, and questions during the course of submissions are the exception rather than the norm.

At present, though, in the UK the preponderance of legal argument takes place in court. There are rarely any time limits for the delivery of submissions and, if any are imposed, they are not usually insisted upon once the argument is under way. Skeleton arguments or (in the House of Lords) the statements of case are frequently not referred to at all. From an advocate's perspective it is crucial to know the identity of the judges well in advance. As one progresses from the specialist cadre of Administrative Court judges to the Court of Appeal (where there may not be a specialist public law Lord Justice of Appeal but where the current policy is to ensure that there is at least one such specialist) to the House of Lords (where there may be no Law Lord who has specialized in administrative law at all), the tactics of oral presentation are likely to alter considerably. For example, an Appellate Committee comprising largely former commercial practitioners will require a very different approach, forensically, from that likely to be deployed before Law Lords known to have strong civil liberties affinities.

---

[5] [1970] Ch 345.   [6] *The Times*, 4 May 1999.

All this may be said to represent the warp and weft of advocacy and part of its intrinsic skill. But that is not the point. The deeper question is whether issues such as the applicable test for reviewing interferences with fundamental rights (proportionality or *Wednesbury*), or the compliance of our planning system with Article 6 of the European Convention on Human Rights should be determined on so slender a thread as the superior skill of the barrister presenting the legal argument or whether there are balancing mechanisms that should be introduced in order to eliminate, so far as is possible, this distorting effect whilst preserving the very real benefits of oral argument.

Ensuring that important constitutional issues are determined effectively raises other considerations than the role of the advocate. The constitution of the Appellate Committees hearing particular cases, the use of judicial assistants, even the physical accommodation in which cases are argued may have significant practical implications for the outcome of litigation.

3. The questions

In an ideal world, perhaps, each case would—in whatever juristic parallel universe it was litigated—have the same outcome. Like the prospect of eternal life, though, how boring that might be. But we should always seek to achieve that objective in public interest cases. How should we do it? In the USA, for example, trial lawyers use a series of sample juries in order to estimate the probability of success. In the House of Lords less extravagant measures are obviously called for.

The following seem to me to be at least some of the questions that may, legitimately, be asked about the current system of public interest litigation before the House of Lords:

- In some civilian legal systems, constitutional courts determine issues without any hearing at all. Should that practice be adopted here in the UK's new supreme court?
- Many top-level courts have quite rigidly structured hearings so that counsel has a strictly limited time to present oral argument. Is this desirable?
- To what extent is there a specialist 'appellate' Bar?
- What might be the advantages or disadvantages of the Law Lords hearing from a small number of counsel frequently?
- To what extent should there be set panels of the House of Lords (or the UK's new supreme court) so that, as in the USA, detailed research can be conducted by legal representatives in order to determine the likely approach to be taken to a particular case? In any event, should members of the House of Lords or the new supreme court have specialized knowledge of the legal context that is being considered?

- Should judicial assistants be used in the House of Lords and the new supreme court?
- Is the physical accommodation in the House of Lords adequate for the determination of complex issues of law?
- Could there be more 'fine-tuning' in ensuring that the right cases are heard by the House of Lords and the new supreme court?

4. THE TIME FACTOR

At different stages, much thought has gone into whether oral hearings could be dispensed with altogether. Lord Woolf of Barnes has reflected this aspiration in the Civil Procedure Rules for judicial review which now enable a 'paper' hearing of judicial review cases if the parties agree. The rationale for dispensing with an oral hearing accords with case management objectives and it has the benefit of greatly reducing the cost of litigation. Judicial review can be an expensive process. Cases that never reach the House of Lords can still involve legal costs close on £1 million. Even permission hearings, coupled with applications for interim relief, have involved costs claims of £55,000 on the claimant's side alone. By contrast, a hearing on the papers is far less costly. In, I suspect, the overwhelming majority of cases the outcome will be the same. Despite this, few have sought to take up the opportunity of a lawyer-free hearing.[7]

In certain jurisdictions—Spain being a good example—constitutional courts typically determine important issues to do with the division of powers between different levels of government, or fundamental rights, without a hearing. Doubtless this is because of the absence of cross-examination in such cases and the notion that, in consequence, there is no need for an oral hearing. Why, after all, is a hearing necessary if the legal issues can be articulated with precision on paper?

Apart from the obvious dichotomy between a hearing that must be oral because witnesses and cross-examination are involved and one that need not be, there are, I believe, important distinctions to be drawn between hearings which require the concentration and focus of oral argument and those that are unlikely to benefit from it.

By definition, all cases that reach the House of Lords are those where the outcome is likely to depend upon an insight into the way in which the issues should be looked at. The intensity with which submissions are crafted and delivered derives its force (I speak from experience) from the certain knowledge the advocate has that he or she will be probed remorselessly during the course of the legal argument.

---

[7] Lawyers have not always been so popular. At the beginning of the 18th century the prevailing view was that the absence of defence counsel would benefit the accused since, if falsely charged, the accused would clear himself through 'the simplicity and innocence' of his responses: see J Robins 'Information Highwayman' *The Times*, 22 April 2003.

I well remember my first experience on my feet in *Caswell*[8] (a seminal case on delay in judicial review). As I started from my prepared script their Lordships remained silent. Their silence gave me initial (and false) confidence and I began to depart from my carefully structured presentation. Eventually, one Law Lord spoke. Then another. And another. Soon they were all (as it seemed to me) speaking one after the other without pause or respite. It was like a scene from Alfred Hitchcock's *The Birds* in which as each bird slowly arranges itself on telegraph wires the menace grows imperceptibly until it reaches the point of sheer terror.

Barristers know that it is in the House of Lords that their arguments, if lacking analytical integrity, will fall apart. That is a most compelling reason for retaining oral submissions as part of the litigation process there. A case such as *Beckwith*[9] illustrates the point. The legal issue was whether local authorities could divest themselves of all responsibility for making direct provision of residential care services under the National Assistance Act 1948 (sections 21 and 26) and contract entirely with private providers so as to make only indirect provision. The issue has become extremely important with the difference in legal protection that, on recent case law, is available to service users if provision is direct as opposed to indirect. I appeared for the appellants. Counsel for the respondent authority had always conceded that some direct provision had to be made by local authorities. The issue, at first instance, had been the extent of the direct provision that had to be made. We won. My advice to the clients had been that we would be likely to win if the concession was rightly made but lose if the concession was wrong. In the Court of Appeal I found myself in the unusual position, in the course of argument, of having to defend a concession made by the other side which, in fact, the other side maintained had been correctly made. We lost. It seemed clear to me (though I had not expected the case to be resolved in that way) that the concession was wrongly made. The Court of Appeal held exactly that. Understandably, however, I was instructed to seek leave to appeal to the House of Lords. How, my clients asked, could we possibly have lost given that the other side had made a concession that it continued to support? I entertained little doubt that the House of Lords would reject our petition. We crafted submissions on paper that read well but they were vulnerable. It all turned on the meaning of the word 'include' in section 26(1). Contrary to my expectation we obtained leave to appeal despite written objections from the respondents who had, by this time, disavowed their concession! The upshot, however, was that on the hearing of the appeal in the House of Lords our arguments were demolished extremely quickly in the verbal cross-fire without the respondents being called upon. This case has always seemed to me to be the clearest instance of the value of oral argument. Written submissions, however well structured, cannot easily be tested. Oral submissions lacking analytic

---

[8] *R v Dairy Produce Quota Tribunal for England and Wales, ex p Caswell* [1990] 2 AC 738.
[9] *R v Wandsworth Borough Council, ex p Beckwith* [1996] 1 WLR 60.

substance cannot easily survive in the House of Lords precisely because they will be tested at the highest level.

But this does not mean that the time allowed for oral argument should be open-ended. What submissions in writing can, and should, provide is the detailed context for the submissions being made. In *Bournewood*,[10] for example, the context required that the House of Lords understood the legislative history behind the drafting of section 134 of the Mental Health Act 1983. The legal submissions had, necessarily, to be directed towards examining the relevance of that history.

I believe that most cases can, once the true context for argument is exposed, be reduced to a few points. In *Alconbury*[11] the House of Lords had to understand the breadth of the scope, in the European Court of Human Rights case law, of the concept of 'civil rights and obligations' within the meaning of Article 6 ECHR. That was, largely, the function of written submissions. It had, also, to understand the detail of the structure of the planning system under scrutiny. Again, this was, or should have been, the function of written submissions. What was, however, the real question in the case—'given that article 6 applied, to what extent did there have to be a *completely*, as opposed to a *sufficiently*, independent and impartial factual enquiry?'—needed to be addressed in oral argument and to be probed.

Currently, there are few limits on the advocate. He or she can address the House of Lords on anything in the 'written case' without restriction of time. This is very different from the situation in many top-level courts. For example, both the US Supreme Court and the Canadian Supreme Court impose strict time limits on counsel for the delivery of oral submissions. In the USA the time allowed is just 30 minutes (timed with a stopwatch to the second!). In the European Court of Justice in Luxembourg it may be as little as 10 minutes. My own experience of imposed time limits is that they work well. In the *Shirley Porter* litigation, before a Divisional Court,[12] strict time limits were laid down for both the presentation of evidence and the delivery of oral argument. In a seven week case I was allowed just two hours to present my case. The discipline that it imposed on what one said and how one said it was considerable. But it worked. Florid phrases and extraneous passages were excised with the ruthlessness of a surgeon's knife. It forced me to think in a more rigorous way than one ordinarily does and the result was, I recall, beneficial rather than disadvantageous in all respects.

The point about imposed time limits is not, necessarily, the actual time allowed. There are, I think, two advantages. First, it enables and encourages the court and the advocate to focus on the true questions. Indeed, I believe that imposed time limits (the length of which should obviously depend upon the nature of the case) should be coupled with identification of the points that have

---

[10] *R v Bournewood Community and Mental Health NHS Trust, ex p L* [1999] 1 AC 458.
[11] See *Alconbury* (n 2).
[12] *Magill v Porter* (1997) 96 LGR 157 (Div Ct); [2000] 2 WLR 1420 (CA); [2001] UKHL 67; [2002] 2 AC 357.

been directed to be argued. Secondly, by such means, the distortions that can be created by superior forensic skill to which I have earlier referred is, thereby, minimized.

5. A SPECIALIST BAR?

The types of cases that this essay is principally directed to require both specialist knowledge and 'feel.' That much is probably uncontroversial. The outcome of a decision such as *Alconbury*[13] has a different 'feel' to a pure planning lawyer than it does to a pure administrative lawyer. A far more difficult question, however, is whether—given this fact—there should be restrictions placed on the advocates that can argue such cases in (at least) the House of Lords. Should there, for example, be a selected 'panel'? The advantages are, at first, clear. Legal argument is more likely to be directed to the points that matter. Cases will be relied on in a way that is not mechanistic but that reflects their true contemporary relevance. I have, for example, seen distinguished City lawyers invoking cases on natural justice decided in the 1970s which now bear little relevance to the current 'climate' of fairness or to the extent to which the Administrative Court will intervene by way of declaratory relief in circumstances in which it would certainly not have done when those cases were decided.

The extent to which outcome or remedy will differ over the years is, truly, a question of 'feel' but it is extremely important to the development of the law. One can see this in many areas. I will choose one for the purpose of illustration— commercial judicial review.

In an address to the Administrative Law Bar Association many years ago, Sir Thomas Bingham MR considered the grounds upon which the courts may legitimately exercise their discretion to refuse relief in judicial review.[14] He identified eight well trodden and familiar grounds: delay, standing, acquiescence, the conduct and motives of the applicant, the exhaustion of other remedies, the inevitability of the outcome, the fact that a remedy will serve no useful purpose, and adverse public consequences. Then, significantly, he suggested what he called 'restricted areas'. He singled out as an example of a restricted area what he termed 'the growing willingness of commercial opponents to pursue their policies by other means, namely by litigation'. Whilst recognizing that the courts were right not to declare financial regulation a 'no go' area in cases such as *Datafin*[15] and *R v Monopolies and Mergers Commmission, ex p Argyll Group plc*[16] (which arose out of rival bidding for Distillers), Lord Bingham concluded that historic ALBA talk by observing thus:

[13] See *Alconbury* (n 2).
[14] Subsequently published as T Bingham 'Should Public Law Remedies Be Discretionary?' [1991] *Public Law* 64.
[15] *R v Panel for Take-overs and Mergers, ex p Datafin plc* [1987] 1 QB 815.
[16] [1986] 1 WLR 763.

It would seem to me wise for the courts to venture into this uncharted minefield with considerable circumspection lest the cure be more damaging to the wider investing public than the disease. I would expect the developing case law to define with greater precision the grounds upon which the court will exercise its discretion to refuse relief, but for the moment perhaps the courts have got the balance right.

In that brief extract Lord Bingham said it all. The 'balance' that he was referring to was the balance whereby the court—if it thought that the decision-maker had erred as a matter of law—would grant but an educative and after-the-event declaration which would not take the commercial applicant where he wanted to go. And, indeed, it is hard to find a commercial judicial review case in the late 1980s and throughout the 1990s succeeding even to that limited extent. Commercial judicial review was, to all practical intents and purposes, an effective 'no go' area. The *Argyll* case decided by the Court of Appeal in 1986 was really the high-water mark for any commercial applicant. The Court held that the decision-maker (the MMC) had no power to take the decision that it did but that relief would be refused in the Court's discretion because, amongst other things, speed of decision was vital in the financial arena and if relief were to be granted there would be further delay.

Even as one moved into the 1990s, commercial judicial review fared not much better. In a little reported speech in *TSW Broadcasting*[17] (about the grant of commercial franchises for television companies) in the House of Lords, Lord Templeman warned of the dangers of advocates trespassing on the facts. And in *R v LAUTRO, ex p Ross*[18] (on intervention notices under the FSA) the Court of Appeal held that whilst the applicant might have had a complaint in relation to his not being allowed to apply to set aside a decision which he had (rightly) not had the chance to make representations before being made, since the argument had not been raised by his counsel in argument relief on that ground would be inappropriate.

But, going back to Lord Bingham's words, the 'balance' that the court had then arrived at was, necessarily, temporary. It is a balance that has shifted as the judges and the Courts have become familiar with the world of commercial regulation. What was once—if not a 'no go' area—at least an area marked with a huge health warning advertisement has become an area familiar to our judges.

I need only mention some cases decided in the last few years for one to see how fashionable prohibitions become fashionable practice areas amongst the shifting tectonic plates of modern judicial review. See, for example, the *Camelot* case[19] in which the Lottery Commission was held to have acted unfairly and compelled by judicial review to reach a new decision according to law, and *Interbrew*[20] in

---

[17] *R v Independent Television Commission, ex p TSW Broadcasting, The Times*, 30 March 1992; [1996] EMLR 291.

[18] [1993] 1 QB 17.

[19] *R v National Lottery Commission, ex p Camelot Group plc* [2001] EMLR 3.

[20] *R (Interbrew SA) v Competition Commission* [2001] EWHC Admin 367; [2001] UKCLR 954.

which, again, fairness led to the quashing of a decision made by the Competition Commission.

My basic point is that whether it be the once (article of faith) public/private law divide, or procedural-only legitimate expectation or commercial judicial review or, indeed mistake of fact, proportionality in domestic law or even *Wednesbury* itself (incontestably, the longest standing ex tempore judgment ever delivered) very little is sacred in judicial review *for ever*.

What specialist advocacy can often do is to guide the court in a way that the non-specialist cannot through the morass of case law for the purpose of detecting trends and patterns in the law. In the sensitive area of constitutional litigation this is, I believe, a very important function. Indeed, given that the caseload of the House of Lords is becoming, significantly, one of public law,[21] the specialism needed at the Bar is, arguably, one that embraces both public law and appellate expertise. This need is particularly strong at the present time where most Law Lords are not public lawyers by training or experience.

And yet, and yet... I remain deeply sceptical of rigidly limiting advocacy rights. However well intentioned, specialist panels of advocates to which compulsory recourse must be made for access to the court is antithetical to the strongest traditions of the Bar. The strength of the Bar lies in its independence and in the fundamental right of the citizen to choose his or her lawyer. The Lord Chancellor's legal aid franchise scheme for solicitors doubtless has its admirers but it remains, in my opinion, vulnerable to the charge that it is likely to hinder access to the court if, and to the extent that, it discourages ordinary people from litigating because (for example) their high street solicitor does not have a franchise to conduct the particular case.

The other problem with specialist panels is that the criteria by which they are selected and renewed are rarely free from controversy. Without wishing to be overtly critical, the Treasury panel of appointed counsel has (at least so far as recent appointments are concerned) missed out a number of extremely able junior counsel. Such anomalies are intrinsic to any selection process. Certainly, so far as litigation against central government is concerned, one would have thought that the market would be the true test of merit.

Regrettably, the same is not always true of litigation before the House of Lords. The most important cases do not necessarily fall into the career paths of the most able or specialized lawyers. The reason for this is obvious. Clients choose solicitors and solicitors choose barristers for a variety of reasons that are not, inevitably, linked to specialist merit.

It seems to me that the answer is not to have compulsory specialist panels of counsel but for the House of Lords to establish a general system for appointing an amicus in most, if not all, cases coming before it. This was, of course, done in *Alconbury*[22] but it is, so far as I am aware, by no means the norm. The amicus system would, I believe, have a significant effect if it became the rule as opposed

---

[21] See Le Sueur (n 1).　　[22] See *Alconbury* (n 2).

to the exception to the rule. And, to be most effective, the amicus should be selected for his or her individual specialist and advocacy skills in relation to the case rather than from a general (and, necessarily, not 'fine tuned') panel.

6. Panels

Some lawyers, as for example Lord Lester of Herne Hill, are highly critical of the fact that there are no set panels in the Law Lords. Counsel does not know until quite close to the date of the hearing who will be sitting. This is, of course, contrary to the jurisprudential beliefs of those who espouse the American tradition of pragmatism. In the USA, lawyers will often research in detail how each of the Supreme Court judges is likely to approach particular issues. One could, doubtless, have a system of (for example) two set chambers of Law Lords which might enable lawyers to predict the approach of the House of Lords (or new supreme court) with more certainty.

I believe that there are good arguments for set panels of Law Lords in constitutional cases of importance. They are not, however, to be derived from considerations of pragmatism. As I have earlier sought to argue, pragmatism ought to have no place in how public interest cases are argued or determined. Such considerations introduce a distorting and logically undesirable element into what should be the true objective of the forensic process.

Why, however, set panels would be a good idea is because of the danger—to which I have also earlier referred—of unspecialized Law Lords deciding cases that require an understanding of the dynamics as well as the literal meaning of the relevant case law. Specialized (as opposed, perhaps, to 'set') panels could have a variety of useful functions. First, such panels could play a greater part in the selection of cases which are heard by the House of Lords at all than the ostensibly arbitrary method that seems to prevail at present (see below). Secondly, the amicus system—which I argue should be extended—would be assisted in its implementation by specialist panels who could be relied upon to determine whether a specialist neutral advocate was required for the particular case and who it should be. Thirdly, a specialist panel could have a useful part to play in imposing appropriate time limits on counsel and directing the issues upon which it wished to be addressed (see above). Finally, of course, such panels would have greater facility in probing and testing the oral submissions made in court.

None of these reasons suggest, to my mind, that panels should be 'set' in the sense that some Law Lords would only sit with particular Law Lords. Such a conclusion would prevent the 'chemistry' of different combinations of specialist Law Lords which, I believe, is healthy and certainly not to be discouraged. However, I believe that constitutional cases should be heard by a panel consisting entirely of specialist Law Lords whatever its precise combination of talent. It is, surely, an anomaly that we have a specialist body of Administrative Court judges ('the nominated judges') who deal with every judicial review case whereas there is no parallel system of 'nomination' in either the Court of Appeal or the House of Lords for exactly the same cases.

It is, in my view, desirable that such specialists take a more active role in 'case management' well before the hearing of the appeal. To this extent, at least, I believe that the composition of the particular panel for any given case should be determined well in advance. As in the European Court of Human Rights in Strasbourg, one Law Lord should be given overall charge of a case as soon as the petition is lodged. That Law Lord should be responsible for ensuring consideration of the case at the leave stage and, if leave is granted, at the stages where consideration is being given to time limits, case directions[23] and the appointment of an amicus. I outline below the anomalies that can occur by cases not being given specialist consideration at the leave stage.

Focused treatment of a case prior to its reaching the hearing is, in my opinion, highly desirable. It avoids the kinds of problems that can occur otherwise, such as the case being given an inadequate or over-generous time limit and issues surfacing at a very late stage in the course of argument.[24] I believe that the case for panels of judges with the functions that I have outlined is extremely strong.

7. OTHER QUESTIONS

Most of the questions that occur to me would be resolved by the use of specialist panels specifying well in advance the parameters of litigation in the House of Lords or the new supreme court. There are a few discrete areas that I would also like to see addressed. The use of judicial assistants or clerks is something that I have long thought to be a good idea. I have already sketched the importance of the context of a case in determining both the 'shape' of the legal argument and identification of the true issues. I have also suggested that context should receive detailed written treatment rather than being the subject of oral submissions.

At present the only background material will be that which the parties choose to put before the House of Lords[25] or that which the diligent researches of the Law Lord(s) hearing the case manage to uncover. The latter, of course, are circumscribed by the present system which does not enable the Law Lords to know which cases they will be hearing until shortly before the hearing. It seems to me to be obvious that judicial assistants, coupled with the system of specialist committees for which I contend, could greatly enhance the provision

---

[23] Including interlocutory relief, a subject shrouded in (unacceptable) mystery once a case has left the CA.

[24] A recent and notable instance is the debacle in the recent *Pinochet* litigation before the HL. See *R v Bow Street Metropolitan Stipendiary Magistrate, ex p Pinochet Ugarte (no 1)* [2000] 1 AC 61; *R v Bow Street Metropolitan Stipendiary Magistrate, ex p Pinochet Ugarte (no 2)* [2000] 1 AC 119; *R v Bow Street Metropolitan Stipendiary Magistrate, ex p Pinochet Ugarte (no 3)* [2000] 1 AC 149.

[25] Hence the importance of an amicus.

of background information necessary to deciding what issues are relevant and how those issues should be argued. The concern that some have expressed about the 'distancing' that can occur between the Bar and the court with the introduction of judicial assistants who will have their own input that is unseen by counsel can be solved by a sensible case management process.

Judicial assistants ought not to express any view on the legal submissions being made. They should provide a detailed note on the background which should be provided to the parties' advocates before it is placed before the Appellate Committee. So too, I believe, should any research conducted by individual Law Lords. The relationship between this background and directions to be given as to oral submissions should be explored between the Appellate Committee and the advocates in a case management hearing similar to those now conducted routinely in the Administrative Court (though not, as yet, in the Court of Appeal).

If all this suggests a more modern approach to litigation in the UK's top-level court I make no apology for it. Nor, at this stage, can I resist urging that larger accommodation than the traditional Committee Room 'A' or 'B' in the House of Lords be provided for the hearing of the appeal—something accepted by the government in July 2003 in its consultation on the new supreme court. Litigation in the House of Lords is terrifying enough (see above) without making it doubly nerve wracking by having to make submissions with hardly any space to spread one's papers and notes. By comparison the High Court is luxury and even that can, in some courts (Court 26 and Court 27) be bad enough. I do not seriously pretend that litigation will produce a different outcome if more space can be found but it is an anomaly of the way this country conducts its affairs that the higher one goes the less privileged the facilities that seem to be accorded!

Finally, a comment on the leave stage.[26] I remain concerned that the House of Lords misses cases that are important and sometimes takes on cases that (at least relative to those rejected) should not be considered. Many years ago I appeared in *R v Canons Park Mental Health Review Tribunal, ex p A*.[27] It was a case about whether psychopathic patients who are untreatable could, lawfully, be detained under the Mental Health Act 1983. We won in the Divisional Court but lost in the Court of Appeal. We applied for leave to appeal to their Lordships' House confident that the House of Lords would entertain an appeal on so important a point. In the event the petition was dismissed without a hearing. Five years later, a Scottish case—*Reid v Secretary of State for Scotland*[28]—reached the House of Lords (no leave was needed for the case to get there) on exactly the same point. The House of Lords overruled *ex p A*.

It is highly undesirable that important cases, like *A*, are not admitted to the House of Lords and I can only think that it is because of the absence of

---

[26] See ch 12.
[27] [1994] 1 All ER 481 (QBD); [1995] QB (CA).
[28] [1999] 2 AC 512.

sufficiently detailed and/or specialist consideration at the leave stage. A related problem is the obviously crucial case where—as recently occurred in *R (H) v Mental Health Review Tribunal*[29]—a declaration of incompatibility is made by the Court of Appeal but neither party appeals so that so fundamental a point as the constitutionality of an Act of Parliament is never considered by the highest court in the land.

8. CONCLUSION

In the middle of *Caswell*[30] my opponent and I asked their Lordships to rule on a point, not directly in issue, but relevant to the profession and arising from the facts of the case. One of their Lordships leaned forward and, declining the invitation, said 'that wouldn't be a good idea; we're very remote when we get up here you know'. My tentative suggestions for reform of the present system will not be accepted by everyone. They are all, nonetheless, directed towards removal of the 'remoteness' of the House of Lords and bringing it into line with the real challenges that constitutional litigation now poses for advocates and courts alike. Views may differ as to how these challenges should be resolved. All are, though, I hope agreed that they must be resolved.

---

[29] *R(H) v Mental Health Review Tribunal for North and East London* [2001] EWCA Civ 415; [2002] QB 1.
[30] See *Caswell* (n 8).

Bibliography

Journal articles and chapters in books

'Merely a Landmark or a Change of Course: the Federal Constitutional Court Hears Arguments in the Strategic Concept Case' (2001) 2(11) *German Law Journal*

'The Irish Lords of Appeal in Ordinary' in DS Greer and NM Dawson *Mysteries and Solutions in Irish Legal History* (Dublin Four Courts Dublin 2001)

'The Statistics' (2001) 115 *Harvard Law Review* 545

'The Statistics' (2002) 116 *Harvard Law Review* 461

Anderson, D 'Shifting the Grundnorm (and other tales)' in O'Keeffe, D (ed) *Judicial Review in European Union Law, Liber Amicorum in honour of Lord Slynn of Hadley* (Kluwer The Hague 2000) 343–360

Arndt, N and Nickel, R 'Federalism Revisited: Constitutional Court Strikes Down New Immigration Act for Formal Reasons' (2003) 4(2) *German Law Journal*

Beardsley, JE 'Constitutional Review in France' (1975) *Supreme Court Review* 189

Beetz, J 'Les Attitudes changeantes du Québec à l'endroit de la Constitution de 1867' in Crepeau, PA and Macpherson, CB (eds) *The Future of Canadian Federalism /L'avenir du fédéralisme canadien* (University of Toronto Press Toronto and Les presses de l'Université de Montréal Montréal 1965)

Bingham of Cornhill, Lord 'Dicey Revisited' [2002] *Public Law* 39

Bingham of Cornhill, Lord 'The Evolving Constitution' [2002] *European Human Rights Law Review* 1

Bingham, T 'Should Public Law Remedies Be Discretionary?' [1991] *Public Law* 64

Böckenförde, E-W 'Grundrechte als Grundsatznormen' ('Fundamental rights as fundamental norms') (1990) *Der Staat* 1

Boskey, B and Gressman, E 'The Supreme Court Bids Farewell to Mandatory Appeals' 121 *Federal Rules Decisions* 81

Bradley, A 'Judicial Independence under Attack' [2003] *Public Law* 397

Brennan, WJ 'The National Court of Appeals: Another Dissent' (1973) 40 *University of Chicago Law Review* 473

Bryde, B-O 'Die bundesrepublikanische Volksdemokratie als Irrweg des Demokratietheorie' ('Democratic theory on a wrong track—the concept of a German people's democracy') (1994) *Staatswissenschaften und Staatspraxis* 330

Burger, W '1972 Report on the State of the Judiciary' (1972) 58 *American Bar Association Journal* 1049, 1053

Canor, I '*Primus Inter Pares*: Who is the Ultimate Guardian of Fundamental Rights in Europe' [2000] *European Law Review* 3

Carey, N 'Judicial Review of Acts of Parliament: the French Experience' [1998] *Trinity College Law Review* 71–86

Carrington, PD 'Crowded Dockets and the Courts of Appeals: The Threat to the Function of Review and the National Law' (1969) 82 *Harvard Law Review* 542

Cooke of Thorndon, Lord 'The Law Lords: An Endangered Heritage' (2003) 119 *Law Quarterly Review* 49

Cornes, R 'McGonnell v United Kingdom, the Lord Chancellor and the Law Lords' [2000] *Public Law* 166

Davis Michael, H 'The Law/Politics Distinction, the French *Conseil Constitutionnel*, and the US Supreme Court' (1986) 34 *American Journal of Comparative Law* 45

Davis Michael, H 'A Government of Judges: An Historical Review' (1987) 35 *American Journal of Comparative Law* 559

Devlin, R, MacKay, W and Kim, N 'Reducing the Democratic Deficit: Representation, Diversity and the Canadian Judiciary, or Towards a "Triple P" Judiciary' (1999) 38(3) *Alberta Law Review* 794

Dickson, B 'Northern Ireland's Troubles and the Judges' in Hadfield, B (ed) *Northern Ireland: Politics and the Constitution* (Open University Press Milton Keynes 1992) ch 9

Dickson, B 'A Unionist Legal Perspective on Obstacles in the South to Better Relations with the North' in Forum for Peace and Reconciliation *Building Trust in Ireland* (Blackstaff Press Belfast 1996) 55–83

Drewry, G 'Leap Frogging and a Lord Justice's Eye View of the Final Appeal' (1973) 89 *Law Quarterly Review* 260

Drzemczewski, A 'La prévention des violations des droits de l'homme: les mécanismes de suivi du Conseil de l'Europe' (2000) 43 *Revue Trimestrielle des Droits de l'Homme* 385–428

du Parcq, Lord 'The Final Court of Appeal' (1949) *Current Legal Problems* 1

Esser, J [1975] *Juristenzeitung* 555

Ewing, K 'A Theory of Democratic Adjudication: Towards a Representative, Accountable and Independent Judiciary' (1999) 38(3) *Alberta Law Review* 720

Fish, S 'La pensée juridique moderne' in *Respecter le sens commun* (LGDJ Paris 1995)

Fletcher, J and Howe, P 'Canadian Attitudes towards the Charter and the Courts in Comparative Perspective' (2000) 6(3) *Choices* 22 (Institute for Research on Public Policy Montreal)

Forsey, EA 'Our Present Discontents' (1970) published as essay no 24 in Forsey, EA *Freedom and Order* (McLellan and Stewart Toronto 1974) 310

Fraser, Lord 'The House of Lords as Court of Last Resort for the United Kingdom' (1986) *Scots Law Times* 33

Gearty, C 'What are Judges For?' *London Review of Books* 25 January 2001

Gibb, AD 'The Inter-relation of the Legal Systems of Scotland and England' (1937) 29 *Law Quarterly Review* 61

Gibb, F 'Lord Chief Justice Warns Ministers He is not Crying Wolf' *The Times* 2 August 2003

Goodall, K 'What Defines the Roles of a Judge? First Steps towards the Construction of a Comparative Method' (2000) 51 *Northern Ireland Legal Quarterly* 535

Goodall, K 'The Legitimacy of the Judge' in John Bell, J (ed) *Studies in UK Law 2002* (BIICL London 2002)

Hadfield, B 'Whether or Whither the House of Lords?' (1984) 35 *Northern Ireland Legal Quarterly* 313

Hale, B 'Equality and the Judiciary: Why Should We Want More Women Judges?' [2001] *Public Law* 489–504

Hart, WO 'The Inter-relation of the Legal Systems of Scotland and England' (1937) 29 *Law Quarterly Review* 61

Hartnett, E 'Deciding What to Decide, The Judges' Bill at 75' (2000) 84 *Judicature* 120

Hartnett, E 'Questioning Certiorari: Some Reflections Seventy-five Years After the Judges' Bill' (2000) 100 *Columbia Law Review* 1643

Hellman, AD 'Light on a Darkling Plain: Intercircuit Conflicts in the Perspective of Time and Experience' (1998) *Supreme Court Review* 247

Henneke, Hans-Günter 'Föderalismusreform kommt in Fahrt *(Reform of Federalism gains pace)*' [2003] *Deutsches Verwaltungsblatt* 845

Higgins, R 'The Relationship between International and Regional Humanitarian Law and Domestic Law' (1992) 18 *CLB* 1268

Hoffmann, Lord 'Human Rights and the House of Lords' (1999) 62 *Modern Law Review* 159

Hope of Craighead, Lord 'Edinburgh v Westminster & Others: Resolving Constitutional Disputes—Inside the Crystal Ball Again?' (1997) 42 *Journal of the Law Society of Scotland* 140–143

Hope of Craighead, Lord 'Taking the Case to London: Is It All Over?' (1998) 43 *Juridical Review* 136

Horowitz, D 'Decreeing Institutional Change: Judicial Supervision of Public Institutions' [1983] *Duke Law Journal* 1265

Howden, CRA 'The House of Lords Its History and Constitution' (1909–10) 21 *Juridical Review* 358

Hunter, L 'Bora Laskin and Labour Law: the Formative Years' (1984) 6 *Supreme Court Law Review* 431

Jahrbuch des öffentlichen Rechts Vol 6 (1957)

Kelsen, H 'Judicial Review of Legislation: A Comparative Study of the Austrian and American Constitution' (1942) 4 *The Journal of Politics* 183

Khan-Freund, O 'On Uses and Misuses of Comparative Law' (1974) 37 *Modern Law Review* 1

Kirchhoff, P 'The Balance of Powers between National and European Institutions' (1999) 5 *European Law Journal* 225

Kommers, DP 'An Introduction to the Federal Constitutional Court' (2001) 2(9) *German Law Journal*

Kühne and Nash [2000] *Juristenzeitung* 996

Lajoie, A 'Égalité et asymétrie dans le fédéralisme canadien' in Le Pourhiet, AM (ed) *Liberté et égalité locales* (Economica Presses universitaires d'Aix-Marseille Aix-en-Provence 1999) 325–340

Lajoie, A 'I valori delle minoranze sociali nelle giurisprudenza costituzionale delle Corte suprema del Canada', in Rolla, G (ed) *Lo sviluppo dei diritti fondamentali in Canada fra universalità e diversità culturale* (Giuffre Milano 2000)

Lajoie, A Mulazzi, P and Gamache, M 'Political Ideas in Québec and the Evolution of Canadian Constitutional Law, 1945–1985' in Bernier, I and Lajoie, A (eds) *The Supreme Court of Canada as an Instrument of Political Change* (University of Toronto Press Toronto 1986)

Lajoie, A Gervais, MC Gélineau, E and Janda, R 'When Silence Is no Longer Acquiescence: Gays and Lesbians under Canadian law' (1999) 14 *Canadian Journal of Law and Society* 101–126

Lajoie, A, Gélineau, E, Duplessis, I and Rocher, G 'L'intégration des valeurs et des intérêts autochtones dans le discours judiciaire et normatif canadien' (2000) 29 *Osgoode Hall Law Journal* 143–188

Lajoie, A Gervais, MC Gélineau, E and Janda, R 'Les valeurs des femmes dans le discours de la Cour suprême du Canada' (2000) 34 *Revue Juridique Thémis* 563–605

Lamprecht, R 'Ist das BVerfG noch gesetzlicher Richter?' 2001 *Neue Juristische Wochenschrift* 419

Laskin, B '"Peace, Order and Good Government" Re-examined' (1947) 25 *Canadian Bar Review* 1054

Laws, J 'Law and Democracy' [1995] *Public Law* 72

Le Sueur, A 'New Labour's (surprisingly quick) next steps in constitutional reform' [2002] *Public Law* 368

Le Sueur, A 'The Influence of the House of Lords on the Administrative Court and Vice Versa' in Gordon, R (ed) *Judicial Review in the New Millennium* (Sweet and Maxwell London 2003)

Le Sueur, A and Cornes, R 'What Do the Top Courts Do?' (2000) 53 *Current Legal Problems* 53

Lederman 'Unity and Diversity in Canadian Federalism' (1975) 53 *Canadian Bar Review* 597

Levin, AL 'Uniformity of Federal Law,' in Harrison, C and Wheeler, R (eds) *The Federal Appellate Judiciary in the 21st Century* (Federal Judicial Centre Washington DC 1989) 133–34

Linseth, P 'Law History and Memory: 'Republican Moments' and the Legitimacy of Constitutional Review in France' (1996/97) 3 *Columbia Journal of European Law* 49–83

Liptak, A 'Federal Appeals Court Decisions May Go Public' *The New York Times* 25 December 2002

Livingstone, S 'The House of Lords and the Northern Ireland Conflict' (1994) 57 *Modern Law Review* 333

Llera Ramo, Francisco José 'La sangría etnicista' *El País* 7 November 2002, 13. Available at <perso.wanadooes/laicos/2002/752S-etnicista.htm> (6 August 2003)

Lovat-Fraser, JA 'The Constitutional Position of the Scottish Monarch Prior to the Union' (1901) 17 *Law Quarterly Review* 252

Lowry, Lord 'The Irish Lords of Appeal in Ordinary' in Greer, DS and Dawson, NM (eds) *Mysteries and Solutions in Irish Legal History* (Four Courts Dublin 2001)

Lyall, A 'The Irish House of Lords as a Judicial Body, 1783–1800' (1993–95) 28–30 *Irish Jurist* 314

Lysaght, CE 'The Irish Peers and the House of Lords' (1967) 18 *Northern Ireland Legal Quarterly* 277

MacDermott, J 'Tribute to Lord Lowry' (1999) 50 *Northern Ireland Legal Quarterly* 8

MacDiarmid, C 'Scots Law: The Turning of the Tide' [1999] *Juridical Review* 156

MacDonald, RA 'Pour la reconnaissance d'une normativité juridique implicite et inférentielle' vol XVIII no 1 *Sociologie et sociétés* 47–58

MacDonald, VC 'The Privy Council and the Canadian Constitution' (1951) 29 *Canadian Bar Review* 1021

MacKay, AW 'The Supreme Court of Canada and Federalism: Does/Should Anyone Care Anymore?' (2001) 80 *Canadian Bar Review* 241

Mackenzie, DC 'Lord Colonsay and his Island' (1931) 43 *Juridical Review* 1

MacLean, AJ 'The 1707 Union: Scots Law and the House of Lords' (1983) 4 *Journal of Legal History* 50

MacLean, AJ 'The House of Lords and Appeals from the High Court of Justiciary, 1707–1887' [1985] *Juridical Review* 192

MacLean, AJ 'The House of Lords' in *Stair Memorial Encyclopaedia* (Butterworths Edinburgh 1988)

Malleson, K 'Assessing the Performance of the Judicial Service Commission' (1999) 116 *South African Law Journal* 41–45

Marshall, G 'Remaking the British Constitution' John Tait Memorial Lecture, Faculty of Law, McGill University, Montreal, 5 October 2000 (published jointly by the Department of Justice and McGill University)

Maurer, A 'Federal Constitutional Court to Decide Whether to Issue a Temporary Injunction Against Germany's New Lifetime Partnerships Law for Homosexual Couples' (2001) 2(12) *German Law Journal*

Mauro, T 'Clerks Follow New Path to High Court' *Legal Times* 21 October 2002

McMillan, ARG 'The Evolution of the Scottish Judiciary' (1940) 52 *Juridical Review* 1, 126, 293 (in three parts)

Megarry, RE 'The House of Lords and Scottish Appeals' (1956) 19 *Modern Law Review* 95

Munday, R 'All For One and One For All' [2002] *Cambridge Law Journal* 321–350

Munday, R 'Judicial Configuration, Permutations of the Court and Properties of Judgment' (2002) 61 *Cambridge Law Journal* 612

Neuborne, B 'Judicial Review and Separation of Powers in France and the United States' (1982) 57 *New York University Law Review* 363

Newark, FH 'Notes on Irish Legal History' (1947) 8 *Northern Ireland Legal Quarterly* 121

Newark, FH 'The Constitution of Northern Ireland: the First Twenty-Five Years' (1948) 8 *Northern Ireland Legal Quarterly* 52

Newman, WJ '"Grand Entrance Hall," Back Door or Foundation Stone? The Role of Constitutional Principles in Construing and Applying the Constitution of Canada' (2001) 14 *Supreme Court Law Review* (2d) 197

Nickel, R 'Juristenzeitung: Zur Zukunft des Bundesverfassungsgerichts im Zeitalter der Europäisierung' ('On the Future of the FCC in the Era of "Europeanization"') (2001) *Juristenzeitung* 625

Normand, Lord 'Editorial' (1953) *Scots Law Times News* 184

O'Connor, SD 'Altered States: Federalism and Devolution at the "Real" Turn of the Millennium' (2001) 60 *Cambridge Law Journal* 493

O'Neill, A 'The European Convention and the Independence of the Judiciary—The Scottish Experience' (2000) 63 *Modern Law Review* 429

O'Neill, A 'Judicial Politics and the Judicial Committee: the devolution jurisprudence of the Privy Council' (2001) 64 *Modern Law Review* 603

O'Neill, A 'Fundamental Rights and the Constitutional Supremacy of Community Law in the UK after Devolution and the Human Rights Act' [2002] *Public Law* 724

Palmer, B '"The 'Bermuda Triangle?" The Cert Pool and Its Influence over the Supreme Court's Agenda' (2001) 18 *Constitutional Commentary* 105

Paterson, AA 'Scottish Lords of Appeal, 1876–1988' (1988) 33 *Juridical Review* 236

Pernice, I (2000) 40 *Jahrbuch des Öffentlichen Rechts der Gegenwart* 205

Rawlings, R 'Taking Wales Seriously: Devolution, Human Rights and Legal System' in Campbell, T, Gearty, C and Tomkins, A (eds) *Sceptical Approaches to Human Rights* (Hart Publishing Oxford 2001)

Ricoeur, P 'Le problème de la liberté de l'interprète en herméneutique générale et en herméneutique juridique' in P Amseleck (ed) *Interprétation et droit* (Editions Emile Brulyant Bruxelles; Presses Universitaires d'Aix-Marseille Aix-Marseilles 1995)

Riles, A 'Introduction: The Projects of Comparison' in A Riles (ed) *Rethinking the Masters of Comparative Law* (Hart Publishing Oxford 2001)

Robbins, I 'Justice by the Numbers: The Supreme Court and the Rule of Four—Or Is It Five?' (2000) 36 *Suffolk University Law Review* 1

Rozenberg, J 'Trying to Keep the Scales of Justice Imperial' *Daily Telegraph* 30 January 2001

Rubio Llorente, F 'El bloque de constitucionalidad' in *La forma del poder (Estudios sobre la Constitución)* (CEPC Madrid 1993)

Rubio Llorente, F 'Tendencias actuales de la jurisdicción constitucional en Europa' in Rubio Llorente, F and Jiménez Campo, J *Estudios sobre jurisdicción constitucional* (McGraw Hill Madrid 1998) 170

Russell, P Ziegel, J 'Federal Judicial Appointments: An Appraisal of the First Mulroney Governments Appointments and the New Judiciary Advisory Committees' (1991) 41 *University of Toronto Law Journal* 4

Scarman, L 'Foreword' in Shetreet, S *Judges on Trial: A Study of the Appointment and Accountability of the English Judiciary* (North-Holland Amsterdam 1976)

Schmidt, CU 'All Bark and No Bite: Notes on the FCC's "Banana-Decision"' (2001) 7 *European Law Journal* 95

Scott, FR 'The Privy Council and Mr Bennett's "New Deal" Legislation' and 'The Consequences of the Privy Council Decisions' (1937), articles combined and reprinted in Scott, FR *Essays on the Constitution* (University of Toronto Press 1977)

Scott, FR 'Centralization and Decentralization in Canadian Federalism' (1951) 29 *Canadian Bar Review* 1095

Scott, FR 'Labour Conventions Case' (1956) 34 *Canadian Bar Review* 114

Selway, BM 'The Constitution of the UK: A Long Distance Perspective' (2001) 30 *Common Law World* 3, 22

Sherlock, A 'Government in Wales and the Development of a New Legal System Within a System' (2002) 8 *European Public Law* 16

Smith, K 'Certiorari and the Supreme Court Agenda: An Empirical Analysis' (2002) 54 *Oklahoma Law Review* 727

Smith, TB 'The House of Lords as Supreme Court of Appeal' 1950 *Scots Law Times News* 98

Starmer, K 'Two Years of the Human Rights Act' [2003] *European Human Rights Law Review* 14

Stevens, R 'A Loss of Innocence: Judicial Independence and the Separation of Powers' (1999) 19 *Oxford Journal of Legal Studies* 390

Stevens, R 'Government and the Judiciary' in Bogdanor, V *The British Government in the Twentieth Century* (Oxford University Press Oxford 2003)

Stevens, RB 'The Final Appeal: Reform of the House of Lords and Privy Council 1867–1876' (1964) 80 *Law Quarterly Review* 343

Steyn, Lord 'Incorporation and Devolution—A Few Reflection on the Changing Scene' [1998] *European Human Rights Law Review* 153

Steyn, Lord 'The Case for a Supreme Court' (2002) 118 *Law Quarterly Review* 382

Stone, KVW 'The Post-War Paradigm in American Labor Law' (1981) 90 *Yale Law Journal* 1509

Tierney, S 'Scotland and the New Legal Order' (2001) 5 *Edinburgh Law Review* 49

Tobias, CW '*Anastasoff*, Unpublished Opinions, and Federal Appellate Justice' (2002) 25 *Harvard Journal of Law and Public Policy* 1171

Tomuschat, C 'Die Europäische Union unter der Aufsicht des Bundesverfassungsgerichts' (1993) *Europäische Grundrechte-Zeitschrift* 489

Tremblay, A 'Judicial Interpretation and the Canadian Constitution' (1991/92) 1 *National Journal of Constitutional Law* 163

Turberville, AS 'The House of Lords as a Court of Law 1784–1837' (1936) 52 *Law Quarterly Review* 189

Vaughan, D and Randolph, F 'The Interface between Community Law and National Law: The United Kingdom Experience' in Curtin and O'Keeffe (eds) *Constitutional Adjudicationin European Community and National Law, Essays for the Hon Mr Justice T F O'Higgins* 228

Vesterdorf, B 'The Community Court System Ten Years from Now and Beyond: Challenges and Possibilities' (2003) 28 *European Law Review* 303–323

Vroom 'The Constitutional Protection of Individual Liberties in France: The *Conseil Constitutionnel* since 1971' (1988) 63 *Tulane Law Review* 265

Walker, DM 'Some Characteristics of Scots Law' (1955) 18 *Modern Law Review* 321

Walker, DM 'Equity in Scots Law' (1964) 66 *Juridical Review* 103

Weiler, JHH 'The State "*über alles*", Demos, Telos, and the German Maastricht decision' in *Festschrift für Ulrich Everling* (Nomos Baden-Baden 1996) vol 1, 1651

Winetrobe, BK 'Scottish Devolved Legislation and the Courts' [2002] *Public Law* 31

Yale, DEC 'The Third Lord in *Rylands v Fletcher*' (1970) 86 *Law Quarterly Review* 311–12

Ziegel, J 'Merit Selection and Democratization of Appointments to the Supreme Court of Canada' (1999) 5(2) *Choices* 14 (Institute for Research on Public Policy Montreal)

Working papers, pamphlets, reports, etc

Bondy, V *The Impact of the Human Rights Act on Judicial Review: an Empirical Research Study* (Public Law Project London 2003)

Bingham, Lord 'A New Supreme Court for the United Kingdom' The UCL Constitution Unit Lecture 1 May 2002 (UCL Constitution Unit 2002)

Blair, C *Judicial Appointments* (Research Paper 5, published in conjunction with the Report of the Criminal Justice Review March 2000)

JUSTICE 'A Supreme Court for the United Kingdom Policy Paper' (JUSTICE London 2002)

Le Sueur, A and Cornes, R *The Future of the United Kingdom's Highest Courts* (UCL Constitution Unit 2001)

Limbach, J 'The Effects of the Jurisdiction of the German Federal Constitutional Court' EU Working Paper LAW 99/5 European University Institute Florence 1999)

McKenna, J *Structural and Other Alternatives for the Federal Courts of Appeals* (Federal Judicial Center Washington DC 1993)

Malleson, K *The Use of Judicial Appointments Commissions: A Review of the US and Canadian Models* LCD Research Paper No 6 (Lord Chancellor's Department London 1997)

Mossberger, K and Wolman, H 'Policy transfer as a form of prospective policy evaluation' Future Governance Discussion Paper 2 (ESRC Hull 2001)

O'Neill, A 'Scotland's Constitution and Human Rights' (a paper delivered at a Law Society of Scotland conference on human rights Edinburgh 28 March 2003)

Rose, R 'Ten steps in lesson learning from abroad' Future Governance Discussion Paper 1 (ESRC Hull 2001)

Walker, N 'The Idea of Constitutional Pluralism' EUI Working Paper Law 1/02 (European University Institute Florence 2002)

Books

Abellán, JL *Historia crítica del pensamiento español* (Espasa Calpe Madrid 1988)

Alison *Practice of the Criminal Law of Scotland* (1833)

Andenas, M (ed) *Article 177 References to the European Court: Policy and Practice* (Butterworths London 1994)

Anderson, A and Demetriou, M *References to the European Court* (2nd edn Sweet & Maxwell London 2002)

Arnot, H *A Collection and Abridgement of Celebrated Criminal Trials in Scotland, 1536 to 1784* (W Smellie Edinburgh 1785)

Baker, TE *Rationing Justice on Appeal: the Problems of the US Courts of Appeal* (West Publishing St Paul 1994)

Bermant, W Schwarzer, W Sussman, E Wheeler, R *Imposing a Moratorium on the Number of Federal Judges* (Federal Judicial Center Washington DC 1993)

Bliss, M *Right Honourable Men* (Harper Collins Toronto 1994)

Blom-Cooper, L and Drewry, G *Final Appeal: A Study of the House of Lords in its Judicial Capacity* (Clarendon Press Oxford 1972)

Boch, C *EC Law in the UK* (Longman Harlow 2000)

Bogdanor, V *Devolution in the United Kingdom* (Oxford University Press Oxford 2001)

Boulding, KE *The Image* (University of Michigan Press Ann Arbor 1957)

Brazier, R *Constitutional Reform* (2nd edn Oxford University Press Oxford 1998)

Browne, GP *The Judicial Committee and the British North America Act* (University of Toronto Press Toronto 1967)

Calvert, H *Constitutional Law in Northern Ireland: A Study in Regional Government* (Stevens London 1968)

Carr, R (ed) *Spain: A History* (Oxford University Press Oxford 2000)

Collins, L *European Law in the United Kingdom* (4th edn Butterworths London 1990)

Costa, J *Reconstitución y Europeización de España* (Instituto de Estudios de Administración Local Madrid 1900 edition of 1981)

de V White, T *Kevin O'Higgins* (Anvil Dublin 1948)

Dickson, B *The Legal System of Northern Ireland* (3rd edn SLS Belfast 1993)

Dickson, B *The Legal System of Northern Ireland* (4th edn SLS Belfast 2001)

Dickson, B and Carmichael, P (eds) *The House of Lords: Its Parliamentary and Judicial Roles* (Hart Oxford 1999)

Dion, M *Canadian Bijuridism and Harmonization of the Law* (University of Ottawa Ottawa 2000)

Donaldson, AG *Some Comparative Aspects of Irish Law* (Duke University Press Durham 1957)

Dworkin, R *Law's Empire* (various editions 1986)

Eaglin, J *The Pre-Argument Conference Program in the Sixth Circuit Court of Appeals* (Federal Judicial Center Washington DC 1990)

Fountainhall's *Decisions of the Lords of Council and Session* (Hamilton & Balfour Edinburgh)

Frankfurter, F and Landis, J *The Business of the Supreme Court: A Study in the Federal Judicial System* (Macmillan New York 1928)

Friedland, M *A Place Apart: Judicial Independence and Accountability in Canada* (Canadian Judicial Council Toronto 1995)

Gadamer, HG *Vérité et méthode* (Editions du Seuil Paris 1976)

Gatfield, G *Without Prejudice: Women in the Law* (Brookers Wellington 1996)

Genn, H *Paths to Justice: What People Do and Think about Going to Law* (Hart Oxford 1999)

Gibb, AD *Law from over the Border* (W Green Edinburgh 1950)

Gibb, AD *Judicial Corruption in the United Kingdom* (W Green Edinburgh 1957)

Griller, GM and Stott, EK (eds) *The Improvement of the Administration of Justice* (American Bar Association Chicago 2002)

Guggenberger, B and Würtenberger, T (eds) *Hüter der Verfassung oder Lenker der Politik? Das Bundesverfassungsgericht im Widerstreit* ('Guardian of the Constitution or Ruler of Politics? The FCC in dispute') (Nomos Baden-Baden 1998)

Hadfield, B *The Constitution of Northern Ireland* (SLS Belfast 1989)

Hartley, T *Constitutional Problems of the European Union* (Hart Oxford 1999)

Hogg, PW *Constitutional Law of Canada* (4th edn Carswell Scarborough 1997)

Hume *Commentaries on the Law of Scotland Respecting Crimes* (Bell and Bradfute Edinburgh 1844) vol 2

Hunt, M *Using Human Rights Law in the English Courts* (Hart Oxford 1997)

Jolowicz, JA *On Civil Procedure* (Cambridge University Press Cambridge 2000)

Kommers, DP *The Constitutional Jurisprudence of the Federal Republic of Germany* (2nd edn Duke University Press Durham NC 1997)

Lajoie, A *Jugements de valeurs: le discours judiciaire et le droit* (Presses Universitaires de France Paris 1997)

Lasso Gaite, JF (ed) *Crónica de la codificación española* (Ministerio de Justicia Madrid 1970–1979)

Limbach, J *Im Namen des Volkes* (Deutsche Verlags-Anstalt Stuttgart 1999)

MacGregor Dawson, R *Constitutional Issues in Canada 1900–1931* (Oxford University Press Oxford 1931)

Mallory, JR *The Structure of Canadian Government* (Macmillan Toronto 1971)

Mason, AT *Brandeis: A Free Man's Life* (Viking Press New York 1946)

McCrone, D *Understanding Scotland: The Sociology of a Stateless Nation* (Routledge London 1992)

McDonnell, AD *The Life of Sir Denis Henry, Catholic Unionist* (Ulster Historical Foundation Belfast 2000) 106

McKenna, J *Structural and Other Alternatives for the Federal Courts of Appeals* (Federal Judicial Center Washington DC 1993)

McKenna, J, Hooper, L and Clark, M *Case Management Procedures in the Federal Courts of Appeals* (Federal Judicial Center Washington DC 2000)

Monahan, PJ *Constitutional Law* (Irwin Law Concord 1997)

Moreno, L *Spain: The Federalization of Spain* (Frank Cass London 2001)

Munro, JEC *The Constitution of Canada* (Cambridge University Press Cambridge 1889)

Neill, P *The European Court of Justice: A Case Study in Judicial Activism* (European Policy Forum London 1995)

Newark, FH *Elegantia Juris: Selected Writings* (Faculty of Law Queen's University Northern Ireland Legal Quarterly Belfast 1973)

Newman, WJ *The Quebec Secession Reference—The Rule of Law and the Position of the Attorney General of Canada* (York University Centre for Public Law and Public Policy Toronto 1999)

Niemic, R *Mediation and Conference Programs in the Federal Courts of Appeals* (Federal Judicial Center Washington DC 1997)

Nolan, Lord and Sedley, S *The Making and Remaking of the British Constitution: The Radcliffe Lectures at the University of Warwick 1996–1997* (Blackstone Press London 1997)

Oliver, D *Constitutional Reform in the United Kingdom* (Oxford University Press Oxford 2003)

Ortega y Gasset, J *La pedagogía social como programa político* (1910)

Page, A, Reid, C and Ross, A *A Guide to the Scotland Act 1998* (Butterworths Edinburgh 1999)

Paterson, AA St J N, Bates, T and Poustie, MR *The Legal System of Scotland: Cases and Materials* (4th edn Sweet & Maxwell Edinburgh 1999)

Pattenden, R *English Criminal Appeals 1844–1994* (Clarendon Press Oxford 1996)

Perelman, C and Foriers, P *La motivation des décisions de justice* (Etablissements Emile Bruylant Bruxelles 1978)

Perry, HW *Deciding to Decide, Agenda Setting in the United States Supreme Court* (Harvard University Press Cambridge 1991)

Posner, RA *The Federal Courts: Crisis and Reform* (Harvard University Press Cambridge 1985)

Posner, RA *The Federal Courts: Challenge and Reform* (Harvard University Press 1996)

Quekett, AS *The Constitution of Northern Ireland Parts II* (HMSO Belfast 1933)

Roach, K *The Supreme Court on Trial, Judicial Activism or Democratic Dialogue* (Irvine Law Toronto 2001)

Robertson, D *Judicial Discretion in the House of Lords* (Oxford University Press Oxford 1998)

Romero Moreno, JM *Proceso y derechos fundamentales en la España del siglo XIX* (CEC Madrid 1983)

Russell, M *Reforming the House of Lords: Lessons from Overseas* (Oxford University Press Oxford 2000)

Sainz Guerra, J *La Administración de justicia en España (1810–1870)* (Eudema Madrid 1992)

Scholz, J-M (ed) *El tercer poder: hacia una comprensión histórica de la justicia contemporánea en España* (V Klostermann Frankfurt am Main 1992)

Schuppert, Gunnar-Folke *Bundesverfassungsgericht und gesellschaftlicher Grundkonsens* ('The FCC and the basic social consensus') (Nomos Baden-Baden 2000)

Scott, FR *Essays on the Constitution* (University of Toronto Press 1977)

Silver, AI *The French-Canadian Idea of Confederation 1864–1900* (University of Toronto Press Toronto 1982)

Slaughter, A-M, Sweet, A and Weiler, JHH (eds) *The European Courts and National Courts: Doctrine and Jurisprudence* (Hart Oxford 1998)

Smith, TB *The Doctrines of Judicial Precedent in Scots Law* (W Green Edinburgh 1952)

Smith, TB *A Short Commentary on the Law of Scotland* (W Green Edinburgh 1962)

Smith, TB *Studies Critical and Comparative* (W Green Edinburgh 1962)

Stern, RL, et al. *Supreme Court Practice: for Practice in the Supreme Court of the United States* (8th edn Bureau of National Affairs Washington DC 2002)

Stevens, RB *Law and Politics The House of Lords as a Judicial Body 1800–1976* (Weidenfeld and Nicolson London 1979)

Sunkin, M and Le Sueur, A *Public Law* (Longman London 1997)

Taylor, P *Taylor on Appeals* (Sweet & Maxwell London 2000)

Timsit, G *Les noms de la loi* (Presses Universitaires de France Paris 1991)

Tomás y Valiente, F *Manual de historia del Derecho español* (4th edn 1983) in *Obras completas vol II* (CEC Madrid 1997)

v Bogdandy, A *Supranationaler Föderalismus* ('Supranational Federalism') (Nomos Baden-Baden 1999)

Walker, DM *The Scottish Legal System: An Introduction to the Study of Scots Law* (6th edn W Green Edinburgh 1992)

Walker, DM *The Scottish Legal System: an Introduction to the Study of Scots Law* (7th edn W Green/Sweet & Maxwell Edinburgh 1997)

Wall, EH *European Communities Act 1972* (Butterworths London 1973)

Wheeler, R and Harrison, C *Creating the Federal Judicial System* (2nd edn Federal Judicial Center Washington DC 1994)

White, RM and Willock, DM *The Scottish Legal System* (Butterworths Edinburgh 1993)

Whyte, J *Interpreting Northern Ireland* (Clarendon Press Oxford 1990)

Official publications

Administrative Office of the US Courts *History of the Authorization of Federal Judgeships* (Analysis and Reports Branch of the Administrative Office of the US Courts Washington DC 1999)

Administrative Office of the US Courts *Judicial Business of the US Courts, 2001*

Bill of Rights Implementation Working Group 'Report Bill of Rights for Northern Ireland: Reports of the Independent Working Groups to the Northern Ireland Human Rights Commission' (NIHRC Belfast 2001)

Bowman, J *Review of the Court of Appeal (Civil Division): A Report to the Lord Chancellor* (Lord Chancellor's Department London 1997)

Bureau of Justice Statistics *State Court Organization 1998* (2000)

Commission on Revision of the Federal Court Appellate System *Structure and Internal Procedures: Recommendations for Change* (The Commission Washington DC 1975)

Commission on Structural Alternatives for the Federal Courts of Appeals *Final Report of the Commission on Structural Alternatives for the Federal Courts of Appeals* (The Commission Washington DC 1998)

Council of Europe Parliamentary Assembly Legal Affairs and Human Rights Committee *Office of the Lord Chancellor in the Constitutional System of the UK* (Doc 9798)

Criminal Justice Review Group (Northern Ireland) *Review of the Criminal Justice System in Northern Ireland* (HMSO Belfast 2000)

Department of Constitutional Affairs *Constitutional Reform: A New Way of Appointing Judges* (DCA London 2003)

Department for Constitutional Affairs *Constitutional Reform: A Supreme Court for the United Kingdom* (DCA London 2003)

Evershed MR, Lord *Final Report of the Committee on Supreme Court Practice and Procedure* (1953) Cmd 8878

Federal Courts Study Committee *Report of the Federal Courts Study Committee* (1990)

Home Affairs Select Committee *Judicial Appointments Procedures: Report* (HC Paper (1996) 52i)

Home Affairs Select Committee *Judicial Appointments Procedures: Minutes of Evidence and Appendices* (HC Paper (1996) 52ii)

Institute of Public Policy Research *Written Constitution for the United Kingdom* (Mansell London 1991)

Judicial Conference of the United States *Report of the Proceedings of the Judicial Conference of the United States* (Judicial Conference of the United States 1990)

Judicial Conference of the United States *Long Range Plan for the Federal Courts* (Judicial Conference of the United States Washington DC 1995)

National Center for State Courts *Examining the Work of State Courts, 1999–2000* (2001)

Northern Ireland Court Service *Judicial Statistics 2000* (HMSO Belfast 2001)

Northern Ireland Human Rights Commission *Making a Bill of Rights for Northern Ireland* (Belfast 2001) available at <www.nihrc.org> (6 August 2003)

Peach, L *An Independent Scrutiny of the Appointment Processes of Judges and Queen's Counsel in England and Wales* (Lord Chancellor's Department London 1999) <http://www.lcd.gov.uk/judicial/peach/indexfr.htm>

Review Group *Review of the Civil Justice System in Northern Ireland—Final Report* (NICS Belfast 2000)

Royal Commission on Criminal Justice Report (1993) Cd 2263

Royal Commission on the Reform of the House of Lords; Report of the Royal Commission on Reform of the House of Lords (2000) Cm 4534

Scottish Executive *Judicial Appointments: An Inclusive Approach* (Consultation Paper 20 HMSO Edinburgh)

Study Group on the Caseload of the Supreme Court (Freund Commission) *Report of the Study Group on the Caseload of the Supreme Court* (Federal Judicial Center Washington DC 1972)

The House of Lords—Completing the Reform (2001) Cm 5291

Woolf of Barnes, Lord *Access to Justice: Final Report to the Lord Chancellor on the Civil Justce System in England and Wales* (HMSO London 1996)

Index